J. REUBEN CLARK

SELECTED PAPERS

J. REUBEN
CLARK

SELECTED PAPERS

Fourth of a multivolume set on the
life and work of J. Reuben Clark, Jr.

David H. Yarn, Jr., General Editor

J. REUBEN
CLARK

SELECTED PAPERS

On International Affairs

EDITED BY DAVID H. YARN, JR.

Brigham Young University

Library of Congress Cataloging-in-Publication Data

Clark, J. Reuben (Joshua Reuben), 1871–1961.
    Selected papers on international affairs.

    Includes bibliographical references and index.
    1. United States—Foreign relations—20th century.
2. World politics—20th century.   3. International
relations.   I. Yarn, David H.   II. Title.
E742.5.C562   1987   327.73   87-17655
ISBN 0-87579-108-5

Brigham Young University, Provo, Utah 84602
©1987 by Brigham Young University. All rights reserved
Printed in the United States of America

Distributed by Deseret Book Co., Salt Lake City, Utah 84130

Contents

Contents

Acknowledgments

It was twenty years ago this fall that I was invited, and I suppose requested, to begin a study of the massive collection of papers of J. Reuben Clark, Jr., with the objective of seeing that a biography was written and that it and selected papers were published. Throughout those years many people have contributed in a variety of ways to the work of what we long ago came to affectionately call the Clark project. In appropriate places acknowledgments have been made. In this fourth volume, I would once again pay tribute to the Trustees of the Clark Estate for their unfailing interest and support and their numberless gestures of love and friendship. The trustees include: Marion G. Romney of the Council of the Twelve of The Church of Jesus Christ of Latter-day Saints; Gordon Burt Affleck, Clark family friend for half a century; the children of J. Reuben Clark, Jr.—Louise C. Bennion, Marianne C. Sharp, J. Reuben Clark III, and Luacine C. Fox; and President Clark's secretary for many years, Rowena J. Miller. Also, President Jeffrey R. Holland of Brigham Young University has been most helpful.

Personnel of the Harold B. Lee Library at Brigham Young University, where the Clarkana Collection is located, gave full measure in their efforts to assist in every way. Hollis Scott, formerly of the University Archives; Dennis Rowley, Director of the Archives and Manuscripts Division; Chad Flake, Director of Special Collections; and Sterling J. Albrecht, Director of the Library, deserve special mention.

In the actual work of publication, I am greatly indebted to Howard A. Christy, Louise E. Williams, and Elizabeth W. Watkins of Scholarly Publications at Brigham Young University. The intense personal interest and meticulous care that they have given to both perspective and detail have been most impressive. I appreciate their professional skills and all they have given of themselves for this phase of the project.

And finally, I must again pay tribute to my dear wife, Marilyn Stevenson Yarn, who has been a devoted and steadfast support in the Clark project these two decades. Her support has in no sense been passive but to the fullest degree active. The work has been essentially a partnership, and I am indeed very grateful to her.

Although I am indebted to many people for all they have contributed to this endeavor, I must accept responsibility for any inadequacies, and I am happy to express my appreciation for the high privilege of having access to the Clark papers and the opportunity of coming to know in a very special way through them the remarkable J. Reuben Clark, Jr.

David H. Yarn, Jr.

Introduction

"If you have an 'A' mind and an 'A' will you'll be an 'A' man, but if you have an 'A' mind and a 'C' will you'll be a 'C' man." So J. Reuben Clark, Jr., counseled a young university student. Reuben Clark had an "A" mind and an "A" will. He grew up in a home where work, initiative, and industry were a way of life. As a boy of eighteen he wrote:

Self control is something that we should all cultivate for upon exercise of our mind over the bodies, which constitutes self control, depends our future prosperity and usefulness in this world, and our salvation in the next. Shakespeare tells us that, "Our bodies are our gardens, to the which our wills are gardeners. . . ." We can scarcely believe what a vast amount of power our mind has over the other parts of our bodies. If we firmly resolve to do anything we generally accomplish it. . . . If we resolve in our minds that we will make of ourselves good, honorable, honest, virtuous, and industrious men, and keep this resolve firmly rooted in our minds, we will surely become that kind of person.[1]

J. Reuben Clark had that kind of mind, that kind of resolve, that kind of will, and became that kind of person. He disciplined himself from his youth to become an assiduous worker. He thrived upon and enjoyed work and accomplishment. After many years of experience he declared, "It is the eternal, inescapable law that growth comes only from work and preparation, whether the growth be material, mental, or spiritual. Work has no substitute."[2]

---

1. Journal of Joshua Clark, vol. 15, 20 January 1890, J. Reuben Clark, Jr., Papers, Harold B. Lee Library, Brigham Young University (Clark Papers hereafter referred to as JRCP).
2. *Conference Report* [The Church of Jesus Christ of Latter-day Saints], April 1933, 103.

Those qualities he developed as a youth paid him great dividends. It was their application while he was a student in the School of Law at Columbia University that opened the door to his future career. As a result of his initiative and industry, and the overall quality of his performance as a student, at the end of his second year in law school he was not only admitted to the New York Bar but was invited to assist one of his professors with a book he was preparing for publication. Reuben spent the summer of 1905 with him, compiling and annotating materials for a case book on quasi-contracts. His work on the 772-page book was so thorough that the following summer, upon his graduation, Professor James Brown Scott employed him again to assist in the preparation of a two-volume work on equity jurisdiction. In the meantime, Professor Scott had been appointed solicitor for the Department of State of the United States. Because of his new responsibilities it became Reuben's lot to compile and annotate the major portion of the work.

On 11 April 1906, two months before Reuben graduated from law school, the United States Senate passed a joint resolution providing for a commission to examine the subjects of citizenship, expatriation, and protection abroad and make a report with recommendations to Congress. The Senate acceded to a recommendation of the House Committee on Foreign Affairs that, instead of appointing a commission, men in the State Department who had to deal with such matters practically should be appointed to prepare the report and propose legislation to Congress. James Brown Scott was one of the three men appointed to do so. Scott, mindful of Reuben Clark's great abilities and capacious talent for work, recommended him; and by the appointment of Elihu Root, secretary of state, on 5 September 1906, Reuben commenced his service as assistant solicitor in the department. During the summer he had completed his work on the two seven-hundred-plus-page volumes for Scott. As soon as his government service began, Scott assigned him to prepare the report for Congress.

After four years Reuben was appointed solicitor for the United States, at that time the highest legal office in the Department of State. Among other things, during these years he prepared the case for the United States against Chile in the famous Alsop Claim (see Part One, Article Three), the decision of which granted the United States one of the largest financial international awards up to that time. Two major memoranda he wrote during this period were

Citizenship of the United States, Expatriation, and Protection Abroad and *Right to Protect Citizens in Foreign Countries by Landing Forces* (see Part Four, Article Two).

During his tenure as solicitor, he also served as chairman of the International Relief Board of the American Red Cross, prepared an extensive report urging vital humanitarian assistance to the wounded and suffering of both belligerent parties even in revolutions or insurrections, and had an exciting encounter in the international meeting with General Nicholas Yermoloff of Russia (Part Four, Article Three).

Near the end of this period he was appointed chairman of the American Preparatory Committee to represent the United States on the International Preparatory Committee for the Third Hague Conference. His general discussion, detailed study of the previous Hague conferences, and preparation for the third conference constitute hundreds of pages. The conference was not held, however, due to the outbreak of World War I in 1914.

After his resignation as solicitor, Reuben was named general counsel for the United States in the American-British Claims Arbitration. He was responsible for preparing claims for the United States against Great Britain and defending the United States against Great Britain's claims (see Part One, Article Four). The chief justice of Canada, a member of the international tribunal, said of one of Reuben's major presentations that "it was one of the ablest legal arguments he had ever heard."[3] A decade later he served not only as special counsel but also as American agent in the American-Mexican Claims Commission.

In the meantime he had entered private practice, with an office in Washington, D.C., another in Salt Lake City, and still another in New York City. Preston D. Richards, one of his assistants when he was solicitor, became his partner in and conducted the affairs of the Salt Lake City office. Reuben himself conducted the affairs for both eastern offices. Usually he would work all day Monday in Washington, board a near-midnight train for New York; work Tuesday, Wednesday, and Thursday in New York; then board a late evening train for Washington and work Friday and Saturday there.

Although he was in his mid-forties and therefore beyond draft

---

3. Quoted in J. Reuben Clark, Jr., to Preston Richards, 10 December 1913, Box 345, Correspondence, Richards, Preston, 1909–1919, JRCP.

age at the outbreak of World War I, Reuben volunteered for military service and entered with the rank of major. Because of his training and experience, the attorney general of the United States requested that Reuben be assigned to work in his office, and later he became adjutant to the provost marshal general of the United States Armed Forces, Enoch H. Crowder. For Reuben's work in the war—which included assistance in the preparation of the selective service regulations, plans for the demobilization of the armed forces, and more particularly his 1,150-page book *Emergency Legislation and War Powers of the President*—he was awarded the Distinguished Service Medal in 1922. His devotion to country and principle is in part suggested by the fact that his salary as a major was one-tenth of what it had been in civilian life the year before he enlisted.

When the war was over and it was decided that a conference on the limitation of armament would be held in Washington, the Department of State called him to Washington from Salt Lake City. He was asked to outline the conference, with many of its details, regarding not only the limitation of armament but the serious problems involving the Far East as well. He planned the conference in large part; assisted Charles Evans Hughes, the secretary of state and leading U.S. delegate to the conference, as his personal adviser and counsel in the conference itself; and prepared drafts of some of the treaties signed at the conclusion of the conference.

Twice in the 1920s, at the encouragement of many friends, he sought the Republican party nomination for a United States Senate seat from Utah; but both times an opposing political machine proved too strong. After the second defeat in 1928, he acceded to efforts to get him to accept the post of undersecretary of state, which for months the secretary of state, Frank B. Kellogg, had been urging upon him. Although in office only ten months, he served under both Kellogg and his successor, Henry L. Stimson, and made two major contributions. The first was a book which became famous as the Clark *Memorandum on the Monroe Doctrine* (see Part Four, Article Seven). Second, during the Mexican Revolution of 1929—which began the weekend before Hoover was inaugurated president—Reuben's prompt action in what the press described as "shirtsleeve diplomacy" was credited with minimizing American losses in life and property.

Reuben had long had an interest in Latin American affairs, and especially in American-Mexican relations. In fact, both prior to and after serving as undersecretary of state, he worked as the personal legal adviser to Dwight W. Morrow, United States ambassador to Mexico. Relations between the two countries were extremely delicate, and the ambassadorship was a major United States diplomatic post. Reuben succeeded Morrow as ambassador to Mexico and continued the work in trying to resolve the difficult problems rooted in the petroleum controversy (see Part Three, Articles One and Two), agrarian land matters, the religious situation, claims, and particularly the boundary dispute involving the Rio Grande. In the negotiations he conducted while he was there with Morrow and during his own two and one-half years as ambassador, he won the friendship and confidence of many Mexican people and their officials. General Plutarco Calles was reported never to have spoken more affectionately of anybody, either foreign or Mexican, than he did of Reuben Clark. Before Reuben and his family left Mexico, the minister of foreign affairs held a reception and concert in his honor; and as he left Mexico City, more than three hundred friends—officials of the Mexican government, members of the U.S. diplomatic corps, and others—assembled to honor him and bid him farewell (Part Three, Article Three).

In March 1933 he returned to Utah and on 6 April 1933 he was sustained as second counselor to President Heber J. Grant in the First Presidency of The Church of Jesus Christ of Latter-day Saints. This high calling did not preclude continued demands for his service to government and business. For example, almost two decades earlier Reuben had made an intensive and exhaustive study of foreign bonds, producing a five-hundred-page manuscript on the subject. Doubtless because of this and because he had had extensive experience in international finance in his work with the American International Corporation while in private practice, he was soon appointed by President Franklin D. Roosevelt to a "committee to create an adequate and disinterested organization for the protection of American holders of foreign securities." This group organized the Foreign Bondholders Protective Council, Inc., in New York City. President Clark was named a director and then elected a member of the executive committee. He was appointed acting president, then served as president for four years, as chairman of the executive committee for seven and one-half years, and finally as director for another seven and one-half years. President Roosevelt also appointed him a delegate of the United States to the Seventh International

Conference of the American States at Montevideo, Uruguay, in December 1934.

J. Reuben Clark, Jr., was thirty-five years of age when he entered the Department of State in 1906, shortly after his graduation from law school, and he spent twenty-seven years in government, legal, and diplomatic service prior to his call to the First Presidency. He was sixty-one years old at that time, near the age at which many people retire; but he would yet live twenty-eight more years, during which he would energetically serve his church. However, there would yet be demands on him to serve his country and to give counsel to government, political, civic, banking, business, industrial, communications, and educational leaders. Thousands of individuals would seek his advice—and all in addition to the immense responsibilities he carried in the First Presidency of the Church.

When he was in Mexico, Reuben was once asked to what he attributed his success in life. His answer was simply "work," which he said he found was "the best substitute for ability and genius."[4] But, characteristically, though he was amply endowed with both he never allowed them to be a substitute for work.

Through the years J. Reuben Clark wrote a multitude of memoranda and papers and gave a host of addresses on a great variety of issues. Obviously, those selected for inclusion in this volume on international affairs are only a sampling of his vast work; but they have been chosen with the purpose in mind of fairly representing his views, many of which were farseeing and astonishingly accurate. That they have done so is my estimation and hope.

---

4. Joseph C. Satterthwaite to Seymour Halpern, 3 February 1931, Box 38, R 11, JRCP.

Editor's Note

As explained in the General Introduction, the series *The Life and Work of J. Reuben Clark, Jr.*, consists of three major divisions. The first two are biographical, Volume One of the series, *J. Reuben Clark: The Public Years*, by Frank W. Fox, treating JRC's legal, diplomatic, and public service career, and Volume Two, *J. Reuben Clark: The Church Years*, by D. Michael Quinn, dealing with his Church service career as a counselor in the First Presidency of The Church of Jesus Christ of Latter-day Saints. The third division, *J. Reuben Clark: Selected Papers*, consists of three volumes of selections from JRC's memoranda, articles, addresses, letters, and verse. Manuscripts of most of these are included in the J. Reuben Clark, Jr., Papers (JRCP), Mss. 303, Special Collections, Harold B. Lee Library, Brigham Young University, Provo, Utah.

This book, Volume Four of the *Life and Work*, is the second volume of the *Selected Papers* and contains selections on a variety of subjects within the broad field of international affairs. The articles have been arranged by subject and divided into four parts as follows:

Part 1. International Arbitration and an International Court
Part 2. War and Peace
Part 3. Mexico
Part 4. Miscellany

The papers in each part are arranged in chronological order, and the title of each is given in the table of contents. The original spelling, grammar, and punctuation of the articles have been retained for the most part, except in cases where confusion would have resulted. Obvious typographical errors have been corrected. Also, certain terms and variant spellings have been standardized throughout the articles to avoid distracting the reader with mechanics. For the same reason, variant editorial treatments of format have been standardized. Exceptions to this treatment are the outline forms chosen by JRC himself.

Documentation has been standardized as much as possible. Legal style references have been changed to the historical format, except for the one reference to a British law. References to certain old legal works reprinted in many editions have been treated as classics, citing chapter and section rather than page. Biblical references correspond with the King James Version of the Bible. Where possible, the shortened titles JRC chose have been preserved. To aid the flow of reading, some of the references have been "ganged"; but generally they occur where JRC placed them. However, Article Eleven of Part Four, which is published here for the first time in an unfinished state, is an exception to nearly all these rules to some extent. Additionally, sources of quotations not cited by JRC have been added wherever possible, and excerpts misquoted by JRC from major American historical documents (e.g., Declaration of Independence, Constitution, Washington's Farewell Address, Monroe Doctrine, Lincoln's Gettysburg Address, etc.) have been corrected, and, in a few instances, reformatted.

Explanatory Notes in Text

Throughout this volume, explanatory notes prepared by the general editor are inserted prior to each of JRC's papers, and, in a few instances, between excerpts of a paper. These notes are set off by hairlines—as shown here.

PART ONE

International Arbitration

Practical Phases of International Arbitration and an International Court

May 1910

In March 1910 JRC was invited to be one of the speakers at the seventeenth annual meeting of the Lake Mohonk Conference, which was held in May of that year. The stated purpose of the conference was "to create and direct public sentiment in favor of international arbitration and an international court; generally, to encourage the substitution of pacific methods for war in settling disputes between nations" ("Answers to Ten Questions about the Lake Mohonk Conference on International Arbitration" [Lake Mohonk, NY, 1910], 1). JRC accepted the invitation conditionally, expressing uncertainty as to whether his work would permit him to attend. The conference came at the time he began to function as acting solicitor for the Department of State and it was probably due to pressures in the office that he did not attend the conference. However, it was for that conference that he prepared this undelivered address. Box 46, Book 1, 1910, Arbitration, E 9.2, JRCP.

Tradition has it that Solon, the great law-giver, declared in reply to the taunt "Are these the best laws you can devise," "No! but they are the best the Greeks can bear."

There is always a wide margin between the theoretically perfect and the practically enforceable law, and the following observations (none of them it is believed new) are offered upon certain practical phases and difficulties involved in unlimited compulsory arbitra-

11

tion, since it is believed that to be successful such arbitration must be practical. It is a trite remark that most of the failures of human endeavor result from a want of understanding and appreciation of the difficulties involved, and that there is no discovery or achievement which might not have been made or attained years earlier had the workers known the real conditions. Yet as this sometimes is overlooked these remarks are ventured with the hope that perhaps some idea or fact herein set forth may, because pointing out practical difficulties, at some time be of possible value in steadying the growth of arbitration, or in really hastening its ultimate secure and permanent establishment. As the necessities of the occasion make impossible any elaboration or argument, the points raised must per force be merely sketched out broadly, concisely, and even bluntly, thus leaving rough and unmodified statements that in a fuller discussion might demand exception and qualification.

It must at the outset be laid down that in all human probability no general universal rule could be successfully enforced regarding or governing unlimited, compulsory arbitration, which lost sight of the omnipotent necessity of self-preservation. There is no escape from this great, perhaps fundamental, natural law.

This means, to bring the matter home, that we Americans must act upon the fact, for so it is for us, that our civilization with its art, its science, its literature, and its ideals must be kept as a living, growing organism, and that "government of the people, by the people, for the people" must not be permitted to "perish from the earth." For it surely must be that today our civilization and our government, are each worth saving for the world, no matter what the cost of preservation shall be, and that our tomorrow's advancement will be equally precious. If this is so, there must be this practical limit to matters arbitrarily justiciable in unlimited compulsory arbitration, even if in rare instances this principle of limitation shall be made by some nation the subject of abuse.

Obviously, if unlimited compulsory arbitration is to be a judicial determination rather than a diplomatic compromise, it must be by the application of law to the facts and circumstances involved, and the law to be so applied must, of course, exist. Is there such arbitral law?

It is a notorious fact often deprecated that the international law thus far developed is not only fragmentary, but covers, with precision and definiteness of any degree, little beyond the belligerent relations of states, the law having been framed when nations as such principally dealt with or touched one another upon the battle field. Moreover, the art of war being now grown to a highly developed science, these rules of belligerency, developed in a simple state of society, have required great revision to meet our present highly specialized needs. There is, however, a fairly adequate and perhaps workable law of war.

But this period of maximum contact in war from which came these faulty belligerency rules, was reciprocally the period of minimum intercourse in peace from which developed far more faulty rules governing the relations of peace. These rules, formulated in the days of the oxcart, the stage coach, and the slow sailing vessel, when every frontier was a practical Chinese wall, naturally fail to meet modern conditions of steam and electric communication and transportation, with the thousand-fold augmented social and commercial intercourse. The new conditions have resulted in a complete shifting of the point of view. Today the learning and tact of foreign offices is no longer exhausted solely to answer questions of precedents of diplomatic representatives resident near the sovereign, but to solve the many and intricate questions concerning the security of person and protection of property of unaccredited subjects. Among the questions to which these new conditions give rise are such as what amount of protection is due, in cases of mob violence, from the local sovereign to aliens, either in the hands of the law or at liberty, whether it shall be the protection given nationals or a greater protection; does the local sovereign, failing to protect an alien, remedy his original default by punishing the mob or by a bona fide, conscientious but unsuccessful attempt to discover and punish the offender, or is an indemnity also due in either or each case; if a government official injures an alien in the course of his duty or outside of it, is it sufficient satisfaction to dismiss the official or must he also be punished as a private individual, leaving the same question as to indemnity; must a State grant to alien laborers the indemnifying relief for injuries which it grants to nationals laboring at the same work under the same conditions, and if so, must such provisions extend to non-resident aliens; what are the rights as to diplomatic intervention of alien stock and bond holders in a local corporation, first where all the stock and bonds are held by aliens and next where only a part thereof are so held, the balance being in the hands of nationals; is it proper for a State to invite investment of foreign capital in local corporations and then proceed to legislate or adjudicate away the value of the investment; may private property be taken for public use without adequate compensation; to what extent may a State control the influx of aliens and upon what grounds might it exclude or expel them, and shall such grounds be physical, moral, educational, ethnological, economic or any or all of these; has a foreign state the right to object, should it appear that the application of these principles resulted in the exclusion of all of its nationals and the admission of the nationals of every other country?

These and a thousand other questions are daily presenting themselves to the Chancelleries of the world, which find neither accepted precedent nor formula for their solution. There is no adequate and workable international law governing these and many others of the commonest, as well as most complicated, relations of peace.

Two ways at once suggest themselves to meet this want,—the first, an official codification of international law to be supplemented, where the law is not already developed, by the necessary legislative enactment by the codifiers; and the second, the building up by an arbitral court of a sort of international common law, in the same way that the English Common Law was built by the English Courts.

But official codification will scarcely answer as to the matters concerning which the law is not yet developed. Being the voluntary and unconstrained agreement of equal sovereigns every official codification of international law must be a compromise, balancing not only different laws, rules, and customs, but different primary national interests. It is difficult enough and sufficiently unsatisfactory where those elements are reasonably settled and well defined, for example, the codification embraced in the Declaration of London. But where, as in those branches of law suggested by the queries enumerated above, the laws and customs of many nations are still forming, where as in the United States the vital national interests in those respects are not only at present undefined, but largely unknown; where some of the nations themselves are not yet thoroughly established; and lastly, where the nations would find themselves sharply divided between those emigrating and those immigrating with a resulting direct conflict of interests,—the framing of a satisfactory and serviceable code covering all these questions, becomes not only most difficult but as a practical matter well nigh impossible. Moreover, even if it were possible finally now to frame a code, which might in a measure partially meet the existing conditions of today, such a code would in all human probability prove inadequate to cope with the development in the formative nations ten years from today. It is obvious that in such cases either the code would give way and be overturned, or the nations suffering would repudiate it, or the code must be revised. Either of the first two suggestions would be a serious menace to arbitration. The remedy remaining would be revision. But the experience thus far had by the world in codification does not encourage the thought that real codification is practicable every decade.

If these premises are sound, as it is believed they are, a proper appreciation of arbitration and its mission would indicate that we should for the present avoid attempts to stereotype into an official international code important undeveloped laws and customs arising from opposing interests. This is not to say that private, as distinct from official, codification of those parts of the law yet undeveloped may not be serviceable and indeed desirable in the development of international law, providing the codifiers have a practical knowledge of the undeveloped portions of the international law and of the conflicting national interests.

Considering now the development of international law by a sort of common law legislation by the arbitral court itself, it is believed this would prove even more unsatisfactory than codification. It seems a reasonable certainty that the young nations by reason of their measurably unsettled and undeveloped territories and governments, to which foreign capital, labor, and immigrants must inevitably and irresistibly resort, will constitute one class. These nations will, of course, subdivide among themselves, because of differences in climate, topography, products, tastes, civilization, resources, and racial characteristics, and will cleave roughly into groups having more or less identic interests. These countries among which under present conditions belongs the United States, will in a majority of cases be defendants before any international arbitral court. The other general class is composed of what may be termed the reservoir nations, from which will be drawn the capital, labor, and immigrants. Broadly the interests of the first group are and will be to exploit and of the second, the reservoir group, to conserve these elements of national wealth and greatness,—that is to say, there will be a direct and essential conflict based upon different social, economic, and at times racial conditions and interests between these two classes. The history of arbitration is sufficient to show that arbitral judges are but human, that they are subject to their peculiar national prejudices, national economic principles, and great national interests. The result has been and we must assume will be, while men and nations are as they are socially, economically and racially, that the judgments of an arbitral court will accord with the broad national interests of the majority of the nations represented. Now, might no more makes right in peace than it does in war. The result will almost certainly be, as has been foreshadowed by the experience of the past, that the nations which consider these vital and essential interests thus arbitrarily sacrificed by these judgments will finally either repudiate the law thus made by the arbitral court or they will decline further to resort to the court. In either case there will result a legal chaos worse than that which exists today.

Those who advocate the development of international law by such judicial legislation sometimes cite, to support their view, the development of the English Common Law, but these advocates overlook that the analogy is entirely false, because the English Courts in developing the English Common Law were acting upon a homogeneity of people, custom, ideal, interest and economic condition, with a single and all-enforcing sanction,—a situation radically and fundamentally different from that which would confront an international arbitral court.

It is believed, therefore, that a proper regard for the development of unlimited compulsory arbitration in the settlement of international disputes and for the peace of the world requires that before it is sought to impose such unlimited arbitration upon the nations, there should be developed with reasonable detail the law which shall be applied in the arbitral decision; and that pending this the nations should be left free to choose the questions they will submit to arbitration, and the conditions under which the submission shall be made. The past shows that real and permanent advancement may be had along these lines.

It is, of course, unnecessary to remark that where any two states or two groups of states are homogeneous in ideal, custom, judicial standards, interest, and economic condition, such nations or groups of nations are prepared, as between themselves, generally to submit their difference of whatever name or nature to arbitral decision in a court constituted between themselves, even though the law as to particular phases be undeveloped; since, though a decision may seem now to bear more hardly against nation A, circumstances are sure to arise where reciprocally the same burden of the decision will fall with equal force upon nation B. And in the end because of these facts the law so made by judicial decision will be applicable to both.

There are moreover certain phases of arbitral jurisdiction which are worthy of consideration and for our purposes we may conveniently consider first the nature of the jurisdiction and secondly, the subject matter of the jurisdiction.

While it is often assumed that all present arbitrations are judicial determinations rather than compromise, it must not be overlooked that a number of The Hague decisions thus far rendered really embody diplomatic compromises rather than judicial determinations. The trouble seems to lie deep, perhaps in the training and standards of some of those called to the arbitral bench. For example, recent articles written by a very noted continental jurist characterize certain arbitral awards (notoriously compromises) as strict judicial determinations. Either the learned writer does not know a judicial determination from a compromise or he is not entirely candid. This raises the query whether it may not be doubted that until there is a fundamental change in judicial standards we may properly hope for strict judicial arbitration.

But, however this may be, it is certain that so long as it continues to be regarded proper for arbitrators sitting on a case to be in close secret and confidential touch with general agents and counsel engaged in that case; so long as members of the tribunal see no impropriety in promiscuously consulting their professional friends and acquaintances not connected with the court upon matters before the court for decision; so long as it is possible for the diplomatic corps and official circles of the capital in which the tribunal sits to gossip authoritatively and accurately as to the attitude of the various members of the tribunal upon the questions at issue and then pending before it; so long as arbitrators consider themselves obligated to look to their foreign offices for directions in determining the questions before them; and so long as the arbitrators believe they must balance their decisions with the local interests of their own particular countries,—it is not only idle but foolish to talk of strictly judicial determinations of international disputes.

So far as the subject matter of arbitral jurisdiction is concerned, it has been already indicated that questions involving that broad but vaguely defined principle of self-preservation must be regarded as excepted from arbitral jurisdiction. Two thousand years of Christianizing influences and centuries of law and order as between individuals have left us still authorized individually to use force for self-preservation. A man is not obliged to stand with arms down and permit another man to take his life, leaving it to his heirs or his personal representatives to litigate the legality of the murder. He may meet force with force, even to the extent of taking life, to protect himself or in defense of his home. The law between nations will scarcely find sanction for principles more advanced than these. A sudden invasion threatening the life of a state, the seizure of a province, the arbitrary and hostile extension of an accepted boundary, the oppression and slaughter of citizens resident abroad, the collection of large numbers of aliens necessarily destructive of the social and governmental order of the state,—all may justify the immediate use of force without the obligation to await the law's delay.

But not only are such rights as these not justiciable as between nations, but there must also be added to this class matters of purely internal administration or policy. For example, the government of the United States could not arbitrate its tariff policy, its conservation policy, its method of levying customs, its right to restrict the privileges of aliens, the right of suffrage, its treatment of its own citizens, or any of a hundred other questions that might be enumerated.

There are therefore serious matters of arbitral jurisdiction still remaining to be settled,—matters which if left unsettled may wreck the entire arbitration plan.

It seems quite obvious that with arbitral law and jurisdiction unsettled it would be unwise to establish at this period of arbitral development, a tribunal with too great rigidity either as to form, jurisdiction, or duration. The arbitral machinery already constituted or proposed seems calculated to secure an orderly growth. In the first place, (save as to the Prize Court, where the law has in the main been settled and therefore removed from the objections urged above as to the law) the proposed machinery does not provide for or contemplate unlimited compulsory arbitration but only the adjudication of questions specifically referred to the court by the parties litigant. The Convention establishing the Permanent Hague Tribunal provides a permanent court panel from which the arbitrators for any given case are selected, and specifies the procedure which shall govern the court when constituted, in the absence of special stipulations by the parties themselves. It has been objected to this Court that much time may be consumed in the selection of judges for a particular case, but this has not been found a practical difficulty worth considering. It has also been objected that the expense of referring to the temporary tribunal is very great because of the temporary character of the particular arbitral court. We have, however, the assurance of a member of the Court (who, by the way, was paid some $25,000 for four months' work) that the expenses of a tribunal are largely the result of the excessive compensation paid to counsel. This latter expense will, of course, be incident to any such tribunal, because the interests of nations being involved in the cases going before the court, they will necessarily be represented by the highest legal talent available.

Perhaps the principal practical difficulties of this Convention system, lie in the matters of procedure,—first, in the opportunity it offers to gamble in the choice of an umpire; and secondly, the arbitrary power which it bestows upon the tribunal, and which (as it works out in practice) makes the adequate hearing of the parties by the tribunal rather a matter of favor, subject to the arbitrary discretion of the tribunal, than a matter of right. More precise rules governing this point would enable the agents and counsel in a given case to spend less time cultivating the personal good will and meeting the peculiar tastes of the members of the tribunal and more time in the preparation of their argument for the court. Or, to state the same point in another way, the tribunal should be so constituted that it would give up the idea that it was a diplomatic body, controlled and administered by court etiquette and graciously giving its time to the consideration of a case, and settle down to the fact that it is a regular judicial tribunal created by the parties resorting thereto whose creature and servant it is.

The present permanent court was constituted by the First Hague Conference by way of a compromise after the Conference refused to adopt Secretary Hay's broad and comprehensive plan for an international court of arbitration which should "be of a permanent character and shall be always open for the consideration of cases that might be referred to it." Under the direction of Secretary Root, the American delegates presented the Hay plan anew to the Second Hague Conference, this time with better success, as the Conference adopted a *voeu* embodying the fundamental conceptions of the Hay plan, supplemented by certain procedural provisions copied from the Conventions for the Pacific Settlement of International Disputes and the Prize Court Convention. Possibly the weak point of this plan is to be found in one of its excellences, that is, the permanency of its personnel. Were the court to be constituted today, it would be possible to name with reasonable certainty, a number of its members who would begin with a prejudice against this nation, its institutions, and its Government, that would operate in any case in which the United States was a party, for experience has demonstrated that these same men find it difficult if not impossible to lay aside their prejudices when sitting on cases in which this Government is a party. As the total number of judges provided in the *voeu* referred to is but fifteen, it is obvious that two or three powerful men of this kind might exert a most undesirable influence against this Government.

It cannot, however, be doubted that this plan marks a well defined step in advance and if the proposal of Secretary Knox to invest the Prize Court when constituted with the functions of a court of Arbitral Justice is adopted, the nations will be given another opportunity to demonstrate their belief in arbitration.

But this paper has already trespassed far beyond the limits assigned to it. As was indicated at the beginning, the sole object of the paper has been to point out certain practical phases or difficulties connected with unlimited compulsory arbitration. It should be unnecessary to say that this does not indicate hostility to arbitration. The course taken has been followed because of the fact that not infrequently it seems to be forgotten that there are many and great difficulties; because it will generally be much easier successfully to plan the arbitral campaign with its difficulties known; and because any arbitral movement to be permanently successful must take true account of the obstacles.

Moreover, it should be understood that nothing that has been said means or is intended to mean that merely because the ideal may now be unapproachable we should cease to reach after it; on the contrary, we should still hitch our wagon to the star. But what has been said does mean that this ideal is probably like every other ideal, impracticable in its fullness for the age that conceives it. But it is still worth striving for. Since the ultimate end of all arbitration is to crush out war with its misery and sufferings we are not unlikely to look with disfavor upon any scheme which does not seem to bring us immediately to the end sought. But there should be no contempt for the shorter steps that make for progress in the right direction.

War, the product of all the ages, cannot be obliterated in a day. Indeed, its elimination may still be the work of centuries. And if the present Permanent Hague Court, or the Hague Arbitral Court, when constituted, shall not (as they probably will not) usher in the millennium, this should not bring despair, for it is surely too much to hope that we shall be able with the "Whereas" of an Arbitral Court charter to change men's hearts, hardened as they are by ten thousand years of strife and tradition.

Arbitration Treaties

26 November 1911

In November of 1911 treaties of arbitration between the United States and Great Britain and the United States and France had been negotiated and were pending before the United States Senate. There was much political unrest in the world; and, in compliance with a suggestion made by officials of the Peace and Arbitration League in New York, "Peace Services" were held on Sunday, 26 November 1911, in the Salt Lake Tabernacle. JRC was the concluding speaker. Box 46, 1911, Arbitration, F 13.1, JRCP.

My brethren and sisters, I sincerely feel that it would have been better had we closed the meeting with the excellent address of Apostle [Orson F.] Whitney. The sentiments which he has expressed are those which find a resting place in the hearts of all of us, and they are good and proper thoughts for us to carry home with us. However, as the meeting is called for the purpose of indicating the desire of the people of this state that the Senate of the United States give its advice and consent to the treaties of arbitration which have been negotiated between the United States on the one hand, and Great Britain and France, in separate treaties, on the other hand, it seems not altogether improper that a few words should be said directly regarding those treaties.

It may in the first place be remarked that our people—by that I mean the American people—appear to have divided themselves into two general classes, so far as these treaties are concerned,—perhaps I should say three: First, the class which believes that the treaties do not go sufficiently far; secondly, the class which believes that the treaties go too far; and lastly the class, to which the negotiators of the treaty belong, which believes that the treaties go far enough but not too far. It is for the purpose of meeting, so far as I may be able, the objections raised by those who think that the treaty goes too far, that I shall frame my remarks.

In order that our attitude and relation to the peace movement and our duty to ourselves and to the other two contracting powers in the matter of these treaties, may be more truly appreciated, it may be well to trace most briefly the part which the United States has played in arbitration. Our record is one of which we may all be justly proud. As early as 1794 John Jay, negotiating a treaty with Great Britain and finding it impossible to agree with that country regarding our northern boundary, incorporated into the treaty a provision which stipulated that the question of that boundary should be arbitrated; and it should be said to the credit and honor of the Mother Country that though she was powerful enough to have forced us to have accepted, in the end, her view of that boundary, she was willing to join with us in settling the matter not according to might but according to right. John Jay, upon his return to America, found his treaty very unpopular, and it is said he was burned in effigy in Boston Common because of the arbitration clause. Alexander Hamilton, however, said at the time that it was a horrible and despicable thing to think that nations could not settle their difficulties by arbitration rather than by the sword. From that time until the present this government has always and consistently urged arbitration as the proper means of settling international disputes, and as a demonstration of its good faith in the matter it has submitted more than seventy international difficulties to actual arbitration. This excludes a considerable number of agreements to arbitrate which were not carried out because of a settlement of the controversies otherwise than by arbitration, as well as all conventional or diplomatic arrangements, delimitation commissions, and domestic commissions for the settlement of international claims. The questions submitted to arbitral tribunals for decision and award have oftentimes been of the greatest importance, both potentially and intrinsically, and include boundary disputes, rights of fishing, the rights and duties of neutrals, the interpretations of treaties, and the personal and property rights of American citizens resident in foreign countries.

The present peace movement with reference to the United States had its inception about 1851 when Senator Foote introduced in the Senate a resolution which contemplated that this government should make arrangements with other powers for the peaceful settlement of our disputes. A similar resolution was introduced in 1853. In 1872 Senator Sumner proposed a like resolution and in 1874 the House of Representatives actually passed such a resolution. In 1878 Italy suggested that there be added to our treaties already negotiated with that country a provision stipulating that all differences arising under the treaty should be submitted to arbitration and that the same article should be added to all future treaties but Secretary of State Evarts replied that "the government of the United States is not prepared at present to adopt a general measure of the character stated, but it will give the question an early consideration." In 1883 the Swiss government approached us with reference to a general arbitration treaty, and following that, in 1888, the British Parliament sent over some two hundred and thirty-five members of that body with a view to ascertaining if there were not some way of reaching an arrangement between Great Britain and the United States for the arbitration or peaceful settlement of our disputes with that country. In 1890 Congress passed a concurrent resolution which requested the President of the United States to negotiate to the end of settling "any differences or disputes arising between the two governments." In 1893 the British House of Commons passed a resolution expressing their satisfaction at learning of this resolution, and stating that they hoped that the British government would lend its cordial cooperation. In 1895 a similar resolution was passed by the French Chamber of Deputies, and in 1897 Secretary Olney and Sir Julien Pauncefote, British Ambassador at Washington, negotiated a treaty which provided that all differences arising between the United States and Great Britain should be submitted to arbitration for settlement under a plan set forth in the instrument. This treaty was sent to the Senate, but notwithstanding the body had as stated requested the President to negotiate such a treaty, it declined to give its consent and approval, although urged so to do both by President Cleveland and by President McKinley. The treaty was therefore never ratified and proclaimed.

In 1899 the First Hague Peace Conference was called at the instance of the Czar of Russia. In that Conference the United States played a prominent part. Among the most important pieces of work accomplished by that conference, at least for our present purpose, was the adoption of a convention providing for the establishment of a permanent Court of Arbitration at The Hague. This Convention, in the framing and adoption of which the United States largely participated, provides the following plans for the settlement of international disputes: First, it stipulates that when two countries are about to go to war a third country may intervene as mediator without giving cause for offense, and may by mediation attempt to settle the differences existing between the other countries. In the second place it provided that where there was an occurrence immediately threatening the peace of the nations, there might be established a court of inquiry, and it was to such a court as this that Great Britain and Russia sent representatives during the Russo-Japanese war in connection with the Dogger Bank incident. In the third place, it provided for the creation of a permanent court. Each nation becoming a party to the convention was entitled to name four persons illustrious for their learning in the law, their integrity, their uprightness and ability to pass upon matters in an impartial and judicial manner. These four persons from each nation comprise together a permanent tribunal, or perhaps it would be better to say a permanent panel from which, in any given case, there may be selected judges to pass upon the case referred to them.

Under that convention and pursuant to its spirit, Mr. Hay, when Secretary of State, negotiated a number of general arbitration treaties which provided that we should submit to the Hague court for determination all differences of a legal nature, or arising out of the interpretation of treaties, and not affecting the vital interests or honor or the independence of this government, and not affecting third parties. These treaties also provided that in addition to this general arbitration treaty there should be negotiated in each case of difference a special arbitration treaty, submitting such case for decision, which special arbitration treaty it was contemplated, should not go to the Senate for its advice and consent. The Senate, feeling that some of its prerogatives would thereby be taken away and that it would lose certain rights conferred by the Constitution itself, refused to advise and consent to the ratification of these treaties except with an amendment. President Roosevelt declined to submit the treaties in this amended form to the nations with whom they had been negotiated, and the matter there rested until Secretary

Root became Secretary of State, when he negotiated new treaties incorporating the Senate amendment, and those treaties are the general arbitration treaties which we have today. These various treaties and activities constitute the antecedents of the present treaties and suggest the moral obligation under which we rest to complete them.

The two treaties which are now before the Senate, the one with Great Britain and the other with France, are treaties which are in addition to and in a way supplemental of the general arbitration treaties negotiated by Mr. Root. The arbitration treaties now before the Senate provide for the submission to a tribunal, either chosen from the permanent court at The Hague or established by a special agreement, of all claims of right whether arising out of a treaty or otherwise when such claims are justiciable in their nature. It also provides, as to those questions which are not justiciable, that there shall be formed a Joint High Commission, to which Commission all such questions shall be referred. The Joint High Commission, having impartially and conscientiously examined the question is to make a report upon matters not justiciable, but such report is not an award. There may also be submitted to this Joint High Commission the question whether or not a given question is justiciable.

The majority report of the Senate Committee on Foreign Relations finds the following objections to these treaties: In the first place, they say that the treaty deprives the Senate of its prerogative of advising and consenting. This however appears not to be true. Indeed, the treaty was most carefully framed with a view to maintaining and retaining for the Senate its full share of the treaty-making power. The difficulty of the majority of the Committee appears to have arisen from the failure of the Committee to read two sections in connection one with another. A proper reading will show that all special agreements for arbitration under these treaties must go before the Senate for its advice and consent.

Another difficulty has been found in the use of the word "justiciable." It has been charged that this is a new word, particularly as to international relations; that its meaning and scope are thus far undetermined; that it invites uncertainties and disputes, and that therefore it marks no gain over the old treaty.

Before suggesting a reply to this contention permit me to digress for just a moment. There are two general classes of questions which come to a foreign office of a government for consideration and settlement. One class has to do with the rights and the duties of nations under the principles and rules of international law, or of treaties; and the other has to do with these questions of policy which go beyond international law and its principles and rules, and beyond the provisions of treaty. The present treaty is designed to meet both questions; first, those which are justiciable, by submitting them to arbitration; second, those which are not justiciable, that is, which are not able to be judged, by submitting them to the Joint High Commission for investigation and report for the information or guidance of the two governments, but without the Commission's finding upon such latter questions partaking of the nature of an award or being binding upon the two governments.

Now, as to the meaning of the term "justiciable," as Secretary Knox has aptly put it, a thing is justiciable which is able to be judged, just as a thing is edible which is able to be eaten, or tangible which is able to be felt. There is nothing of mystery or secrecy about the term. Therefore those matters are justiciable which are susceptible of being determined by law, and these, and these only, will go to this permanent court for arbitration, or before the special court created by the treaty for it. If the matter is not justiciable it does not go to arbitration. There can be no difficulty therefore in the matter of the meaning of the word "justiciable." That the term is new in international arbitration must be admitted, but it is scarcely newer in such connection than the phrases "vital interests," "honor," and "independence" found in our existing treaties and it has this manifest advantage over them, that it is a term of art with a definite meaning, while the others are inartistic terms meaning whatever the individual nation may choose to suggest.

A third objection urged by the majority of the Committee is that the treaties may involve us in the arbitration of questions which according to the universal opinion of the world may not be arbitrated. The explanation and comments just made regarding the word "justiciable" show, however, that this contention is not sound, for only those things which are justiciable, that is, governed by law and so able to be judged, can be arbitrated. Therefore the great mass of questions of policy are outside of the arbitration feature of the treaty and may only be considered in an advisory way by the Joint High Commission whose findings upon these matters have not the character of an award. The majority report of the Senate indicated and quite properly, three things which they regarded as beyond arbitration, which three things are preeminently matters, as the majority said, which no country on the face of the earth would think of arbitrating. The first one was the question of the Monroe Doctrine. The Monroe Doctrine, as you know, is to the effect roughly that we should regard as an unfriendly act any further colonization by European powers on this hemisphere. But this is not a matter of law and so justiciable and to be settled by arbitration. It is a question of high policy. It has been recognized by the nations of the earth for nearly a hundred years, because no nation has felt it worth its while to challenge it. It will be observed so long as we are able to maintain it, and the moment we are unable to maintain it some nation will challenge and overturn it. We announced the doctrine, not as a mere arbitrary matter, but because we regarded it as a matter of self-preservation to this government, to the American people, and to the institutions for which we stand. We obviously could not consent to arbitrate that question and no nation would be likely to suggest arbitrating it.

Another question which the majority of the Committee say we might be asked to arbitrate under this treaty is the question of immigration, and they undoubtedly have in mind the question of the great influx of immigration that might come to us from the East. But so far as international law recognizes anything at all it recognizes the sovereign right of every nation to say what class of people shall become a part of it, and if for any reason, either economic, or religious, or political, it is concluded by a government that a certain people are not proper people to be incorporated into the body politic, there is an unassailable sovereign right of the nation to exclude those people.

The third point raised by the committee is the question of our territorial integrity, they fearing, apparently, that under these treaties we might be asked to arbitrate the question as to whether or not we own a certain piece of territory which had been seized and occupied by some other power. Of course, they would not include here those questions as to boundaries merely which we have arbitrated from the earliest foundation of this government. There can be no question therefore on that point as the precedent is set. But if another nation should wish to invade us and take possession of our lands and then arbitrate as to whether or not they had a right to remain, it is quite obvious that we could not, and under the well established and recognized principles of international law, we need not submit such a proposition to arbitration. Such a situation is not dissimilar from that arising when a man invades forcibly and wrongfully your home. The municipal law in such a case does not require that you sit quietly down or that you permit him to expel you from your home, and then litigate with him as to whether he has the right to your home. A man entering by force may be repelled with force. Nor are you obliged to let a man shoot you down, and leave it to your heirs or personal representatives to litigate with him as to whether he was justified in his action. If a man threatens to kill you, you may if necessary, to protect your own life, take his. The same principle applies in international relations. Therefore we shall not be called upon to arbitrate any such question and this objection of the committee falls to the ground also.

These are the objections which the Senate has urged to these treaties. I am fully confident that none of them are well founded. It is perfectly true, and has to be true as they say, that until we have a law governing a certain state of circumstances there can be no arbitration of that, because arbitration implies the application of principles of law to a given state of facts. But as we have no law covering the Monroe Doctrine, as we have no law save a positive affirmation of our right covering the question of immigration, and as we have no law that recognizes the right of one country to invade or take possession of the territory of another, those questions are beyond the scope of the present treaties, and any objections to those treaties, based upon those matters, are ill founded in fact. As a practical matter, it is, I am sure, necessary for those who are guiding this government, to look carefully into the question of what they will arbitrate. We owe it as a duty to humanity to see to it that this government which, as Lincoln said, was "conceived in Liberty, and dedicated to the proposition that all men are created equal"—shall continue to exist in order "that government of the people, by the people, for the people, shall not perish from the earth." We owe it to humanity to see that, in those countries of our own, over which we are ruling and in which there is not a civilization equal to our own, the blessings of life, liberty, and the pursuit of happiness shall be extended. This is our duty and our destiny. Therefore we must look with care at the kind of treaty that we make in order that this high end may not be interfered with. But the present treaties amply protect these ends. They are sufficient and safe, and should be ratified.

The Alsop Claim

1910-12

Perhaps JRC's most widely known legal action while he was the solicitor of the Department of State was the Alsop Claim. He made the initial study of the case while he was an assistant solicitor and it led to the revival of diplomatic negotiations with Chile in 1907 that finally resulted in the claim's being submitted for arbitration. An agreement was framed on a protocol under which the arbitration was to be conducted with the king of England acting as Royal Amiable Compositeur. Forty pages of JRC's case were devoted to his introductory statement on the origin of the case, and thirty-one pages were so used in his countercase.

When the Amiable Compositeur made his award to the United States, JRC had the responsibility of preparing the official opinion of the Department of State on its distribution. The following excerpts come from a five-page statement within that opinion.

In 1820 a group of American citizens organized a partnership know as Alsop & Company for the purpose of doing business in Valparaiso, Chile, and Lima, Peru. This house continued doing business in Valparaiso (the Chilean firm being the one interested in the transactions hereinafter referred to) from that date, 1820, until December 31, 1873. The uniform plan followed by this group of men appears to have been to organize a firm for a period of five years

31

(except the last term, the eleventh, which was for three years), the affairs of each term being wound up at the end of that term. . . .

Beginning with 1860 and continuing down to 1870, one Pedro Lopez Gama had certain dealings and negotiations with the Government of Bolivia with reference to the exploitation and exportation of guano from the Bolivian Littoral. . . . Terms No. 9 and No. 10 of Alsop & Company financed Gama in these operations. It would seem that by the end of Term No. 9, namely, December 31, 1865, Gama owed Alsop & Company on account $90,000. . . . This sum had been increased . . . [by] December 31, 1870 . . . to [$732,406.46 and eventually amounted,] with interest, plus certain other advances in 1875 . . . to $1,287,595.76. . . .

. . . On April 9, 1875, Pedro Lopez Gama, in order to cancel this indebtedness, transferred to John Wheelwright and George Frederick Hoppin, "acting in their capacity as liquidating partners of the Commercial firm of Alsop & Company of Valparaiso . . ." all his (Gama's) claim against the Government of Bolivia arising out of the various transactions in connection with which he had been financed by Alsop & Company. . . . This transfer was recognized by the Government of Bolivia in a decree or resolution of the Bolivian Cabinet Council under date of February 7, 1876. . . .

Under date of December 26, 1876, a contract was entered into by and between "the Minister of Finance and Industry, Dr. Manuel Ignacio Salvatierre, in representation of the national interests, and John Wheelwright, partner and representative of Messrs. Alsop & Company of Valparaiso, for the consolidation and amortization of the credits which he had pending against the State," by virtue of and derived from the assignment made by Gama. . . . This contract incorporates two resolutions of the Bolivian Cabinet Council, one dated December 23, 1876, and the other dated December 24, 1876. . . .

The resolution of December 23 provided for a concession for the operation of certain government mines located in the Bolivian Littoral. The proceeds derived from the operation of these mines under the concession were to be divided . . . between the concessionaires and the Government of Bolivia. . . . The resolution of December 24 recognized the transfer from Gama to Wheelwright of Gama's claims against the Government and acknowledged the sum of 835,000 bolivianos as being due to Wheelwright "as representative of the firm of Alsop & Company" in satisfaction of these claims, which sum was to draw interest at 5 per cent until paid. This resolution provided . . . for the payment of the debt out of the Bolivian customs collected either at Arica or at a national customs house. There were thus two sources to which the Alsop creditors might look for payment of the debt recognized as due them by this contract of December 26, 1876: The first was the Bolivian customs collected at the Arica customs house or at a national customs house if established, and the second was the Government's share of the proceeds derived from the operation of certain government mines by the concessionaires. The concessionaires received nothing from the customs house on this debt and comparatively nothing from the mines.

* * *

The obligation was thus . . . primarily against Bolivia. The United States contended, however, that the obligation ran also against Chile and pressed that Government for payment. The case was presented to the United States and Chilean Claims Commission of 1893, but the Commission expired without passing upon it. The revived Commission of 1901 dismissed the claim for want of jurisdiction but without prejudice. . . .

From 1901 until 1909 the claim was from time to time called to the attention of Chile, but in August of the latter year it was again presented to Chile and vigorously pressed until the two Governments on December 1, 1909, signed a protocol referring the claim to the King of England for adjustment as *Amiable Compositeur*. This protocol provided:

Whereas the Government of the United States of America and the Government of the Republic of Chile have not been able to agree as to the amount equitably due the claimants in the Alsop claim,

Therefore, the two Governments have resolved to submit the whole controversy to His Britannic Majesty Edward VII who as an "amiable compositeur" shall determine what amount, if any, is, under all the facts and circumstances of the case, and taking into consideration all documents, evidence, correspondence, allegations, and arguments which may be presented by either Government, equitably due said claimants.

The full case of each Government shall be submitted to His Britannic Majesty, and to the other Government through its duly accredited representative at St. James, within six months from the date of this agreement; each Government shall then have four months in which to submit a counter case to His Britannic

Majesty, and to the other Government as above provided, which counter case shall contain only matters in defense of the other's case.

The case shall then be closed unless His Britannic Majesty shall call for further documents, evidence, correspondence, or arguments from either Government, in which case such further documents, evidence, correspondence, or arguments shall be furnished within sixty days from the date of the call. If not so furnished within the time specified, a decision in the case shall be given as if such documents, evidence, correspondence, or arguments did not exist.

The decision by His Britannic Majesty shall be accepted as final and binding upon the two Governments.

At the solicitation of the two Governments, his late majesty Edward VII indicated his willingness to act as *Amiable Compositeur* under the protocol. But before the arrival of the date fixed by the protocol for the submission of the Cases of the respective Governments His Majesty died. His successor, George V, upon renewed inquiry by the two Governments, expressed his willingness to act as *Amiable Compositeur* under the protocol. Accordingly, the Cases of the two Governments were submitted under date of August 1, 1910. On December 1, 1910, the Counter Cases of the two Governments were submitted.

The Government of the United States contended before the *Amiable Compositeur* that the obligation of Chile to meet the indebtedness recognized by Bolivia in the contract of December, 1876, rested upon three grounds (see Case of the United States, 232-314):

First. The Government of Chile was liable for such indebtedness because it had deliberately and with knowledge appropriated the funds specifically set apart and appropriated to the payment of this obligation by the contract aforesaid.

Secondly. The Government of Chile was liable for such indebtedness because of repeated solemn undertakings made to the Government of Bolivia to pay such indebtedness, the Government of the United States for and in behalf of the claimants having the rights of a beneficiary under these formal undertakings.

Thirdly. The Government of Chile was liable for such indebtedness to the Government of the United States because of many diplomatic undertakings and agreements made and repeatedly renewed by the Government of Chile directly to the Government of the United States and based upon ample consideration.

The Government of the United States also insisted before the

Amiable Compositeur that the Government of Chile was liable in tort because of the wrongful action of that Government not only in failing to recognize certain specified mining rights conveyed by the Cabinet Council resolution of December 23, 1876, but in actually depriving the concessionaires of such rights. . . .

On July 5, 1911, the *Amiable Compositeur,* acting under the protocol, denied recovery on the tort, but did

award and determine that the sum of two million two hundred and seventy-five thousand three hundred and seventy-five (2,275,375) bolivianos is equitably due to the representatives of the firm of Alsop & Company.

The Commissioners, to whom the *Amiable Compositeur* referred the matter for study, stated in their Report that

as the debt admitted by Bolivia was payable in bolivianos, the award must be payable in the same currency or in gold at the current rate of exchange.

On August 11, 1911, the Government of Chile, through its duly accredited representatives at London, delivered to the American Ambassador at London a ninety-day draft for £186,059 6s. 2d. At maturity on November 10, 1911, this draft was cashed in London and the proceeds thereof, minus $464.92 for exchange, were transmitted to the Secretary of State. On November 16, 1911, $906,201.86 was covered into the Treasury of the United States to await distribution to the beneficiaries by the Secretary of State.

Representatives of the estates of Joseph W. Alsop, Henry Chauncey, Edward McCall, Stanhope Prevost, Theodore W. Riley, George J. Foster, George G. Hobson, John Wheelwright, and George F. Hoppin, all deceased, are appearing before the Department claiming to participate in the fund on the ground that "the award belongs to, and has been made for the benefit of, the following-named estates"—naming them as above. Each of the persons named except John Wheelwright and George F. Hoppin were partners in Alsop & Company, Term No. 9.

Other parties are appearing before the Department, some as assignees, some as payees of orders, some as creditors, and some as persons claiming apparently upon a theory of *quantum meruit* for services rendered. (Opinion by the Solicitor for the Department of

State, *Distribution of Alsop Award* by the Secretary of State [Washington, D.C.: Government Printing Office, 1912], 7-11) (Box 74, G. 10, JRCP)

Although most of the work in the preparation of the case was done by JRC while he was assistant solicitor, the case itself was submitted according to the protocol on 1 August 1910, which was one month after he became the solicitor. In publication the arguments for the case of the United States fill a volume of 352 pages (*The Alsop Claim. The Case of The United States of America versus The Republic of Chile before His Majesty George V* [Washington, D.C., 1910]), supplemented by the evidence in an appendix of two volumes, one of 529 pages and the other of 591 pages (*The Alsop Claim. Appendix to the Case of The United States of America versus The Republic of Chile before His Majesty George V*, 2 vols. [Washington, D.C., 1910].) Four months later, after having examined the case of the Republic of Chile, JRC submitted his countercase of the United States in a 198-page volume (*The Alsop Claim. The Counter Case of The United States of America versus The Republic of Chile before His Majesty George V* [Washington, D.C., 1910])—supplemented by a 400-page volume of evidence (*The Alsop Claim. Appendix to the Counter Case of The United States of America versus The Republic of Chile before His Majesty George V* [Washington, D.C., 1910].)

In contrast with the case, countercase, and evidence prepared by JRC for the United States is the following description of the Chilean materials given by the British Commission to whom the materials from both governments were referred by the Amiable Compositeur.

The Chilean Case is of 54 folio pages, the Counter-Case of 335 folio pages, but, the material documents being quoted over and over again in the Cases [*sic*] and Counter-Cases [*sic*], only a short appendix of documents is annexed. (*Award pronounced by His Majesty George V as "Amiable Compositeur" between The United States of America and The Republic of Chile in the Matter of the Alsop Claim*, London, July 5, 1911 [Washington, D.C., 1911]) (Box 71, G1.1, JRCP)

*   *   *

To Dr. John Bassett Moore, one of his teachers when he was in law school and later a good friend, JRC wrote expressing some of his thoughts on the decision of "His Britannic Majesty, George V," in the Alsop case.

You are quite right in assuming that the results must be satisfactory to this Department. We are entirely satisfied. Having insisted before the agreement to refer to the King was made that Chile should either arbitrate or pay us a million dollars, we are, of course, quite content with the $900,000 plus which we received. As of possible interest to you and for your own information, I may say that in proposing to the Secretary that the sum so named should be fixed at $1,000,000 I had in mind the fact that if we should be awarded the face value of the Wheelwright contract with the interest thereon at the rate stipulated, with permission for payment in Bolivianos at their present value, we should get just about $900,000. To this I added $100,000, first, in order to make the sum a round one, and second, to make some allowance for what we regarded the tort side of the claim. You will observe from the award that the Amiable Compositeur actually adopted this plan (though excluding the tort), and gave us an award as stated.

The only personal complaint I have with the award is that the matter having been referred to the King as Amiable Compositeur, he proceeds to hand down, or rather to incorporate in his decision, what purports to be a legal opinion in the form of a report of the committee to which the matter was referred for examination. It seems rather incongruous that an Amiable Compositeur should give us legal decision, and our arbitral courts compromises; particularly when the Good Book assures us that grapes are not gathered from thorns nor figs from thistles.

The King's award is somewhat unfortunate in my judgment in at least two particulars, not so much from the standpoint of this case but from the standpoint of general diplomacy: First, it seems to refuse to find that the Wheelwright contract constituted an actual pledging of the customs. I think this finding is erroneous. Secondly it refused to regard, as having a binding force, promises made in diplomatic correspondence. If some of our weak sisters get the idea that they can promise in diplomatic correspondence in order to relieve a situation, and then not be obliged later to live up to such promise, I am apprehensive that our difficulties may be hereafter increased. The opinion of the King's committee is also rather strange where it finds that the Wheelwright mining rights were "options" (whatever they may be) and then holds that such options are not property rights.

However, these are mere incidents, not to say small disappointments, which I suppose come in almost every lawsuit, and therefore I have no real complaint to make. (J. Reuben Clark, Jr., to John Bassett Moore, 23 August 1911, Box 345, Moore, John Bassett, 1911-1940, JRCP)

Jurisdiction of American-British Claims Commission

May 1913

Based on an 18 August 1910 agreement between the United States and Great Britain, a tribunal was assembled on 13 May 1913 in Washington to commence arbitrations. After five days of meetings, the tribunal recessed for three weeks, then reassembled in Ottawa for a week and a half of meetings. At that time, the tribunal adjourned until 9 March 1914, when it reconvened in Washington. In the fourth meeting of the initial Washington assemblage, Robert Lansing, agent for the United States, "announced that, in view of their general application to a number of cases, the United States desired to present its views upon the meaning and interpretation of certain provisions of the Special Agreement and Terms of Submission annexed, particularly as regards the meaning of the terms 'Equities' and 'Admissions' as there used" (*American and British Claims Arbitration—Protocols of the First Session of the Tribunal,* n.p., n.d., 15). When the president of the tribunal approved the request, JRC, who was counsel for the United States, addressed the tribunal. Sir Charles Fitzpatrick, chief justice of Canada and a member of the tribunal, paid JRC a high compliment at the end of his address, saying that "it was one of the ablest legal arguments he had ever heard." When reminded of the compliment by a friend, JRC said, "I feel the more embarrassed as the argument has since appeared in print. . . . And as you will see from glancing over it, it nowise merits the praise which he gave to it. . . . In view of the real character of what I said, this, however, seems to me a real reflection upon the character of the arguments he had heretofore heard, rather than upon the excellence of this one" (J. Reuben Clark, Jr., to Preston D. Richards, 10 December 1913, Box 345, Richards, Preston, 1909-1919, JRCP). The address is preceded by a brief account of the specific circumstances which prompted it. Both the brief account and the address appear here as printed in the *American Journal of International Law* in October, 1913. Box 7, JRCP.

This argument was delivered by J. Reuben Clark in connection with the defense made by the United States to the claim presented by His Britannic Majesty's Government for compensation for the losses sustained by William Hardman at Siboney, Cuba, during the Spanish-American War. The occasion for the making of the argument arose from the following circumstances:

During the course of the argument made by the Honorable E. L. Newcombe, Assistant Agent for Great Britain, in presenting the claim of the Canadian Government against the United States in what is known as the "Yukon Lumber" case, His Excellency, Henri Fromageot, President of the Tribunal, inquired as to the existence in American and English law of a certain principle of the French law. In the course of the brief discussion which followed on this point, Mr. Newcombe stated that in his judgment the provisions of French law were wholly inapplicable to the case under discussion which was to be decided entirely under and in accordance with the principles of American and English law.

During his argument presenting the Hardman case to the Tribunal, the Honorable C. J. B. Hurst, C. B., K. C., Agent for Great Britain, took the position that in its decision of the case, the Tribunal must be bound by the strict rules of international law. Thereupon, the President of the Tribunal referred to the provisions of Article 7 of the Special Agreement under which the Tribunal is organized and acts, and particularly to that provision of the article which speaks of "equity." The clause in question reads:

Each member of the tribunal, upon assuming the function of his office, shall make and subscribe a solemn declaration in writing that he will carefully examine and impartially decide, in accordance with treaty rights and with the principles of international law and of equity . . .

Mr. Hurst, in discussing the question thus raised, contended in substance that the use of the word "and" instead of "or" connecting "international law" and "equity" showed clearly that the intention was that equity should apply only in cases where international law did not cover the ground but that where international law did cover the ground, the Tribunal was to apply that law.

Mr. Clark's argument was made primarily for the purpose of setting forth the position of the United States with reference to the provisions of Article 7.

There had also arisen in connection with the argument in the case of the "Lindisfarne" presented by Great Britain, the question as to the meaning of the second clause of the Terms of Submission which provides:

> The arbitral tribunal shall take into account as one of the equities of a claim to such extent as it shall consider just in allowing or disallowing a claim any admission of liability by the Government against whom a claim is put forward.

It appeared from the argument presented by Mr. Hurst on behalf of Great Britain that His Britannic Majesty's Government was prepared to take the position that communications from a subordinate officer to the head of a department, between the different heads of different departments, from the head of a department to the President, as also communications from the President to Congress, might be invoked as admissions of liability on the part of this Government for the injury complained of, where such communications had come to the notice of His Britannic Majesty's Government. Moreover, the view was seemingly entertained by the British Agent that it was immaterial whether or not such communications had been brought officially to the attention of His Majesty's Government by the Department of State.

This offered the occasion for the presentation of the last half of Mr. Clark's argument.

MR. CLARK. Mr. President and members of the Tribunal:

In this discussion not only of the general jurisdiction of the Tribunal but also of "admissions" and "equities," I am happy in this thought—that so far as I understand the comments made by the learned Agent of Great Britain on the points mentioned, we are, from what he has said today, in substantial accord. I am therefore led to hope there will be no great differences developed between us on the questions to be discussed.

I shall be as brief as possible, in order not unduly to weary the Tribunal, with a necessary regard, of course, to the discussion, in an appropriate measure, of the points upon which I desire to speak.

It seems to me, in the first place and laying the foundation for a consideration of the meaning of the principles of equity as stated in Article 7 of the Special Agreement, that it must be kept in mind that arbitrations may be of two kinds: that is to say, a nation may arbitrate questions of policy, either its international policy or its national policy, as to which it may become involved in matters of difference with other nations. Certainly two nations in disagreement over any matter are entitled to submit that question to arbitration if they so desire.

That is one kind of arbitration.

The other kind of arbitration is an arbitration of legal differences; that is, differences which arise between two governments on questions and matters of law.

As I have remarked, either kind of question is arbitrable; that is to say, two nations may agree to submit either to arbitration. Only the latter kind, however, I take it, is to be subject to the rules and principles of law, unless otherwise laid down in the terms of submission.

There has been considerable confusion in the use of the term "arbitration," and not infrequently even governments, in discussing the matter, have used the term, one government having in mind one concept of the meaning of the word and the other government another meaning, thus often leading to misunderstandings and disagreements otherwise entirely unnecessary.

It seems to me essential to understand, as affecting this Tribunal, the precise kind of an arbitration in which we are engaged; that is whether we are engaged in an arbitration in which questions of policy or questions outside of the domain of law are to be considered, whether we are engaged in an arbitration in which other considerations than legal considerations are to enter; or whether we are engaged in an arbitration of matters of law, before a judicial tribunal created by the parties, because they had otherwise no common court to which they could submit their claims or questions of legal difference.

As bearing upon this question in a general way, but not specifically (because the Special Agreement is not thereunder) I wish to refer you to the language of the general treaty of arbitration between the United States and Great Britain of 1908.

Article 1 says:

> Differences which may arise of a legal nature or relating to the interpretation of treaties existing between the two contracting parties and which it may not have been possible to settle by diplomacy, shall be referred . . .

and then follow provisions not pertinent to the present discussion.

Now, the essential element to be noted in this article is that the treaty relates to and governs differences which may arise of a legal nature, or relating to the interpretation of treaties. Those were the differences in contemplation of the parties when they made this general treaty of arbitration.

Article 2 of this same treaty provides:

> In each individual case the high contracting parties, before appealing to the Permanent Court of Arbitration, shall conclude a special agreement defining clearly the matter in dispute, the scope of the powers of the arbitrators, and the periods to be fixed for the formation of the arbitral tribunal and the several stages of the procedure.

The point that I wish to get from this article is that there is to be under this treaty a special agreement, a *compromis,* defining the scope of the powers of the arbitrators.

It is unnecessary for me to observe that there is in the present proceeding such a special agreement as this convention calls for. Taking up that Special Agreement and turning to its preamble, the following provision is found:

> Whereas Great Britain and the United States are signatories of the convention of the 18th October, 1907, for the pacific settlement of international disputes, and are desirous that certain pecuniary claims outstanding between them should be referred to arbitration, as recommended by Article 38 of that convention,
>
> Now, therefore, it is agreed that such claims as are contained in the schedules drawn up as hereinafter provided shall be referred to arbitration, under chapter 4 of the said convention, and subject to the following provisions.

Turning now to Part 4 of the Hague Convention for the Pacific Settlement of International Disputes, which is thus incorporated in this Special Agreement, it is to be noted that Article 37 (which is the first article under Part 4, Chapter 1) provides:

> International arbitration has for its object the settlement of disputes between states by judges of their own choice, and on the basis of respect for law.

I desire here to emphasize that the disputes are to be settled by *judges*. Article 38, which follows, says:

> In questions of a legal nature, and especially in the interpretation or application of International Conventions, arbitration is recognized by the Contracting Powers as the most effective, and, at the same time, the most equitable means of settling disputes which diplomacy has failed to settle.
>
> Consequently, it would be desirable that, in disputes about the above-mentioned questions, the Contracting Powers should . . .

and then follow stipulations not presently pertinent.

In other words, Part 4 of the Pacific Settlement Convention itself, in positive terms, contemplates the settlement of legal differences and matters, as distinguished from non-legal controversies, and such settlement is to be made under and in accordance with that part of the convention dealing with the mode of such settlement.

The method of settling other difficulties—difficulties with reference to policy or difficulties with reference to acts that are beyond or outside the domain of law, are provided for in the earlier parts of that convention,—those parts dealing with good offices and mediation, and with international commissions of inquiry.

If, therefore, this is to be a decision by judges on the basis of respect for law, in accordance with the terms of the Hague Convention, I submit that this means the constitution of a court, a court of law, and as I shall explain a little later on, this establishment of a court, this appearance before a court, must be taken to mean that the Tribunal itself will administer law.

I wish at this point to draw a distinction between a tribunal sitting as a court to administer law, and a body sitting as a legislature to make law. The functions of the two bodies are wholly distinct, and should not be confused. This Tribunal sits as a court, not as a legislature. It is to administer, not make, law.

Turning, now, to Articles 51 and 52 of the Convention for the

Pacific Settlement of International Disputes, it will be observed that provision is there made for the making in each particular case of a *compromis*. In these articles it is also provided—I shall not take the time of the Tribunal by reading them—that the *compromis* so to be made shall define the scope and the powers of the arbitrators.

Looking now, pursuant to these provisions, to the Special Agreement in order to determine the powers of the arbitrators on the point in question, it is to be observed that Article 7 provides:

> Each member of the tribunal, upon assuming the function of his office, shall make and subscribe a solemn declaration in writing that he will carefully examine and impartially decide . . .

Note what follows—

> in accordance with treaty rights and with the principles of international law and of equity, all claims presented for decision, and such declaration shall be entered upon the record of the proceedings of the Tribunal.

Under this Special Agreement three things are to be looked to by the arbitrators, in their determination of cases coming before them: (1) treaty rights, (2) the principles of international law, and (3) the principles of equity.

I take it that there is no necessity for developing, at this time at least, any argument regarding treaty rights. That matter will hereafter come up for very full discussion in later cases, and treaty rights are not involved in the cases now before the court.

As to the principles of international law, as used in the Special Agreement, the matter stands differently. As the learned Agent for Great Britain pointed out this morning, until we began with the Hardman case we have had before the Tribunal no case presenting a question of international law. I may say that what is true of the two cases already presented, the "Lindisfarne" and the "Yukon Lumber,"—will be true of any number of cases that will hereafter come before this Tribunal for consideration, determination, and award. This fact leads me to this suggestion, perfectly obvious I submit, that the domain of strict international law as thus far developed and recognized by the nations, fails wholly and absolutely to cover all of the activities and all of the intercourse in which nations under modern conditions are engaged. Therefore such international law fails to provide a remedy for many of the disputes which arise between nations on matters concerning questions purely of a legal nature, and arising out of their intercourse.

Looking at the matter from a slightly different angle: I think it must be conceded that in considering the growth and present development of international law, we begin with each nation of the family of nations as an absolute power in itself, an individual unit subject to no rules and to no regulations. However, as nations came together and formed a family, a society of nations, each nation gave up a certain amount of the autonomy, of the independence which, as a separate and distinct unit, it had theretofore enjoyed. The sum of these national surrenderings, if you will, constitutes the body of international law as we have it today. But the nations have reserved to themselves, and have declined to surrender one to another, perfect freedom in a great mass of activities, some of which are in process of delimitation and subjection to rules of action, though not yet sufficiently defined to be generally recognized as international law, while other activities still remain wholly beyond the reach of rule or restraint.

This Tribunal, to repeat what I said a moment ago, has already had presented to it two cases that do not fall within the domain of prescribed rules of international law. For that reason the learned arbitrators will not be able to go to the books of international law as was observed by my honored Colleague this morning, and find one word there which will be of assistance to them in the determination of the two cases presented yesterday and the day before.

The question then comes, where is the Tribunal to look, where is this Tribunal to go, for the law which it has to apply in cases involving purely questions of law, but as to which there is no applicable principle of strict international law?

It seems to me that the answer to this question is more or less obvious.

In the first place, I assume the Tribunal should apply in such a case the principles of private international law, so-called, in so far as they may be applicable—and there will be cases arise, I am confident, where the principles of private international law will be invoked by the one or the other party to this arbitration.

In the next place, the Tribunal will invoke in appropriate cases the principles of maritime law, the principles which were involved in the case of the "Lindisfarne" already presented to you.

Again, where there is no international law, and where neither the principles of private international law nor the almost equally co-existing principles of maritime law apply, it seems to me that the Tribunal should look for their guidance to the fundamental principles of the jurisprudence of the various systems of laws, particularly the common law (and I include in that term the common law and equity as understood in the United States and Great Britain) and the principles of the civil law. Whatever is fundamental to those two main systems of law that control the civilized world, is properly applicable by this Tribunal as a guide in its decisions.

But suppose that those fail—and I am not certain but that under certain conditions the principle that I am now going to suggest would control and override any of the three preceding, even did any or all of the sources indicated contain principles applicable to and sufficient to dispose of the case—then inasmuch as this is an arbitration between two countries having more or less similar systems of government, two countries of essentially the same race, with the same language and the same fundamental laws, this Tribunal should go to the fundamental principles of the laws of the two countries for the guidance which it may need in a particular case. To this point and conclusion I understood my learned friend, Mr. Newcombe, yesterday to speak when he suggested that the law of France as to possession did not apply with reference to the discussion of the case of the "Yukon Lumber," but that the laws and principles common to the two countries interested should be exclusively invoked.

Again, I take it that if these all fail that then the plaintiff government in a given case has a right to call the Tribunal's attention to any positive principle of law of the defendant nation and insist that such a provision of law shall be administered in favor of the plaintiff government in that particular case.

And finally, possibly, in the absence in such cases, of a principle of positive law of the defendant obligating the defendant to give the relief asked for by the plaintiff government, that then an affirmative principle of law of the plaintiff government might be invoked.

I submit these observations as the views of the Government of the United States as to the scope and meaning of the phrase of the Special Agreement "principles of international law" as it is to be understood and applied in this particular arbitration between the two governments concerned. It is from the various sources indicated that in the appropriate cases this Tribunal should gather the principles of so-called international law which it is to administer in these proceedings.

I come now to the third provision, and I have to request the Tribunal to look carefully at the language of Article 7: The decision is to be "in accordance with treaty rights and with the principles of international law and of equity." As was pointed out by my learned friend this morning, this provision does not say "or equity." To that observation I would desire to add this: It does not, moreover, say "with equity;" it does not say "or with equity;" nor does it say "and equity." It says, "the principles of international law and of equity." That is to say, under any proper grammatical construction, "principles" comes over from "international law" and is to be understood before the phrase "of equity," so that the sentence should read in the same way as if it had been written "the principles of international law and the principles of equity."

Taking that as a starting point, I take it that "the principles of equity"—not merely "equity" or "justice and equity"—must by this Tribunal be given a technical interpretation. There has been a great looseness of usage and interpretation of the term *equity* by international tribunals. For example, international tribunals have said where they were operating under a convention requiring that they should do justice and equity, that what they were to do was to administer abstract equity regardless of the law; that they were to try to conceive what was the abstract equity involved in any particular case, and apply that to the case in hand. It is an error, far-reaching and fatal, for international tribunals charged with the enforcement of law to undertake to administer international justice in accordance with the conceptions of equity which may be entertained by the particular arbitrator who may be sitting upon the case.

Fortunately for the development of international arbitration, this general theory of making equity equal the conscience of the judge sitting as a court, is not new; it was widely applied in the earlier years of the development of English equity. It was thoroughly tried and found wanting. In the course of that experience it became perfectly evident that law and order, stability and progress, did not lie along that road. On this point may I call the attention of the Tribunal to the words, oft quoted, of the great Selden, who made use of this expression—and I may say that Mr. Spence, the very learned English commentator upon equity, says that nobody knew more about equity than Selden,—

"Equity," says Selden, "is a Roguish thing, for law we have a measure, know what to trust to; Equity is according to the conscience of him that is Chancellor, and as that is larger or narrower, so is Equity. 'Tis all one as if they should make the Standard for the measure we call (a foot) a Chancellor's foot, what an uncertain measure this would be! One Chancellor has a long Foot, another a short Foot, a third an indifferent Foot; 'Tis the same thing in the Chancellor's Conscience."

May I repeat that the question of developing a jurisprudence by virtue of the individual conscience of the judge passing upon the cases presented to him was tried out in the development of English equity long before we brought it to this country and incorporated it as a part of our law.

Later, however, the fundamental fallacy of the system having become apparent, there was a change, so that Lord Mansfield, one of the greatest English judges, was able to say that—

A court of equity is as much bound by positive rules and general maxims concerning property (though the reason of them may now have ceased) as a court of law is.

In other words, it was found absolutely necessary in order that justice might be certain, in order that people might know what their rights were, might know what they could do and what they could not do, that the principles of equity should be fixed and determined within certain general broad lines; and Lord Eldon still later said, speaking in the case of *Gee v. Pritchard,* a case involving an injunction against the printing of certain letters:

If I had written a letter on the subject of an individual for whom both the person to whom I wrote and myself had a common regard, and the question arose for the first time, I should have found it difficult to satisfy my mind that there is a property in the letter; but it is my duty to submit my judgment to the authority of those who have gone before me; and it will not be easy to remove the weight of the decisions of Lord Hardwicke and Lord Apsley. The doctrines of this Court ought to be as well settled, and made as uniform almost as those of the common law, laying down fixed principles but taking care that they are to be applied according to the circumstances of each case. I cannot agree that the doctrines of this court are to be changed with every succeeding judge. Nothing would inflict on me greater pain, in quitting this place, than the recollection that I had done anything to justify the reproach that the equity of this court varies like the Chancellor's foot.

The point that I wish to make from this is that in developing an international jurisprudence—and this honorable Tribunal will have its due and a great share in such development—the question of what is equity broadly and generally must be carefully considered in order that it may not be, as was the earlier equity of the English courts, made synonymous with individual personal conscience to the almost certain scandal of international arbitration.

It moreover appears to me that the term "principles of equity" are "terms of art," since they are principles which are common to both countries. Now it is well settled that where terms of art are used in a treaty the terms should be interpreted in accordance with the law of the two countries concerned.

In this case the meaning of these terms is the same in both countries. Therefore, it seems to me that "principles of equity," as used in the Special Agreement, is to be understood as meaning, broadly and generally, the principles of equity invoked and applied in the equity jurisprudence as understood and administered in the two countries.

Under the interpretation which is thus given to Article VII of the Special Agreement, treaty rights, the principles of international law, and the principles of equity become amply sufficient and adequate to determine all questions coming before the Tribunal, without the necessity of resort to the varying and indefinite conceptions of abstract equity or conscience.

Turning now again to the Terms of Submission. Article II of these Terms provides:

> The Arbitral Tribunal shall take into account as one of the equities of a claim to such extent as it shall consider just in allowing or disallowing a claim any admission of liability by the Government against whom a claim is put forward.

Article III provides:

> The Arbitral Tribunal shall take into account as one of the equities of a claim to such extent as it shall consider just in allowing or disallowing a claim, in whole or in part, any failure on the part of the claimants to obtain satisfaction through legal remedies which are open to him or placed at his disposal, but no claim shall be disallowed or rejected by application of the general principle of international law that the legal remedies must be exhausted as a condition precedent to the validity of the claim.

And Article IV stipulates:

"The Arbitral Tribunal if it considers equitable may include" a certain amount of interest.

That is, there are in the Terms of Submission themselves three things that are noted as equities to be considered by this court—the question of admission, the question of exhaustion of legal remedies, and the question, under favorable circumstances, of awarding interest.

What is the meaning of equities in those terms of submission? In my judgment it means the same thing here that it would mean in the equitable jurisprudence of the two countries. That is, the same fundamental propositions that would guide and control courts acting under the equitable jurisprudence of the two countries should guide and control here.

On the point of the meaning and purpose of equity, I should like to read the statement of the Master of the Rolls, Sir John Trevor, who made the following comment:

Now, equity is not part of the law, but a moral virtue which qualifies, moderates, and reforms the rigor, hardness and edge of the law, and is a universal truth. It does also assist the law where it is defective and weak in the constitution, which is the life of the law; and defends the law from crafty evasions, delusions, and new subtleties invented and contrived to evade and delude the common law, whereby such as have undoubted rights are made remediless. And this is the office of equity, to protect and support the common law from shifts and contrivances against the justice of the law. Equity, therefore, does not destroy the law, nor create it, but assists it.

Story, the first great commentator upon Equity Jurisprudence in the United States, makes the following comment:

Sir James Mackintosh, in his Life of Sir Thomas More, says: "Equity in the acceptation in which the word is used in English jurisprudence, is no longer to be confounded with that moral Equity, which generally corrects the unjust operation of law, and with which it seems to have been synonymous in the days of Selden and Bacon. It is a part of laws formed from usages and determinations, which sometimes differ from what is called Common Law in its subjects; but chiefly varies from it in its modes of proof, of trial, and of relief. It is a jurisdiction so irregularly formed, and often so little dependent upon general principles, that it can hardly be defined or made intelligible, otherwise than by a minute enumeration of the matters cognizable by it." There is much of general truth in this statement; but it is, perhaps, a little too broad and undistinguishing for an accurate equity lawyer. Equity, as a science, and part of jurisprudence, built upon precedents, as well as upon principles, must occasionally fail in the mere theoretical and philosophical accuracy and completeness of all its rules and governing principles. But it is quite as regular, and exact in its principles and rules, as the Common Law; and, probably, as any other system of jurisprudence, established, generally, by positive enactments, or usages, or practical expositions, in any country, ancient or modern. There must be many principles and exceptions in every system, in a theoretical sense, arbitrary, if not irrational; but which are yet sustained by the accidental institutions, or modifications of society, in the particular country where they exist. There are wide differences between the philosophy of law, as actually administered in any country, and that abstract doctrine, which may in matters of government, constitute, in many minds, the law of philosophy.

This last is the point I desire to bring forth particularly,—that a distinction must be drawn between the law of philosophy and the law which may be applicable as between two countries at difference over legal questions.

One more quotation on this matter from Mr. Pomeroy, one of our modern American authorities on Equity:

I am now prepared to examine, and if possible determine, the true nature of equity considered as an established branch of our American as well as of the English jurisprudence. We are met at the very outset by numerous definitions and descriptions taken from old writers and judges of great ability and high authority, many of which are entirely incorrect and misleading, so far at least as they apply to the system which now exists, and has existed for several generations. These definitions attribute to equity an unbounded discretion, and a power over the law unrestrained by any rule but the conscience of the Chancellor, wholly incompatible with any certainty or security of private right. For the purpose of illustrating these loose and inaccurate conceptions, I have placed in the foot-note a number of extracts taken from the earlier writers.

It is very certain that no court of chancery jurisdiction would at the present day consciously and intentionally attempt to correct the rigor of the law or to supply its defects, by deciding contrary to its settled rules, in any manner, to any extent, or under any circumstances beyond the already settled principles of equity jurisprudence. Those principles and doctrines may unquestionably be extended to new facts and circumstances as they arise, which are analogous to facts and circumstances that have already been the subject-matter of judicial decision, but this process of growth is also carried on in exactly the same manner and to the same extent by the courts of law. Nor would a chancellor at the present day assume to decide the facts of a controversy according to his own standard of right and justice, independently of fixed rules,—he would not attempt to exercise the *arbitrium boni viri;* on the contrary, he is governed in his judicial functions by doctrines and rules embodied in precedents, and does not in this respect possess any greater liberty than the law judges.

From these authorities there may be gathered the meaning of equity and the purpose of equity.

Coming now to the question of admissions, on this point I wish briefly to say: The United States did not intend nor does it desire, to avoid any undertaking, any obligation which it has consciously made or incurred; and I am perfectly sure that His Britannic Majesty's Government are animated by the same spirit; moreover, neither government will wish to secure an award before this Tribunal on any undertaking not consciously given.

I think we cannot overlook the fact that we are here something more than mere litigants before a private tribunal. We are facing each other here practically as sovereign to sovereign and everything that is due from sovereign to sovereign is due to and from us here.

But this brings with it the necessary accompaniment. We must protect each the rights of his own sovereign or, to put it otherwise, the rights of sovereignty. Neither is in a position to permit to pass unchallenged any contention or argument which would in any way impair the sovereignty he represents. Moreover, I take it the Tribunal would wish to lay down no principles that would impair the rights of sovereignty of either party; nor, I apprehend, do they wish to lay down new principles which will either affect generally or override the already settled fundamental principles and rules of the law of nations.

It is with these considerations in view that as representing the United States, I must take exception to any doctrine or principle which would erect into the dignity of a formal obligation against the Government of the United States the statements of subordinate executive officers or any officers not duly authorized to represent and speak to a foreign government for the United States with a view to creating obligations.

It is impossible to tell where a contrary doctrine would lead. Should we stop with communications from the President to the Congress; or from the head of a department to the President; or from the head of one department to the head of another department; or from the head of a subordinate office or bureau of the department to the head of the department? One could not tell where to draw the line if one did not look strictly to the rules and laws that govern in such cases.

Moreover, if the principle were established that a report, that an expression of an opinion by different officers of government one with another, created an obligation in favor of a foreign government or of a citizen or subject of a foreign government, government itself would be paralyzed and destroyed; for no one can tell how far that matter would reach. It would be impossible to foresee what might be said by some ill-advised, inefficient or even corrupt subordinate officer and then invoked against the government itself as establishing a legal liability against it.

On this point I might refer to the fact, well known, of how carefully nations guard against the contracting of obligations when they fully sense and know they are engaged in such a transaction; for example, the negotiation, conclusion, and ratification of treaties. No country concludes a treaty of any importance with another country without demanding the exhibition of full powers from the person authorized to negotiate and sign the treaty. Governments perfectly understand that in dealing with one another in the creation of obligations they deal in certain prescribed ways and in accordance with certain conventional forms, and that if those forms and those ways are not followed the nation is not bound.

On this point I must ask the indulgence of the Tribunal to follow me in a few quotations showing the attitude of the Government of the United States on these points.

First, I wish to say that with the Government of the United States the Executive is the national spokesman with reference to foreign governments. When the United States has anything to say to a foreign government it is said through the Executive.

Mr. Moore, narrating an incident in 1793, says:

The French Minister, having in 1793, requested an exequatur for a consul whose commission was addressed to the Congress of the United States, Mr. Jefferson replied that as the President was the only channel of communication between the United States and foreign nations, it was from him alone "that foreign nations or their agents are to learn what is or has been the will of the nation;" that whatever he communicated as such, they had a right and were bound to consider "as the expression of the nation;" and that no foreign agents could be "allowed to question it," or "to interpose between him and any other branch of Government, under the pretext of either's transgressing their functions." Mr. Jefferson therefore declined to enter into any discussion of the question as to whether it belonged to the President under the Constitution to admit or exclude foreign agents. "I inform you of the fact," he said, "by authority from the President." Mr. Jefferson therefore returned the consul's commission and declared that the President would issue no exequatur to a consul except upon a commission correctly addressed. ("Mr. Jefferson, Secretary of State, to Mr. Genet," 22 November 1793, quoted in John Bassett Moore, *A Digest of International Law,* 8 vols. [Washington, D.C., 1906], 4:680)

Again, the Secretary of State is the organ of official communication between the Government of the United States and foreign governments. He only speaks authoritatively.

(I may remark that I am reading only selected extracts and you will find a great many precedents herein collected with which I do not trouble you.)

As I said, the Secretary of State is the organ of official communication. On this point I desire to read from Moore, vol IV, page 780:

There shall be at the seat of government an executive department to be known as the Department of State and a Secretary of State, who shall be the head thereof.

The Secretary of State shall perform such duties as shall from time to time be enjoined on or intrusted to him by the President relative to correspondences, commissions, or instructions to or with public ministers, or consuls from the United States, or to negotiations with public ministers from foreign States or Princes, or to memorials, or other applications from foreign public Ministers or other foreigners, or to such other matters respecting foreign affairs as the President of the United States shall assign to the Department, and he shall conduct the business of the Department in such manner as the President shall direct. (Revised Statutes, Section 202, quoted in Moore, 4:780)

Mr. Seward when Secretary of State, in an instruction to the American Minister to France, said:

This Department is the legal organ of communication between the President of the United States and foreign countries. All foreign powers recognize it and transmit their communications to it, through the dispatches of our Ministers abroad, or their own diplomatic representatives residing near this Government. These communications are submitted to the President, and, when proper, are replied to under his direction by the Secretary of State. This mutual correspondence is recorded and preserved in the archives of this Department. This is, I believe, the same system which prevails in the governments of civilized states everywhere. (Moore, 4:781)

Turning now to the question of the effect of communications from the President to the Congress, in connection with this question of admissions, it has always been the position of the United States that such communications were private communications, passing, if you will, between members of the family; that foreign nations were not entitled to question them, were not bound by them, and that the foreign government became interested only when the determination of Congress was conveyed to them.

In 1835 Mr. Forsyth, Secretary of State, in writing to Mr. Livingston, our Minister to France, said:

The President corresponds with foreign governments through their diplomatic agents, as the organ of the nation. As such he speaks for the nation. In his messages to Congress he speaks only for the Executive to the legislature. He recommends, and his recommendations are powerless, unless followed by legislative action. No discussion of them can be permitted. All allusions to them, made with a design to mark an anticipated or actual difference of opinion between the Executive and legislature, are indelicate in themselves. (Moore, 4:684)

Mr. Marcy, Secretary of State, in 1856, said:

The President's annual message is a communication from the Executive to the legislative branch of the Government; an internal transaction, with which it is not deemed proper or respectful for foreign powers or their representative to interfere, or even to resort to it as the basis of diplomatic correspondence. It is not a document addressed to foreign governments. (Moore, 4:685)

Again, in 1875, Mr. Fish, addressing a communication to our Minister to Turkey, said:

The Turkish Minister having produced a volume of Foreign Relations of the United States, and commented on the circumstance that the correspondence of the Department of State with its consular officers in Tripoli and Tunis was arranged under the head of "Barbary States" instead of "Turkey" his attention was called to the fact "that the volume to which he referred . . . was a communication addressed by the President to Congress, and not one addressed to foreign governments (although we furnished them with copies of this, as we do of all or nearly all of our public documents)," and "that the arrangement to which he had referred was not intended to convey any special political significance, but was one of usage and of domestic convenience." (Moore, 4:686)

In this connection it may be observed that if communications on matters such as those under discussion with Turkey are not for the cognizance of foreign Powers, that is, if foreign Powers are not bound by them or have no interest in them, then where the President transmits to Congress a recommendation for the payment of a claim made by an alien against the Government of the United States as a matter of grace, as a matter of sovereign favor, it surely cannot be that that recommendation can be taken as an admission of liability upon the part of this government to compensate said alien. If it is to be ruled that the President of the United States cannot recommend to Congress as a matter of grace and favor any claim of an alien against the Government of the United States without thereby raising against the United States an obligation of liability, obviously such matters of favor and grace must cease; because as the President has no control over Congress, no control over the appropriations of Congress, can only recommend to Congress, he cannot afford to undertake, nor can the Government of the United States afford to have him attempt to undertake to do the proper, the right, the just, or the equitable thing without running the danger of having invoked against the United States the admission of a positive legal liability in the case.

Again, I say that only statements made by the Secretary of State are to be regarded as binding upon this government, and even then, and in respect to that, I would add the further contention and argument that it must be understood that foreign governments, and they have been dealing with the United States for 125 years, must know that the Secretary of State himself has not full powers to bind this government, that he himself is circumscribed, that the President whom he represents is circumscribed, that they cannot by themselves, that is the Executive, obligate this government to pay a claim; and foreign governments receiving assurances from the national Executive would, I take it, be taken to know that the Secretary of State in making any such declaration, was exceeding his well recognized and established authority, and was giving an undertaking of no force or value.

I do not need, however, to go that far with reference to the cases before us.

As to the "admissions of liability" contemplated in the Terms of Submission, I must observe that this expression cannot mean duly authorized and binding admissions of legal liability by the proper officer of government, since if such an admission were produced I see little left for the Tribunal to decide unless it be the question of the amount. Surely such an admission would be entitled to more consideration than an equity; it would be of the essence. It cannot be that such admissions were in contemplation.

Now I want to draw a distinction, however, between such duly authorized admissions of legal liability and certain so-called admissions which have been used in the course of the argument here before the Tribunal—and, I submit, properly used.

If a subordinate officer of the American Government, either a Cabinet officer or one subordinate to a Cabinet officer, has made an "admission," so-called, of legal liability, if he has said that in his opinion the United States is legally liable on some claim, I submit that such an "admission" does not impose upon the United States an obligation, though it may be appropriately used for what it is worth—little, I think—as an evidence of what the law is on that transaction. But it may not be used as evidence that the United States has admitted a liability, because the party making it has no authority to make such an admission. Moreover, admissions of persons as to facts may be appropriately used. For example, if in a collision case the captain of the American boat in a report to his chief says that the facts of this transaction were so and so, I submit that His Majesty's Government has a right to introduce such a report as evidence of the facts and the report should be so considered. But such a statement as that does not constitute, and was never intended to constitute, an admission of legal liability by this government.

And to repeat what I said a few moments ago, if that does constitute an admission of liability, then I say to you that government is threatened.

In this connection I submit that Mr. Newcombe's use of the letter yesterday from Lieutenant Tillman regarding the time of delivery of those logs was a pertinent and proper use. He invoked it as evidence of the time when the logs were delivered, and however much I would disagree with him—as I would—as to the interpretation which he placed upon that letter, nevertheless that was evidence which he had a right to introduce and upon which the Tribunal has a right to rely, or at least to consider, in the matter of determining the facts.

One word more and I will have finished.

As covering this whole question of the meaning of the terms of the Special Agreement and the danger that will come from this Tribunal or any arbitral tribunal undertaking to do anything other than administer the law, and in some few cases consciously and carefully probably extending it, I may be permitted to observe that if nations come to feel in submitting differences to arbitration that the decision will probably not be according to the law involved but will be according to the ideas of the Tribunal, as to abstract right and justice, then I say to you arbitration cannot live. No nation would know where an arbitral tribunal might go in a controversy to which it was a party. As I understood the position taken by my learned friend today, it was that the decisions of this Tribunal must be in accordance with the law, international law, with treaties, with the principles of equity—

SIR CHARLES FITZPATRICK. Are those alternative or cumulative expressions—international law and equity?

MR. CLARK. The agreement contemplates the principles of international law and the principles of equity.

SIR CHARLES FITZPATRICK. Yes; the principles of international law as governed by the principles of equity, or are they disjunctive?

MR. CLARK. I think they are disjunctive, sir.

SIR CHARLES FITZPATRICK. Alternative?

MR. CLARK. Yes, sir.

SIR CHARLES FITZPATRICK. Where there is a principle of international law that principle has to be applied in its entirety. Failing in the principle of international law, then in the alternative you take the principle of equity?

MR. CLARK. Yes; but understanding international law to comprise the other matters which to my mind coordinate with the strict international law and complement it, and which I referred to and discussed in the beginning of my remarks.

SIR CHARLES FITZPATRICK. Quite right.

MR. CLARK. Unless the Tribunal develops the law in that way and unless the principles governing the Tribunal are these, arbitration is certainly in a precarious condition, because nations will not, they cannot afford, under the existing conditions of the world, to submit questions to determination by arbitral tribunals unless they have the confidence and assurance that the tribunal will in its deliberations and determinations be guided by the fixed and settled rules and principles properly applicable and controlling.

The Next Advance in the Judicial Settlement of International Disputes (Compulsory)

3 May 1915

This article was written by JRC in response to a request from Theodore Marburg, president of the American Society for Judicial Settlement of International Disputes. It was solicited to be published in the May quarterly of the society. JRC spelled out clearly what he proposed to write and expressed doubt that it was what Marburg would want to print; however, Marburg urged him to prepare the article. In submitting the article to Marburg, JRC again said that Marburg might not wish to publish it as a judicial settlement matter, "for among other things it in a small way uncovers certain deities worshipped in high places" (J. Reuben Clark, Jr., to Theodore Marburg, 3 May 1915). Marburg described the first part of the article as "critical or destructive of present aspirations" and the latter parts as "constructive . . . highly suggestive and useful" and proposed publishing the latter part with several "omissions or modifications . . . of statements in line with the position taken . . . in the first parts of the paper." He then made what appears to have been a confession to JRC: "As you are probably aware, the main object in founding the 'Judicial Settlement' Society was to promote the Court of Arbitral Justice. . . . It would therefore never do for the Society to attack, in its Quarterly, the wisdom of the project" (Marburg to Clark, 4 May 1915). JRC said he knew the society was committed more or less to the Court of Arbitral Justice, but "had not appreciated that the promotion of that court was the main object in founding the

Society, and had assumed from its name that the primary purpose of the organization was the promotion of the judicial settlement of international disputes" (Clark to Marburg, 5 May 1915). In his first letter to Marburg, JRC said he could not write (and he was sure Marburg did not wish him to attempt so to do) anything which did not commend itself fully to his own judgment and which set forth anything else than that which he firmly believed (Clark to Marburg, 5 April 1915). Under the circumstances, he could not in good conscience make the deletions and other modifications necessary to satisfy Marburg; therefore, the article was not published.

In his letter of 5 April 1915 to Marburg, JRC described the position he took in the paper as follows:

> I came to the conclusion that the real line open for advance in the extension of the judicial settlement of international disputes lay not in the direction of the creation of a new court . . . not in the direction of providing some machinery for the enforcement of arbitral awards . . . but in the direction of the establishment of the principle in however limited a field at first, of what is sometimes known as compulsory arbitration; or to put it in a slightly different way, in the establishment of a principle and procedure which would enable an injured government in certain specified matters to hale into court the offending government, whether that government would or not, securing a judgment thereon by default, if the defendant nation proved indifferent or obdurate. While fully recognizing that any such plan would have its disadvantages and that such disadvantages would be great, I am convinced in my own mind that it promises the greatest real advancement for world's peace that is open from the standpoint of the judicial settlement of international disputes.

For letters, see Box 24, Correspondence, "Judicial Settlement of International Disputes," 3–5 May 1915, JRCP. For article, see Box 46, Book 3, 1915, Arbitration, J 9.15, JRCP.

It is a familiar fact that because of varying conditions of wind, tide, current, and numerous other elements affecting successful navigation, a straightaway sailing course between two ports is rarely or never feasible. The vessel tacks now in this direction, now in that, perhaps never sailing for any great space along the direct line. The navigator is content if his advance be in such general direction as shall ultimately bring him seasonably to his port.

So it is with progress towards the judicial settlement of international disputes. Varying, changing, and crossing currents and conditions of finance, government, industry, and thought; permanent elements of race and physical environment; half permanent factors such as national ideals, aspirations, and religion; the all important infinity of the human mind and character with the resulting complexity of human society,—all these elements and others working simultaneously in direct current, and in cross and counter-current, force the conclusion that a direct course to the universal judicial settlement of international disputes may not now be made. A wise direction of progress towards this end would therefore seem to require both a recognition of these facts and an accommodation to them of all measures taken to reach the end.

As it must seemingly be admitted that a plan for the judicial settlement of all international disputes may not be and probably is not in fact now possible in practice, wisdom counsels that attention and determination should not be unalterably fixed on an impracticable, if not an actually unattainable end. Yet, as it is certain that human welfare and happiness will be augmented and conserved by the nearest possible approach to that end, human effort should be employed in making every possible real advance towards an attainable approximation, for every approximation is a real gain, not a loss for humanity.

But just as it would be unwise to direct a ship along a course over which progress was no longer possible because of adverse conditions of waves, tides, currents, or wind, or along a course which no longer afforded the greatest possible advance towards the port of destination, so is it unwise to head the judicial settlement movement in directions in which developed opposition appears either to bar further true progress or to make real advancement less rapid than could be made on some other course.

In what direction therefore does it appear wise that the judicial settlement movement should seek now to proceed?

One discussing judicial settlements is oppressed by the fact and embarrassed by the knowledge thereof, that the subject has long since been written out in its essentials. No one can hope, with any real justification, to advance anything new. The most one can do is to re-survey the question from some slightly different angle and bring old ideas into new relationships and juxtaposition, so possibly pointing out the way for further progress in this matter of vital human concern. No further excuse will therefore be offered for the triteness of the observations which are to follow.

The peace crusader frequently appears to overlook the basic consideration that the actual state of mind of the world is as much a fact and factor in this whole problem of peaceful settlement of international disputes as is anything else; and further that this state of world mind is not necessarily either what the crusader desires, or thinks it should be. Man is what he is, not necessarily what he ought to be. Every peaceful settlement movement must reckon with the facts as they are.

Again, it has become the fashion to speak of the world of today as something quite different in essence from what it was a thousand or even a hundred years ago; to talk of the operation of new forces upon humanity; and to consider that the nature and mind of man have somehow recently undergone a metamorphosis from lower to higher forms, so eliminating former baseness. But it is to be doubted whether so far as man is concerned, any new forces of any kind exist, either in physical nature or in the human mind. Forces that have always worked, are working today. So far behind us as we can reach with history, tradition, or myth, there are in man the same selfishness, envy, avarice, cruelty, ambition, domination, love, and hate, that exist in him today, no other or different. These were, are, and, while man is man, ever will be the main springs of human action. They materialize now in one form, now in another, sometimes their dormancy seems like extinction, but still they are there. What man sought yesterday, the means he used, and what he wrought to get it, he will seek, use, and do today and tomorrow. It is true he has in his normal state somewhat softened his manner, he has restrained somewhat his animal instincts, but in times of great stress, when he thinks his existence threatened, man is again the primal brute. The elemental still wells up in him and bursts out from him, and when it comes it is naked, with all its primitive ferocity and attended by all its accompanying virtues and vices.

It seems clear on reflection, that any wise statesmanlike plan for advancement in the peaceful settlement of international disputes must be framed to meet and deal with man and his attributes as they have been and are.

Quite obviously in the judicial settlement of international disputes, four things are necessary: First, a justiciable dispute to be settled; second, an agreement to submit the dispute to an international tribunal for judicial settlement; third, a tribunal to which the dispute may be referred for adjudication; and fourth, the satisfaction of the award made by the tribunal.

For our purposes, international differences may be divided into two classes: first, those justiciable—that is those involving disputes which are determinable under and in accordance with the established and applicable principles of international law and therefore fit for judicial settlement; and, second, those non-justiciable—that is those involving disputes as to matters of political or other policy which are outside the domain and beyond the guidance, regulation, or control of existing international law, and therefore unfit for judicial settlement.

It is believed that, for illustration, an analogy may be here appropriately drawn between the conduct of individuals under our own laws and Constitution and the conduct of states under the law of nations. As to the former, it may be remarked that while pursuant to the laws and the Constitution certain rules of behavior are prescribed both for our personal and business relations as individuals, as also for the mutual relationship of government and individual, yet our fundamental instrument places certain matters such as freedom of speech and of the press, and freedom of religion, beyond the control of law or government, thereby creating what the continental civil lawyers have termed a realm of anarchy. Within the ascertained boundaries of this realm, individuals move with the most complete and absolute freedom, wholly without legal restraint,—each person being a law unto himself. So it is with states. They have organized themselves into a society; they have as to certain matters set for themselves more or less clearly defined rules of action and conduct which make up the body of so-called international law, in accordance with which they are to regulate their intercourse, both in peace and in war. But they have also reserved to themselves, as individual units, a very large domain of political life in which each state moves without legal limitation, and works out its own will and purpose unrestrained, in the last analysis, by anything save the superior will of its more powerful associates. This is a realm of international anarchy and within it every state acts with its original, primal freedom—indeed license—each a law unto itself.

It may be questioned whether it is either more possible or more desirable, to delimit one of these realms than the other, for thus far human progress has been founded on both.

The Judicial Settlement Society is organized for the purpose, as its name shows, of advancing the *judicial* settlement of international disputes, that is the settlement by judicial processes of those disputes and controversies which are amenable to the rules and principles of law which nations have set up for their guidance and control. It has nothing to do with the settlement of those political questions which lie outside the domain of international law and within the realm of international anarchy. But even as thus delimited, the field is of such wide extent that it will not be fully covered in this generation.

So far, therefore, as the international dispute is concerned, the suggestions made hereinafter apply only to those that may be settled by invoking those rules and principles of law which are applicable and controlling.

Regarding the satisfaction or enforcement of awards, it is to be noted that considerable agitation has recently taken place over the alleged necessity of providing some sort of international marshal, supported and assisted by an adequate international police, whose duty it shall be to enforce the awards of international tribunals; and not a little effort has been spent in promoting this suggestion. There are, however, a number of considerations which indicate that the establishment of an international constabulary is by no means a pressing necessity now, and further that the present agitation is unwise, because involving a diffusion of effort that should be concentrated for advancing the general cause.

It must not be overlooked that, unfortunately but not without justification, the small powers have a basic and universal suspicion, sometimes growing into fear and dislike, of the large powers, which makes them unwilling to consent to the creation of any engine of possible oppression. It must, however, be assumed that the *sine qua non* of the establishment of any serviceable international constabulary would be the cooperation of practically all the powers, great and small. A constabulary created by a few powers to operate among themselves only would, at best, be of doubtful advantage to the general cause, and for a part of the powers to join in imposing the plan upon the others would be monumental tyranny. But a majority of the small powers have already indicated their unwillingness, except under reservations rendering the plan practically useless, to enter into a convention which provided *inter alia* for the use of force in enforcing the award of a tribunal on a contract debt, even though this force was to be exercised by the creditor nation only. The history of this proposition before the Second Hague Conference, as disclosed in its published proceedings, seems to leave little justification for hope that the small powers would join in a plan for a general international constabulary.*

Moreover, the same natural indisposition which an individual would have against participating in a measure that would subject him to national police in matters not theretofore under police cognizance and that would deprive him of any liberty of movement theretofore enjoyed, would operate adversely upon and probably control the action of some of the larger powers in this delimination of their former freedom of action. Again, it is almost a certainty that some of the larger powers would see in the establishment of any such arrangement such a potential threat of armed interference with them as to make them hostile to the suggestion. Both of these considerations would make seriously against and probably prevent the establishment of such a force.

But yet the effort to set up such a constabulary might and ought to be made if it be a necessity. But it is not. Little real difficulty is experienced or ever has been experienced in getting self-respecting nations to carry out the awards of international tribunals, and where hesitation has been shown there has usually been found some way successfully to meet it without serious trouble or inconvenience. The energies and resources at the command of the workers for judicial settlement are far too scanty to be frittered away on non-essentials; they should go to the actual necessaries. It would be an inexcusable blundering to arouse among the nations any unnecessary

---

*Of the forty-four states represented at the Second Hague Conference, ten (Belgium, Brazil, China, Liberia, Luxembourg, Roumania, Siam, Sweden, Switzerland, and Venezuela) refused to sign the Convention governing the use of force in the collection of contract debts. None of these, except China and Liberia, have since adhered. Ten other states, to wit: Argentine Republic, Bolivia, Colombia, Dominican Republic, Ecuador, Greece, Guatemala, Peru, Salvador, and Uruguay, signed with reservations. None of these has ratified the Convention. Nicaragua has since adhered with a reservation. Yet under normal conditions and judging by the past, it may be fairly assumed that among these states there are some against which it may be found at some time useful to be in a position to invoke the provisions of the Convention. Yet they are not as yet parties to it, and therefore not subject to its terms.

irritation or hostile feeling over a matter which at best is now but of merely auxiliary importance.

Effort devoted to this phase of the subject might much better be directed along other lines where the necessities are greater and the chances of success larger.

As to the forming of a tribunal to hear and determine the difference, it should in the first place be observed that the nations have already created a general court of arbitration—the Permanent Court of Arbitration at The Hague,—to which they have agreed generally to resort. This court has heretofore fully and promptly responded to every demand made upon it, and has risen to every opportunity presented to it. Moreover, the terms under which resort to it may be had are so all-embracing and elastic, that one can scarcely imagine a difference that could be submitted to it which it would prove incompetent to hear and adjudge. Such being the facts, the necessary tribunal can be regarded as now in being. As will be pointed out later, there are certain amendments to the Pacific Settlements Convention that must still be made to enable it to handle certain cases, but nothing so formidable and difficult as the erection of a new court (adverted to below) need now be considered. The cause of arbitration does not presently require a new court, and will be now only indirectly benefitted by it.

This conclusion is supported by the fact that the history of modern arbitration shows no insurmountable obstacle or even real difficulty in constituting a court, once an agreement is reached to arbitrate the dispute. Indeed in recent years the difficulties attached to the forming of the court have been all but negligible. The great difficulty, and this in some instances has led to the very brink of war, has been found in securing an agreement to arbitrate. This being secured, the other steps have followed, even in the extreme cases, almost as a matter of course.

For the present therefore, a tribunal being already provided, the problem of creating some new or other court, however desirable it may ultimately prove, for a perfect system, may be safely held in abeyance, and the energy which would be spent for that purpose be applied at other points.

Before leaving this subject, however, one or two observations may be offered regarding the plan for a Court of Arbitral Justice as formulated at the last Hague Conference, and referred to in the Final Act of the Conference.

Some appear to entertain an impression that if this plan were put into operation, it would provide as to the powers signatory thereto, a scheme of compulsory arbitration, that is, a scheme which would enable a power signatory to its establishing convention, to compel any other power signatory to arbitrate any difference between them. This is not the fact. The plan would not impose nor does it contemplate compulsory arbitration. Indeed the constitution of the new court would not widen at all the present field of arbitration. The powers could properly decline to arbitrate any question then as freely as they may now. Indeed they would not be under any obligation even to resort to the proposed new court to settle the differences they are already under obligation to arbitrate, but they might refer such differences either to a special tribunal, to the Permanent Hague Court, or to the new court, as best suited their fancies, their policies, or their interests.

There would of course under the proposed plan be the advantage of having a court already formed which could sit upon every case, and there might be a resulting continuity of decision which might or might not be greater than will be maintained in the Permanent Court. But the present advantages of both of these and the danger of non-continuity of decision by the Permanent Court, are all so slight as practically to eliminate the necessity for the satisfying of these advantages in anything less than a highly perfected organization.

Some emphasis has also been laid on the fact that the proposed plan would bring as members of the court men of high standards, learning, and legal ability. Quite aside from the obvious bad taste and even stultification involved in an argument thus severely reflecting not only upon the character of the general personnel of the Hague Permanent Court panel, but of our own representatives on the court (from whom judges are taken for the hearing of cases submitted under the Pacific Settlement Convention) but also upon the men who have actually sat upon the cases going before the Permanent Court, always with rectitude and generally with a judicial attitude, learning, and ability, this argument is not one of great strength. A glance at the Permanent Court panel will show that governments have usually appointed thereon as their representatives at least some of their strongest men—men who would almost certainly be appointed to a "permanent" court were it established. It is these same men whom the powers have chosen for service in the various arbitrations at The Hague. But if such men on a tribunal formed under the Pacific Settlement Convention, are undesirable, what just reason is there for thinking that if they were appointed to another court they would lose their undesirability? A man's fitness for office can hardly depend on the wording of his commission. Moreover, if these men or any of them are regarded as unfit, why create for them a "permanent" court where you would be compelled to try your case before them, rather than leave them as a panel, where, in the constitution of a tribunal for any particular case, they can be so easily overlooked?

But aside from this point, it may be well to observe that the forty-four powers represented at The Hague refused, or at least failed, to enact the proposed plan into a Convention and so to inaugurate such a "permanent" court.* They did, however, express a *wish* that this might be done, that is they wished for the doing of an act which they had it in their power to do and might do if they so wished. Moreover, in expressing even this *wish,* in itself a logical absurdity, almost fifty per cent of the powers made a reservation (such as would render the whole scheme lamentably ineffective) on the only really critical point in the whole scheme, namely, the representation of the constituting powers in the court.†

---

*The records of the Second Hague Conference show, regarding the scheme accompanying the *voeu,* the following situation:—Belgium, Denmark, Greece, Roumania, Switzerland, and Uruguay abstained from voting. Mexico, Brazil, Colombia, Persia, Guatemala, Haiti, Venezuela, Paraguay, Dominican Republic, Panama, Ecuador, China, Bolivia, and Nicaragua, either made reservations to the effect that the court when established must recognize the absolute equality of states, (which would make the organization of an effective, useful court impossible), or made declarations of like tenor.

†It is of interest to observe that the powers in making their final vote on the Prize Court Convention (which contains the plan of choice and distribution of judges seemingly in the minds of those promoting the Arbitral Court plan) divided as follows: Dominican Republic, Japan, Russia, Siam, Turkey, and Venezuela abstained from voting; Brazil voted no; Chile, China, Colombia, Cuba, Ecuador, Guatemala, Haiti, Persia, Salvador, and Uruguay voted under reserves regarding the choice and distribution of judges. Later the following powers, though voting for the convention, refused to sign: China, Greece, Luxembourg, Montenegro, Nicaragua, Roumania, and Serbia. Liberia did not vote on the proposition and has not signed. Japan, Siam, and Turkey signed the Convention, the latter two under reservation. Russia, Dominican Republic, and Venezuela, abstained from voting and have not subsequently signed.

If some plan were devised to meet the objections inherent in this one, and this seems not impossible, it would, at the right moment, considerably advance the cause of judicial settlement to adopt it. But no such plan has been yet considered. Viewing the matter not from the standpoint of building a perfect system, but from that of doing what needs doing most and can be most easily done, from the standpoint of advancing the cause of arbitration at the greatest possible speed, one is constrained to believe that the continued overemphasis of this plan at this time is most inexpedient. The effort expended on this would better be put on something else which is really now needful.

Of the four things stated as necessary for the judicial settlement of international disputes one remains for comment,—the agreement of the differing powers to submit their dispute to judicial settlement.

As has been already intimated, the real difficulty in the way of bringing about the peaceful settlement of international disputes comes in securing an agreement to arbitrate. The history of accomplished peaceful settlements makes this so clear and certain that no time will be spent in demonstrating it beyond referring to one already well known illustration. At the First Hague Conference, Germany seems to have made her support to the Pacific Settlement Convention dependent upon the dropping of the proposal to provide for the compulsory arbitration of certain questions, and the proposal was dropped. At the Second Hague Conference, Germany was an ardent advocate of compulsory arbitration in the abstract; she joined in amending and perfecting the Pacific Settlement Convention; and she not only worked and voted for, but seemingly assisted in the elaboration of the scheme for a Court of Arbitral Justice as to which the Conference finally expressed a *voeu;* but Germany, though heart and soul for the abstract principle, though cordially favoring and supporting all plans for establishing the auxiliaries of arbitration, would have nothing to do with and secured the defeat of a plan which if erected into a Convention would have gone appreciably towards the root of the difficulty by putting the signatory powers under a treaty obligation actually to settle by arbitration certain specified subjects. That is to say the one thing Germany was unwilling to do was to sign an agreement putting her under a definite treaty obligation to arbitrate her differences with other powers. Her unwillingness so to do killed the plan.

The basic problem, therefore, in promoting arbitration is how to meet and overcome the difficulty of securing, particularly at critical stages of negotiations, an agreement to arbitrate international differences. It is of the essence that to be truly effective the agreement must require no auxiliary action before it becomes operative upon a given dispute.

Experience, it may by way of preliminary remark be observed, suggests that agreements to arbitrate differences may be most easily made before the actual specific difference arises and becomes a matter of an active discussion, for discussion unduly magnifies the difference by reason of the efforts of both foreign offices to support their own and combat the other's case. In part and in some of its aspects the pecuniary claims arbitration now carrying on between the United States and Great Britain illustrates this point. For notwithstanding both parties were signatories to the Pacific Settlement Hague Convention, and had in addition a general agreement between themselves to arbitrate the exact class of cases under discussion, yet it was not possible to make the necessary special agreement except by an elimination of certain cases which, though justiciable and therefore properly fit for arbitration, yet were excluded, because the discussion thereof had developed an unwillingness to arbitrate on the part of the one party or the other.

It necessarily follows from these facts that a general agreement to arbitrate international differences, effective without special agreements for each case, will be of almost infinitely greater value and service and will mark far greater progress in the cause of judicial settlement, than will a general agreement which to be effective in a particular case must be supplemented by a special agreement that must be framed in the heat and distortion of a current argument.

For obvious reasons (some already suggested) a general preliminary agreement of this kind is now possible only as to international differences that are justiciable, that is governed by ascertained law. The powers, large or small, will almost certainly be unwilling now to agree to go further than this. The attitude of Great Britain towards the constitution of the International Prize Court makes this clear.

From the point of view of the field to be covered,—the jurisdiction,—there are two forms of general agreement (for each of which there is something to be said) by which the desired object might be accomplished. The first is a general agreement to arbitrate all differences arising between the signatory powers *except* those belonging to specified classes, (and) or *except* those found upon an enumerating list. The American delegation to the Second Hague Conference proposed, as permitted by their instructions, an arbitration plan in which the exceptions were designated by classes, the classes named being vital interests, honor, and independence of the power arbitrating, and the interest of third powers (see Annex 1 [not printed herein]). So far as advancing the cause of arbitration is concerned, one of the fatal defects of this plan lay in the principle embodied in the second article of the proposal which gave to each of the powers the right to determine whether the particular difference fell within the named exceptions. It is not easy to think of any controversy arising between states which would not in some aspect affect the vital interests of one of the states. It may in passing be remarked that the treaties making such broad initial exceptions, particularly when supplemented by the determinative clause of this plan, do not make any real progress in the cause of arbitration. Indeed such treaties mark a long retreat from the advanced position taken nearly a half a century ago by the United States and Great Britain in the Treaty of Washington, under which Great Britain arbitrated matters affecting her vital interests, her honor, and her rights as an independent neutral nation.

The second kind of possible general agreement is that in which it is agreed to arbitrate questions falling in specified classes, or included in an enumerating list, all other differences than those specified being beyond the purview of the treaty. At the Second Hague Conference, the scheme finally elaborated, known as the Anglo-American project, was a combination of both sorts of agreement, that is, it contained an exemption of all questions of vital interests, honor, and independence, with the further pernicious provision that each state should judge for itself whether any of these were on its part involved, and it also added a list of subjects which it was agreed could be submitted to arbitration without the reserves or exemptions noted, i.e., such listed matters were not to be subject to exemption on the ground that they involved the vital interests, honor, or independence of the parties. A further clause provided for the making of a *compromis* for each particular case that should arise.

As the plan contemplated a scheme of semi-obligatory arbitration, the vote on the project is not without interest and significance.

Thirty-two states voted for the proposal; nine voted against it,

73

and three abstained. Those voting nay were Austria-Hungary, Belgium, Bulgaria, Germany, Greece, Montenegro, Roumania, Switzerland, and Turkey. Those abstaining were Italy, Japan, and Luxembourg. Mr. Higgins' comment upon the result is, "The opposition of Germany and Austria-Hungary and the abstention of Italy were fatal." Propositions considered in connection with the elaboration of the scheme were made by Serbia, Portugal, Sweden, Brazil, San Domingo [Dominican Republic], Denmark, Mexico, Switzerland, United States, Great Britain, Greece, Austria-Hungary, Italy, Russia, and Uruguay,—an indication, it may be safely said, of the widespread willingness, if not desire, for some arrangement of this sort. Mr. Fromageot's excellent table analysis of these various proposals is printed as an Annex to this paper (Annex 2) [not printed herein].

Looking at the scheme dispassionately and away from the heat of the conflict that waged over it, one is compelled to the view that as it finally emerged from the attacks of its enemies, it marked slight, perhaps no real progress in arbitration. It was little, if any, better than the *voeu* finally adopted, which Mr. Choate attacked so vigorously and for which the delegates of the United States abstained from voting. Viewed as a plan even of limited obligatory arbitration, it had two fatal defects, one of commission and one of omission,—it provided for the making of a special agreement in each case before arbitration could be had, and it failed to provide that if one of the parties was unwilling and refused to arbitrate, the other party could proceed to arbitration alone. No scheme can be properly regarded as providing for compulsory arbitration which does not provide for the latter. Considered side by side with the truly great Prize Court Convention, which provides against both these defects, the obligatory arbitration plan was unworthy [of] the Commission that evolved it.

It is a curious circumstance that notwithstanding thirty states (including, and this is of practical importance, nearly all of the states that have frequently resorted to arbitration in the past as also those with which we seem most likely to have differences in the future) voted for this plan of obligatory arbitration, defective though it is, still almost nothing has been done to advance obligatory arbitration which seems thus so promising and which, as shown, is the essence of the whole problem. And yet the proposal to create a Court of Arbitral Justice under a plan that called for the reservations (which would make its effective establishment impossible) from nearly half the world, including many of these same powers, has had most vigorous, even though as yet ineffective, support.

As already suggested no agreement for compulsory arbitration will meet its name which does not provide some method by which a dispute may be judicially settled where one of the parties is unwilling and refuses to proceed. And a difference is to be taken between compelling the arbitration of a dispute and compelling its settlement.

There are two ways that immediately suggest themselves in which to accomplish this: The first is by the plan adopted by the Second Hague Conference for the collection of contract debts, by which a signatory power recognizes the right of collection by force "when the debtor State refuses or neglects to reply to an offer of arbitration, or after accepting this offer, prevents any *compromis* from being agreed on, or after the arbitration, fails to submit to the award." Or shortly put, it is probably accurate to say that in effect this convention recognizes the right to use physical force to compel arbitration or settlement, or putting it in another way, this convention really legalizes war under given conditions, and in this view is not properly to be considered as in essence a measure looking to judicial settlement. Having in mind the attitude (already alluded to) of the smaller powers, constituting practically half of the world's nations, towards this plan, it can hardly be regarded as satisfactory.

But there is a further point. The Contract Debt Convention is not, as a fact, a plan for compulsory arbitration, since under it a recalcitrant power need never go to arbitration. It is, as stated, merely designed to compel arbitration or settlement. It is true the Contract Debt Convention plan provides for *obligatory* arbitration, that is, it places states under a treaty obligation to arbitrate. But *compulsory* arbitration requires that arbitration may be secured when desired by one only of the powers, and no plan which does not enable one power actually to present a difference before a tribunal for hearing and determination, no matter whether the other party is willing or not, can be regarded as a compulsory arbitration plan.

After an agreement is secured giving the right thus to compel arbitration, quite obviously there must be a practically self operative provision for the forming of a tribunal to hear the case, in cases where one of the parties does not participate.

It would appear that this latter might be accomplished without great difficulty by so amending the Pacific Settlement Convention as to provide in such cases for the empaneling of a court to whom the power desiring to arbitrate could present its petition and prayer for hearing and determination, notwithstanding the other party declined to participate at all in the proceedings. It would seem this might be done by a provision stipulating that in cases of difference between two powers signatory to such an arbitration agreement, the matter should be referred to a tribunal composed of the senior member of the Hague Court from each of the countries to the dispute, and an umpire, who should have the decisive vote, to be chosen by these two, or in default of a choice by this means, then the umpire to be chosen (for example) by the ruler of Holland (when Holland was not a party, and by some other power if Holland were involved), the umpire to be neither a subject of Holland (or of the other nominating sovereign) nor of either of the differing states, any two of these three to constitute a tribunal authorized to proceed to a hearing and determination of the case. The smaller powers would not be likely seriously to object to such a plan for it gives them what they insist upon (and rightly, so long as nationals are chosen to sit in arbitration cases), namely their own nationals upon the tribunal hearing the case in which they are parties.

If it be suggested that such a plan would require an equivalent of the Court of Arbitral Justice, and therefore why not go on and seek to establish that court, it may be answered first, that the smaller powers have already declared their unwillingness to constitute such a court except upon conditions that would not provide an effective tribunal; that there is no apparent reason for supposing that they have changed or will change their views in the immediate future; and that it seems unwise if not indeed impracticable to establish a world's court with one-half or less of the world in it. In the second place, it is easier to modify an existing plan by amendment than it is to frame and adopt an entirely new plan. In other words, there are in the suggested amendment fewer difficulties to overcome,—a most important factor in all such matters. And in the third place, and accessory to the second, such a modification as proposed would give to the smaller powers, in the special court when constituted, the precise recognition and participation which they desire and demand in the Court of Arbitral Justice, to its destruction as an effective tribunal.

As to the feasibility of providing for such a scheme of compulsory arbitration, among the powers, it is to be said that this is precisely what has been done in the International Prize Court Convention, for under that Convention, resort may be had to the International Prize Court by a neutral power dissatisfied with the decisions of the local prize court; by a neutral individual, under conditions stated; or by the subject or citizen of an enemy power, whose property is injuriously affected by the decision of the local prize court. Moreover, the Convention distinctly provides (Art. XI) that either party failing to appear or to comply with the rules of the court the case proceeds without him and judgment is given "in accordance with the material at its disposal."

In this connection the attitude of the Senate of the United States is of interest. That body has declined to advise and consent to the ratification of the Olney-Pauncefote Treaty; to general treaties of arbitration which did not specifically provide for a special agreement requiring its advice and consent in each particular case before the case could go to arbitration; to the Pacific Settlement Convention of the Second Hague Conference, except upon a proviso that the provision making it possible for the Permanent Court to frame a *compromis* in case of failure so to do by the two interested powers should not be operative as against the United States; to the treaty regarding contract debts save upon the understanding that the contemplated recourse to the Permanent Court could be only by virtue of other arbitration conventions, general or special; and to the Taft-Knox treaties with France and Great Britain, save upon the express reservation of the right (which indeed it was intended the treaty should give) of that body to pass upon a special agreement to arbitrate any question arising. The Senate also eliminated from these latter treaties a proposed agreement to submit to a Joint Commission for determination [of] the question whether any given difficulty was arbitrable under the treaty. And yet the Senate advised and consented to the ratification of the Prize Court Convention without any reservation whatsoever as to the two vital points of the plan as just discussed.

The powers have thus joined in one truly compulsory arbitration convention. No reason is seen why the principle may not be extended. It can be if properly handled.

As to the enforcement of the judgment given in cases where one of the parties does not participate, the successful power would have the same remedies that are open to it when the whole proceeding is participated in by both parties. It is, moreover, to be seriously doubted that this would give any further trouble than is now experienced in enforcing ordinary arbitral awards. A power refusing to join in an arbitration before such a tribunal, would normally get scant sympathy or encouragement in a declination to meet the award made.

How far thirty-two powers (nearly seventy-five per cent of the nations of the world) might be willing to go along some such course as is suggested above, a survey of the obligatory arbitration plan they voted for (Annex 3 [not printed herein]) will indicate. How short a distance half the nations were willing to go along the lines of establishing an arbitral court as proposed, is shown by reservations made by them to the Hague *voeu*,—reservations of [a] kind that makes the establishment of a true, effective *world court* impossible.

The more the subject is considered without bias or predilection, the clearer it seems to grow that a movement to secure truly compulsory arbitration, as outlined above, of all justiciable questions, is the most promising, the most important, and will be the most effective, in promoting the judicial settlement of international disputes of any of the movements heretofore suggested. It is certainly far and away more important than movements looking to the establishment either of an international constabulary or of a "permanent" court. On this point one may well rest with the words of M. Bourgeois who said in discussing the matter at the last Hague Conference:—

> The very just criticism is made that there are no judges at The Hague; but there would be something more unfortunate than the failure to have judges at The Hague, namely, the failure to have cases to present to them after they have been appointed. This, however, would be the danger if the compulsory principle is rejected. It would be to set at nought the growing confidence of the world in arbitration. It is prudent, it is necessary, to secure for the Court not only judges, but a clientele as well.

Probably the wisest way to begin to bring about such a result will be to secure a compulsory agreement to arbitrate a limited number of subjects, however few or unimportant they might be. A beginning once made, it would be found a much simpler matter to enlarge it.

On this point also, the words of M. Bourgeois, President of the First Commission at the Second Hague Conference, are well worth consideration. He is reported as saying:—

A provision for compulsory recourse to arbitration, without restriction, and in every case, is not possible at the present time in a general convention.

But the same thing is not true with respect to certain accurately defined subjects concerning which obligatory recourse to arbitration is in international practice already quite largely adopted. The greater number of States, if not all, acting individually, have accepted the obligation to resort to arbitration for the settlement of a certain class of disputes. Would it not have a considerable moral effect to consolidate, in a general agreement, stipulations now separately entered into between the different nations, and to ratify by a common signature, provisions to which we have already fixed our signatures for the most part in pairs?

Finally, attention should be drawn to the *voeu* adopted by the Second Hague Conference which expressed its views on this matter in these words:—

It is unanimous—

1. In admitting the principle of compulsory arbitration.

2. In declaring that certain disputes, in particular those relating to the interpretation and application of the provisions of International Agreements, may be submitted to compulsory arbitration without any restriction.

Finally, it is unanimous in proclaiming that, although it has not yet been found feasible to conclude a Convention in this sense, nevertheless the divergences of opinion which have come to light have not exceeded the bounds of judicial controversy, and that, by working together here during the past four months, the collected Powers not only have learnt to understand one another and to draw closer together, but have succeeded in the course of this long collaboration in evolving a very lofty conception of the common welfare of humanity.

As it is the style to find in the present world war and the circumstances leading up to it, a vindication for every theory, it may not be amiss to contemplate what would have been the resulting condition if after Austria refused Serbia's offer of arbitration of the questions between them, Serbia had been in a position to take her case before an international court despite Austria's unwillingness, and had been able to secure from that court a determination either that her offers to Austria were all that could be demanded, or that she should make to Austria further concessions specified by the tribunal.

America's Part in the World Court Movement

2 December 1920

Early in 1923, in sending Senator William E. Borah a copy of this article, JRC explained, "Something over two years ago, in a spell of indignation (possibly it was indigestion) over an article which appeared in one of our leading magazines . . . I went over the old material pretty carefully and prepared an article which I thought somewhat of printing. However, it has never been put in type" (J. Reuben Clark, Jr., to Senator William E. Borah, 28 February 1923, Box 25, World Court, "America's Part in the World Court Movement," 2 December 1920, J 11.1, JRCP). Senator Philander C. Knox called it "an exhaustive and accurate article" and felt it was probably prompted by an article of Chandler P. Anderson's published a short time before in the *North American Review*. Knox said that JRC believed—and Knox entirely agreed with him—that the Anderson article was neither exhaustive nor accurate and that it would "be helpful to lay before the public a complete history of the movement, the principles involved, and the story of their development." Knox suggested to Colonel George Harvey of the *North American Review* that he might wish to publish the Clark article, although he thought it would take about twenty pages of the magazine and so far as he could see it could not well be cut (P. C. Knox to Colonel George Harvey, 4 December 1920, Box 503, Book 1, JRCP).

After examining the manuscript, the editors showed great interest but said that "its length unfortunately . . . [was] prohibitive for the purposes of the Review" unless JRC could contrive "to reduce it by half. . . ." (The Editors to P. C. Knox, 20 December 1920, Box 92, J 11, World Court, 1920–1926, No. 1, JRCP). Reluctant to reduce it, fearing that its purpose (its "effectiveness," or "accuracy," or both) would be defeated, and apparently assuming that other journals would have the same "mechanical situation," it appears that JRC did not submit it to anyone else for publication. Because the article was not published, the documentation within it was never put into a final form. In attempting to do so here, documentation has been completed in cases where JRC's marginal notes made the source clear enough to track down. In other cases, JRC's marginal note has been reprinted as is, sometimes with an alternate source for the citation given in brackets. Box 92, World Court 1920–1926, No. 1, 2 December 1920, J 11, JRCP.

For more of JRC's views on the World Court, see also "Statement of Hon. J. Reuben Clark, Former Solicitor, State Department, Former Ambassador of the United States to Mexico," and "Statement of J. Reuben Clark, Jr., on the Entry of the United States into the World Court," in *The World Court: Hearing before the Committee on Foreign Relations, United States Senate, Seventy-third Congress, Second Session, Relative to the Protocols Concerning the Adherence of the United States to the Permanent Court of International Justice, May 16, 1934* (Washington, D.C., 1934), 124–97. Box 148.

First Period

The reconsideration, necessary and imminent, of fundamental problems of our foreign policy as they affect the adjustment of disputes, pending and potential, between ourselves and other nations, will require, for the working out of a sane and wise progress, that there be freshly in mind some of the essentials underlying our past relationships in these respects. Moreover, the inadequacy of facts set out in current discussions regarding American participation in these matters, is so great and so calculated to misplace responsibility or credit, as the case may be, for the situations and developments of the past, that it seems desirable we should put before ourselves a rather complete, even though prosaic, account of the steps heretofore taken.

Before proceeding to the details of development, it should be in mind there are four interrelated factors involved in the pacific adjustment of international disputes.

First: The principle of adjustment of disputes by such means must be accepted by the nations. This has been already sufficiently done, for even the most bellicose of imperial governments has left unsaid nothing that was necessary on this point.

Second: And growing from *First,* a definition or enumeration of the disputes which nations agree shall be settled by peaceful means must be made, that is, there must be an agreement as to the extent of jurisdiction. This definition or enumeration must provide whether disputes shall be submitted for peaceful determination irrespective of the desire of the defending nation—in other words whether the jurisdiction is obligatory; or whether such disputes are to be settled by peaceful means only when the defending nation consents—that is, whether the jurisdiction is purely voluntary; or whether the jurisdiction shall be partly obligatory and partly voluntary, by being obligatory as to some matters and voluntary as to others.

Next to the adoption of the fundamental principles first set out, this becomes the most vital point of consideration in the whole question. It has so demonstrated itself before the Hague Conference, for while the nations there represented expressed the fullest willingness to adhere to the principle of the peaceful settlement of international disputes, yet certain nations were immovable in their determination not to consent to any list of important subjects as to which there could be obligatory arbitration. But, if the peaceful settlement of disputes is ever to take the place of adjustment by force, it must be made possible, first, to take a recalcitrant offending nation into court whether it wishes to go or not, and second, having the nation so in court, to obtain a decision against it, if necessary even a decision by default, if the case made out by the complaining nation shall *prima facie* warrant it. So fundamental is this consideration that real progress in peaceful adjustment may be measured by the extent to which obligatory arbitration of international disputes is adopted by the nations. All else is largely an expression of fine intention which may or may not fructify into useful action.

Obligatory arbitration was provided for as to matters of prize, by the International Prize Court Convention of the Second Hague Conference.

Third: The machinery by which peaceful adjustments shall be worked out, that is the functioning tribunal or tribunals, must be agreed to and set up by the nations.

The Hague Convention for the Pacific Settlement of International Disputes sets up a tribunal which has never yet failed fully, and more or less adequately, to respond to any demand made upon it for the adjudication of international disputes, and no serious difficulty has ever arisen under this Convention, in setting up a special tribunal for a particular case. The real trouble experienced, as already stated, has always come in securing the agreement to submit the dispute to arbitration.

It is not necessary now to note the arbitral tribunals set up by various two-group nations among themselves.

Fourth: The sanction which shall be placed behind the peaceful settlement as determined by the international tribunal must be provided for. Though theoretically the existence of a sufficient sanction is indispensable to the effective operation of any adjustment plan, and its setting up in a satisfactory manner a problem not without difficulty, yet as a practical matter the question is one of simplicity. For once an agreement to arbitrate has been arrived at and the arbitration thereunder completed, we have yet to see any of the larger states refusing to do one of two things, either to comply with the award or, if it were found preferable, to make a satisfactory adjustment with the other interested power.

Of course, if the field of obligatory arbitration be enlarged, the question of sanction will become more important. For though a nation voluntarily assenting to a particular adjudication must have had in mind the possibility of its losing the cause and, therefore, must have determined beforehand its willingness to accept and obey even an adverse award, yet where the jurisdiction is obligatory, the nation might not in the particular case at issue have so determined, and, therefore, conceivably it might refuse to abide by an award given in such a cause. But a dispute in which such an unacceptable award might be given would, if it remained unadjusted, in the last analysis almost certainly mean war whether the matter were arbitrated or whether it were not; and the use of force, or war, to carry out an arbitral award is on a quite different footing from war to enforce a mere claim before an award is made.

The Convention of the Second Hague Conference, stipulating

concerning the use of force for the collection of contract debts, sanctioned war to enforce an arbitral award.

With the foregoing principles freshly in mind we shall be able to appraise more accurately the ensuing resumé of the various steps which have from time to time been taken by this government in its efforts to promote the peaceful adjustment of international disputes.

While the whole history of the United States from the time of the Jay treaty with Great Britain (1794) is a record of unwavering devotion to the peaceful adjustment of international disputes, this present so-called World Court Movement may be conveniently dated from the First Hague Conference of 1899. The prior great Treaty (the Olney-Pauncefote Treaty) of 1897, between the United States and Great Britain will be more fully noted later, for it, along with most of the other peaceful adjustment plans considered by the United States since the First Hague Conference, has had a direct bearing and influence on the general movement.

The Russian Circular of 1899, proposing the First Hague Conference, suggested submitting "for international discussion at the Conference" eight different projects, the last of which reads as follows:

> To accept in principle the employment of good offices, of mediation and facultative arbitration in cases lending themselves thereto, with the object of preventing armed conflicts between nations; to come to an understanding with respect to the mode of applying these good offices, and to establish a uniform practice in using them. (For. Rel. 1898, 541, 551 [James Brown Scott, *The Hague Peace Conferences of 1899 and 1907,* 2 vols. (Baltimore, 1909; reprinted 1972), 2:4-5]; Frederick W. Holls, *The Peace Conference at The Hague and Its Bearings on International Law and Policy* [New York, 1900], 25, 26)

The proposal by Russia for a Conference was accepted by the various powers, including the United States.

In his instructions (dated April 18, 1899) to the American delegates to this Conference, Mr. Secretary Hay after quoting the proposed Russian program for the Conference and referring to its first seven projects, commented upon the eighth one as follows:

> The eighth article, which proposes the wider extension of good offices, mediation and arbitration, seems likely to open the most fruitful field for discussion and future action. "The prevention of armed conflicts by pacific means," to

use the words of Count Mouravieff's circular of December 30, is a purpose well worthy of a great international convention, and its realization in an age of general enlightenment should not be impossible. The duty of sovereign States to promote international justice by all wise and effective means is only secondary to the fundamental necessity of preserving their own existence. Next in importance to their independence is the great fact of their interdependence. Nothing can secure for human government and for the authority of law which it represents so deep a respect and so firm a loyalty as the spectacle of sovereign and independent States, whose duty it is to prescribe the rules of justice and impose penalties upon the lawless, bowing with reverence before the august supremacy of those principles of right which give to law its eternal foundation.

The proposed Conference promises to offer an opportunity thus far un-equalled in the history of the world for initiating a series of negotiations that may lead to important practical results. The long-continued and widespread interest among the people of the United States in the establishment of an international court, as evidenced in the historical resumé attached to these instructions as Annex A, gives assurance that the proposal of a definite plan of procedure by this Government for the accomplishment of this end would express the desires and aspirations of this nation. The delegates are, therefore, enjoined to propose, at an opportune moment, the plan for an international tribunal, hereunto attached as Annex B, and to use their influence in the Conference in the most effective manner possible to procure the adoption of its substance or of resolutions directed to the same purpose. It is believed that the disposition and aims of the United States in relation to the other sovereign Powers could not be expressed more truly or opportunely than by an effort of the delegates of this Government to concentrate the attention of the world upon a definite plan for the promotion of international justice. (For. Rel. 1899, 512 [Scott, 2:8-9])

The Annex B to which Secretary Hay refers is so comprehensive in its plan and so far reaching in its vision on this subject, that it is worth quoting in full. It reads:

Resolved, That in order to aid in the prevention of armed conflicts by pacific means, the representatives of the Sovereign Powers assembled together in this Conference be, and hereby are, requested to propose to their respective Governments a series of negotiations for the adoption of a general treaty having for its object the following plan, with such modifications as may be essential to secure the adhesion of at least nine Sovereign Powers.

1. The Tribunal shall be composed of judges chosen on account of their personal integrity and learning in international law by a majority of the members of the highest court now existing in each of the adhering States, one from each sovereign State participating in the treaty, and shall hold office until their successors are appointed by the same body.

2. The Tribunal shall meet for organization at a time and place to be agreed upon by the several Governments, but not later than six months after the general treaty shall be ratified by nine Powers, and shall organize itself by the appoint-

ment of a permanent clerk and such other officers as may be found necessary, but without conferring any distinction upon its own members. The Tribunal shall be empowered to fix its place of sessions and to change the same from time to time as the interest of justice or the convenience of the litigants may seem to require, and fix its own rules of procedure.

3. The contracting nations will mutually agree to submit to the International Tribunal all questions of disagreement between them, excepting such as may relate to or involve their political independence or territorial integrity. Questions of disagreement, with the aforesaid exceptions, arising between an adherent State and a non-adhering State, or between two Sovereign States not adherent to the treaty, may, with the consent of both parties in dispute, be submitted to the International Tribunal for adjudication, upon the condition expressed in Article 6.

4. The Tribunal shall be of a permanent character and shall be always open for the filing of cases and counter cases, either by the contracting nations or by others that may choose to submit them, and all cases and counter cases, with the testimony and arguments by which they are to be supported or answered, are to be in writing. All cases, counter cases, evidence, arguments, and opinions expressing judgment are to be accessible, after a decision is rendered, to all who desire to pay the necessary charges for transcription.

5. A bench of judges for each particular case shall consist of not less than three nor more than seven as may be deemed expedient, appointed by the unanimous consent of the Tribunal, and not to include a member who is either a native, subject, or citizen of the State whose interests are in litigation in that case.

6. The general expenses of the Tribunal are to be divided equally between the adherent Powers, but those arising from each particular case shall be provided for as may be directed by the Tribunal. The presentation of a case wherein one or both of the parties may be a non-adherent State shall be admitted only upon condition of a mutual agreement that the State against which judgment may be found shall pay, in addition to the judgment, a sum to be fixed by the Tribunal for the expenses of the adjudication.

7. Every litigant before the International Tribunal shall have the right to make an appeal for re-examination of a case within three months after notification of the decision, upon presentation of evidence that the judgment contains a substantial error of fact or law.

8. This treaty shall become operative when nine sovereign States, whereof at least six shall have taken part in the Conference of The Hague, shall have ratified its provisions. (Scott's Am. Instructions (Carnegie) 14 [Scott, 2:15-16; *Proceedings of the Hague Peace Conferences; The Conference of 1899*, trans. Carnegie Endowment For International Peace])

This is the most noteworthy plan that has appeared in connection with the project for a world court, and it deserves careful consideration from the point of view of the fundamentals already named.

1. It postulates, and events showed correctly so, a willingness

among the powers to accept the principle of the peaceful adjustment of international disputes.

2. In the matter of jurisdiction its proposal goes beyond that of any other general plan yet projected because it proposed the obligatory arbitration (as it seems) of *"all questions* of disagreement" between the contracting nations, only "excepting such as may relate to or involve their political independence or territorial integrity."

A passing criticism might be made of this, first, that the classification proposed is unscientific and leaves open for discussion and a possible unadjustable difference (without suggesting a means of settling the same), the question as to what disagreements between nations do "relate to or involve their political independence or territorial integrity;" and, second, that the exceptions specified are not stated in scientific form. A more substantial point is that in excepting territorial claims from arbitral jurisdiction, the plan runs counter to the uniform practice of the United States during the whole of its national existence; and a further one that it is not easy to conjure up a likely situation where it would be proposed to arbitrate our "political independence." But these objections may be passed in view of the general excellence of the plan.

The comprehensiveness of the Hay proposal is also evidenced by the fact that it includes the adjustment of disagreements between a state adhering to the plan and a non-adhering state, and also between two non-adhering states, by providing voluntary jurisdiction over such disagreements,—that is to say such disputes are to be adjusted by the proposed international tribunal if the two states concerned agree so to settle them.

Provision was also made for the re-examination of a case after decision and award, upon presentation of evidence of a "substantial error of fact or law."

3. In the matter of the machinery of a tribunal for accomplishing the pacific adjustment of disagreements between nations, the Hay plan is also, in its elemental concepts, of the most advanced.

The judges are to be chosen "on account of their personal integrity and learning in international law,"—a test of qualification which has not in essence been added to in any plan since proposed.

The tribunal to be constituted was to be "of a permanent character,"—and *permanency* has been one of the things chiefly talked about by world court enthusiasts.

The tribunal projected was to be "always open for the filing of cases and counter cases, either by the contracting nations or by others that may choose to submit them." This is the most advanced suggestion that has been made on this point.

While it provided for the choosing of judges "one from each sovereign State participating in the treaty," it also stipulated that individual cases coming before the tribunal were to be heard by "a bench of judges . . . of not less than three nor more than seven as may be deemed expedient, appointed by the unanimous consent of the Tribunal,"—thus providing a tribunal of workable size.

Again, this *bench* so chosen was not to include any judge who was "either a native, subject, or citizen of the State whose interests are in litigation in that case." In this respect the proposed plan goes beyond any which has since been seriously considered.

The project further provided that it should come into operation without waiting for all the states to adhere to it. This principle reappears in later plans under a claim of novelty.

4. No special sanction was provided by the plan, a further postulate being indulged in here, namely, that (as the history of arbitration to that time had shown) self respecting nations obey awards made against them.

When the Conference began its work at The Hague, a Committee was named to consider the Russian project regarding good offices, mediation, international commissions of inquiry, and arbitration. The drafting of a proposed text of Convention was in turn referred to a Special Committee of Examination (Comité d'Examen), which, as Mr. Holls says, "rapidly and quite unexpectedly became the center of interest in the entire Conference" (Holls, 170). Of this Committee certain American delegates, acting under the foregoing instructions and with the foregoing plan, were members.

It would be going beyond the purview of the present discussion to consider the working of the Conference or the results accomplished by it save as it relates to arbitration. All this may be gained from Mr. Holls' excellent work on "The Peace Conference at The Hague." It is enough to say that the Conference drafted and adopted, among others, a Convention for the Pacific Settlement of International Disputes.

Considering this Convention in respect of the four fundamentals already referred to, we note the following:

1. In loftiest expression (which ought long since to have regenerated the world under the theory, increasingly appealing in some

quarters, that fine words equal good deeds) the principle of the friendly settlement of international disputes was asserted in the preamble and in Article 1. No comment on this is necessary.

2. The provisions regarding the jurisdiction to be exercised under the Convention were divided into three primary branches, evidently intended to embrace all disputes between states.

The first dealt with good offices and mediation. The powers signatory agreed that in case of serious disagreement or conflict, before an appeal to arms, they would have recourse as far as circumstances allowed "to the good offices or mediation of one or more friendly powers," and it was declared that voluntary interposition under this branch of the treaty by powers strangers to the dispute should "never be regarded by one or the other of the parties in conflict as an unfriendly act." Provision was also made that in cases of special mediation the states in conflict should for a period of not to exceed thirty days cease all direct communication on the subject of the dispute. This latter was the origin of the "cooling off"* principle which later formed one of the two prime elements of the so-called Bryan peace treaties, and which was so much commended by pro-Leaguers, in the discussions concerning the League Covenant, as the specific against all war.

The United States in the dispute threatening war between Ecuador and Peru, was (at the instance of Mr. Secretary Knox) the first power to invoke these provisions of this Convention.

The second branch of the jurisdiction was bestowed upon Commissions of Inquiry which, in case of differences between powers, were "to facilitate a solution of these differences by elucidating the facts by means of an impartial and conscientious investigation." The invocation of this provision of the treaty in the Dogger Bank incident probably averted a war between Great Britain and Russia. This principle of the Convention was the other of the two Hague Convention ideas that made up the essentials of the Bryan peace treaties of 1913.

The third branch of the jurisdiction related to international arbitration and provided both the jurisdiction and the machinery for such adjustments.

---

*This was Holls' suggestion (see Holls, 188). See also Carnegie's Translation [*Proceedings of the Hague Peace Conferences*], 112, 170, *188, 694, 696, 832, 836.*

As to the arbitral jurisdiction, the Convention provided that:

> In questions of a legal nature, and especially in the interpretation or applica-
> tion of international conventions, arbitration is recognized by the signatory pow-
> ers as the most effective, and at the same time the most equitable means of
> settling disputes which diplomacy has failed to settle. (William M. Malloy,
> *Treaties, Conventions, International Acts, Protocols, and Agreements between the United
> States of America and Other Powers, 1776-1909,* 2 vols. [Washington, D.C.,
> 1910], 2:2023)

It will be observed that there is in one respect and as to one class
of disputes a gain here over the designated jurisdiction of the Hay
plan because a part of the jurisdiction is put now on a scientific
basis, namely "questions of a legal nature," thus postulating a decision according to the law involved. It is not clear whether "the
interpretation or application of international conventions" was to be
regarded as a matter of a *legal nature* or otherwise under this Convention. However, under this plan, even questions regarding Mr. Hay's
excepted classes, those relating to "political independence or territorial integrity," might be submitted to arbitration if the questions
involved were of a *legal nature.*

On the other hand, there is a distinct falling off from the Hay
standard which provided for the arbitration of *all disputes,* with the
exception of those involving political independence or territorial
integrity, because many questions arise between nations which are
not legal in their character and yet which do not fall within the
exceptions noted by Mr. Hay.

With reference to the obligatory or voluntary character of submission to arbitration under the Convention, there was a great loss
from the Hay plan, because under the Convention a resort to the
Hague Tribunal was to be had only under a special act (*compromis*)
negotiated by the parties in each particular case, the subject of the
international difference to be defined therein as well as the extent of
the arbitrators' powers (Art. 31).

This, of course, destroyed all obligatory arbitration and made
the submission of disputes entirely voluntary in every case. In the
matter of obligatory submission, the signatory powers merely reserved to themselves the right of concluding "either before the
ratification of the present act or later, new agreements, general or
private, with a view to extending obligatory arbitration to all cases
which they may consider it possible to submit to it."

Thus there was a fundamental failure to meet the standard of the Hay plan in matters of jurisdiction.

Because of its bearing on the development of the World Court Movement, it should be noted that, as a practical matter, a necessary incident of the making of any award in any dispute of a legal nature, is the determination of facts which constitute a breach of the international obligation; and, furthermore, that the making of any award involves the fixing of the nature and extent of the reparation to be made for such breach. All arbitration is conducted in this way unless the particular agreement provides otherwise.

Having these facts in mind (and the two latter points are adverted to merely because a special virtue has been applied to them in connection with the wording of the arbitral jurisdiction clause in the Covenant for the League of Nations) it is clear that the First Hague Convention carried the matter fully as far as the much lauded League Covenant which provides in Article 13 that:

> Disputes as to the interpretation of a treaty, as to any question of international law, as to the existence of any fact which if established would constitute a breach of any international obligation, or as to the extent and nature of the reparation to be made for any such breach, are declared to be among those which are generally suitable for submission to arbitration.

As to the arbitral machinery, the essential provisions of the First Hague Convention were these:

Each state, party to the plan, was to nominate four persons "of known competency in questions of international law, of the highest moral reputation, and disposed to accept the duties of arbitration," who were to form the permanent panel of the Hague Court. From this panel, the powers signatory or adhering to the plan were to choose the arbitrators in any given disputes between them which they were submitting to arbitration. Special provision was made for selecting an umpire for such a tribunal so constituted.

This followed generally the outline of Mr. Hay's plan, but differed from it in three important particulars, first, the parties themselves and not the full panel (as suggested by Mr. Hay) selected the arbitrators for a particular case; second, nationals of the disputing powers were eligible as members of the court chosen to try the particular case, whereas under the Hay plan nationals might not sit; and third, the Court was not "always open," as suggested by Mr. Hay (Art. 32).

It will be observed in recapitulation that this Convention failed to meet Secretary Hay's plan in a number of vital matters, as follows:

1. Its arbitral jurisdiction was narrower than that proposed by Mr. Hay.

2. It failed to provide any obligatory jurisdiction.

3. The Tribunal created lacked the "permanent character" which Mr. Hay appears to have had in mind.

4. It was not "always open for the filing of cases and counter cases" because before resort could be had to the Court a special agreement must be negotiated.

5. It did not exclude nationals of an interested power from sitting on the Court trying the case.

6. It made no specific provision for the constitution of the Court by a less number of powers than that signatory to the Convention, though this may perhaps be implied.

To the United States and Mexico came the honor of submitting the first case taken before the Hague Tribunal,—The Pious Fund case,—which was submitted under a special agreement signed by the United States (by Mr. Secretary Hay) and Mexico under date of May 22, 1902.

However, influences now became operative on Mr. Hay which induced him to negotiate and conclude (December 1904-January 1905) with Great Britain, France, Switzerland, Germany, Portugal, Italy, Spain, Austria-Hungary, Mexico, and Sweden and Norway, a series of supplemental treaties (one with each power), which were a distinct retreat from the advanced position Mr. Hay had embodied in his Hague plan.

After reciting in the preamble that by Article XIX of the Hague Convention "the High Contracting Parties have reserved to themselves the right of concluding Agreements, with a view to referring to arbitration all questions which they shall consider possible to submit to such treatment" (For. Rels. 1907, pt. 2, 1134) the new treaties (which were alike in terms) provided in Articles I and II as follows:

Art. I. Differences which may arise of a legal nature, or relating to the interpretation of Treaties existing between the two Contracting Parties, and which it may not have been possible to settle by diplomacy, shall be referred to the Permanent Court of Arbitration established at The Hague by the Convention of the 29th of July, 1899, provided, nevertheless, that they do not affect the vital interests, the independence, or the honor of the two Contracting States and do not concern the interests of third parties.

Art. II. In each individual case the High Contracting Parties, before appealing to the Permanent Court of Arbitration, shall conclude a special agreement defining clearly the matter in dispute and the scope of the powers of the Arbitral Tribunal, and fixing the periods for the formation of the Arbitral Tribunal and the several stages of the procedure. (Confidential Executive G. 58th Cong., 3d Sess.)

The Senate amended the treaties when submitted to them, by striking out the word "agreement" in Article 2 and by inserting in lieu thereof the word "treaty," which made it necessary that the Senate advise and consent to every special agreement (*compromis*) which might be negotiated under the treaties.

This was distinctly a step backwards, because time and again this Government had submitted the claims of its own citizens against other governments to arbitration under Conventions to which the Senate was not asked to advise and consent and upon which the Senate did not function. Moreover, it seems Mr. Hay had in mind the securing from the Senate of authority, through these proposed treaties, to conclude all special agreements (*compromis*) for the arbitration of particular cases, even those against the United States, without again consulting the Senate. If this were his plan, the Senate amendment made its carrying out impossible.

Furthermore, providing as they did for submitting to arbitration only questions "of a legal nature" or concerning "the interpretation of treaties," from which categories were excepted all questions affecting the "vital interests, the independence, or the honor of the two contracting states" (a phrase incorporated from the then recent Anglo-French treaty, and since much and properly criticized as wholly inapplicable to American arbitration), these treaties fell far short of meeting not only the wide powers proposed in the plan Mr. Hay sent to The Hague, but also the scope of arbitration as theretofore practiced by the United States from the formation of the Government.

Mr. Hay declined to go forward to the ratification of the amended treaties, which lay in the Government files until Mr. Root, upon becoming Secretary of State, resuscitated them.

But apparently Mr. Hay was unwilling to regard these treaties, even as he negotiated them, as sufficient. Accordingly, using as a basis a resolution of the Interparliamentary Union, adopted at its meeting held at St. Louis, Mr. Hay, coincidentally with his beginning of negotiations for the arbitration agreements just referred to, instructed American diplomatic officers, accredited to powers signatory of the Hague Convention of 1899, to sound out those powers as to the holding of a second Hague Conference. Most of the Powers addressed replied expressing sympathy with the proposal. Russia, however, then at war with Japan, announced that she could not become a party "at this moment" in such a conference, while Japan reserved from the subjects for the consideration of the conference, questions "relative to the present war" (Folio correspondence in re Second Hague Conference)

Not quite two months after the first note, Mr. Hay addressed a second note to the same Powers in which he communicated the results following the sending of his first note, and suggested that the purpose of President Roosevelt in undertaking to initiate the second conference had been sufficiently realized so that the matter might be left for completion to the International Bureau under the control of the Permanent Administrative Council of The Hague. He also intimated that the Government of the Netherlands should call the second conference.

This was the condition of affairs when Mr. Hay died on July 1, 1905, and Mr. Root became Secretary of State six days later—July 7, 1905.

Second Period

For reasons which the public correspondence fails to explain, the Russian Government in September 1905 took the initiative in calling the Second Conference, instead of allowing the matter to go forward at the instance of the Government of the Netherlands as Mr. Hay had suggested (Folio Correspondence in re Second Hague Conf., 5). Nor does it appear that the United States made any objection to this procedure notwithstanding the Power calling the Conference always assumed such a recognized relation to it as practically to dominate its entire proceedings. As one of the American delegates to one of the Conferences has said, substantially the control of the proceedings of the conference goes into the hands of the Power whose representative is made President, who, without consulting the Conference, names the presiding officers of the commissions among which the work of the Conference outlined in the program is distributed (Report of Preliminary Committee for Third Hague Conf.). Moreover, these commissions, because they follow what is known as the continental method as distinguished from parliamentary methods of procedure established in England and America, center in their presiding officers such an undue proportion of power as to deprive the commissions of that freedom of action on the business brought before them which seems to be necessary for the proper conduct of the work. Finally, this delegate affirmed that everything seemed to be so arranged as to prevent as far as possible a direct and straight vote upon any proposition presented—the whole Conference being so far within the domination of the Power having the chief presiding officer, as to make it better, in the opinion of this delegate, to have no further conference than to have it controlled by any single Power in that way.

The first main point proposed by the Imperial Russian Government for consideration by the Second Conference reads as follows:

1. Improvements to be made in the provisions of the Convention relative to the peaceful settlement of international disputes as regards the Court of Arbitration and the international commissions of inquiry. (Folio Correspondence, 21 [Scott, 2:176])

In his instructions to the American delegates to the Second Conference, Mr. Root (then Secretary of State) made some general observations, which should be in mind, regarding the general policy of the United States to the effect that the "object of the Conference is agreement, and not compulsion;" that "after reasonable discussion, if no agreement is reached, it is better to lay the subject aside, or refer it to some future conference in the hope that intermediate consideration may dispose of the objections;" that "the immediate results of such a conference must always be limited to a small part of the field which the more sanguine have hoped to see covered;" that "it may well be that among the most valuable services rendered to civilization by this Second Conference will be found the progress made in matters upon which the delegates reach no definite agreement;" and that "the policy of the United States to avoid entangling alliances and to refrain from any interference or participation in the political affairs of Europe must be kept in mind, and may impose upon you some degree of reserve in respect of some of the questions which are discussed by the Conference" (For. Rel. 1907, pt. 2,

1128 et seq. [Scott, 2:183-86]). He then quoted the declaration (in respect of our relations to and freedom from entanglement with Europe) made by the American delegates to the First Hague Conference, in connection with their vote upon the report of the Committee on the limitation of armaments, and the declaration of like import made by the same delegates before signing the arbitration convention, and concluded with this observation: "These declarations have received the approval of this Government, and they should be regarded by you as illustrating the caution which you are to exercise in preventing our participation in matters of general and world wide concern from drawing us into the political affairs of Europe."

The limitation of armaments, the limitation upon force for the collection of ordinary public debts arising out of contract, the general field of arbitration, the immunity of private property at sea, rules for the government of military operations on land, the rights and duties of neutrals, all received special consideration in these instructions.

As to arbitration,—Mr. Root stated there were two lines of advance clearly indicated. "The first is to provide for obligatory arbitration as broad in scope as now appears to be practicable, and the second is to increase the effectiveness of the system so that nations may more readily have recourse to it voluntarily" [Scott, 2:189].

Referring to the Senate amendment to the Hay treaties, Mr. Root said:

> The amendment, however, did not relate to the scope or character of the arbitration to which the President had agreed and the Senate consented. You will be justified, therefore, in assuming that a general treaty of arbitration in the terms, or substantially in the terms, of the series of treaties which I have mentioned will meet the approval of the Government of the United States. (For. Rel 1907, pt. 2, 1134 [Scott, 2:190])

Then after quoting the first article of the Hay treaties already quoted above, he added: "To this extent you may go in agreeing to a general treaty of arbitration, and to secure such a treaty you should use your best and most earnest efforts."

Then followed the frequently quoted paragraph from Mr. Root's instructions which reads:

There can be no doubt that the principal objection to arbitration rests not upon the unwillingness of nations to submit their controversies to impartial arbitration, but upon an apprehension that the arbitrations to which they submit may not be impartial. It has been a very general practice for arbitrators to act, not as judges deciding questions of fact and law upon the record before them under a sense of judicial responsibility, but as negotiators affecting settlements of the questions brought before them in accordance with the traditions and usages and subject to all the considerations and influences which affect diplomatic agents.

He directed the delegates to use their efforts "to bring about in the Second Conference a development of The Hague Tribunal into a permanent tribunal composed of judges who are judicial officers and nothing else, who are paid adequate salaries, who have no other occupation, and who will devote their entire time to the trial and decision of international cases by judicial methods and under a sense of judicial responsibility" [Scott, 2:190-91].

A subsequent sentence of his instructions called attention to the desirability of having all the principal systems of law represented in any court,—which, of course, would inevitably happen were any considerable group of nations to associate themselves together under such a plan.

Mr. Root did not, however, submit, with his instructions, any project for the establishment of the court which he had in mind.

From the point of view of the four principal features involved in the peaceful settlement of international disputes, the following observations may be made on these instructions:

1. The general principle of the desirability of settling international disputes by peaceful means is taken, as it properly may be—as already accepted by the powers.

2. In the matter of arbitral jurisdiction, there is an avowed adoption of the Hay treaties provision, which is a practical abandonment of obligatory arbitration—as already defined and explained—and a substantial curtailing of the subject matters recognized as suitable for arbitration and actually arbitrated by us in the century and a quarter of our national existence.

3. Prime emphasis (as to arbitration) was placed on the machinery of arbitral tribunals, and primarily on one point of this, namely, the character and qualification of the judges. But the suggested requirements contained nothing essentially new from that already existing in the Hague Convention. As a matter of fact men nominated to the Hague Court under the First Convention, were, seem-

ingly, without exception, among the best men for the work which each country possessed. If nations were to appoint men under any other court plan, they would inevitably be the same men or men of like calibre. The American members of the Hague Tribunal at the present time are Mr. Elihu Root, Mr. John Bassett Moore, Judge George Grey, and Mr. Oscar Straus.

No one would suggest that any of these gentlemen would bring more wisdom or learning or integrity to his task as judge in an arbitral proceeding, merely because he happened to be appointed to the tribunal under a slightly differently worded formula.

Moreover, while Mr. Root's suggestions regarding the amount of salary and the exclusive employment of the judges in their court work, are undoubtedly useful considerations in the setting up of the proper kind of a court, they can hardly be called fundamental in principle.

The fact is (and it is submitted Mr. Root was in error here) nations do not hesitate to submit differences to arbitration solely or mainly because they fear the judges may act as negotiators and presumably compromise claims, whereas they would be willing to arbitrate if they could be assured of impartial judicial determinations from a tribunal panel acting as judges, because it is not too much to say that few important judicial decisions in the domestic courts of any nation, even our own, are devoid of far reaching compromises reached by the court members acting as negotiators on even vital matters. Humans live and work together by compromise. The real reason nations fear unlimited, obligatory arbitration is, first, because as to many most essential things affecting international relations there are no accepted, controlling, and governing rules by which the nation may guide its action when taken, or by which its action when so taken can be judged by any kind of tribunal, and in such cases a negotiated compromise would be inevitable and might be a fatal thrust at the nation; and second, because in other matters where there is a rule of conduct established and accepted by which a nation may steer its course and by which it may be judged, nations are unwilling to submit their acts falling within the rule to the judgment of any tribunal however constituted because the question involves too vitally their growth and destiny, to warrant their hazarding an unfavorable opinion from any court. Moreover, and this is perhaps conclusive as to what may be expected from the members of any international tribunal, until the concept of nationality is wiped out, until the pride of race and that love of country, in which generations have traditioned us, are destroyed, it is idle to expect that any patriotic man, sitting on any tribunal, will as to vital interests, involving the future existence of his own country, cease to effectuate compromises, no matter what the occasion or the compulsion may be, and no matter what the verbiage of the formula under which he may be acting.

4. No sanction was adverted to by Mr. Root except in connection with the collection of contract debts, where it was proposed that force be authorized to collect an arbitral award under conditions specified.

The Second Hague Conference held its opening session on June 15, 1907. On August 1, there was submitted by the American delegates to the First Sub-Commission of the First Commission, an American plan of arbitration which being short may be quoted here in full:

I. A permanent Court of Arbitration shall be organized to consist of fifteen judges of the highest moral standing and of recognized competency in questions of international law. They and their successors shall be appointed in the manner to be determined by this Conference, but they shall be so chosen from the different countries that the various systems of law and procedure and the principal languages shall be suitably represented in the personnel of the court. They shall be appointed for —— years, or until their successors have been appointed and have accepted. (Second Hague Conf. II, 309, 1031 [Scott, 1:821])

II. The Permanent Court shall convene annually at The Hague on a specified date and shall remain in session as long as necessary. It shall elect its own officers and, saving the stipulations of the convention, it shall draw up its own regulations. Every decision shall be reached by a majority, and nine members shall constitute a quorum. The judges shall be equal in rank, shall enjoy diplomatic immunity, and shall receive a salary sufficient to enable them to devote their time to the consideration of the matters brought before them. (Scott's Status of International Court of Justice, 80 [Scott, 1:821])

III. In no case (unless the parties expressly consent thereto) shall a judge take part in the consideration or decision of any case before the court when his nation is a party therein.

IV. The Permanent Court shall be competent to take cognizance and determine all cases involving differences of an international character between sovereign nations, which it has been impossible to settle through diplomatic channels and which have been submitted to it by agreement between the parties, either originally or for review or revision, or in order to determine the relative rights, duties or obligations in accordance with findings, decisions, or awards of commissions of inquiry and specifically constituted tribunals of arbitration.

V. The judges of the Permanent Court shall be competent to act as judges in any Commission of Inquiry or Special Tribunal of Arbitration which may be constituted by any power for the consideration of any matter which may be specially referred to it and which must be determined by it.

VI. The present Permanent Court of Arbitration might, as far as possible, constitute the basis of the court, care being taken that the powers which recently signed the Convention of 1899 are represented in it.* [Scott, 1:822]

Considering this as a broad, comprehensive, outline plan, the following observations may be made:

As events showed, it was obviously and palpably impracticable at that time to create an arbitral court of only fifteen judges.

The suggestion that the judges be chosen so that the various systems of law and procedure and the principal languages should be suitably represented in the personnel of the court, was unnecessary and not fundamental, because any court of nations must inevitably be so constituted.

The provisions regarding the annual meeting of the tribunal were probably designed to secure what afterwards came to be called the *permanency* of the court; those regarding a quorum and voting by majority were mere details of procedure already covered in the existing Hague Convention; and those stipulating equality of rank, amount of salary, and diplomatic immunity for the judges likewise were details not running to the essence. The provision against nationals sitting as judges is a repetition of a clause in the Hay plan, but to this there is an exception which is not found in the Hay plan.

As to jurisdiction, the court was to be merely *competent* "to take cognizance and determine all cases involving differences of an international character between sovereign nations," but no obligatory jurisdiction was proposed. Moreover, while the phrase "all differences" could embrace any and all difficulties arising between nations and would, therefore, if unmodified be broader than the Hay plan, yet the phrase "of an international character" must be noted as restrictive, widely or narrowly, and in any event so nebulous in meaning as to render the whole phrase quite unuseful, because any dispute between nations might be considered *ipso facto* as of "international character." If the intention were to exclude domestic questions by this provision, it might have been much more definitely

---

*Another plan has been printed under the heading, "Project for a Permanent Court of Arbitration drafted by the American Delegation upon which the joint project of Germany, Great Britain, and the United States was based," but this plan does not appear to be in the record.

and happily stated. However, the limitation that the court would only consider cases referred to it under special agreements was probably designed to protect the states against the indefiniteness of the earlier clauses.

The proposal clearly does not conform to Mr. Root's instructions which directed that as to jurisdiction, the delegates follow the provisions of the Hay treaties.

Attention is directed to the fact that this plan falls short of the advanced position embodied in the Hay plan in the following particulars:

1. It does not provide for the constitution of the court upon adhesion to the plan by a minimum number of nations.

2. The court was not to be "always open for the filing of cases and counter cases, either by the contracting nations or by others that may choose to submit them," and on the contrary was merely open to parties who had agreed to submit a specific controversy to it.

3. No provision was made for the re-examination of a case except by the agreement of the two parties.

By the time the Hague Conference came fairly into its work, there were four projects before it providing for the pacific adjustment of international disputes.

The first involved the revamping of the First Hague Convention for the Pacific Settlement of International Disputes.

The second was a plan for the creation of an International Prize Court.

The third was a plan for the establishment of a "Judicial Arbitration Court"—this grew out of the consideration of the American plan last quoted. In so far as the published instructions go, it would seem that this latter plan was developed by the American delegates at the Conference without specific direction from the Department of State.

The fourth was a project for a Convention limiting the use of force in the collection of contract debts to cases where "the debtor State refuses or neglects to reply to an offer of arbitration, or, after accepting the offer, prevents any *compromis* from being agreed on, or, after arbitration fails to submit to the award."

As to the first project, the perfecting of the Convention for the Pacific Settlement of International Disputes, the plan was here and there perfected (particularly in respect of provisions regarding Commissions of Inquiry) but no fundamental changes were made by the

Conference. This Convention may, therefore, for present purposes, be dismissed without further comment.

The second project—The International Prize Court—seems to have been essentially a European product, two original projects—a German and British—having been presented to the Conference. Out of these grew a draft prepared by a commission of which the rapporteur was Mr. Louis Renault who is credited with having been mainly responsible for the plan as finally worked out. The project as finally adopted by the Conference is worthy of consideration because offered and apparently framed before the presentation of the elaborated plan for the Judicial Arbitration Court (to be next considered), it was quite evidently the model upon which the latter court plan was based in all its fundamental particulars. How far indeed this is true, may be judged by the fact that more than half of the provisions of the Judicial Arbitration Court plan have been carried over bodily—in many cases without any essential change even in the verbiage—from the International Prize Court plan. This is conspicuously true of the one feature of the arbitral plan which ultimately caused its rejection by the Conference, namely the proposed schedule for the appointment of judges. Others of the more elemental provisions are identical (save for necessary verbal changes) with the Second Hague Convention for the Pacific Settlement of International Disputes.

In certain fundamental respects the provisions of the Prize Court go beyond those of any other convention actually agreed to and signed by the Hague Conferences.

Its distinguishing provisions cover,

First: Obligatory arbitration of matters of prize. The defendant nation may be taken before the International Prize Court whether it wishes to be so taken or not (Arts. 3 and 28 et seq.);

Second: Authority to give judgment against a nation in a prize case even though that nation failed to appear before the court in answer to the petition of the complaining party (Art. 40);

Third: Decisions of the tribunal are to be rendered, first, by applying principles of law covered by treaty between the two powers, and in accordance with the treaty (Art. 7); or in the absence of treaty provisions then by the rules of international law; or in the absence of the two foregoing "in accordance with the general principles of justice and equity;"

Fourth: A court was set up which was to be "always open" for the filing of cases;

Fifth: This court was of workable size, namely, a court of fifteen judges (Art. 14).

Thus this court meets the three great principles of the original Hay plan,—obligatory jurisdiction, a permanent court always open, and a tribunal of workable size.

It went beyond the expressed provisions of the Hay plan in providing for judgment by default, and in stipulating that the decisions should be rendered in accordance with law, though on this latter point it is to be noted that Mr. Hay was proposing a tribunal with very much broader jurisdiction than that given to the International Prize Court which was to deal only with matters of prize.

The third project before the Conference, that for a Judicial Arbitration Court, encountered at the Conference, practically from the outset, insurmountable difficulties. Without attempting to follow the maze of discussion which attended its consideration by the committee charged with its drafting, it is enough to say that the Conference finally declined to do more with the draft than to express in the Final Act of the Conference the following *voeu* (wish):

> The Conference calls the attention of the Signatory Powers to the advisability of adopting the annexed draft Convention for the creation of a Judicial Arbitration Court, and of bringing it into force as soon as an agreement has been reached respecting the selection of the Judges and the Constitution of the Court. (Malloy, 2:2379)

The last named matters, the selection of the judges and the constitution of the court were the subject of spirited, almost bitter debate before the framing committee and were the cause, judging from the records, of the rejection of the plan by the Conference.

These same matters have lain at the root of the failure of all efforts since made to bring about the establishment of this particular court. Moreover, inasmuch as these difficulties arise from the necessity, first, of providing a sizeable court, that is, a court of sufficiently few members to be workable, and, secondly, and resulting from that, of providing on the one hand for continuous representation on the Court of the great powers and on the other hand of intermittent representation of the smaller powers, it would seem to be not a hazardous forecast to say that until the small powers lose their sense of nationality and state equality, any court founded on such a plan must continue to fail.

Aside from this feature of the constitution of the proposed court, there was nothing in the plan which the most timid of states might not have accepted for it lacked all of the great essentials, save as to this constitution of the court, which were possessed by the Prize Court.

First, there was no provision for obligatory arbitration or adjudication. The court was merely declared *competent* to deal with "all cases" which the parties might *agree* thereafter to submit to it.

Second, since there was thus no obligatory jurisdiction, there naturally was no provision for proceeding against a state against its will, as in the case of the Prize Court.

Third, although the court was termed a "judicial arbitration court," there is no provision whatsoever that the decisions should be in accordance with law as in the International Prize Court Convention. It is true there is in the Judicial Arbitration Court project, much language used regarding the judicial qualifications and capabilities of the so-called judges, but it is not laid down among the rules which are to control these persons that their decisions shall be in accordance with law.

Fourth, a curious provision of the proposed plan (and this is brought bodily from the Prize Court Convention which in this respect is likewise deficient) stipulates that in reaching a decision "if the number of judges is even and equally divided the vote of the junior judge . . . is not counted."

The proposal to determine which side is right in a given controversy by arbitrarily disregarding the vote of the member last elected to the court is sufficiently novel, certainly in a system where law, equity, and justice are proclaimed as solely controlling, and particularly where the issue may conceivably be peace or war, to challenge attention. It is true the proposal is not without precedent in principle, because the Romans hazarded battle or remained in camp depending upon the voracity with which the sacred chickens ate their corn.

No further mention need be made of the Convention respecting the Limitation of the Employment of Force for the Recovery of Contract Debts, other than to note the criticism made of it, that until it became operative the use of force was never justified in collecting contract debts. The convention was the result of the work of the American Delegation to the Conference, who, in urging its adoption, were following out their instructions. Mr. Root, had earlier expressed himself to the Russian Ambassador, in the preliminary correspondence leading to the Conference, as believing that in narrowing the causes of war and reducing its frequency, the agreement to observe some limitations upon the use of force for the collection of ordinary public debts arising out of contracts might be effective. In this connection it might be observed that it is not easy to recall any war which resulted from the use of force to collect contract debts even prior to the Convention. The Convention is, however, of interest because it marks the maximum to which nations have gone in the matter of authorizing the enforcing of arbitral awards by the use of force.

In the years 1908 and 1909, Mr. Root renegotiated (as they were amended by the Senate) the treaties which Mr. Hay had concluded and then filed in the archive of the State Department without ratification. The Senate now approved them and they were ratified. The putting into effect of these Hay-Root treaties with their far-reaching limitations, is regarded by foremost authorities on our international relations as the most serious blow ever dealt to arbitration in this country.

But to return to the plan for Judicial Arbitration Court,—which the Conference declined to adopt.

Those who have followed the development of the arbitration movement subsequent to the Second Hague Conference, will recall that immediately upon the return of the American Delegates from the Second Hague Conference, a movement began to establish the primacy of this plan over any other, indeed over all others, theretofore proposed for the pacific settlement of international disputes. The motives which lay behind this well financed publicity, if not indeed, propaganda, which has been persistent and continuous almost to the present time, are probably not heretofore unknown, but they are immaterial to our purposes. It is enough to say that from that time to this no occasion deemed propitiatory, has failed to see haled into the public view the desirability of consummating this as the only plan worthy of consideration. It has been again and again brought to the attention of the nations even by interested private individuals who so tampering with our foreign affairs, have pleaded for its adoption.

But in tracing the course of these efforts to secure the adoption of this plan, we must return to the Prize Court Convention. Reference has already been made to the fact that Article 7 of this latter Convention provided that the determinations of the Prize Court should be in accordance with law. Accordingly Great Britain called a maritime conference to meet in London to frame the prize law which the court should administer. To this conference the United States, upon invitation, sent delegates.

One of the defects of the Prize Court Convention, as adopted by the Hague Conference, was the provision for a direct appeal from the decisions of national courts. Therefore, pointing out that because of this stipulation the ratification on the part of the United States of the Prize Convention was rendered difficult by reason of objections of a constitutional and internal nature not obtaining in other countries, Mr. Root embodied in his instructions to the American delegates to this Maritime Conference, a draft protocol, to be agreed to by the powers signatory of the Prize Convention. This protocol, to meet the situation of the United States, stipulated that instead of prize cases going to the international court as a matter of appeal from our national courts, they should be taken up by the Prize Court for examination *de novo* and the question of liability so determined.

Mr. Root's instructions to the American delegates contained no reference to the erection of the Prize Court into a Judicial Arbitration Court.

Mr. Root retired as Secretary of State on January 27 and was succeeded by Mr. Robert Bacon.

The Conference was held in London beginning December 4, 1908, and closing February 26, 1909. There were in attendance representatives of Austria-Hungary, France, Germany, Great Britain, Italy, Japan, the Netherlands, Russia, Spain and the United States (For. Rels. 1909, 304, et seq.).

In the early part of February, Mr. Bacon instructed the American delegates to propose that the powers represented at the Maritime Conference in addition to adopting the provision suggested by Mr. Root providing that the International Prize Court should as to certain countries consider prize cases *de novo,* should also formally agree to invest the Prize Court when constituted with the jurisdiction and procedure of a court of arbitral justice for arbitration, which court when so acting should accept jurisdiction and adopt for its consideration and decision in the case submitted to it, the project of the convention for the establishment of a court of arbitral justice concerning which a *voeu* was adopted by the Second Hague Conference (Series In. No. 8, 35).

Obedient to their instructions the American Delegates made both proposals to the Maritime Conference.

As the Conference progressed the American Delegates, acting under instructions, yielded (rather unaccountably at first sight) American prize principles to continental European prize principles in a number of most important matters (For. Rels. 1909, 306).

As the end of the Conference approached, Mr. Bacon, anxious for the projects, stated that in exchange for an acceptance by the Maritime Conference of the two American propositions above set out, the United States would yield its former doctrine and consent that nationality should be the test of enemy character; and, further, would agree that as to continuous voyages, the destination of merchandise would be presumed innocent when it was to be discharged in a neutral port, though proof to the contrary would be allowed.

Finally, as the Conference was near closing, Mr. Bacon, invoking the fact that he had made concession after concession to assure the success of the Conference and out of deference to a feeling for Great Britain and in the hope that Great Britain would accede to the American proposals, made a final appeal to the British Government to accomplish the adoption of the American projects. He accompanied his plea with a further concession (contrary, he said, to American tradition) made on the same day with a view to propitiating Great Britain (Feb. 10 Series In. No. 8, 36-37).

However, notwithstanding these requests and national offerings, the members of the Maritime Conference, while accepting the offerings in full, adhered to their position originally taken, that the adoption of either project was beyond the purview of the Conference, though they yielded as far as to adopt a *voeu* to the effect that the powers should agree that where the constitutional principles of any power required it, cases should go before the International Prize Court not on appeal, but *de novo* (For. Rels. 1909, 318).

Thus the announced sacrifice of American prize principles was in vain so far as the establishment of the Judicial Arbitration Court was concerned.

On March 5, 1909, the day after Mr. Taft became President and the same day on which Mr. Knox was made Secretary of State, Mr. Bacon advised our Ambassador to Great Britain, and directed him to advise the American representative at the other courts concerned, that the United States would upon receipt of the texts of the Maritime Conference send an identic circular note to each of the participating powers, suggesting in the first place the way in which the International Prize Court could be enabled to treat prize cases *de novo,* and in the next place, again take up the question of empowering the Prize Court to act as an arbitral court under the Judicial Arbitration Court plan, now called "Court of Arbitral Justice," or "Arbitral Court" (see Identic Circular Note, For. Rels. 1910, and Series In. No. 8, 12).

In compliance with this seeming but pseudo-commitment of the new administration to this Arbitral Court plan, Mr. Knox, in October 1909, did send to the Powers an Identic Circular Note* in which he proposed an amendment to the Prize Court Convention in accordance with the recommendation of the London Maritime Conference, and also proposed that the Prize Court so constituted should be authorized to act under conditions named, as a Court of Arbitral Justice (For. Rels. 1910, 597).

This step was followed by a Confidential Conference at Paris in March 1910 at which representatives of the United States, France, Great Britain, and Germany agreed upon two draft protocols to accomplish the two purposes proposed in the Identic Circular Note.

For a number of reasons, the most important of which was the failure of Great Britain to accept and ratify the Declaration of London, the Prize Court Convention did not go into effect, and, therefore, neither of the protocols ever became operative.

Third Period

The conclusion of the Pecuniary Claims Convention of August 8, 1910, the decision of the North Eastern Coast Fisheries case by the Hague Tribunals in September 1910, and the conclusion of the arrangement regarding the capture and killing of fur seals of July

---

*This identic note has been printed (by interested parties) with a headline "Proposed to and adopted by" Mr. Knox. There is in this an implication wholly erroneous. For instead of being proposed to Mr. Knox, the matter was initiated and handled entirely in the Department of State, in the usual course of business by Mr. Secretary Knox and those assisting him, without outside suggestion or proposal.

1911, had so cleared the Department of State and the British Foreign Office of pending differences between the two governments, that Mr. Knox felt it opportune, in order that "no future differences shall be a cause of hostilities between them or interrupt their good relations and friendship," to negotiate a general treaty of arbitration between the United States and Great Britain.

Moreover, having in mind the failure of the United States to secure an agreement by the powers to establish an arbitral machine along the lines urged by the American delegates at the Second Hague Conference and by the Department of State thereafter, and aware of our success in eliminating our differences with Great Britain notwithstanding the absence of the much advertised and panegyrized machinery provided by this Court of Arbitral Justice plan, Mr. Knox concluded that the lines of true advance in the peaceful adjustment of international disputes lay in securing agreements to settle by peaceful means all differences instead of agreements to set up a machinery without work to do. That is, he was convinced the real crux of the problem was the establishing of an arbitral or pacific settlement jurisdiction over the greatest possible number of subjects, and that the maximum progress could be found in making the peaceful adjustment of differences obligatory in the maximum number of cases, if this could be worked out in a way that would command the approval of the Senate. He, therefore, undertook negotiations to this end with Great Britain and France, and certain beginnings were made with Germany.

Before proceeding to a consideration of the Knox treaties, the provisions of the great Olney-Pauncefote Treaty—the forerunner of the Knox treaties and urged upon the Senate for its favorable action not only by President Cleveland under whose direction the treaty was negotiated but also by President McKinley—should be briefly considered.

The Olney-Pauncefote Treaty stipulated for the submission to arbitration by the United States and Great Britain of "all questions in difference between them which they may fail to adjust by diplomatic negotiations" (Art. 1). This was all-embracing and without exception.

For the purpose of such arbitration, differences were divided into three classes: first, "pecuniary claims or groups of pecuniary claims which do not in the aggregate exceed £100,000 in amount, and which do not involve the determination of territorial claims"

(Art. 2); second, all "pecuniary claims or groups of pecuniary claims which shall exceed £100,000 in amount and all other matters in difference, in respect of which either of the High Contracting Parties shall have rights against the other under Treaty or otherwise, provided that such matters in difference do not involve the determination of territorial claims" (Art. 4); and third, "any controversy which shall involve the determination of territorial claims" which in a subsequent part of the treaty were defined to include "all claims to territory and all claims involving questions of servitudes (Art. 6), rights of navigation and of access, fisheries and all rights and interests necessary to the control and enjoyment of the territory claimed by either of the High Contracting Parties" (Art. 9).

Classes one and two were to be submitted to one tribunal (with provision for review by another tribunal) and class three was to be submitted to a third tribunal, for the creation and functioning of all of which provision was made in the treaty (Arts. 3, 5, 6, 10). Provision was also made for the taking away from the tribunals exercising jurisdiction over classes one and two, if the tribunal having it should so determine, any claim which necessarily involved "the decision of a disputed question of principle of grave general importance affecting the national rights of such party as distinguished from the private rights whereof it is merely the international representative" (Art. 7).

It is obvious that this jurisdiction is far and away greater than that provided for in any of the plans afterwards proposed, even including the great Hay plan itself, because under the Olney-Pauncefote plan nothing was exempt from the matters which were to be subjected to possible adjustment by the tribunals created, whereas under the Hay plan questions relating to or involving political independence or territorial integrity were excepted. It is, however, to be said that a classification of claims based merely on the amount involved is not scientific and in this respect the treaty was at fault though the fault was in one sense slight because *all disputes* were, under the treaty, to be peacefully adjusted.

This is the background upon which Mr. Knox now began to work. He considered all disputes as divisible into two (instead of three) classes, namely, justiciable disputes and non-justiciable disputes. Disputes were "justiciable in their nature by reason of being susceptible of decision by the application of the principles of law or equity." Therefore, the treaty provided for the submission to arbitration, for hearing and determination, of all questions as to which there was controlling and governing rule of conduct known beforehand and accepted. In all such differences, the first and primary task of an arbitral tribunal would consist in determining the facts in controversy; the second, in applying the predetermined rule to such facts. Warned by the fate of the Hay treaties, Mr. Knox (after mature consideration) did not attempt to make this jurisdiction obligatory under the general treaty, but left to the Senate the power to approve the special treaty concluded for the arbitration of each particular case.

It was provided that non-justiciable disputes—that is to say— all those disputes which concerned questions of policy or other matters as to both of which there are no governing and controlling rules accepted as among nations—should be referred to a Joint High Commission of Inquiry "for impartial and conscientious investigation" the commission being authorized "to examine into and report upon the particular questions or matters referred to it, for the purpose of facilitating the solution of disputes by elucidating the facts, and to define the issues presented by such questions, and also to include in its report such recommendations and conclusions as may be appropriate" which reports and conclusions were not to "be regarded as decisions of the questions or matters so submitted either on the facts or on the law, and shall in no way have the character of an arbitral award" (Art. 2). In other words as to all those differences over matters concerning which and concerning the conduct of nations with reference to which, there was no accepted, controlling rule or principle to be invoked by the parties or applied by the tribunal, no decision was to be given by the Commission, because there being no pre-known accepted rules the question becomes purely one of national interest backed by national power; and until selfishness disappears from the nations, it is likely that important questions to which no accepted rule of conduct attaches, may not be safely submitted to obligatory arbitration by some general tribunal, but must be either settled by diplomacy or by submission to special tribunals constituted to consider them.

It was also provided in the Knox treaties that at the request of either party, the submission of any question to the Joint High Commission of Inquiry should be "postponed until the expiration of one year after the date of the formal request therefor, in order to afford an opportunity for diplomatic discussion and adjustment of the questions in controversy" (Art. 2).

In case the parties disagreed as to whether or not a given dispute was justiciable or non-justiciable, the matter was to be referred to the Joint High Commission of Inquiry composed of three citizens of the United States and three subjects of Great Britain, "and if all or all but one of the members of the Commission agree and report that such difference is within the scope of Article 1 (that is, that the dispute is justiciable) it shall be referred to arbitration in accordance with the provisions of this treaty" (Art. 3).

The provisions of these Knox treaties by dividing disputes into the two classes (justiciable and non-justiciable) by providing a means of determining, in case of differences between the powers regarding it, to which category any given dispute was to be assigned, by affording adequate machinery for facilitating the disposition of non-justiciable disputes, and by specifically stipulating that justiciable disputes should be decided according to law and equity, mark a renewed advance by the United States in the matter of the peaceful adjustment of international disputes—a reoccupation of a considerable part of the ground lost by the Hay-Root 1904-1905 treaties—and likewise indicate the only road along which further real progress may be made.

For as stated at the beginning the real impediment to pacific settlement of international differences is not to be found in the existing Hague arbitral machinery, faulty though it is, but in the absence of an adequate jurisdiction in the tribunal,—a jurisdiction which must be made obligatory in as large measure as is possible in the present national temper on the general subject.

But the Senate was unwilling to approve of this recovery of lost ground by Mr. Knox, and so amended the treaties by striking out the clause providing for determination by the Commission of Inquiry of the question whether or not a given dispute was justiciable, and by withdrawing from the jurisdiction conferred by the treaty certain specified matters.

Mr. Knox rightly considered that these changes destroyed in great part the advance made by the treaties, and he therefore declined to proceed with their ratification. It is submitted, however, that they still hold enough of gain over the present situation to justify putting them into operation.

During the year 1913, Mr. Bryan as Secretary of State initiated the negotiation of a series of treaties embodying what was known as "President Wilson's Peace Proposal." These treaties were however mere applications of the Hague Commissions of Enquiry, and the "cooling off" of the mediation clauses of the Hague Pacific Settlement Convention, as amplified in the Knox treaties. The Bryan treaties therefore contained no new essential element, and made no real advance.

It appears that in 1914 interested private parties, seemingly unauthorized by our own government, importuned certain powers to vitalize the *voeu* arbitral court plan through the adoption of a supplemental convention which was apparently actually drafted. But nothing seems to have come of this.

This brings the matter to the arbitration clauses of the League of Nations Covenant, the jurisdiction provision of which has already been quoted and commented upon. A draft arbitral convention to implement the Covenant provisions, has been drawn by a special committee appointed therefor by the Council of the League. But according to press reports this draft plan was found unacceptable to the Council because certain of its provisions—particularly those relating to obligatory arbitration—went beyond the powers and authority given under the Covenant,—or in other words, from the standpoint of the Covenant, these provisions were illegal. The press also reports the Assembly of the League did not approve the scheme as drawn by the Special Committee, certain large powers objecting to the obligatory arbitration feature. However, as this new plan is probably still not fully formed, it would be beside the present purpose to speculate on its final terms. If the final project conforms to the Covenant provisions, it must fall far short of the plan in the Olney-Pauncefote Treaty, the Hay Hague plan, and the Knox treaties, and must disprove the assumption, frequently made by unthinking pacifists, that real progress in arbitration, as practiced between the United States and other powers, has been made in the current world movement for the pacific settlement of international disputes.

Outline Suggestion on the Establishment of Courts of International Justice

15 June 1923

Apparently on his own initiative, JRC prepared this memorandum for President Warren G. Harding. Inasmuch as the president was getting ready to make a trip, JRC sent the memorandum to his friend Warren F. Martin, a special assistant attorney general, asking him to deliver it so that the president would be sure to get it before leaving Washington. President Harding acknowledged receiving the memorandum and wrote, "I . . . am taking it with me in my travels for a more leisurely study than I can give amid the rush of my preparation for my Western trip" (Warren G. Harding to J. Reuben Clark, Jr., 20 June 1923, Box 503, Book 3, JRCP.) President Harding had no opportunity to respond or act on the Clark suggestions because, after visiting Alaska and British Columbia, he became ill in Oregon and died in San Francisco on 2 August. Both the memorandum and its cover letter are reproduced here. Box 47, Book 2, 1923, World Court, J 11.8, JRCP.

Letter to President Harding

June 15, 1923

Honorable Warren G. Harding,
  White House,
    Washington, D.C.

My dear Mr. President:

Firmly convinced of the national necessity for the solidarity and success of our Party, particularly as to a sound and constructive foreign policy, and deeply interested in your own welfare, I am venturing again to write to you touching the establishment of a system of international justice.

I have prepared the enclosed memorandum on the matter which is, I hope, sufficiently explicit to require no further elaboration here. In its larger aspects it is the fruit of at least some experience and of considerable reflection running over many years. The memorandum is in three parts,—a preliminary resumé, an enumeration of some favorable considerations for the plan, and an outline of the plan itself.

I am most anxious that you may devise some program that will put the whole Party behind a great, constructive plan for a safe and wise world association and organization for justice,—a plan that shall have no connection whatever with the League of Nations or with any of its instrumentalities, that the Party can call its own by creation not adoption, and that will use and perpetuate so far as is possible the existing, tried, and effective international instrumentalities which the Party has had so large a share in creating. To the support of such a plan, you can, I am confident, Mr. President, rally an undivided Party without a well-founded feeling by any member either of stultification or apprehension as to the future of our country.

I regret that I cannot be in Utah to join the hearty welcome which I know my native State will give you. When you contemplate our stark and rugged mountains in endless chains, our great free, open desert stretches, our wonderful monuments carved by the mighty hand of Nature—all the handiwork of God—you will, I feel, be willing to excuse, perhaps to tolerate (because you will fully understand and appreciate) the extreme tenacity with which some of us cling to our freedom, national and individual, and to our great free institutions; you will know why we shun the very appearance of every destructive entanglement.

Allow me to wish a pleasant, restful, health-giving trip,—for yourself and for Mrs. Harding.

With every personal good wish, I am
Faithfully,

P.S. I am sending this by the hand of Mr. Martin that you may surely get it before you leave.

Memorandum

Outline Suggestion on the Establishment of Courts of International Justice

A. PRELIMINARY RESUMÉ

The First Hague Conference (1899) framed and the Second Hague Conference (1907) amplified and amended the Convention for the Pacific Settlement of International Disputes. This Convention provided for three methods of peacefully settling international disputes, as follows:—

1. Good Offices and Mediation on the part of disinterested nations.

The United States was the first to invoke this method of peaceful adjustment when it mediated between Ecuador and Peru while Mr. Knox was Secretary of State, and by so doing prevented those countries from going to war.

2. Commissions of Inquiry.

This machinery was used for investigating the Dogger Bank incident between Russia and Great Britain, during the Russo-Japanese war, and so averted what seemed to be an imminent possible war between Russia and Great Britain.

3. Arbitration.

The United States and Mexico were the first to use this method of adjustment under the Hague Convention, while Mr. Hay was Secretary of State, when the two nations took the Pious Fund Case to The Hague.

The United States as well as other powers have since that time used the Hague Tribunal to secure the adjustment of a number of matters of the last international importance and danger.

That part of this Hague Convention which dealt with arbitration provided for the creation of what was termed a "Permanent Court of Arbitration" which consisted of (at most) four persons nominated by each of the nations ratifying or adhering to the Convention, the national groups so named by the nations constituting in reality a panel or list of persons from whom nations, desiring to arbitrate their differences under the Convention, were to choose a court to try and to adjudicate the controversy between them.

A special treaty (*compromis*) was usually framed for creating a court for a particular case. The "Permanent Court of Arbitration" had no compulsory (affirmative) jurisdiction.

The Second Hague Conference also framed a Convention for the establishment of an International Prize Court which provided for compulsory (affirmative) jurisdiction in matters of prize.

The same Conference also provided—in the Convention respecting the Limitation of the Employment of Force for the Recovery of Contract Debts—that as to contract debts force might be used against a power which neglected to reply to an offer of arbitration or refused to arbitrate such a matter, or which, having agreed to arbitrate, refused to proceed, or which declined to carry out an award.

The Statute creating the League Court provides that the personnel of that Court shall be elected by the Assembly and Council of the League from a list of persons proposed by the various national groups composing the "Permanent Court of Arbitration" (described above) and by groups named by nations who are not members of that Court.

The present suggestion is that a new international Supreme Court shall be created, entirely unconnected with the League, and that the personnel of this new court shall not only be nominated by the national groups composing the "Permanent Court of Arbitration," but shall be elected by that Court also. This conforms to the principles of organization which are already operative in the selection of the personnel of the League Court, thus overcoming the great obstacle (heretofore unsurmountable) of how to elect a court of few members which should be regarded by the small powers as sufficiently representing them.

The suggestion is also made that courts inferior to the Supreme

Court should be provided for, so as to localize international justice as far as possible (a principle that has gone far to establish justice in the lives of the great nations), and so as to curtail as much as possible the expense of international litigation which is almost prohibitive to the small poor powers.

The jurisdiction of these Courts of First Instance and of the Supreme Court should be partly voluntary or permissive and partly compulsory (affirmative),—perhaps compulsory as to treaty rights and voluntary as to international law rights as defined by an international code to be framed and agreed to by the nations.

A sanction of force might or might not be put behind the decisions of the Supreme Court, and the final decisions (if any) of the Courts of First Instance.

The "Permanent Court of Arbitration" should be left as it is, so far as its jurisdiction in international affairs is concerned, while its functions should be enlarged to make it a deliberative body with the power or recommendation only as to its conclusions on general matters or on specific matters which may from time to time be referred to it by the nations.

B. SOME CONSIDERATIONS FAVORABLE TO THE PLAN

The foregoing suggestions provide a plan which will,—

1. Build upon the Hague Tribunal, which is an already existing and accepted institution to which all the nations of the earth (not a part of them only) are now or may become parties, and to which a great majority of the nations have consented and to whose functions they are accustomed.

2. Establish a world judicial system under conditions involving no new instrumentalities for the creation of the system,—the Hague Tribunal groups already function in creating the League Court.

3. Involve no new principle in the election of the judges of the proposed Supreme Court,—the judges of the League Court are now elected by representatives of the nations (in the Council and the Assembly), and this suggestion is to have them elected by the representatives of the nations assembled in The Hague Tribunal.

4. Bring international justice to the doors of the component national units by providing for local courts of first instance from which appeals may, in necessary cases, be taken to the Supreme Court (as in the American judicial system).

5. Make the initial trial of international disputes less expensive than the trial thereof before the Supreme Court in Europe. At

119

present a small nation can fight a decisive battle for what it costs to try its dispute in Europe.

6. Provide a real compulsory (affirmative) jurisdiction in at least a part of the field of international relationships, instead of the weak and ineffectual jurisdiction of the League Court, which has been strangled by the Powers and not permitted to function upon any important controversy.

7. Preserve the great provisions of the Hague Convention relating to Good Offices and Mediation and to Commissions of Enquiry.

8. Give to the Hague Tribunal certain deliberative, quasi-legislative functions which can serve as a safety valve for and a crystallizer of world opinion and as a formulator of desirable actions and policies, but without any sanction except the power to recommend,—thus securing in these respects all the advantages of the League Assembly without any of the disadvantages arising from the domination of the League Council and of the Council of Ambassadors.

9. Create a real judicial system with the minimum amount of innovation upon existing, accepted instrumentalities, and at the same time separate that judicial system from international political influences.

10. Eliminate entirely all connection with the League and with any and all of its instrumentalities, and thus eliminate all bases of criticism founded upon unwillingness to become affiliated with the League.

11. Eliminate all possibility of involvement in League matters, commitment to League policies, connection with the enforcement of the iniquitous, peace-destroying war treaties, and participation in the enforcement of the League sanctions in arbitral matters.

12. Provide a system of world association which shall in no way sacrifice our own interests, our free institutions, or our sovereignty.

13. Unite the Party behind a great constructive plan which shall be its own, which shall build upon existing instrumentalities that the Party was largely instrumental in establishing, and to which its members can be called in whole-hearted support without stultification or apprehension as to the effect upon their country.

C. THE PLAN IN OUTLINE

I. *The Hague Tribunal*

This Tribunal shall be continued as at present constituted, except that the members shall be appointed for a definite term of years (say five) and the American members thereof shall be appointed by and with the advice and consent of the Senate. The functions of the Hague Tribunal shall be,—

1. To act as a court under and perform all the functions specified for it in the Hague Convention for the Pacific Settlement of International Disputes.

2. To have the following additional functions, to which it shall be duly authorized by an international convention:

(a) To elect the members of a Supreme Court, hereinafter described, from a list of persons nominated by the national groups who are members of the Tribunal and by national groups named (in the same manner as are the Hague Tribunal groups) by nations who are not members of the Tribunal.

(b) To meet in session at regular, prescribed intervals, and in special sessions upon the request of two powers, to discuss and recommend changes in an international code, to be drafted and agreed to by the Powers, and to deliberate upon and make recommendations concerning matters referred to the Tribunal by any nation or concerning such general matters as to the Tribunal shall seem to call for consideration or action. All actions recommended by the Tribunal shall be carried out as determined by the nations, either immediately or after consideration by international conferences specially called for that purpose by the interested nations.

II. *A world judicial system* shall be created consisting of three classes of courts,—

1. *The Hague Court* which shall stand as it is and have the powers and perform all the functions specified and provided for in the Hague Convention for the Pacific Settlement of International Disputes.

2. *Courts of Original Jurisdiction, that is, Courts of First Instance.* These courts shall sit at the capital of the defendant nation; each court shall be composed of three judges,—one member representing and chosen by the defendant nation, and a third member [*sic*] who shall be a national of a third nation, neutral to the controversy, who shall preside over the court, and who shall be chosen by the Supreme Court (provided for hereinafter) from among its members.

There shall be no fixed number of Courts of First Instance; such a court shall be constituted each time the need therefor arises by reason of a controversy between two or more nations.

Each member of each such court must be a member of the Hague Tribunal panel.

If more than two states are parties to a controversy, then each additional state shall appoint an additional member of the Court, of the same qualifications as the other national members of the Court. In such an event the Court shall sit at the capital designated by the Supreme Court.

3. *A Supreme Court.* This Court shall be of appellate and of original jurisdiction. It shall sit at The Hague, and be composed of nine (eleven) judges who shall be elected for a term of six years by the Hague Tribunal from a list of persons nominated by the national group members of the Tribunal or by national groups chosen by States not members of the Tribunal, as heretofore set out. The original members of the Supreme Court shall upon election be divided by lot into 3 groups, A, B, and C; Group A's term to expire two years from the date of election; Group B's, four years; and Group C's, six years. The successors of the members of these groups (who serve out the Group term) shall each hold office for a full six years.

This plan would call for the election of three members every two years. No member shall be eligible for election to succeed himself more than once.

III. *The jurisdiction of the Courts*

1. *Courts of First Instance* shall have permissive jurisdiction of all questions arising between states and involving the interpretation of treaties and the application of the rules and principles of international law as defined by the international code; and compulsory (affirmative) jurisdiction of all questions as to which an agreement for such jurisdiction has been reached between the parties.

These courts shall have authority to find the facts, determine upon and fix the remedy, and make an award. From the decisions of these courts, an appeal shall lie to the Supreme Court unless otherwise stipulated by the parties.

2. *The Supreme Court* shall have permissive jurisdiction as to all matters of original jurisdiction, which shall comprise all matters referred to the Court by the parties disputant—and compulsory (affirmative) jurisdiction (1) of all appeals from decisions of the courts of original jurisdiction except those as to which the parties disputant shall in each case expressly agree otherwise; and (2) of all matters which the parties have agreed shall be referred to Courts of First Instance and which one of the parties afterwards shall refuse to submit to such a court.

Each party to a controversy before this Court shall be entitled to have one of its nationals sit as a member of the Court during the trial of such controversy, and if one of its nationals is not a regular member of the Court, then the Court shall appoint from the Hague Court Panel, a national of such disputant nation to sit with the court during the trial of the controversy.

In cases of original jurisdiction, it shall have the same powers as the Courts of First Instance and its awards therein shall be final. In cases of appeals, this Court shall have authority to reexamine the facts, redetermine and fix the remedy, and make a final award. The awards of this Court may or may not have such sanctions as are specified in the Hague Convention covering the Employment of Force for the Recovery of Contract Debts.

IV. *Compulsory (affirmative) jurisdiction to be given to Courts of First Instance and to the Supreme Court*

Compulsory (affirmative) jurisdiction shall be given, after some such plan as is provided in the Hague Prize Court Convention,—

1. Of all disputes regarding the interpretation of treaties, except those which the parties shall expressly reserve.

2. Of all disputes involving matters of international law as defined in and by an international code to be framed and agreed to by the nations, in so far as such jurisdiction may from time to time be agreed to by the nations.

Pacific Settlement of International Disputes

20 July 1923

Having sent President Warren G. Harding the memorandum reproduced as Article Seven in this section, some five weeks later JRC prepared the following memorandum, which became the feature article in the 4 October 1923 issue of *Unity* and was published again in the December 1923 *Advocate of Peace*. The *Deseret News* in Salt Lake City published it on 29 December 1923. Box 47, Book 2, 1923, World Court, J 11.9, JRCP.

Summary

The attached memorandum, after calling attention to some of the background—the Grand Design of Elizabeth [I] and Henry IV, the Holy Alliance, and the League of Nations,—points out there are now before the American people for their consideration, three proposals involving plans for the pacific settlement of international disputes, which, in the order of their announcement, are,—

1. Membership in the League of Nations, which the people unquestionably rejected at the last Presidential election.

2. The plan outlined in Senator Borah's Resolution providing for the "outlawry of war," the codification of international law, and the establishment of an international judiciary with affirmative (compulsory) jurisdiction.

3. President Harding's plan of adhesion to or participation in the Permanent Court of International Justice established by the League of Nations, either as the Court now is or after it has been separated from the League.

This memo sketches a plan—and gives reasons therefor—for consolidating the plans of President Harding and Senator Borah, and for amplifying the same in a way that will add to the machinery proposed by them a deliberative body—a World Congress—which shall have authority to consider general matters affecting the world or special matters referred to it by two or more of the nations, such a Congress to be composed of representatives of *all* the nations.

This plan is to be worked out,—

1. By an international convention declaring international war a crime and its aggressive wager a criminal, with possible reparations, restitutions, and penalties.

2. By an international convention codifying international law, so that, a judicial system being set up with compulsory jurisdiction, nations may be able to know, *first,* what they ought to do under a given set of circumstances, and, *second,* the rules by which their conduct under such circumstances is to be judged if and when such conduct is called in question before the international judiciary.

3. By an international convention which shall accomplish the following purposes,—

    a. Perpetuate, as now constituted, the present Hague Permanent Court of Arbitration for such use as the nations may from time to time care to put it.

    b. Create a new permanent World Supreme Court to be constituted as follows:—

Its first members shall be the members of the present League Permanent Court of Arbitration.

Members elected to take the place of these first members shall be not only nominated by the present Hague Permanent Court of Arbitration but shall be *elected* by that court also. For this purpose of election the Hague Permanent Court might, if such were desirable, be divided into a *first* and *second* electoral college, the memberships of each college being made up in some such manner as the League Council and Assembly.

This court should have compulsory jurisdiction in certain matters, perhaps those affecting interpretation of treaties and a part, at least, of those covered by the international code.

c. Provide for the creation of Courts of First Instance which should sit in the capital of the defendant nation to the controversy, the members of the Court (three) to be chosen *one* by the plaintiff nation, *one* by the defendant nation, and a *third,* a national of neither party, to be one of the members of the World Supreme Court bench. The national members must be members of the Hague Permanent Court of Arbitration panel.

The jurisdiction of such courts should be compulsory in some such manner as the Supreme Court.

d. Enlarge the functions of the Hague Permanent Court panel so as to make of that body a deliberative assembly—World Congress—which should sit at regular intervals (American members to be appointed by and with the advice and consent of the Senate) and should have *recommendatory* powers as to all matters coming before them either of general import considered on the initiative of the Congress, or on special matters referred to it by two or more powers.

Some of the advantages which such a combined plan—with the amplification suggested—would have are pointed out on pp. 18–19 of the memo.

*   *   *

Preliminary

The Grand Design

Certainly since the Grand Design (conceived, as it is said, in the brain of Elizabeth [I] of England) was elaborated by Henry IV of France and published to the world by his great minister, Sully, statesmen and philosophers (obedient to the divine principles of Sinai and Gethsemane) have visioned and struggled for the abolition of war and the peaceful adjustment of international disputes.

The Grand Design provided for a disarmed, organized, leagued world, with national boundaries adjusted to fit the views—perhaps whims—of its proponents; it provided an international army to maintain the *status quo* which it was to establish; it set up an assembly of the representatives of the nations composing it, for the discussion and adjustment of international disputes; it operated upon the consciences of the constituent national peoples by fixing the religion to which they should belong.

The immediate purpose of the Grand Design was the curtailment of the power and influence of Austria; its impelling motives were fear and hate of the Empire. It was in essence an alliance aimed against the then great dominant power which was to be stripped of possessions and confined within curtailed boundaries.

The Grand Design died with Henry.

The Holy Alliance

Two hundred years later, in the early part of the past century, a plan involving the basic elements of the Grand Design was insinuated into the visionary mind of Alexander of Russia, one of the most powerful and perhaps the most absolute of Europe's monarchs, who accomplished the formation of the Holy Alliance which was to guarantee the territorial adjustments following the reduction of Napoleonic France through an international army made up of the Allied Powers, and was to maintain the existing governmental status and form.

The purpose of the Holy Alliance—though cloaked by words of beatific benevolence—was the destruction of the dominating military power and influence of France and the perpetuation of the prestige, influence and paramountcy of the nations forming it.

The Holy Alliance crumbled and fell.

The League of Nations

One hundred years later the same ideas became again current in world affairs and the League of Nations was organized to give a sanction to the Treaty of Versailles, the purpose of which was to destroy Germany and to give France (who was to be backed by Great Britain and the United States) that position of dominating influence in Europe at which Germany aimed.

In essence, the League of Nations is, by intention and by actual operation, a military alliance among the Great Powers of Western

Europe which, with their possessions and dominions and the flattered weak and small powers of the world, have regrouped themselves in a new "balance of power" arrangement. The real purpose of this alliance is to make secure to themselves the world-wide territorial, strategic, political, economic, and financial gains with which, through the intervention of the United States, they were able to enrich themselves at the end of the Great War.

These Great Powers (or at least France) hope, plan, and expect to retain these gains through the maintenance and enforcement of the pernicious, peace-destroying yet so-called peace treaties of which the Treaty of Versailles is the prototype.

To give to this purpose a semblance of respectability, legality, and justice, these Powers work, when it best suits their ends, through the instrumentalities of the League of Nations. They manipulate at will, and have always done so, the Secretariat, the Assembly, and the Council: they even tamper with the Permanent Court of Justice itself. Behind this whole panoply of pseudo-world organization sits the Council of Ambassadors—successors of the Supreme Council—the "Big Four"—dominating, directing, compelling the course of Europe and of much of the world,—all for the benefit of the newly-grouped Great Powers. A narrow national selfishness, never exceeded in the history of the world, is the driving force of the whole system.

Thus the League of Nations perpetuates the worst features of the Grand Design and the Holy Alliance and adds no new fundamental element of virtue. If history repeats itself, the League must fall.

Present Situation

There are now before the American people for consideration (in the order of their presentation),—

1. The taking on of membership in the League of Nations.
2. The Borah Resolution plan, involving the outlawry of war, the codification of international law, and the establishment of an international judiciary with compulsory jurisdiction over international disputes.
3. President Harding's plan of adhesion to or participation in the Permanent Court of International Justice established by the League of Nations, either as it is or after it has been separated from the League.

The vote cast against it by the overwhelming majority of the American people at the last election, seems to eliminate membership in the League of Nations from present consideration.

This leaves President Harding's Permanent Court plan and Senator Borah's plan for further consideration.

In considering these two matters, there should be in mind certain existing international machinery framed to the same general end, that is the machinery provided for or set up by the Hague Convention for the Pacific Settlement of International Disputes.

The First Hague Conference (1899) (to which delegates were sent by President McKinley) framed, and the Second Hague Conference (1907) (to which delegates were sent by President Roosevelt) amplified and amended the Convention for the Pacific Settlement of International Disputes. This Convention provided for three methods of peacefully settling international disputes, as follows:

1. Good Offices and Mediation on the part of disinterested nations.

The United States was the first to invoke this method of peaceful adjustment when it mediated between Ecuador and Peru while Mr. Knox was Secretary of State, and by so doing prevented those countries from going to war.

2. Commissions of Inquiry.

This machinery was used for investigating the Dogger Bank incident between Russia and Great Britain, during the Russo-Japanese war, and so averted what seemed to be an imminent possible war between Russia and Great Britain.

3. Arbitration.

The United States and Mexico were the first to use this method of adjustment under the Hague Convention, while Mr. Hay was Secretary of State, when the two nations took the Pious Fund Case to The Hague.

The United States as well as other powers, have since that time used the Hague Tribunal to secure the adjustment of a number of matters of the last international importance and danger.

That part of this Hague Convention which dealt with arbitration, provided for the creation of what was termed a Permanent Court of Arbitration which consisted of (at most) four persons nominated by each of the nations ratifying or adhering to the Convention, the national groups so named by the nations constituting in reality a panel or list of persons from whom nations, desiring to arbitrate their differences under the Convention, were to choose a court to try and to adjudicate the controversy between them.

A special treaty (*compromis*) was usually framed for creating a court for a particular case. The Permanent Court of Arbitration had no compulsory (affirmative) jurisdiction.

The Second Hague Conference also framed a Convention for the establishment of an International Prize Court which provided for compulsory (affirmative) jurisdiction in matters of prize.

The same Conference also provided—in the Convention respecting the Limitation of the Employment of Force for the Recovery of Contract Debts—that as to contract debts force might be used against a power which neglected to reply to an offer of arbitration or refused to arbitrate such a matter, or which, having agreed to arbitrate, refused to proceed, or which declined to carry out an award.

The Statute creating the *League Court* provides that the personnel of that Court shall be elected by the Assembly and Council of the League from a list of persons proposed by the various national groups composing the Permanent Court of Arbitration (described above) and by groups named by nations who are not members of that Court.

A Suggestion

The plans of President Harding and of Senator Borah should be combined and then should be amplified by an incorporation therein of the Hague Tribunal which should have its functions enlarged so as to provide for a deliberative World Congress that should have powers of recommendation as to the general matters coming before it or as to the special matters which might from time to time be referred to it by the nations.

To carry out such a plan, the necessary international conferences should be called to accomplish the following matters.

I. A convention (treaty) should be framed for adoption by *all* the nations of the world that should declare international war to be an international crime and the nation waging it an international criminal to be punished by the nations in accordance with provisions and stipulations which the convention should set out and which might require the offending nation to make for its illegal action any or all of the following restitutions, restorations, and guarantees:

    a. To give up any and all advantages, whatever their nature or character, which it had secured through its illegal acts.

    b. To restore completely any and all property taken or destroyed in the course or as the result of its illegal acts.

    c. To pay the cost of all operations of whatever kind which were incident to the defensive or other measures taken by the other nations.

    d. To reimburse the nation attacked for all expenditures incurred by it in defending itself against the aggression of the offending state.

    e. To surrender for a period of years to be determined by the World Congress, such and so many of its customs houses as might be determined by the Congress which should provide a system for administering the same during the periods named and which should apply the proceeds thereof to the purposes enumerated under (b), (c) and (d) hereof, unless sums sufficient therefor should be earlier paid by the offending state from other sources.

    f. To pay as a penalizing indemnity such sums as the World Congress might determine. This indemnity might be used for the development, particularly the building of lines of communication, of such of the poorer nations as might be designated by the World Congress.

    g. To have applied against it, in cases of great gravity where the laws of war had been broken, the doctrines of retorsion and reprisal, the World Congress determining the extent to which these doctrines should be applied.

    h. To deliver to the World Congress for trial and punishment, those of its authorities who were responsible for the hostile acts.

But the Convention should further provide that war waged as an act of self defense upon attack, or as an act of self preservation either prior to attack or otherwise, or as a means of compelling an aggressive belligerent to desist, shall be justifiable and shall not entail the punishment hereinabove provided for.

Intervention pursuant to the terms of a treaty obligation or right, and interposition for the protection of oppressed citizens and their rights shall not be regarded as war within the meaning of the Convention.

The Convention should make provision for determining the aggressor, in case of threatened or actual international war, (it might be done by the World Congress); and it must be considered whether it ought not also to make provision for concerting (when deemed desirable or necessary) common measures of defense or control by the defending or non-aggressive nation or nations against the aggressors, and for cumulative measures of pressure and restraint which the nations might use in their discretion to avert a threatened war.

While war will scarcely be abolished by resolution, and therefore the value of a convention outlawing war, judged as a measure to bring immediately the actual abolition of war, may be questioned, yet the making of such a convention would not be a vain thing, for it would crystallize a growing world sentiment against war, would declare a standard by which the nations and the peoples thereof would be entitled to judge every future war (condemning or otherwise the parties thereto in accordance with the standard set up) and would so give direction and form to the great operative moral forces of the world by which alone the ultimate disappearance of war from the earth may be accomplished.

II. A convention should be framed which should codify international law, both that relating to war and also, and particularly, that relating to peace.

While there may at first sight appear to be some incongruity in outlawing war and then providing rules by which war shall be waged, such an incongruity is rather a matter of abstraction than reality. The practical fact cannot be ignored that war will hereafter be waged, and it is of the highest importance that the rules by which future belligerents shall conduct their operations shall be laid down and agreed to beforehand. Otherwise future wars will be mere welters of atrocities.

That the rules of peace should be codified is also necessary, particularly and indispensably so if an international judicial system, with compulsory jurisdiction, is to be created.

Just as under our Constitution there are certain individual rights which are beyond the reach of law,—for example, freedom of speech, of the press, and of religion, so there are among nations certain individual national rights which are not the subject of international law—for example, the control of immigration and of naturalization. Some such individual international rights are now recognized as beyond the scope of international law: but others are in the border land, and whether or not these latter should fall within the rules and prescriptions of international law, or should be left wholly outside its purview, and if brought within what should be the rule of conduct prescribed with reference thereto, are wholly unsettled questions.

Obviously a compulsory jurisdiction over international disputes by an international judicial system must be predicated upon an accepted rule of conduct pursuant to which a nation may frame its course and according to which its course when taken may be judged by an international tribunal. No nation may safely submit its conduct to compulsory review when it does not know *first* what it ought to do or is expected to do under the given circumstances, and *second* by what rule its conduct under such circumstances will be judged.

This marks the true distinction between *justiciable* disputes—those concerning matters which may be determined under and in accordance with a recognized rule of law of which the offending nation knew and by which it should have guided its conduct, and *non-justiciable* disputes—those which concern matters as to which there is no accepted rule by which nations may shape their conduct or by which that conduct may be judged.

Thus a full codification of existing international law is indispensable to the creation of any wise and effective international judicial system with powers of compulsory jurisdiction.

III. A Conventional arrangement must be made which shall set up an international judicial system with a compulsory jurisdiction covering as many subjects as it may be possible and wise so to provide for.

Senator Borah's Resolution calls for such a court but makes no specific provision therefor.

President Harding's plan contemplates participation in the Permanent Court of Arbitration set up by the League. The creating statute of that Court provides a way by which its jurisdiction may be made compulsory.

While President Harding's original plan called for a limited membership in the League, his present proposal is to divorce the Court from the League and to make it self perpetuating. This would mean that the Statute of the Court should be so revised that any nation might—or if and in so far as compulsory jurisdiction were adopted must—submit its international controversies to this court for determination. After the re-creation of the Court under such a

Statute, none of the nations would have anything further to do with it except to support it financially, to obey its mandates, or to revise from time to time its Statute.

Whether European powers will be willing to set up, and whether the United States ought to be willing to join in setting up, in the present state of world affairs, with its lack of prescribed international rule in so many matters of vital importance to the very life of nations, an independent, self perpetuating small body of men with the extraordinary, far reaching powers which that body would possess and which would inevitably touch on occasion the very vitals of national existence, may be legitimately and respectfully questioned. An apprehension is justified that such a plan will not be acceptable.

But however that point may be concluded, neither President Harding's plan nor Senator Borah's plan makes provision for a further necessary element of a world organization that shall be responsive to the present thought and aspiration of the peoples of the world in this matter, in that no body is in contemplation by either of them which shall act as a deliberative body upon matters that are not strictly legal but that affect and have to do with the general relations of all nations or the relations between groups thereof. The present League Assembly purports to act as such a body, but so many of the peoples of the world are outside of it (either from choice or because admission has been denied), it is so much a part of the political purposes, adjustments, and machinery of the Treaty of Versailles, and it is so completely, and under the circumstances inevitably, dominated by the local interests of Europe, that it fails adequately to respond to the requirements of a world organization.

It is therefore suggested that, to meet this further need, existing international instrumentalities be combined and their functions enlarged in order to provide, *first,* an international judicial system with compulsory jurisdiction, and *second,* a deliberative world body—*World Congress.*

A new international Supreme Court should be created, entirely unconnected with the League, the members of which court should *not only be nominated* by the national groups composing the Hague Permanent Court of Arbitration (as is the case with the League Permanent Court under its Statute), *but also elected* by the Hague Court panel. By thus conforming to the principles of organization which are already operative in the selection of the members of the League Court, the great hitherto unsurmountable obstacle—namely, how to choose the members of such a court in a manner satisfactory both to the large and small powers—would be overcome.

It is also suggested that courts inferior to the Supreme Court should be provided for, so as to localize international justice as far as possible (a principle that has gone far to establish justice in the lives of the great nations), and so as to curtail the expense of international litigation which is almost prohibitive to the small poor powers.

The jurisdiction of these Courts of First Instance and of the Supreme Court should be partly voluntary or permissive and partly compulsory (affirmative), perhaps compulsory as to treaty rights and compulsory or voluntary (as and to the extent agreed upon) as to international law rights as defined by an international code to be framed and agreed to by the nations.

A sanction of force might or might not be put behind the decisions of the Supreme Court, and the final decisions (if any) of the Courts of First Instance.

The Hague Permanent Court of Arbitration should be left as it is, so far as its jurisdiction in international affairs is concerned, while its functions should be enlarged to make it a deliberative body with the power of recommendation only as to its conclusions on general matters or on specific matters which may from time to time be referred to it by the nations.

In greater detail this plan is as follows:

I. *The Hague Tribunal set up under the Hague Convention.* This Tribunal (that is the Hague Court "panel") shall be continued as at present constituted, except that the members shall be appointed for a definite term of years (say five) and that American members thereof shall be appointed by and with the advice and consent of the Senate. The functions of the Hague Tribunal shall be,—

1. To act as a court under and perform all the functions specified for it in the Hague Convention for the Pacific Settlement of International Disputes.

2. To have the following additional functions, to which it shall be duly authorized by an international convention:

   a. To elect the members of a Supreme Court, hereinafter described, from a list of persons nominated by the national groups who are members of the Tribunal and by national groups named (in the same manner as are the Hague Tribunal groups) by nations who are not members of the Tribunal. (In order to simulate more nearly the League machinery for the election of members of the League Permanent Court, the Hague Tribunal might be divided into *first* and *second* electoral colleges which should, as to their component members, conform as nearly as possible to the groupings in the League Council and the League Assembly, and which should vote in electing court members in the same manner that the Council and Assembly now vote to elect members of the League Court.)

b. To meet in session at regular, prescribed intervals, and in special sessions upon the request of two powers, to discuss and recommend changes in an international code, to be drafted and agreed to by the Powers, and to deliberate upon and make recommendations concerning matters referred to the Tribunal by any nation or concerning such general matters as to the Tribunal shall seem to call for consideration or action. All actions recommended by the Tribunal shall be carried out as determined by the nations, either immediately or after consideration by international conferences specially called for that purpose by the interested nations.

II. *A world judicial system* shall be created consisting of three classes of courts,—

1. The *Hague Court* which shall stand as it is and have the powers and perform all the functions specified and provided for in the Hague Convention for the Pacific Settlement of International Disputes.

2. *Courts of Original Jurisdiction, that is, Courts of First Instance.* These Courts shall sit at the capital of the defendant nation; each court shall be composed of three judges,—one member representing and chosen by the plaintiff nation, a second member representing and chosen by the defendant nation, and a third member who shall be a national of a third nation, neutral to the controversy, who shall preside over the court, and who shall be chosen by the Supreme Court (provided for hereinafter) from among its members.

There shall be no fixed number of Courts of First

Instance; such a court shall be constituted each time the need therefor arises by reason of a controversy between two or more nations.

Each member (other than the presiding member) of each such court must be a member of the Hague Tribunal panel.

If more than two states are parties to a controversy, then each additional state shall appoint an additional member of the Court, of the same qualifications as the other national members of the Court. In such an event the Court shall sit at the capital designated by the Supreme Court.

3. *A Supreme Court.* This Court shall be of appellate and of original jurisdiction. It shall sit at The Hague, and be composed of nine (eleven) judges who shall be elected for a term of six years by the Hague Tribunal from a list of persons nominated by the national group members of the Tribunal or by national groups chosen by States not members of the Tribunal, as heretofore set out. The original members of the Supreme Court shall upon election be divided by lot into 3 groups, A, B, and C; Group A's term to expire two years from the date of election; Group B's, four years; and Group C's, six years. The successors of the members of these groups (who serve out the Group term) shall each hold office for a full six years.

This plan would call for the election of three members every two years.

No member shall be eligible for election to succeed himself more than once.

The initial constitution of this court might be accomplished by adopting as its members the members of the existing Permanent Court of Arbitration of the League of Nations. This would coincide with the plan of President Harding.

III. *The jurisdiction of the Courts.*

1. *Courts of First Instance* shall have permissive jurisdiction of all questions arising between states and involving the interpretation of treaties and the application of the rules and principles of international law as defined by the international code; and compulsory (affirmative) jurisdiction of all questions as to which an agreement for such

jurisdiction has been reached between the parties.

These courts shall have authority to find the facts, determine upon and fix the remedy, and make an award. From the decisions of these courts, an appeal shall lie to the Supreme Court unless otherwise stipulated by the parties.

2. *The Supreme Court* shall have permissive jurisdiction as to all matters of original jurisdiction which shall comprise all matters referred to the Court by the parties disputant—and compulsory (affirmative) jurisdiction (1) of all appeals from decisions of the courts of original jurisdiction except those as to which the parties disputant shall in each case expressly agree otherwise; (2) of all matters which the parties have agreed shall be referred to Courts of First Instance and which one of the parties afterwards shall refuse to submit to such a court; and (3) of all other matters as to which the parties have agreed a compulsory jurisdiction should attach.

Each party to a controversy before this Court shall be entitled to have one of its nationals sit as a member of the Court during the trial of such controversy, and if one of its nationals is not a regular member of the Court, then the Court shall appoint from the Hague Court Panel, a national of such disputant nation to sit with the court during the trial of the controversy.

In cases of original jurisdiction, it shall have the same powers as the Courts of First Instance and its awards therein shall be final. In cases of appeals, this Court shall have authority to reexamine the facts, redetermine and fix the remedy, and make a final award. The awards of this Court may or may not have such sanctions as are specified in the Hague Convention covering the Employment of Force for the Recovery of Contract Debts.

IV. *Compulsory (affirmative) jurisdiction to be given to Courts of First Instance and to the Supreme Court.* Compulsory (affirmative) jurisdiction shall be given, after some such plan as is provided in the Hague Prize Court Convention,—

1. Of all disputes regarding the interpretation of treaties, except those which the parties shall expressly reserve.

2. Of all disputes involving matters of international law as

defined in and by an international code to be framed and agreed to by the nations, in so far as such jurisdiction may from time to time be agreed to by the nations.

Some Considerations Favorable to the Plan

The foregoing suggestions provide a plan which will,—

1. Build upon the Hague Tribunal, which is an already existing and accepted institution to which all the nations of the earth (not a part of them only) are now or may become parties, and to which a great majority of the nations have consented and to whose functions they are accustomed.

2. Establish a world judicial system under conditions involving no new instrumentalities for the creation of the system,— the Hague Tribunal groups already function in creating the League Court.

3. Involve no new principle in the election of the judges of the proposed Supreme Court,—the judges of the League Court are now elected by representatives of the nations (in the Council and the Assembly), and this suggestion is to have them elected by the representatives of the nations assembled in The Hague Tribunal.

4. Bring international justice to the doors of the component national units by providing for local courts of first instance from which appeals may, in necessary cases, be taken to the Supreme Court (as in the American judicial system).

5. Make the initial trial of international disputes less expensive than the trial thereof before the Supreme Court in Europe. At present a small nation can fight a decisive battle for what it costs to try its disputes in Europe.

6. Provide a real compulsory (affirmative) jurisdiction in at least a part of the field of international relationships, instead of the weak and ineffective jurisdiction of the League Court, which has been strangled by the Powers and not permitted to function upon any important controversy.

7. Preserve the great provisions of the Hague Convention relating to Good Offices and Mediation and to Commissions of Enquiry.

8. Give to the Hague Tribunal certain deliberative, quasi-legislative functions which can serve as a safety valve for and a

crystallizer of world opinion and as a formulator of desirable actions and policies, but without any sanction except the power to recommend,—thus securing in these respects all the advantages of the League Assembly without any of the disadvantages arising from the domination of the League Council and of the Council of Ambassadors.

9. Create a real judicial system with the minimum amount of innovation upon existing, accepted instrumentalities, and at the same time separate that judicial system from international political influences.

10. Eliminate entirely all connection with the League and with any and all of its instrumentalities, and thus eliminate all bases of criticism founded upon unwillingness to become affiliated with the League.

11. Eliminate all possibility of involvement in League matters, commitment to League policies, connection with the enforcement of the iniquitous, peace-destroying war treaties, and participation in the enforcement of the League sanctions in arbitral matters.

12. Provide a system of world association which shall in no way sacrifice our own interests, our free institutions, or our sovereignty.

PART TWO

War and Peace

International Cooperation to Prevent War

August 1916

The excerpts presented below come from a talk JRC gave before the League of Women Voters. A note attached to the manuscript adds, "Sounds like a speech [given] in Utah (one of the few states having women suffrage before 1919 . . .)." JRC was in Utah during the latter part of August of 1916. Box 24, "World Federation," League of Women Voters, August 1916, J 9.26, JRCP.

So long as there are worse things than death, there will be worse things than war. So long as an individual had rather live than die, he will fight to live; so long as individuals will fight to live, nations will do likewise.

Society has for centuries struggled to eliminate the occasions for life and death struggles between individuals. In early society, possession by A of something B wanted, was an occasion for life and death struggle. This has been gradually changed with a present result of comparative peace. At the beginning—it may be observed in passing—man had before him communism or individualism. One as attainable as the other. It required no greater advance and not so great a subordination of selfishness, to agree that A and B should have the desired property in common, than that it should belong exclusively to A; yet at a time when the possession of that property meant so much in human existence, perhaps in itself either life or death, man determined upon individualism as against communism.

145

Nations are but collections of individuals. The growth of nations seems governed by the same laws that govern the growth of communities. Originally, the clan or tribe seeing desirable territory or property in the hands of another clan or tribe, went and took by force—if it were strong enough—that territory or property. This meant continual war; and while war was thus continuous and promiscuous, man remained savage.

But eventually clans and tribes discovered the law of progress, already discovered by their individual numbers—that safety, happiness, prosperity, progress, came only by continued occupancy of territory, or property, and the law of national ownership came into being.

It seems to be the great law, that rules of conduct develop first between individuals—then between nations. [Consider, for example, the current attitude regarding the] slavery of individuals [as opposed to that regarding] subject nations.

If this be the great law—then how shall we hope to blot out war between nations, so long as we still have life and death struggles between individuals?

On this hypothesis, nations must do as society has done, lessen as rapidly as may be the occasions for life and death struggles.

Furthermore, if laws forbidding murder have not during the centuries been able to abolish the felonious taking of human life, even when extermination of the individual was the penalty attached to the crime, shall we hope to abolish war by a resolution carrying no comparable penalty,—for nations could not be destroyed as the penalty for waging war, and if they could, who would be the executioner?

Finally, the law of the individual is that to take life in self defense is justifiable; are we prepared to say that a nation must suffer extermination rather than to wage war?

Must we not make up our minds that human agency at least is not able by mere fiat to usher in a millennium; that progress must come but slowly; and that the true problem is how can the occasions for war be best curtailed and lessened?

Manacled men may not commit murder, but [neither do they] progress. [We] must educate men. So with nations.

* * *

With the foregoing hypothesis in mind, it is assumed the word *international* may be taken in its usual sense as implying a group of independent, fully sovereign states acting under and in accordance with recognized customs, rules, and principles.

At any rate my observations shall proceed upon the premise that this nation shall cooperate in no way and participate in no measures which will not leave it completely free and independent, wholly sovereign. For it is my abiding faith that this nation has performed and will yet perform a mighty work for human government among the nations of the world. I am not willing to do anything that will lessen its influence or power among the peoples of the world, for there is immeasurably much to do to accomplish the political salvation of the world.

It is not to be assumed that we should be more able to exercise our power for good—the moral influence of which so much is said—if we had been, during the hundred forty years of our national existence, a party to every European War, every diplomatic European squabble, every world difficulty that has arisen during that period.

* * *

We go to a cobbler for shoes; plumbers for plumbing; doctors for surgery.

One of the tragedies of the present situation is that because in the past we have participated so little in world politics—in international matters—now that we are faced with a serious discussion of them we are generally so scantily equipped with information that we may neither adequately discuss nor sufficiently understand the real problem put before us.—It is, under these circumstances, possible for designing persons on either side of a controversy to impose upon our trustfulness. Moreover, as we do not understand the problems, either side presenting a plausible argument, is believed by some one, no matter how unsound basically the precise point in issue may be.

We must look at matters calmly. Apply principles involved in world affairs to a small group—for the world is made up of groups who lose few characteristics by amalgamation in large groups.

For example—not a few persons are under the impression that

world federation, world cooperation is a new idea—a new sun in the political firmament. The fact is of course quite otherwise.

The suggestion of a federated world followed the firm establishment of a number of first class powers.

Concerning this first plan, there is one matter of surpassing interest to you Ladies,—the League of Women Voters.

Government—national or world—is not an end in itself; we do not live that we may have government, we have government that we may live. Government is an incident of life, not the end of its purpose. Life is given for far other and transcendent purposes. Participation in government is therefore necessary and desirable for individuals only in so far as is wise or indispensable for its maintenance. Personally, therefore, I welcome the participation of my mother, my sisters, my wife, and my daughters in matters political. Men need the steadying moral influence of women in all their world contact and action. Furthermore, while I wish to deny to no woman such actual political activity as she may wish, I belong to that old fashioned school which honestly believes that "The hand that rocks the cradle, rules the world;" that the great moral powers lay primarily in the domain of women; and that, speaking generally, the home circle and the religious circle are the basic vantage points from which that moral influence may be most potently and lastingly exercised. When woman shall cease to radiate that moral force, when her activities shall be directed to advancing the ends of narrow selfishness, in business or in politics, the world will be in a precarious stage.

But in the field of moral forces, woman stands unapproached and supreme. When the moral issue arises, she exerts the mastering hand. Hers is the voice that directs, even if some other voice calls the command; she lays off the course, though the hand of man may grasp the helm.

Points on Meeting the Situation Arising from Operations by and against Submarines within Our Marginal Waters

October 1916

Outraged at the inaction of the secretary of state and the president when a German submarine destroyed some boats near Nantucket Shoals off the coast of New York, JRC wrote the following memorandum and sent it to David S. Barry at the National Republican Headquarters. Apparently he thought there was a possibility that the historical precedents he cited in the memorandum, if used judiciously by the Republican National Headquarters, might generate some action on the part of the national officials, who were Democrats. The memorandum follows the letter to Barry. Box 46, Book 3, 1916, Submarines, J 9.27, JRCP.

October 13, 1916

David S. Barry, Esquire
    National Republican Headquarters,
        43rd Street & 5th Avenue,
            New York City.

My dear Mr. Barry:
    Observing that, according to the press, the Secretary of State is scrutinizing the points regarding the way in which U-53 destroyed the boats off Nantucket Shoals, and that the Department is busily hunting precedents to enable them to handle the situation, and

having in mind the stock Democratic query, "What, Mr. Hughes, would you have done," it occurred to me that that gentleman might like to have before him the substance of the stuff I enclose herewith.

The form in which I have put it is somewhat fervid, but it is always easy to cool such stuff off, and the Democratic papers would have us believe that Republican gatherings are always held now days in close proximity to ice plants. At any rate the action of the administration in this emergency is either so painfully incompetent, or so rottenly disingenuous that I feel something may be appropriately said about the matter.

If you agree with me and feel that the enclosed will be helpful, kindly make such use of it as you may deem wise.

Very sincerely yours,

(Enclosure)

*   *   *

The war is now brought to our very doors. Submarines of one belligerent are sinking vessels of the other almost within gun shot of our coasts, and the war vessels of the other are assembling to attack and sink the submarines. If this continues, armed conflict is inevitable at the very entrance to the great sea lanes of our trans-Atlantic and coastwise commerce.

We have long since been warned by one of the belligerents that submarines find difficulty in distinguishing neutral from belligerent merchantmen, and freight ships from passenger boats, particularly because sometimes belligerents, as a ruse of war, fly neutral flags. Grave, war-menacing accidents have already happened because of this difficulty.

The other belligerent, in turn, who now begins operations against these submarines in our marginal waters, warns us that it is difficult to distinguish between neutral and belligerent submarines, and it is of course evident that the use of obvious ruses of war would increase the difficulty to an impossibility.

That is to say, we have been warned by one belligerent that our vessels of commerce may be sunk, our property lost and destroyed, and our men, women and children murdered because of the hostile operations of that belligerent, and we are now warned by the other belligerent that our vessels of war may be sunk and more American property lost, more American citizens murdered because of his operations against the first, all of which is to happen in our closest marginal waters, where under every principle governing war and the peaceful intercourse of nations we have a right to be in absolute safety and with complete freedom from such molestation. It is needless to say that when these warnings become actions, we shall be at war, and I challenge the Administration to give it any other name.

What is the Administration doing to meet this situation, pregnant with so grave a danger?

The President vacillates of course and as usual, and shuttles between Shadow Lawn and various non-partisan Democratic gatherings, dropping by the way irrelevant and beatific platitudes and boasting he has kept us out of war, but we have as yet no tangible evidence that he is even seriously considering this matter, laden with potentialities.

On its part the State Department also delays meeting the situation with any affirmative action, through a minute, one might say microscopic, investigation of the exact way and manner in which already destroyed American property was lost, and the precise formalities followed in putting American life in jeopardy. The Department is also and again hunting for precedents,—and by the way, this is an occupation which, second only to the all-embracing, all-stifling, all-crushing vacillation and indecision of the President, has been the source of most of our international ills.

Indeed, from the beginning of the war the State Department has continuously frittered away its time looking for precedents, for something that happened in exactly the same way, in a precisely similar place, at an identical hour,—some event alike in all details with those they were considering; and failing to find such precedents as fail they must, because of the new conditions, new methods, and new instruments of warfare, they have hesitated, faltered, and wavered in every course in which they have gone forward at all, and have been driven back, in a rout from positions which at first they properly occupied. The State Department has failed from the first to appreciate the fundamental principle of true statecraft that while precedents are most useful to point to an argument, yet the argument itself must be built upon great, broad, underlying principles and rules which are at once the guides for our own course, as also the course which the belligerents must follow. Had the Department of State looked to principle, instead of vainly seeking for

151

precedent, it would have found no important happening in which we have been involved, or by which we have been affected since the beginning of the war, which was not controlled and subject to adjustment by principles which were a century old, and many of them principles which we ourselves laid down, when, leading the world by a hundred years, we announced in the days of Washington the rules of neutrality by which nations were to be and are governed. That those responsible for the handling of our foreign affairs have been ignorant of these, our own rules and principles, has been at once our shame and our calamity.

As to the present emergency it may be said that one hundred years ago, in the days of small sailing vessels and smaller cannon, Madison, then Secretary of State, instructed Monroe and Pinckney, our Plenipotentiaries to London, on this precise matter, and laid down the controlling principles, as follows:

> There remains, as an object of great importance, some adequate provision against the insults and injuries committed by British cruisers in the vicinity of our shores and harbors. These have been heretofore a topic of remonstrance, and have, in a late instance, been repeated with circumstances peculiarly provoking, as they include the murder of an American seaman within the jurisdictional limits of the United States.

Referring to documents he enclosed with reference to these matters, Mr. Madison continued:

> They not only support a just demand of an exemplary punishment of the offenders, and of indemnity for the spoliations, but call for some stipulations guarding against such outrages in future. With this view, it is proper that all armed belligerent ships should be expressly and effectually restrained from making seizures or searches within a certain distance from our coasts, or taking stations near our harbors commodious for those purposes.
>
> In defining the distance protected against belligerent proceedings, it would not, perhaps, be unreasonable, considering the extent of the United States, the shoalness of their coast, and the natural indication furnished by the well defined path of the Gulf Stream, to expect an immunity for the space between that limit and the American shore. But at least it may be insisted that the extent of the neutral immunity should correspond with the claims maintained by Great Britain, around her own territory.

Madison also called attention to the fact that Great Britain during the reigns of James I and Charles II, provided by express prohibitions against the roving or hovering of belligerent ships so near the neutral harbors and coasts of Great Britain, as to disturb or threaten homeward or outward bound, as well as against belligerent proceedings generally, within an inconvenient approach towards British territory.

This was the principle we then announced in plain, unambiguous language, without fine words or sounding phrases, and although then among the weakest of the weak, we announced it to the proudest and most powerful nation of the earth, then still smarting over our new won independence.

This is the principle, thus hoary with age, for which the administration professes to be searching to meet the present grave emergency. Let them take it and act on it, unless it desires that now we are powerful among the most powerful we shall abandon this sacred principle and cringe and slink away from this emergency like whipped curs. Insistence upon undoubted rights never yet led to war between responsible, self-respecting nations.

But if the President and the State Department feel any hesitancy in now proclaiming so robust and manly a doctrine, there is still another principle which may be of service to them, and to which therefore I venture to invite their attention in order that they may be able properly to handle the present situation.

Let me begin with a homely illustration. If two quarreling neighbors begin to fight in the street in front of your house, to throw bricks and to shoot at one another, thereby breaking the windows and doors of your house and injuring and killing your family you call the policeman to stop the fight, or no policeman appearing you yourself go out, take the fighters by the scruff of the neck and drive them away; and further when the fight is over you compel them to pay for the property they have destroyed, and to answer for the injury or death of your family, if necessary with their own lives.

An identic principle applies in international law.

In the broad ocean road just in front of our doors two sets of quarreling neighbors have begun to fight. Already they have destroyed our property, have endangered our lives, and further hostilities will bring additional property losses and probably actual loss of life. We have a right to say to them "Get away from here and go fight in your own front yards." We are not bound to sit shivering and spineless suffering this; we may with dignity and right, tell them that this fight is a threatening, destructive nuisance that must be stopped, or moved. The principle upon which such a demand would be based is as old and venerable as the one to which I have just referred. In our own history we have invoked it against others and others have invoked it against us.

In 1817 General Jackson (one of Democracy's patron saints) invaded Spanish territory and by force of arms put an end to the fitting out therefrom of raids against American citizens and their property on American soil, and the United States successfully defended and justified his course in thus abating that nuisance.

In 1837 Great Britain violated our own territory by invading the United States and killing our citizens, and destroying our property—all for the purpose of preventing possible irreparable injury to her own territory, and to the property and lives of her subjects; and while the two countries disagreed as to whether the particular circumstances of the case justified the actual measures taken, they were in complete accord on the principle that the protection of the property and the lives of a nation's citizens or subjects would justify that nation in destroying a sufficiently threatening situation even within the confines of another nation.

This same principle was the fundamental basis upon which we placed our intervention in Cuba in 1898.

In 1896, Mr. Olney, that lately converted champion and apologist of the administration, communicating as Secretary of State with the Spanish Minister regarding the situation in Cuba, formally advised the Minister that the United States could not "contemplate with complacency" a prolonging of existing conditions which he described as a continuation of a struggle "raging almost in sight of our shores," the interruption of "extensive trade relations which have been and should continue to be of great advantage to both countries," the "wholesale destruction of property—which, making no discrimination between enemies and neutrals, is utterly destroying American investments that should be of immense value, and is utterly impoverishing great numbers of American citizens." And a little later the same gentleman, reporting to President Cleveland, asserted that "it is impossible not to discern that a state of things exists at our doors, alike dangerous to good relations, destructive of legitimate commerce—and most vexatious and trying because entailing upon this Government excessive burdens in its domestic administration and its outward relations," and that the continuation of this condition must make the United States consider a change in its policy, which it may be remarked had been theretofore peaceful.

Again, in his message to Congress, just before the resolution recognizing Cuba as free and independent had passed, President McKinley characterized as "of the utmost importance" in his summary of the causes which gave to the United States the right to intervene "to stop the War" that "the present condition of affairs in Cuba is a constant menace to our peace, and entails upon this government an enormous expense;" that "the lives and liberty of our citizens are in constant danger and their property destroyed and themselves ruined;" and that "our trading vessels are liable to seizure and are seized at our very door by warships of a foreign nation."

These are the reasons we gave for intervening in Cuba, for invading the soil of another sovereign, and for ousting that sovereign from his own dominions.

Will anyone say that the continued presence and operation of hostile fleets in our very home waters will not be, to quote Mr. Olney, "destructive of legitimate commerce," will not be "most vexatious and trying because entailing upon this Government excessive burdens in its domestic administration and its outward relations," will not be a struggle "raging almost in sight of our shores," will not involve a "wholesale destruction of property—which, making no discrimination between enemies and neutrals is utterly destroying American investments that should be of immense value, and is utterly impoverishing great numbers of American citizens;" or, to quote President McKinley, "will not lead to a seizure of our trading vessels" at our very doors, will not place "the lives and liberty of our citizens . . . in constant danger," and finally and beyond all, will not be a "constant menace to our peace," and will not indeed be a threat to embroil us in the very war itself?

If these things would legalize and justify, as they would under all the precedents and authorities, a violation and invasion even of foreign territory itself, in order that we might, both in person and in property, be protected and preserved, how much more will they legalize and justify an abating [of] such conditions on our own home seas where, looked at in the most favorable light for the belligerents, we have as much and equal right with them.

The adminstration will find in the doctrines of self-preservation and self-defense, which means merely the safety of the persons and property of our citizens, the maintenance of our peace, and the perpetuation of our institutions, as also in instances of the invocation of such doctrines with which history is filled, full and ample authority and justification for a demand that since you destroy our commerce and our property, endanger our lives, and threaten our peace by embroiling us in the great European conflict, you must either cease your fighting or go elsewhere, and for taking any and all measures which it may be necessary to take in order to see to it that our demands are obeyed.

America's Prime Interest Is a Just and Lasting Peace

June 1917

The circumstances of the writing of this memorandum are not known, but in it JRC presented a statement of views he had often expressed more formally at other times and listed some definite measures he believed should be incorporated in the peace terms at the end of World War I. Many of these were so incorporated; but JRC's important advice on readjustments becoming misadjustments was ignored in the framing of the Treaty of Versailles, and in less than twenty years another European war was brewing. The memorandum is obviously in rough-draft form and incomplete. Box 46, Book 3, 1917, Peace Terms, J 9.34, JRCP.

"Making the world safe for democracy," puts the cart before the horse. [It] is a fine phrase, but like most of its kind, is meaningless when looked at from the point of view of actual conditions, for at best it concerns only the winning of this war, now [become] a struggle between autocracy and democracy, and not the ultimate and basic purpose, namely a just and lasting peace. For though in democracies, wars are less frequent yet they do exist.—*Quaere,* is not Russia democratic, united, self conscious, educated, more to be feared, more of a menace, than Russia autocratic, discordant, unconscious, and ignorant?

The history of the World has shown that every great war sows the seeds of the next great war which follows; the humiliations,

157

indemnities, land adjustments, etc. etc., etc., of the one always produce the other.

The present War has shown that, under the existing conditions attending international intercourse, no great country can keep itself neutral in any great world war.

The United States is, therefore, vitally interested in seeing to it that insofar as is humanly possible no seeds are sown during this war which can produce another war.

Among the principal causes of the present war were Imperial ambitions, racial affinities, race conceit, commercial rivalries, and territorial misadjustments of earlier wars.

To insure a lasting peace it is indispensable, first, that a complete curb be put upon the Imperial ambitions, and this could be accomplished best by promoting in Imperial countries those forms of government which would eliminate predominant influences of the ruling houses.

One of the significant forces of the present age is that of race consciousness and cohesion which must be recognized. Closely associated with this race cohesion is the desire for racial self-government. The feeling is abroad in the land that no race should be a subject race. And, reciprocally, that every race has a right to govern itself.

Insofar as possible unhealthy racial conceit should be eliminated and to this end: Provision should be made for the maximum amount of freedom of thought. Intellectual slavery is the worst of all slavery. The masses of peoples should be permitted to do their own thinking upon matters affecting their own welfare, insofar as such intellectual freedom is possible in a world of unequal intellects.

Economic rivalries are probably inevitable so long as separate nations exist, or any one people lives by and within itself, or as the world is divided into individual coherent units, whether political, racial, or otherwise. Commercial slavery and worse will follow any domination by any single great power, or group of large or small powers. The evils to the world of such a situation are not obviated merely by becoming one of the dominating group.

Therefore, the aim should be to prevent, so far as may be possible, any plan for commercial domination beyond that which may be necessary in order to bring about the other purposes mentioned above, particularly the elimination of Imperial ambition and the discipline of race conceit. This is merely saying that a league for commercial supremacy would constitute a warring league, and that if such a league were formed at the end of this war and operated thereafter, the laying down of arms would merely constitute a cessation of only one form of hostility, and that actual war would continue thereafter. It may be that this will be necessary in order to win a lasting peace, but it should be clearly understood that such a league is a means to an end, and not the end itself which should always be a lasting peace.

Territorial misadjustments of the past should be rectified, but these rectifications should not be new misadjustments. That is to say, only French Alsace-Lorraine should go back to France; German Alsace-Lorraine should remain with Germany. It is not to be forgotten that France stole Alsace-Lorraine originally from German principalities. Difficulties may arise in practice in determining which are French and which are German, but these are not insurmountable and a proper division can be sufficiently approximated.

Our interest at the peace table is to see that these principles are made operative in the peace adjustments and that they are not importantly violated. Except and insofar as these principles are involved we have no concern whatever with European politics and we must never overlook that our sole interest is to see that a minimum amount of war seed is sown at the end of the present conflict.

Among the definite measures which must mark the conclusion of a permanent peace are the following:

The restoration and indemnification of Belgium.

The restoration of French Alsace-Lorraine.

The elimination of the Turk as a ruler either in Europe or Asia; not alone political policy but humanity requires this.

Probably the creation of the independent state of Poland.

Some re-adjustment of the Balkans which shall take into account the principles as to race, etc., commented on above. With the details of the Balkan adjustment we are not interested.

Restorative compensation to France and Belgium for the depredations, etc., which they have suffered.

The question as to the observance and perpetuation of the principles of international law is relatively unimportant. Int. law is under most favorable conditions without sanction and is merely a non-enforceable non-contractual agreement between various completely independent pol[. . .]

1. Enter conference without confidence in one set of negotiators.
2. However difficult it may have been, our entry into the war required infinitely less of wise statesmanship, than will our exit from it.
3. Why we entered—*humanity*—large vague word, anybody dream dreams see visions, must concrete ideas—e.g. elimination of Turk as a ruler; "make world safe for democracy," supra; for vengeance, for outrages inflicted.*

---

* Editor's Note: Again, JRC did not finish this document; thus its sketchy concluding phrases.

America at the Peace Table

Probably 1917

The original, handwritten copy of this memorandum is not dated nor is there noted on it what prompted its writing. However, in 1950 JRC added this note: "Just to blow off steam; not finished." In spite of the title, the real question JRC seems to have been examining is why the United States was at war. Box 46, Book 3, 1917, Peace, J 9.34; Box 90, J 9.34, JRCP.

Of all the great entente powers, the United States alone would have difficulty in precising one single, simple reason why she is at war. Russia can invoke race affinities; Italy an "Irredenta Italia;" France, an Alsace-Lorraine; Japan a treaty obligation; and England a violated Belgium, and all of them interlocking international agreements and undertaking. On our part we winked at Luxembourg and Belgium; we overlooked a long list of premeditated indignities; we condoned the *Lusitania* and other submarine butcheries; we affected not to see repeated serious and carefully planned violations of our sovereignty which actually endangered (perhaps so designed) our peaceful relations with other great powers; and we have disclaimed that we fought for any material advantage from the war.

It is true we have talked in a ponderous way of "humanity." But the word is large, and not in the best repute among diplomats, internationalists, or statesmen. Like liberty, many crimes have been committed in its name,—too many to make it persuasive, particularly when both parties to the quarrel invoke it. As we say it the world smiles cynically, but applauds loudly with its hands, for why offend the naïve amateur who supplies a stream of two millions of men and twenty billions of gold per year? After all, did not Mr. Ford and his Peace Ship party measure up pretty well to our best stature, both in conception and execution?

Data on German Peace Treaty

1919

This document, subtitled "Data presented to the Committee on Foreign Relations—United States Senate—Sixty-Sixth Congress—First Session—Relating to the Treaty of Peace with Germany—Prepared by Major J. Reuben Clark, Jr.," was published in Washington at the Government Printing Office. It is forty-three pages long in an 8½-by-11-inch format.

Regarding JRC and his knowledge of the treaty and the League covenant, Senator Philander C. Knox of Pennsylvania, a member of the Foreign Relations Committee and a former secretary of state, said: "By virtue of his long experience in diplomatic and international affairs, his splendid legal ability and fearless patriotism, I regard his views and opinions on the vital questions involved equal to those of any man in America." Then, speaking of the *Data on German Peace Treaty* document, he added: "In speaking in the senate today, I shall put in the record an analysis of the treaty made by Major Clark with the observation that it displays the most thorough grasp of the intricate subjects involved yet presented and made by a man possessing one of the ablest analytic minds I know" (*Salt Lake Herald,* 30 August 1919).

The document itself must be examined in order for one to appreciate the real scope and nature of the analysis. However, here, inasmuch as it was published, we must limit ourselves to the table of contents only. Box 47, Book 1, 1919, Data Peace Treaty, J 10. 10, JRCP.

CONTENTS

Peace Treaty with Germany and the League Covenant

2 September 1919

The address excerpted here was delivered by JRC in the Salt Lake Tabernacle at a meeting sponsored by a committee announced as representing "every walk of life and political denomination" and "described as a spontaneous movement on the part of those Utahns who want to know the facts" (*Salt Lake Herald,* 27 August 1919). Irrespective of the committee, Utah was strongly pro-League territory, and JRC was vigorously opposed to the conditions of the treaty and especially the League covenant. Still, he came to the podium highly recommended by Senator Philander C. Knox (see introduction to Article Five, above), and his speech was delivered to an overflow crowd.

In the address JRC discussed the theory of the League covenant, the labor organizations which would exist under it, the main contentions of the proponents of the League, and the territorial boundaries which would be established under the treaty. He wanted the United States to have no part in such a treaty, and in one place suggested very prophetically that, should the treaty be adopted, another war with Germany—possibly with Russia, Japan, and China as its allies—was all but inevitable. Box 47, Book 1, 1919, League, Tabernacle, J 10.6, JRCP; also Scrapbook, vol. 1, J 10.6, JRCP.

Near the outset of his address JRC observed that one could hardly speak of the League covenant or the Treaty of Versailles without being charged with political partisanship. He then declared:

But my own discussion will, I assure you, be entirely free from such partisanship. I do not belong either to the class that supports the treaty merely because it is vouched for by distinguished proponents belonging to both great political parties, nor do I belong to the class that opposes it merely because these proponents desire its ratification.

I belong to that great class of American citizens who see in the present situation such a departure from the traditional attitude of our government towards other nations and towards world politics as to constitute this one of the most critical moments in our history.

Taught from my infancy that this constitution of ours was inspired; that the free institutions which it creates and perpetuates were God given, I am one of those who scan every proposal to change or alter either with a critical eye.

I am a member of that class which has a firm and unshakable determination to guard our institutions and our constitution at all costs; that believes that ours is the greatest and best government upon the face of the earth; that believes it is worth all it cost the fathers of the revolution to establish it, and all it cost our own fathers to preserve and perpetuate it in the great civil war; that believes it has performed a mission and has still other missions to perform for the political salvation of the world; and that believes, if you will, that we the American people are the chosen of God for the perpetuation of a government which holds sacred those great fundamental inalienable rights of life, liberty and the pursuit of happiness.

It is with this spirit and with these feelings that I have studied the treaty, whose obligations it is proposed to place upon the American people, and out of such study followed in such spirit, there has come to me the conclusion that nothing looms before us which could be equally disastrous with its ratification by us.

And this conclusion reaches not alone that part which deals with the League of Nations, but also those parts which provide for the treatment of our crushed foe, Germany, and for the international labor organization.

Having reached this conclusion, it would be idle for me to say that I did not approach the subject from a partisan standpoint. I am a partisan insofar as our freedom and independence are at stake and glory in this partisanship.

I am against the League of Nations, I am against the treaty as a whole, not because I am a Republican, not because it is fathered by its distinguished proponents, but because as a patriotic American I believe the effects which would flow from its adoption would constitute the most far-reaching disaster that could by any chance come to us.

* * *

It becomes clear from a reading of the testimony given before the Foreign Relations Committee of the Senate by those who are responsible for its provisions, that they seek to draw a distinction between what they term legal and what they term moral obligations, and this for the purpose of making it appear that we shall be free to meet or repudiate the great burdens of the treaty.

Their arguments go to the point that we may with propriety disregard a mere moral obligation, that we need be bound only by our legal obligations.

Or put in a somewhat plainer and cruder form, that a mere promise of ours, a mere holding out that we will under certain contingencies do certain things, that we will render certain assistance, is not a binding obligation upon us, even though the other nations of the world should go forward in dependence upon them; and that it is only those cases in which there is a legal obligation that we need to be bound.

* * *

In my consideration of the provisions of the treaty I shall decline to make or consider any distinction, even if I were able to grasp the difference between a moral and a legal obligation. I shall consider and maintain that no matter what kind of promise we give, we must keep it when given. Honor lies in no other course; our preservation can be assured in no other way.

If we enter the League and are called upon to perform its obligations, we must not besmirch our fair name, we must not disgrace the memory of our honored ancestors, nor ourselves, nor our posterity, by a refusal based on the plea that the obligation imposed is merely moral.

JRC spoke of the theory of the League covenant, including the organization of an assembly in which each nation would have three representatives and only one vote, and a council consisting of one representative from each of nine nations, each of whom would have one vote. In terms typical of his concern for the infringement of the covenant upon national sovereignty—particularly that of the United States—he said:

In passing upon matters affecting the peace of the world, both the assembly and the council determine whether the subject matter of a dispute is solely within the domestic jurisdiction of the party defendant.

So that if Japan should insist upon the free entry of her nationals into the United States and we contested it, it would be for the council or the League to determine whether the exclusion of undesirable aliens was a matter of our determination, or whether it was a matter of international concern, and if it were the latter, then they would determine what our course should be in a body in which we would have but one vote out of nine or in another body where we would have but one vote out of thirty-two or out of forty-five, as the case might be.

So [it would be] as to our treatment and protection of aliens generally in this country, our tariff system, and many other matters it is not necessary now to enumerate.

JRC's apprehension at the idea of the government of the United States subjecting itself to the decisions of the League assembly and council—both to be composed largely of representatives of nations whose political, economic, and social traditions were different from our own—led him to observe:

Of the European powers who have been asked to join two only are republics, all the rest are monarchies. In this League assembly, when constituted, the Anglo-Saxon race will have seven votes out of a possible thirty-two or forty-five. In the council, the Anglo-Saxon race will have two votes out of nine.

___

He described the labor organization which would exist under the League covenant, then summarized:

___

In other words, under the provision of this labor organization, we, the people of the United States, speaking through our government must have our own choice of our own delegates, whether representative [of] capital, or labor, made subject to the approval of foreign powers.

___

Through a hypothetical case JRC pointed out that a nation which rejected a decision of the international labor organization could be drawn into a war against the members of the League. He then gave his attention to what he called the main contentions which had been put forth by the proponents of the League in support of its adoption. Commencing with the one he designated as least important, he discussed four which required only brief treatment, then said:

___

I come now to the fifth, the last, and the most important of the contentions made by proponents of the League . . . the contention that this treaty will abolish war.

* * *

But the covenant before us is not a league to prevent war; it is, on the contrary . . . a league to ensure war.

* * *

When the world adopts the principle of interference by force by one part to compel another part to do its will, to live according to its standard, then progress, civilization and humanity itself are doomed.

But this League goes beyond even this, for in certain cases it makes war legal and in other cases positive and mandatory. If we associate ourselves in this League we obligate ourselves to join in any measure deemed necessary, even measures of force, "to safeguard the peace of nations," whatever that means.

*   *   *

It is not customary to go into a street brawl and risk your life merely for the abstract idea that a fight is wrong. Why should we go into an international brawl on any such theory? Would it not be wiser to save American life to protect America and her institutions?

Again, if two nations get into a dispute and, pursuant to the terms of the treaty, they refer the matter either to arbitration, or to the council, or to the assembly of the League itself, they may under this treaty go legally to war after three months from the rendering of the decision, if such decision so rendered be not satisfactory to them.

What shall be the alignment of the other powers in such a war so waged is entirely unstipulated in the treaty and we should not know to what lengths a war so sanctioned by the treaty itself might lead us.

Further, if after the determination of such a difficulty by the council, by arbitration, or by the assembly, one of the parties thereto shall fail to observe that decision, war is legalized against such party.

Again a war is not declared illegal where it results from a situation or dispute concerning which, either the council or the assembly has not been able to reach a unanimous decision, excluding the parties in interest.

Finally, if two nonmembers of the League refuse obligations of membership for the purpose of a dispute between them and go to war, then war either for or against either of these parties on the part of members of the League is proper and legal.

What the ultimate line-up of the various parties signatory to this treaty in case of any such conflicts is unprovided for in the treaty, but it is as certain as that day follows the night that the grouping of the powers would be guided by their purely human selfish interest; and any such war so legalized must all but inevitably lead us into a world conflagration far greater than the one we are but now finishing.

*   *   *

But this is not all, we are obliged to go to war whenever it is necessary to protect the League covenants from breach brought through the waging of an authorized war; or to prevent a nonmember from conducting a war which as a member it would not be authorized to conduct.

In these cases we, willing or unwilling, must under the compulsion of a moral obligation furnish for the waging of wars such men, such munitions, and such measures of war as may be recommended to us by the council of the League of Nations in which we have one vote out of nine, and therefore in a war to which we may be opposed and against a participation in which we may have voted and protested.

But even these are not the most drastic or significant of the compulsory war provisions. By Article X of the League covenant we guarantee the territorial *status quo* of the various allied and associated powers as established by the treaty.

I am fully aware of the contention put forth by proponents of the League that this is but a moral obligation; that Congress if it does not wish to go to war may disavow this moral obligation. . . .

Allow me to say again that this contention that it is a moral obligation only is so dishonorable, is so base in its every aspect, so wholly un-American, that even the most ardent proponent should cease to use it.

If we are to have the League, with its obligations, let us take it and let us live up to the full measure of its obligations whatever their character. Do not, I beg of you, lend your support to this instrument with the thought that we may upon our whim breach our duties and responsibilities under it.

At this point in his address JRC turned his attention to the provision in the treaty guaranteeing the territorial boundaries established under the treaty, which boundaries would in effect fragment Germany and her colonies and dismember Russia. He continued, prophetically:

Recalling that Russia will by the proposed dismemberment have deep cause of permanent irritation as against the five great powers; recalling that Germany will inevitably have an undying hatred and a deep-seated determination for revenge against these same powers; that this will likewise be true of Austria, of Bulgaria and of Turkey; that all of these powers have not only been cut out from a part in the League of Nations, but that they have not even as yet been invited to become members—bearing in mind all this, can anyone believe there is any power on earth which can prevent these great powers from immediately consulting together, from immediately forming a secret alliance which shall pledge them to a mutual undertaking for a recovery of the territories and the possessions which they have lost?

And where, I ask you, do you think that the Slavic peoples of the Balkans will go when the break comes; with whom will they associate themselves—with Russia, Turkey, Bulgaria, Germany and Austria, with all of whom their traditions of the past are connected, with most of whom they have racial, religious and linguistic affinities, or with us who are alien and wholly strangers to them?

It would be to deny the uniform lesson of history to assume that they will not follow Russia, and as Russia and Germany and Austria go, so will go Japan in all human probability.

Several paragraphs later JRC said that as a result of the treaty the German people would indeed believe that they had been robbed and there would be

---

created and fostered in the people a spirit of hatred and a spirit of revenge which cannot but end in a further great war; and when that war comes and Germany, using her own immense economic and industrial resources, draws on Russia and possibly on Japan and on

China from their immense resources of raw materials and of men, the mind shudders to contemplate the holocaust which will follow.

When JRC directed himself to the amendments, among the things he said was:

As to the amendment requiring the action of the council to be unanimous, except where otherwise expressly provided for in the covenant or in the treaty, it is to be noted that insofar as the treaty itself is concerned, there is no important practical thing entrusted to the council of the League which is not to be determined by a majority vote.

In the next place, if none of the far-reaching beneficent things, from the standpoint of the proponents of the League, can be done except by a unanimous vote of the council, I say to you that no such things will ever be done if they run counter to the interests present or prospective of any members of the League, nor if such things are contrary to the interests of any power friendly or threatening to any member of the League.

And if this be true, then the League is a delusion and a snare and is a mere rope of sand incapable of bestowing any of the blessings contended for by its proponents.

When JRC finished his remarks on the amendments, he quoted a long passage from President Abraham Lincoln predicting future threats to the government of the United States, then concluded his address with this rousing passage of patriotic oratory:

Are we to permit now that tearing down, for what could be a greater destruction than the loss of our sovereignty in matters vital to our existence?

Are we to permit the consitutional barriers built by our inspired fathers against oppression to be broken down? Are we to lose our freedom, to cease to be the land of the free and the home of the brave? Are we to cease to be the beacon light of liberty for the world?

We entered the war free and independent. Let us not leave it in shackles.

Let us preserve ourselves as we are. Let us maintain our freedom and our independence, that in the future, as in the past, we may act the knight errant succoring the oppressed of all nations.

Let us not barter away our right to look every quarrel squarely in the face and espouse the just course as it shall be made known to us. Let us not waste the strength God has given us to establish an asylum for the heart weary of all nations, in petty squabbles over a few rods of miserable European blood-sodden soil.

Then guided ever by the light of disinterested and impartial justice, we shall see the truth, uphold it and save the world.

The League of Nations

October 1920

The addresses of JRC on the League of Nations alone are sufficient to constitute a volume; but, due to limitations of space, only representative excerpts are reproduced here. These come from a series of five addresses given in Utah as part of JRC's contribution to the political campaign in the fall of 1920. The original typed copies are numbered in a different order from that in which they were presented; what determined this rearrangement is not known. They are listed here in the order in which they were given.

General Analysis of [the] Covenant and Some of Wilson's Fundamental Misstatements Concerning It

18 October 1920

The first address was given in Provo on 18 October. After making a general analysis of the League covenant and discussing some of the more important points advanced by League advocates, he concluded his speech in these words:

No nation shall go farther than ourselves in providing for the peaceful adjustment of international disputes, justiciable in their nature. No nation has gone farther in the past than have we. But we must enter into no plan, we must participate in no scheme, which shall subject our great national policies, domestic and foreign, to the adjudication of nations whose traditions, civilization, and government are not alone different from ours, but actually hostile to ours. We shall not undo the work of the Fathers, and once more place ourselves under the dominion of monarchic Europe. That man or party who undertakes to accomplish this thing and to lead us to destruction and national death, must perish in that oblivion to which his deeds consign him. (Box 91, J 10, vol. 5, JRCP; or see Box 47, Book 1, 1920, League—Provo, J 10.18, JRCP; see also *Salt Lake Tribune,* 19 October 1920)

Failure of League

19 October 1920

The second address in the series, given in Ogden, was devoted to examining the work of the League during the first year of its existence and concluding that it had failed. Beyond the technical inadequacies JRC saw in the League covenant was a fundamental issue with which the Founding Fathers came to grips in establishing the Constitution of the United States—namely, human nature. In light of human nature they formed a government with built-in safeguards to establish and preserve individual freedoms and center sovereignty in the people. JRC cherished our free institutions and wanted our national sovereignty shielded from the influence of foreign nations.

The original typed copy of this address is marked "No. 4," but it was delivered as the second in the series.

I am well aware that it has become the fashion to speak of the world to-day as something quite different from what it was a thousand or even a hundred years ago, to talk of the operation of new forces upon humanity and to consider that the nature and mind of men have somehow out of the tragedy of the war undergone a metamorphosis from lower to higher forms, so eliminating former baseness. But I am here to proclaim that no new forces of any kind do exist either in physical nature or in the human mind. Forces that have always worked are working to-day. So far behind us as we can reach with history, tradition, or myth, there are in man the same selfishness, envy, avarice, cruelty, ambition, domination, love and hate, that exist in him today,—no other and no different. These were, are, and while man is man, ever will be the main springs of human action. They materialize now in one form [and] now in another, some times their dormancy seems like extinction, but still they are there. What man sought yesterday, the means he used and what he wrought to get it, he will seek, use and do today and tomorrow. It is true he has in his normal state softened his manner, he has restrained somewhat his animal instincts. But in times of great stress, when he thinks his existence threatened, man again is a primal brute, the elemental still wells up in him and bursts out from him and when it comes, it is naked with all its primitive ferocity and attended by all its accompanying virtues and vices. We have therefore nothing to hope from the false assumption that man is not what he is. What national pride and arrogance and ambition have done in the past they will do in the future, and I tell you with all the soberness and the earnestness which I possess, that in my judgment this League spells not the beginning of the millennium but the beginning of woe and infinite disaster.

When we shall have christianized the world, when the gospel of Christ shall have been accepted by all the world's people and be lived by them, when as a result of this, man's nature has actually changed, so that all baseness has been wiped out of it, then will come the millennium. Then and not till then shall we safely embark on a scheme which subordinates our sovereignty to the will of other powers and which leaves open to challenge the dearest and most sacred rights our fathers bought for us with their blood. (Box 91, J 10, vol. 5, JRCP; or see Box 47, Book 1, 1920, League—Ogden, J 10, 19, JRCP; see also *Salt Lake Tribune*, 20 October 1920)

Constitutional Functions of [the] Senate

21 October 1970

The third address in the League of Nations series, designated "No. 5" on the original typed copy, was delivered in Price. In it,

JRC discussed the constitutional functions of the Senate of the United States and the manner in which it had exercised its powers on treaty matters in the first century and a quarter of national existence. Then one by one he examined Senate reservations on the League covenant, concluding that there was

---

not one of them that did anything but protect. . . . [the] rights of American citizens against interference by alien races and foreign governments. (Box 91, J 10, vol. 5, JRCP; or see Box 47, Book 1, 1920, League—Price, J 10.20, JRCP; see also *Salt Lake Tribune,* 22 October 1920)

A Case Tried Before the League

22 October 1920

JRC gave the fourth speech in the series in Mount Pleasant, Utah. The original typed copy listed this talk as "No. 3." He began his remarks with a brief description of the nature and complexity of the documents expressing international agreements. Speaking specifically, he said:

Moreover, in the matter of this Covenant of the League, although it is supposed to be perfectly plain and simple, there are so many matters that require for adequate and appreciative understanding, a knowledge of international matters and of the machinery of international intercourse not available to the most of us, that it is difficult, if not wholly impossible, even if one has some knowledge of it, to make an explanation which shall be accurate and which shall carry to the layman a precise picture of the situation as it exactly exists. It is not difficult to talk of the Covenant in general terms. It is not difficult to expatiate upon either its virtues or its vices in broad indefinite phrases; but when the argument is finished, the hearer too often goes away with practically no concrete idea of what it is all about.

In an effort to make his remarks more concrete, JRC took two possible disputes as examples and outlined the process they would undergo if they were being put before the League instrumentalities for decision.

In the first instance he traced out the course that he thought would have been followed had the Japanese government taken the United States before the League tribunal on the question of Japanese immigration. Following the prescribed procedure step by step, he demonstrated how it was possible that a bare majority vote in the assembly of the League could require the United States to admit all Japanese indiscriminately.

In the second instance he traced through the League council and assembly a possible dispute between the United States and Great Britain. Inasmuch as Great Britain and each of her five self-governing colonies had one vote, he argued, in any dispute between the United States and Britain or any of her colonies, Great Britain would effectually have five votes and the United States none, since the United States and the concerned British state could not vote.

In both instances, he concluded, the sovereign power of the United States would be vitiated and the government subjected to the will of an international assembly. (Box 91, J 10, vol. 5, JRCP; or see Box 47, Book 1, 1920, League—Mt. Pleasant, J 10.21, JRCP; see also *Salt Lake Tribune*, 23 October 1920)

League Mandates

30 October 1920

In the Salt Lake Theater in Salt Lake City, Utah, JRC presented the fifth and concluding speech in his comprehensive series on the League of Nations. The original typed copy of this talk lists it as "No. 2." In this address JRC showed how France, Great Britain, and Belgium had taken all of Germany's African possessions; how France, Great Britain, Italy, and Greece had taken Turkish territory in Asia Minor and Mesopotamia; how Japan and Great Britain had divided Germany's Pacific Islands between them; and how these nations had even attempted to induce the United States to take Armenia and Turkey, Lloyd George having stated in Parliament that control of these two countries was too difficult and nonremunerative for any of the European powers to attempt.

With contempt for the greed of the European powers and disgust for President Wilson's part in the entire treaty episode, in part JRC said:

And yet in the face of all this we are told by Mr. Wilson that "a change of mind has come over the world" (p. 104); that "there is not a single act of annexation in the treaty" (p. 13), that this treaty "is an absolute renunciation of spoils, even with regard to the helpless parts of the world, even with regard to those poor benighted peoples of Africa over whom Germany had exercised a selfish authority which exploited them and did not help them," that "in every portion of its settlement every thought of aggrandizement, of territorial or political aggrandizement, on the part of the great powers was brushed aside, brushed aside by their own representative" (p. 337); that "you must not devote your scrutiny to the details and forget the majesty of the plan" (p. 291) [source not found].

Thus the arch Leaguers have cried to the world "Look, look at the beautiful heavens!" and while the world enraptured gazed at the stars, they quietly, deftly, in the time-honored method, picked its pockets. (Box 91, J 10, vol. 5, JRCP; or see Box 47, Book 1, 1920, League—Mandates—SL, J 10.25, JRCP; see also *Salt Lake Tribune*, 31 October 1920)

The Treaty of Versailles

22 June 1921

Early in June of 1921 JRC had a confidential request from his friend Fred Morris Dearing, assistant secretary of state. The hand-written letter began:

Very Confidential—
Dear Reuben:

Henry [P. Fletcher, undersecretary of state] tells me on my return that the mind of Secstate [Charles Evans Hughes] is very open on the subject of the Treaty and that he is disposed to find an alternative to sending the Paris Product back to the Senate. Henry and I want to be ready to produce this alternative when it is called for. He has already spoken in greatest confidence to John Bassett Moore. *Since you have so little to do,* and are a true patriot and authority besides (this by way of escaping the task—the hard work part—myself) I thought I would ask you to give me a concrete memo, as full as you care to make it, setting out your conception of what this country should do when the Knox Resolution is finally passed, *a* Treaty with Germany, *b* relationship with the League and its members, *c* American soldiers in Germany, *d* guaranteeing the interest on indemnity and other foreign bonds, *e* State Department to pass on all Foreign Government or large Foreign bond flotations from point of view of seeing whether we ought not to secure certain things before allowing the flotations in this market, *f* observers in Europe, *g* codification of internation[al] law to exclude barbaric scientific warfare, *h* world court, *i* disarmament conference, *j* mandate policy. And anything else you can think of as flowing out of the general clearing up of the war. (Fred Morris Dearing to J. Reuben Clark, Jr., 6 June 1921, Box 24, Memorandum on Treaty of Versailles, prepared for Fred Morris Dearing, 22 June 1921, J 10.29, JRCP)

Two weeks later, when JRC was in Washington, he visited Dearing and was asked again for his views on the matters enumerated in the letter. JRC then "hastily dictated" to Dearing's secretary what became an eleven-page memorandum (Clark to John Bassett Moore, 1 July 1921, Box 24, Memorandum on Treaty of Versailles, prepared for Fred Morris Dearing, 22 June 1921, J 10.29, JRCP).

A few days after JRC dictated the memo, he received a letter from John Bassett Moore. Having learned confidentially that Moore had been called into conference at the State Department, he sent his copy of the memorandum to Moore for his examination and any criticisms he cared to make.

In part he said to Moore:

I have been convinced for a long time, as I think I have often told you, that what we know as Wall Street, is bending every effort, first to secure the ratification of the Versailles Treaty, or, that failing, to tie us up in some equivalent way with some new treaty. To me the purpose of this seems obvious, namely, to put us behind, as a guarantor, the German indemnity bonds, thus making them easily marketable. This would leave the tax revenues of France, Great Britain, and Italy more available for the service of their own bonds,—some hundreds of millions of which Wall Street has. I can clearly see how such a plan would much help Wall Street, but I cannot see how the rest of us would be helped.

* * *

As to my views on an alliance with the powers, it would be difficult for me to find language which would sufficiently express my abhorrence. This alliance idea is founded on the general principle,—as it seems to me,—of completely crushing and actually making subject the German people. That they have committed crimes is clear; that they should be punished therefor is but elementary justice; but to enslave their entire country is so iniquitous a thing, that modern civilization (to say nothing of the precepts of Christianity) cannot tolerate it. Quite aside from consideration of morality the whole idea is so unsound politically as to be unworthy of serious consideration. How anyone can seriously consider making an alliance of France, Great Britain, and the United States against all the balance of the world,—for that is what it will finally work down to,—is quite beyond my comprehension. (Clark to Moore, 1 July 1921, Box 24, Memorandum on Treaty of Versailles, prepared for Fred Morris Dearing, 22 June 1921, J 10.29, JRCP)

A week later Moore wrote to JRC saying, "In due time . . . I shall expect to see you in the United States Senate, where men of your type are needed. It would be a great thing if you were there now to make a speech on the lines of your present letter and confidential memorandum" (Moore to Clark, 7 July 1921, Box 24,

Memorandum on Treaty of Versailles, prepared for Fred Morris Dearing, 22 June 1921, J 10.29, JRCP).

A year later Fred Dearing became minister for the United States in its legation at Lisbon, Portugal. He had been greatly impressed with JRC's analysis of the Treaty of Versailles while still in the United States, but after his experiences of several months in Europe he seemed amazed at JRC's foresight. In November of 1922 he wrote:

Dear Reuben:

Why I should attempt a letter to you is beyond my comprehension. There is so much that needs talking about that I do not know where to begin. I am sure it would interest you to hear that all of the wisdom you and the dear old Senator [Philander C. Knox] displayed in the matter of the Paris Treaty is apparently substantiated by everything that is happening in this part of the world day after day. In addition I have just come back from Eastern Europe, and assure you that the view one obtains from that point is simply overwhelmingly convincing so far as the rightness of the stand taken by you and P.C.K. during the Senate discussions is concerned. Indeed, it seems to me almost like clairvoyancy or something superhuman that you should have seen and have gauged so clearly what the effects of the damn foolishness at Paris would be. The thing comes back to me again and again, and every time with fresh force, and in your own case, it seems to me all the more remarkable, on account of the fact that you have never been in this part of the world. (Dearing to Clark, 20 November 1922, Box 343, Dearing, Fred, JRCP)

Box 91, J 10, Vol. 5, JRCP; see also Box 47, Book 1, 1921, Peace Treaty, Dearing, J 10.29, JRCP.

Memorandum

June 22, 1921

A. *Treaty with Germany*

There are many reasons why we should not become a party in any sense to the Treaty of Versailles but probably the most cogent of all may be succinctly stated thus:—

It would make us a party to all of the adjustments provided for in that Treaty and by becoming a party to them we would become responsible for them. This would place upon us a task of such magnitude as to be unbearable because we should always be looked to on one pretext or another to enforce the terms of the Treaty. Already British statesmen have pointed out that they have responsibilities which practically exhaust their resources in maintaining the peace in Mesopotamia, Africa, etc. France is equally employed with her possessions. Therefore if the occasion came to use armed forces in Europe we should be asked to furnish them.

Undoubtedly, moreover, when the time came for the use of our forces they would advance the argument, in order to induce us to take on the task, that we were more disinterested than any other power, and that, therefore, our interference would be less obnoxious to the German people, all of which would result in the handling of the situation by us with the least possible friction.

We must not, however, be led into that situation.

Our adjustments with Germany should be carried out in my judgment by three means:—

First, we should rehabilitate the treaties existing between us at the time of the outbreak of the war, with such emendations and eliminations as the war has shown ought to be made.

Second, we should negotiate a new treaty that should in the first place provide for our obtaining the same treatment that is to be given to Allied and Associated Powers under the Versailles Treaty, and in the next place ensure that neither our citizens nor our trade shall be discriminated against. These two matters are obviously closely related and are reciprocal, one of the other.

Third, we should make an arrangement which will provide for the adjustment of our claims against Germany. We should hold the property which we have of German citizens as a guarantee that any judgments which may be obtained before the Joint Tribunal (which we ought to establish to pass upon these claims) shall be satisfied.

The inter-adjustments that may be necessary between ourselves and our co-belligerents ought, it seems to me, to be worked out in bilateral treaties between ourselves and the individual countries concerned.

B. *Relationship with the League and Its Members*

In my judgment we should have no dealings whatsoever with the League as such, and I base this conclusion primarily upon the provisions of Article 17 of the Treaty which to all intents and purposes constitutes League members an alliance against every other state in the world. It is my conviction that we ought not to recognize any such alliance. We must insist on our right to continue to deal with the nations of the earth separately and not collectively. Otherwise we shall be always dealing with and at the mercy of a superior force, diplomatic and physical.

The League as such has not yet acquired any status with reference to any great international matter that in any way requires us to deal with the League as an entity, because it cannot in vital matters speak for the collection of nations which it purports to represent. We should insist that, in the future as in the past, we shall settle our difficulties with different nations, with those nations themselves and not through the instrumentality of any alliance of nations.

C. *American Soldiers in Germany*

It is my belief that the American soldiers should be recalled from Germany at the earliest possible moment. My reason for this conclusion is roughly two fold:

First, the effect on the German people. The presence of our soldiers in Germany must be a constant irritation to the German people who will regard themselves as exploited and tyrannized over by the soldiers. We may grant that the German people have merited punishment and that they ought to have it. At the same time it will be fatal to assume that we are going to make of the German race a subject people, first, because the world has progressed beyond the point of making people slaves, and second, because the character of the German people is such that they could not be successfully held in slavery. This means that we shall ultimately—very [much] more quickly in my judgment than many people imagine—resume our normal relationship towards the people and their trade. Selfishly therefore there is every reason why we ought not to make any more difficult than is necessary future relations of trade and commerce with that nation.

In the second place, the relationship which exists between our soldiers and the German people is such as to be most detrimental to our own army. Army officers are notoriously imperious under the best of circumstances; they lack all, or nearly so, of the saving graces possessed by civilians and to put them among and over a subdued people merely increases this characteristic to the substantial detriment of these officers and their contact with the German people.

D. *Guaranteeing the Interest on Indemnity and Other Foreign Bonds*

It is my deliberate judgment that the United States must not either directly or indirectly undertake to guarantee the interest or principal of any foreign bonds. Our own debt is something like twenty-five billions of dollars which is all the load we ought to carry.

I am convinced there is a determined effort and propaganda to induce us somehow to underwrite the German bonds. That such would be for the benefit of American holders of the bonds of France and Great Britain cannot be doubted, because with our guarantee behind the German bonds, it would be possible to raise money on them for the rehabilitation of France and Great Britain which would relieve the tax incomes of those countries for application to their own bonds. This would obviously make those bonds a better security. But the foreign bond holders among us are comparatively so few in number that the whole people of the United States should not be saddled with this great added burden merely that a few might realize upon their foreign investments. However patriotic the motive that prompted the investment in these foreign bonds, patriotism was intimately mixed with commercialism, and the investors should be required to continue to carry out the chance upon which they gambled when they bought the bonds.

E. *State Department to pass on all Foreign Government or large foreign bond flotations from point of view of seeing whether we ought not to secure certain things before allowing the flotation in this market*

I seriously doubt that the State Department has the machinery available to carry out any such function yet. I admit at once the desirability of having lodged in some executive branch power to pass on such questions, and I appreciate that the branch in which it is lodged ought not to be able to act without consulting the State Department and probably not without the acquiescence or approval of the State Department. It may be that the Treasury Department is the right one to have the determination of this matter, or that the Treasury and Commerce and State together should have it, but I do not believe the State Department alone ought to be charged with such a far-reaching financial and economic matter.

There is a possibility that there may be some constitutional question involved here but I am of the opinion that the power to regulate commerce is sufficiently broad in character to cover the exercise of such a power.

F. *Observers in Europe*

It is my judgment that this Government should immediately relieve itself of all special observers in Europe and should place that work in the hands of our diplomatic representatives. It is my further view that we should build up the existing organization and strengthen it rather than attempt to create a new organization. While I am not intimately acquainted with the functions of those observers I am quite sure that their work would easily fall within the purview of the work which our diplomatic service is supposed to perform. The greater the number of persons that you have in Europe meddling with our foreign relationships, the greater will be the difficulties that will arise, the more enormous will be our commitments, and the more embarrassments that will come.

G. *Codification of International Law to Exclude Barbaric Scientific Warfare*

It is my firm conviction that the President and the Secretary could undertake no greater or more noble work than that of attempting to secure a re-enactment and recognition of the rules governing warfare at the outbreak of the world war. It is perfectly clear that the armies and navies of the world are now straining every nerve and exerting every intellectual and other power which they possess to make of the next war such a holocaust as has not before been seen in the history of the world. They are deliberately planning to devise and develop means of exterminating not armies but entire peoples. With their new explosives, their submersible boats, their air craft, and their gases they intend to fight next time not only the armed forces of the world but the noncombatant including the women and children. This is so fiendish a thought and plan that no effort should be spared to defeat it if possible.

The real difficulty of the situation seems to be a feeling among men ordinarily wise and thoughtful that such a development is certain, so certain that it may not be avoided. The thought is expressed that the last war having shown the power of chemicals it is inevitable that that power will be used to the utmost in the next great war.

To this it may be answered that ever since man fought it has been easier to kill noncombatants, to slaughter women and children, than it has been to kill the opposing armed forces. There never has been a time in the history of the world when it was not possible for an army to exterminate the peoples of the opposite side. It is school boy knowledge that in the early wars this was the course that was followed, and yet the world in the face of this fact advanced from point to point in the protection of the weak and innocent, until noncombatants were largely relieved from the rigors of war. We must not permit this gain of civilization to be destroyed by any ambition of men whose sole purpose and training in the world is to kill, I mean the members of the armies and navies of the nations. No more noble, nor more far-reaching task, nothing more beneficial to the human race, could be undertaken by the President and the Secretary than this work to place the world in these respects back where it was when the last war began.

H. *World Court*

I have no suggestions to make on this subject that are not contained in the article, a copy of which you have, which I prepared on the present World Court movement.

I. *Disarmament Conference*

There is no question but that it is most desirable that we reach some understanding regarding disarmament. Such a conference might appropriately be linked up with the Conference for the Codification of International Law. It might well be that the first approach of disarmament could involve the elimination by the nations of the use of certain weapons for example, submarines, air craft, high explosives and poisonous gases. Heretofore disarmament has been approached from the standpoint rather of the size of the armament than from the standpoint of weapons, the latter being taken up separately. But if the President should call a Disarmament Conference and should point out that that conference must consider two things, first the elimination of certain weapons of war, and second, the curtailment of armies and navies, he would lay a foundation for the most substantial achievement in the cause of humanity which lies before us. Moreover, curtailment in the size of armies and navies involves, as heretofore proved, matters that are possibly quite beyond the reach of agreement, for there is every reason to believe that the considerations which have controlled nations in the past will continue to control them more or less in the future. On the other hand the conclusions reached and advances made with reference to such matters as dum-dum bullets, the use of air craft, etc., have been such as to show that the human mind is prepared to advance on that line even when it may not advance on the curtailment of armies.

J. *Mandate Policy*

You will recall that under the Treaty of Versailles we are co-owners of the German colonies as also of certain of the territory of Memel in Europe. Even if we do not, as we should not, ratify the Treaty of Versailles, and so do not become co-owners of this territory under the Treaty, still the Treaty is a statement of what is the ultimate fact, namely, that as one of the successful co-belligerents we are inevitably co-owners of these territories. Therefore, no matter whether we ratify the Treaty or not, we have the undoubted right to express our views with as much weight as does any one else upon the disposition to be made of the so-called mandates. You will recall moreover that as a matter of fact the distribution of the mandates and the fixing of the terms upon which they shall be held has been determined not by any body created by the Treaty of Versailles but by the Supreme Council which is merely a co-belligerent council to which we have in the past been a party and of which we may continue to be a party if and when we wish. Therefore, we may continue to insist that we be heard on all mandate matters.

In the next place, it seems to me that we should recognize that the allocation of these territories, no matter what the terms may be, is in fact a cession of them to the powers receiving them. It is true that under the terms of the League Covenant there are certain provisions which indicate the possibility that mandates may be taken from powers who handle them unsatisfactorily. But who, it may be asked, and on what compulsion, shall Britain be forced to give up Mesopotamia, or France Syria, or Britain German East Africa? The mandate situation should be faced squarely and the facts viewed in all their nakedness.

However, recalling our position as co-owners by reason of our co-belligerency in the successful war, and remembering that the allocation of the mandated territories and the terms of the mandates are made and prescribed by a non-treaty functioning body, we may appropriately continue to insist upon our views as to mandates—not only Yap, but all of them—and see to it that we obtain an arrangement for the promotion of equal opportunities for our citizens in the mandated territories.

Criticism of Plan to Outlaw War

17 January 1922

Senator Harry S. New of Indiana was a great admirer of JRC and apparently requested this memorandum. It appears to have been dictated extemporaneously; for, in a note of thanks to JRC, New said, "Miss Mummenhoff has just completed typing your memorandum to her" (Harry S. New to J. Reuben Clark, Jr., 17 January 1922, Box 47, Book 1, 1922, Outlaw War, Sen. New, J 11.2, JRCP). In a brief response to New, JRC said, "I am sorry it was not better but I had no opportunity to make any special preparation for its writing" (Clark to New, 24 January 1922, Box 25, "Criticism of Plan to Outlaw War," Memo for Sen. New, 17 January 1922, J 11.2, JRCP). Box 47, Book 1, 1922, Outlaw War, Sen. New, J 11.2, JRCP; see also Box 25, "Criticism of Plan to Outlaw War," Memo for Sen. New, 17 January 1922, J 11.2, JRCP.

The right of a nation to wage a just and necessary war cannot be destroyed by a mere legal prohibition. It would still survive as an extra-legal right like the right of revolution. The American revolutionary war was illegal and criminal according to existing law, but the right of revolution, in just and necessary cases, is now everywhere acknowledged by statesmen and publicists. War cannot be made criminal, in a moral sense, by legal prohibition. That issue must always be determined by the particular facts of the case.

While the moral right of a nation to wage a just war would

survive even a legal prohibition declaring it to be criminal, such a prohibition would seriously handicap the cause of a righteous nation, engaging in a just and necessary war, by giving competitive or hostile nations a technical footing, for resistance, which would likely influence world opinion in a wrong and unrighteous direction.

A just nation, like America does not need to be prohibited from waging unjust and unnecessary war. A criminal nation will not respect such a prohibition. Unrighteous war like murder, to be successful, involves the pretense of innocence, and the manufacture of evidence, which will make the war appear just or defensive. Bismarck's forged telegram in 1870 is an illustration of how a criminal nation would evade the plan to outlaw war.

War as an institution for the settlement of international disputes could hardly be defended by any one, but a war between nations may be for the just and righteous purpose of punishing a criminal nation, not by way of revenge, but as a deterrent to the commission of similar crimes in the future. In such cases, war is a necessary factor in human progress. To prohibit it would be like the abolition of capital punishment in France, which was followed by such a terrible increase of homicide, as to require its restoration.

The prohibition of "annexations, exactions or seizures, by force" would, if effective, deprive a righteous nation in a just cause, of one of the most effective, and often the only possible penalties. Illustration, the treaty with Mexico, in 1848, and with Spain in 1898.

The reserved right to make defensive war against "actual or imminent attack" is altogether insufficient. A nation is charged with the duty of defending not merely its territory, but the rights of its citizens as General Harrison said, "wherever they are." The exercise of such rights may be restricted or denied, in many ways other than by military attack, and their defense may require the instant use, or threat, of force, although there be no actual or imminent military attack.

The prohibition of reprisal would be most dangerous. Suppose international law prohibited the poisoning of drinking water, and the use of poisoned gas. Suppose an enemy were to get control of the New York aqueduct, and poison the water, under circumstances which enabled the enemy to hold its ground and continue the poisoning, as against every attack except by poison gas.

The most dangerous proposal of the plan to outlaw war is the compulsory submission of all international disputes to an international tribunal. We cannot overlook the possibility of a tribunal controlled by hostile nations, urged by adverse interests or unfriendly feelings. No American statesman has a right to subject the future of his country to such a risk. I suggest four illustrations.

A. Suppose Japan by peaceful penetration, intrigue, or other successful policy should acquire control of the foreign policy of China and induce the Chinese government to exclude American commerce, from Chinese ports, as a retaliation for our own immigration law. Might such a question be safely submitted to a controlled or hostile court? Every great commercial nation would benefit by our exclusion. Japan might be in a position to secure support from the great powers, for reasons similar to those which secured for her the promise of Shantung. Nor must it be overlooked that the policy of weakening or limiting the power of our republic has been considered and openly advocated by foreign powers. Guizot, Prime Minister of France, declared this to be his policy, prior to the Mexican War. The British press took the same course, at the same time. The proposal was to found a new state in the southwest, on Mexican territory, and place it under the control of France, or England, or both, for the purpose of limiting the growth of our republic.

B. Suppose Japan should complain to the tribunal, even if she did not use actual force, of our shipments of munitions to the Philippines, as being acts hostile to Japan and endangering her security. Who can be certain that the international tribunal might not be under a similar compulsion to that, by which Japan secured Shantung?

C. Suppose Japan, by agreement with Mexico, and the consent of the Mexican people, were to acquire territory on the western coast of Mexico, populate it and make it a military and naval base. Apparently our only recourse would be to the international tribunal. Can any American statesman guarantee that the tribunal would decide in our favor, declaring Japanese immigration to Mexican territory, with Mexico's consent, such a violation of our Monroe Doctrine, as the world would be bound to prevent?

D. Suppose many Americans in Mexico should be murdered by Mexican police or soldiers acting under orders, and suppose such massacres were to continue. Might not our appeal to the court be met by Mexico with a showing that the Americans were killed resisting arrest, and that the arrests were made on evidence that the Americans were conspiring to overthrow the Mexican government?

Might not the evidence and the witnesses be controlled by Mexico, so as to make a false showing, which we could not technically meet? Might not even a disinterested court hesitate to give us relief, and much more so a court controlled by competitive or hostile nations? Would not the murders be likely to go on or public opinion, among our people force us to break our agreement, thus giving competitive nations a legal ground for war against us?

None of the above objections goes so far as to reach voluntary submission of disputes by both parties to the international tribunal. None goes so far as to oppose an ex-parte investigation and report, by the tribunal, on the complaint of one nation.

The fear above expressed of a prejudiced or hostile tribunal is based largely on what General Harrison told the writer of his experience with the Paris tribunal of 1899, to which he presented the Venezuelan dispute. In that case we agreed, I believe, to the composition of the tribunal, as a part of the submission.

The danger to us of compulsory submission to an international tribunal is one which arises from the nature of things. Nations are separated by the same wide differences which separate judges chosen by or from different nations. Conflicting interests, differences of race, history, language, political systems, legal principles, morals, religion, tradition, and all the rest prevent judges from approaching an international question from the same point of view, and make it impossible for them to decide cases on the lines of justice, which America would expect and need.

Cancellation of Inter-Allied Debt

1922

Listed among the " 'Civic' Speeches, 1921–1929" (Box 114; Clarkana Index, 32) is one for which there appears to be no confirmed date or place of delivery; however, JRC doubtless composed it in response to the efforts of Great Britain, France, Italy, and American international bankers to have the debts of the World War allies cancelled. In it he discussed the moral implications and the business and financial considerations involved in cancelling the war debt. Box 47, Book 1, 1922, Allied Debt, N 11.3, JRCP; and Box 114, first folder, titled "Clarkana Civic Speeches," article no. 3.

Paul, the Apostle, writing to the Corinthians, pointed out that the body is not one member, but many, but that no member could say that because it was not another member, it was not part of the body and that "the eye cannot say unto the hand, I have no need of thee: nor again the head to the feet, I have no need of you" (1 Cor. 12:21). Nothing truer regarding the body and the interrelationship of its members has ever been written; and as it is with the physical body, so it is with the body politic. No one member of the body politic can say it is not part of that body because it is not some other member of it, and, likewise, no member of the body politic can say it has no use for some other member. All members are essential to a healthy vigorous whole.

Not always are these plain, homely facts in the minds of our conglomerated citizenry. Diverse conditions of climate, geographical situation, industry and fundamental interests lead now this section of the country, now that one, to feel that it has no need for some other whose vital interests do not appear immediately to minister to the interests of the first.

Or to make it a little more concrete—not always does the so-called East understand or appreciate the West, or the South; and the latter in turn fail frequently to understand the East; but we are all one body politic together, and the great doctrine of Paul is completely applicable to us.

Just now there is a propaganda partly in behalf of foreign countries, and partly from and in behalf of certain of our own great financial and commercial interests in this country, which is of such far reaching consequences to all of us, and which referring to taxation has a vital interest for all of us. I refer to the agitation that we cancel the ten billion dollar debt which Europe owes to us by reason of our loans to them during the great world war.

I shall not detain you by any lengthy comment upon the general cost of the war to the world, but yet a table prepared by Professor Ernest L. Bogart, of the University of Illinois, the Carnegie Endowment for International Peace may not be without interest. Professor Bogart, as a conclusion to nearly 300 pages of discussion, summarizes, in a tabulation of figures, the direct and indirect costs of the great world war, as follows:

Total direct costs net		$186,333,637,097.
Indirect costs:		
Capitalized value of human life:		
Soldiers	$ 33,551,276,280.	
Civilians	33,551,276,280.	
Property losses:		
On land	29,960,000,000.	
On Shipping and cargo	6,800,000,000.	
Loss of production ..	45,000,000,000.	
War relief	1,000,000,000.	
Loss to neutrals	1,750,000,000.	
Total indirect costs		151,612,542,560.
Grand total		$337,946,179,657.

This estimate, great as it is, is low, because it includes for the United States a direct net cost of only $22,625,252,843 (Ernest L. Bogart, *Direct and Indirect Costs of the Great World War* [New York, 1919], 267). Whereas, as a matter of fact there was disbursed from the United States Treasury from April 6, 1917, the date on which we declared war, to October 31, 1919, a total of $66,606,854,907. If we deduct from this, as does Mr. Bogart, the loan which we made to the allies of $9,455,014,125 (which is the figure Mr. Bogart gives), we would have left approximately $57,151,000,000 (see U.S. Department of Treasury, *Annual Report of Secretary of Treasury on State of Finances* [Washington, D.C., 1919], 29, hereafter referred to as *Treasury Reports*).

Therefore, if Mr. Bogart has made, as to other countries, the same sort of estimate he has made for the United States, the total direct costs of the war will exceed by many billions the figure he gives, namely, $186,333,637,097, and the total direct and indirect costs, which he places at approximately 338 billions, will likewise be materially increased.

I have quoted these figures in order that we might approach an appreciation of the great debt burden under which the world now staggers. This debt is apportioned (giving billions) by Mr. Bogart, as follows:

Great Britain 44 billions, rest of British Empire 4 billions—France 25 billions—Russia 22 billions—Italy 12 billions—Germany 40 billions—Austria-Hungary 20 billions—Turkey and Bulgaria 2 billions (Bogart, 267).

As a matter of fact while our total disbursements, as already given, total 663 billions of dollars, not all of this sum was actually expended because part of it at least was merely refinancing, the taking up of short time notes and other obligations, and the substituting, therefore, of different obligations. It seems probable, however, that after making allowances for this refinancing, we actually collected and disbursed as war expenditures between the dates named—April 6, 1917, to October 31, 1918—better than 40 billions of dollars. Of this amount there has gone over into what is called our public debt, approximately 23 billions of dollars (*Treasury Reports*, 1920, 323) of which foreign governments owe us on account of advances made under the Liberty Bond acts, $9,434,773,829 (*Treasury Reports*, 1921, 33). The amounts advanced to the various governments during the war was in the nearest approximation, as follows:

Belgium 349 millions—Cuba 10 millions—Czechoslovakia 61 millions—France 2 billions 997 millions—Great Britain 4 billions 277 millions—Greece 15 millions—Italy 1 billion 631 millions—Liberia 26 thousands—Roumania 25 millions—Russia 187 millions—Serbia 26 millions (*Treasury Reports*, 1921, 37).

Upon this latter sum there has accrued and was owing us on November 15, 1921, $1,155,502,131.91 interest (*Treasury Reports*, 1921, 35).

In addition to the foregoing sums, foreign countries owe to the United States on obligations received from the American Relief Administrations, 84 millions of dollars; on obligations received from the Secretary of War and from the Secretary of the Navy on account of the sale of surplus war materials, 565 millions; and on obligations held by the United States Grain Corporation, 57 millions (*Treasury Reports*, 1921, 40).

There must be added also to the foregoing, as included within the obligations which foreign governments owe to citizens of the United States, the hundreds of millions of bonds which were taken by various financial institutions and munitions manufacturers in this country in exchange for munitions furnished to those countries.

To all the foregoing there must be added probably 800 millions of dollars of bonds which were issued upon the public market of the United States from January 1, 1921, to March 31, 1922 (Roberts, June, 11 [full source not found]).

The part of this debt which it is urged that we should cancel is the 9½ billions with the interest accrued thereon, which the United States advanced to the allies during the war. Nobody in the East is suggesting that the obligations coming to individuals in this country as munitions profits should be forgiven. Only that part of the foreign debt to us which the people carry is to be made the subject of our munificence.

The arguments advanced by those who urge the forgiveness of this foreign debt are briefly these:

The money having been advanced after we entered the war and having been used to hold the enemy until we could throw our immense army across the water, the money was really expended on our own account and we ought not to ask the repayment of it. Morally we should forgive it.

It is also contended that American industry lags because of lack of foreign markets and that prosperity will come only with a revival of foreign trade; that foreign markets are wanting because of lack of money abroad with which to purchase the products of our farms and industries; that the money which they must pay to us on account of interest and sinking funds could, if we forgave the debt, be spent on the purchase of supplies in this country, thus bringing prosperity to our manufacturers and to our producers of raw materials.

As to the proposition that we ought not in good morals to request the repayment of the money we have advanced to the Allies, not much need be said.

Let me say in the first place, that I am one of those who have always believed that we should have entered the war upon the sinking of the *Lusitania* and that the war was unduly prolonged and the world in general unduly suffered because of our delay. On the other hand, it seems probably that our own loss of life was less than it would have been had we entered the war earlier, to say nothing of the less important but far from minor consideration, that we spent less money than we would have spent had we entered the war earlier. Moreover, the general demoralization of our industries and finance, was probably far less than it would have been if we had been actually at war for a longer time. But these last are selfish considerations which I would not urge as against an earlier entry into the war.

However, there are considerations that go, in my judgment, squarely to the point that we have no moral obligation to forgive this great foreign debt.

In the first place, the war was not of our making. It was exclusively an European affair. Moreover, England, France and Russia were advised by their secret service agents in Germany of what Germany was prepared to do, yet they sat idly by and permitted Germany to complete the armament with which she planned to crush them. I shall not now undertake to suggest what might have been done to meet this situation so disclosed, or to check it, but something might have been done.

Again according to my view, it was neither our right nor our duty to intervene by force of arms in a squabble in Europe, merely because it was a squabble. That principle, while contended for by some in this country, is so contrary to the rules which have governed the growth and progress of Nations that to act upon it would have been to subject us to serious criticism from all the neutral Nations of the world and to establish a principle which invoked against us might [have] at some periods of our career, been disastrous. Nations, like individuals, engage in conflict when their own rights are involved or threatened; we entered the war only when the flagrant violation of our rights had passed all the bounds of longsuffering patience.

Furthermore, the war was virtually lost when we entered the field. What could allied Europe have done to preserve itself against the Central Powers and against the threat of Russia, first, without our money and our supplies, and second, without our men? Can anyone doubt that the Germans would have so long delayed their last "push," or that that "push" when made would not have been successful, if we had been out of the situation? Now, by voluntarily going to help a man against a common enemy, you do not undertake to guarantee that man against a great loss. You may very well be willing to help, and also to bear the burden of the loss which falls upon you personally; you may be willing to concede that there is a moral obligation upon you to bear your own burden; you might even consent, as an act of charity, to indemnify your associates against loss; but you certainly would repudiate the idea that by coming to the assistance of a man you immediately incurred a moral obligation to see that he lost nothing; or if that be a little extravagant, you would hardly admit that morally you were under obligation to forgive him the advance of any funds you might have made to him to enable him to win his own battle. Our entering into the war did not make it solely our cause, with the others merely assisting us to win it. The war, after our entering it, still remained their war, though it also became our war. I am sure no one would advance the argument that Great Britain ought to forgive the debt Italy owes her because of advances made during the Great War, on the ground that it enabled Italy measurably to maintain her position in the Alps, while Great Britain carried out operations in other parts of the world. There is certainly no substance in this argument.

It is true that we stood in a slightly different relationship to France than that in which we stood as to any other power, because of the action of France in helping us in our own Revolution. But remember that in that Revolution, while Frenchmen such as Lafayette, and others, came to us and fought for us because of their belief in our cause, the French Government itself had no such motive. The government came in because it also was at war with England and believed that by aiding us it could strike a blow at its own enemy. It is true the government sent us men and that they shed their blood, for us,—an action we shall never forget, nor cease to be grateful for. The government also lent us money, but she collected every dollar from us, though we were a weak and struggling Nation at the time. We did not whine, we paid. We did not say that there was a moral obligation running against France to forgive our debts, because she had assisted us in fighting a common enemy. We considered ourselves obligated to pay France what we had in the way of money, and as I have said, we met our obligation.

I will not argue the bad taste nor the selfishness which seems to be involved in any suggestions by European powers, that we cancel these debts. I only say there is no moral obligation resting upon us that in the slightest degree is persuasive that we should forgive these debts.

Having so eliminated the question of the moral side of the matter, I shall pass to that which relates to the business and financial aspect.

As to the second argument in favor of the cancelling of this foreign debt, some further analysis of the situation is necessary.

The advances to foreign governments were made under the First and Second Liberty Loan Acts (*Treasury Reports*, 1921, 33); no credits were established under the Victory Liberty Loan Act (*Treasury Reports*, 1920, 53).

There were advanced to foreign governments, 2 billions 114 millions under the First Liberty Loan Act, and 7 billions 320 millions under the Second Liberty Loan Act (*Treasury Reports*, 1921, 33).

These advances began April 25, 1917, with an advance to Great Britain, and ended Sept. 28, 1920, with an advance to France (*Treasury Reports*, 1920, 330–37). These advances were made from funds realized from the various war bans, of which (omitting Treasury certificates, and war saving securities) there were dollars outstanding as of June 30, 1921, the following:—

First Liberty Loan, 1 billion 926 millions (*Treasury Reports*, 1921, 245)
    Maturing June 15, 1947 (*Treasury Reports*, 1919, 344–47)
Second Liberty Loan, 3 billions 132 millions (*Treasury Reports*, 1921, 245)
    Maturing Nov. 15, 1942 (*Treasury Reports*, 1919, 344–47)
Third Liberty Loan, 3 billions 652 millions (*Treasury Reports*, 1921, 245)
    Maturing Sept. 15, 1928 (*Treasury Reports*, 1919, 344–47)

Fourth Liberty Loan, 6 billions 394 millions (*Treasury Reports*, 1921, 245)
    Maturing Oct. 15, 1933 (*Treasury Reports*, 1919, 344–47)
Victory Liberty Loan, 4 billions 245 millions (*Treasury Reports*, 1921, 245)
    Maturing May 20, 1923 (*Treasury Reports*, 1919, 344–47)

For the 9 billions 434 millions, advanced to foreign governments under the loan acts, this government took, and on November 15, 1921, held obligations drawing 5% interest, and payable on demand (*Treasury Reports*, 1921, 33).

The amounts advanced to each government have been already given. November 15, 1921, there was still outstanding of these advances, amounts as follows:

Belgium	347 millions
Cuba	8½ millions
Czechoslovakia	61½ millions
France	2 1/3 billions
Great Britain	4 billions
Greece	15 millions
Italy	1½ billions
Liberia	26 thousands
Roumania	23 millions
Russia	187 millions
Serbia	26 millions

(*Treasury Reports*, 1921, 33)

As already stated there is due on these sums, 1 billion 155 million dollars interest (*Treasury Reports*, 1921, 35).

The annual interest due from Europe in this debt ($9,434,774,829.24 at 5%) is 462 million dollars round numbers.

The interest charge on our public debt for 1921 was approximately a billion dollars (*Treasury Reports*, 1921, 521), while the sinking fund provision for the same year was approximately 255 millions (*Treasury Reports*, 1921, 63), or a total interest and sinking fund charge of 1¼ billions of dollars. The combined charges for 1922 will be approximately 1 billion 272 millions (*Treasury Reports*, 1921, 63).

The result of this is that the interest alone which we should receive from foreign countries on what they owe us amounts to more than one third of the interest and sinking fund charge on our total debt.

The Government expenditures for the fiscal year 1920, were

almost 6½ billions of dollars; for the year 1921 about 5½ billions of dollars—a saving of a half billion of dollars; and for 1922, about 4 billions of dollars,—a saving of 1½ billions of dollars over 1921, and of 2 billions of dollars over 1920 (*Treasury Reports*, 1921, 1).

It would thus appear that the service of our national war debt probably constitutes approximately one third of our total national expenditure for 1922; and of this service fund, approximately one third could be met by the interest due us from foreign countries. Or put in different form, if the foreign governments were to pay their interest, we could reduce our national taxes 11½%.

This of course takes no account of the sinking fund, on the European debt, which if paid and added to the interest, would enable us to make a reduction of approximately 14½% in our year national taxes, or about 1/7 of such taxes.

But the cancellation of the debt means of course much more than the mere default in interest. If the debt were cancelled and then amortized over 10 years, it would mean in effect raising from our tax payers 1 billion dollars a year for each of the ten years, and paying the same over to Europe. There would in addition be a loss of the interest on outstanding principal each year.

No argument is necessary to support the contention that the taxpayers of this country cannot stand, and ought not to stand, the added burden of a cancellation of this debt, which would so materially increase their already crushing taxes.

Nor would the cancellation of this debt have the effect contended for it, even if it could be borne by the taxpayers.

In the first place, the owing of this debt has so far been no real handicap to Europe's purchasing power, because they have paid practically nothing either on principal or interest of the debt. If the interest and some amortization payments had been kept up, there would be the basis for an argument that to relieve them of further payments would enable them to spend these funds in purchasing American products, but such is not the fact. It is true the owing of this debt may have curtailed their borrowing power somewhat, and yet they have floated in this country three quarters of a billion of dollars of bonds in the last fifteen months. It is also true, and this may have some significance, that if these European countries were forgiven this debt they owe the government, the bonds they have issued to our munitions manufacturers and financiers would be materially strengthened.

Furthermore, it is common knowledge that ever since the war American merchants and financiers have been trying to discover some way in which Europe could finance her trade with America. The League of Nations fathered and supported what looked like a feasible plan for the purpose, but it fell because the European countries refused to make the necessary commitments. More recently the bankers of London, Paris, Tokyo, and Rome have tried to work out a plan for a great international corporation, and this has been supported by the Prime Ministers of the Powers, particularly by Lloyd George, at their meeting at Cannes in February, and more recently in Genoa, but it is to be doubted if anything comes of it.

The great difficulty in the way of any trade in Europe is the low exchange rate. The relative values of European currency have fallen enormously as the following table will show:

	Unit Value	Rate May 26, 1922
Belgium	.1930	.0842
France	.1930	.0910
Italy	.1930	.0525
Germany	.2382	.0034

Great Britain, Holland, Denmark, Sweden, and Switzerland are approximately normal (Roberts, June, 10).

One of the most potent causes for this condition as to exchange which prevents purchasing here, is the failure of practically all European countries to balance their budgets—that is to live within their incomes. They spend more than their revenues and then issue paper money to cover the difference. Russia appears to be the worst offender in this connection. A Soviet journal published in Moscow asserts that at the beginning of the war Russia had a billion 630 million rubles; by the end of 1917, it had 27 billion 300 million rubles; at the end of 1919, it had 225 billion rubles; and at the end of 1920 it had 1 trillion 168 billion rubles. This journal states that the needs for 1920 are 48 trillions 500 billions of rubles (Roberts, January, 11.) The value of a gold ruble is 49 cents to 77 cents.

There is no hope for a revival of trade with Europe, until their budgets balance, and they go to work. They will have no exchangeable currency so long as matters run as they are. The forgiveness of the debt they owe us, would have no effect on this situation, as is shown by the fact that they have never paid us anything on account of that debt during all the time they have been following this course. Probably the real cause of all this inflation, is the maintenance by France of enormous armies, which reflects on adjacent countries, and the failure to determine the size of the German separation payments.

But even if—as is contrary to the fact—the forgiveness of this debt would give Europe money to buy American produce, still it would have little or no effect upon us here in the West, for the reason that Europe is now producing practically all the foodstuffs she needs, and other countries near at hand are furnishing her mineral raw materials. While agriculture in Europe will not get back to normal in 1922 for various reasons, the production of food will be restored, barring crop failure, as will also the fruit and vegetable crop. So with potatoes, rice, and corn.

The count of animals is being restored, though lack of purchasing power prevents their buying the necessary feeding stuffs to bring it up to pre-war levels. But it is said that Europe will—looking to the whole situation—reach an agricultural equilibrium in 1922, and this is accomplished in part by the new methods of milling by which the average extraction of flour is increased from 72% for wheat and 76% for rye before the war, to 85% and 90% now (Roberts, April, 2).

Thus Europe will make few purchases in any event from us of the West.

Moreover, even if the cancellation of the debt meant more purchases in the United States, it would, for reasons I have already stated, merely constitute putting money in one pocket for the sales made, and taking it out of the other to pay the extra and excessive taxes, occasioned thereby.

The League of Nations and Its World Court

28 May 1923

In the early part of May 1923 Salmon O. Levinson of Chicago, chairman of the American Committee for the Outlawry of War, wrote a letter to JRC saying that Philander C. Knox was their "connecting link," Knox having given Levinson "a super-abundance of confidence in" Clark (S. O. Levinson to J. Reuben Clark, Jr., 9 May 1923, Box 355, JRCP). He explained that he would be in New York during the latter part of the month and said he would like to see JRC at that time. On 28 May 1923, at the home of Mrs. Willard Straight, Mr. Levinson met JRC and received from him the following brief statement. Box 47, Book 3, 1923, Outlawry War, J 11.7, JRCP.

For more on JRC's views regarding a world court, see the introductory note to Article Six of Part One.

In essence, the League of Nations is, by intention and by actual operation, a military alliance among the Great Powers of Western Europe which, with their possessions and dominions and the flattered weak and small powers of the world, have regrouped themselves in a new "balance of power" arrangement. The real purpose of this alliance is to make secure to themselves the world-wide territorial, strategic, political, economic, and financial gains with which, through the intervention of the United States, they were able to enrich themselves at the end of the Great War.

These Great Powers (or at least France) hope, plan, and expect to retain these gains through the maintenance and enforcement of the pernicious, peace-destroying yet so-called peace treaties of which the Treaty of Versailles is the prototype.

To give to this purpose a semblance of respectability, legality, and justice, these Powers work, when it best suits their ends, through the instrumentalities of the League of Nations. They manipulate at will, and have always done so, the Secretariat, the Assembly, and the Council: they even tamper with the Permanent Court of Justice itself. Behind this whole panoply of pseudo-world organization sits the Council of Ambassadors—successors of the Supreme Council—the "Big Four"—dominating, directing, compelling the course of Europe and of much of the world,—all for the benefit of the newly-grouped Great Powers. A narrow national selfishness, never exceeded in the history of the world, is the driving force of the whole system.

I am unwilling that the United States—our country, my country—with its great free institutions, its liberty-loving people, its great traditions, shall become to any extent or to any degree a part of or a participant in this solemn travesty of a proclaimed world organization, which is dominated by governmental theories and systems hostile to and destructive of our own, which by virtue of number of votes will be able to impose its will upon us, which purporting to be a world organization, excludes a great portion of the civilized people of the earth from its membership, which not only fails to keep but is subversive of the peace of the world, which announces the doctrine of self-determination and then denies to peoples the right of choosing their allegiance, and whose deep underlying motive force—always operative—is not the lofty precept of the Covenant, but the base self-interest of its component separate Great Powers.

I am unwilling that the United States, with its glorious record for the peaceful adjustment of its own international disputes—its arbitration of its boundaries, north and south, of its rights under treaties, of its rights of fishery in foreign coastal waters, of its rights as a belligerent upon the high seas, of its rights as a belligerent upon land, of its rights and duties as a neutral, of the rights of its citizens in foreign countries, of the rights of aliens in its own domains, of the propriety under the rules and principles of international law of the decisions of our Supreme Court,—our country whose reputation for fairness and justice induced the British Empire to arbitrate questions touching Britain's honor,—I am unwilling that our country shall compromise this glorious past by adherence to a Court whose achievements with a world organization behind it seem never yet to have reached the dignity of an actual decision on any matter and whose advisory opinions have thus far related to the most trivial of the disputed questions that have beset Europe. I am unalterably opposed to our country having any association of any kind or degree with the League of Nations or with any of its instrumentalities. I cannot support any plan which proposes such an association, or which equivocates with the fundamental question [of] whether we shall make such an association.

The plan for the outlawry of war already announced, contemplates three things,—the outlawry of aggressive war, the building up of an international code, the establishment of a court of justice. Let the proponents of this plan frankly announce this as a plan for the whole world, not for a part of the world, and let them announce it as a substitute plan for the present League of Nations. Let them declare for a rule of law and justice, as against the existing rule of force.

Let them demand,—

(1) The calling of a Conference of the nations which shall solemnly covenant that hereafter aggressive international war is a crime, for waging which the aggressor shall take no advantage but shall be punished,—the covenant to make proper reserves as to defensive measures, the protection of citizens, and the enforcement of arbitral awards.

(2) The calling thereafter of a second conference for the codification of the international law of peace as well as of war.

(3) The creation thereupon of Courts of Justice which might be closely modelled after our own Federal judicial system, with district and circuit courts, and a supreme court of last resort, which courts shall have affirmative (compulsory) jurisdiction of matters covered by the international code in some such manner as is provided by the Hague Prize Court Convention, and whose decisions shall have some such ultimate sanction as is provided in the Hague Convention for the Enforcement of Contract Debts.

A bold, honest espousal of a far-reaching constructive program such as this will command the approval of the millions of citizens who voted against the League of Nations at the last election, and the active support of the great bulk of them. Show them practicable measures for the advancement of world peace and international justice outside the League, and they will rally to you to a man. Go to them with an equivocal, half-hearted, timid proposal that may be twisted into a suggestion that they adopt something they have already repudiated, and you will merit and you will probably receive not only their disapproval but their repudiation.

Power to Confiscate Ex-Enemy Property in Time of Peace

9 February 1926

On 6 October 1917, six months after the United States entered World War I, Congress passed "the trading with the enemy act, which provided for the taking over of all German-owned property in the United States" (Warren F Martin and J. Reuben Clark, Jr., *American Policy Relative to Alien Enemy Property*, 69th Cong., 2d Sess., S. Doc. 181, 16). As early as June 1914, almost two years before the United States entered the war, JRC had expressed his concern for the protection of aliens and their rights in a letter to ex-President William Howard Taft (William H. Taft to J. Reuben Clark, Jr., 19 June 1914, Box 503, Book 3, JRCP).

When JRC wrote the present memorandum, entitled *Power to Confiscate Ex-Enemy Property in Time of Peace, or Status of Ex-Enemy Property* (Clifton, N.J., n.d.), his friend Warren F. Martin—former secretary to Senator P. C. Knox and former special assistant to the United States attorney general—was busy in the East lobbying on the matter. Because of his connections in the Congress, he had the memorandum published with his name on it as well as JRC's.

The memorandum is an interpretation of treaties and the Constitution and discusses both international and domestic aspects of the issue. Its opening sentence is this question: "May the property of German nationals, which is still held by the Alien Property Custodian, be now confiscated by the Federal Government or must it be returned to those (or their representatives or assignees) from whom it was taken?" In the remainder of the first twenty-six pages, not reproduced here, JRC discussed his response to that question under these topic headings: "International Aspect," "Domestic Aspect," "War and Peace Powers," and "Confiscation of Enemy Property." The following excerpt, more than one-third of the entire memorandum (pp. 27-43), commences with the last paragraph of the topic, "Confiscation of Enemy Property," and continues through to the conclusion. Box 48, Book 1, 1926, Ex-Enemy Property, N 7.2, JRCP; see also Box 113, N 7, JRCP.

Now there are at least four dates on which the World War could be said, for the United States, to have ended.

1. The date on which, as a fact, the war ended, after which no fighting was engaged in either by the United States or by Germany, the date on which, as Marshall Foch said, the enemy capitulated, namely, November 11, 1918, the date of the Armistice.
2. The date on which, according to the Treaty of Versailles, the war ended as a matter of law, namely, January 10, 1920,—the date of the going into effect of the Treaty of Versailles.
3. The date of the joint Resolution of Congress which declared the state of war existing between the United States and Germany to be at an end, namely, July 2, 1921.
4. The date of the proclamation of the Treaty of Berlin, providing for post war adjustments between the United States and Germany, namely, November 14, 1921.

Confiscation in Time of Peace, under the Principles of International Law

Grant that at any time prior to any of these dates, the Congress of the United States in the exercise of its war powers—for the Supreme Court has expressly declared, as we have already seen, that the confiscation of enemy property is an exercise of the war power—

might have confiscated German owned property in the United States because a state of war still existed; yet not having confiscated the property prior to the end of the war, Congress may not now, in times of peace, authorize such confiscation.

This conclusion is, as it is submitted, justified by reason and on principle, and is in accord with the authorities.

Mr. Justice Field declared in Miller v. United States (John William Wallace, *Reports of Cases Argued and Adjudged in the Supreme Court of the United States,* 23 vols. [Washington, D.C., 1864-76], 11:315-16) that:

> The war powers of the government have no express limitation in the Constitution, and the only limitation to which their exercise is subject is the law of nations. That limitation necessarily exists. . . . And it is in the light of that law that the war powers of the government must be considered. The power to prosecute war granted by the Constitution, as is well said by counsel, is a power to prosecute war according to the law of nations, and not in violation of that law. The power to make rules concerning captures on land and water is a power to make such rules as Congress may prescribe, subject to the condition that they are within the law of nations. There is a limit to the means of destruction which government, in the prosecution of war, may use, and there is a limit to the subjects of capture and confiscation, which government may authorize, imposed by the law of nations, and is no less binding upon Congress than if the limitation were written in the Constitution. The plain reason of this is, that the rules and limitations prescribed by that law were in the contemplation of the parties who framed and the people who adopted the Constitution.
>
> Whatever any independent civilized nation may do in the prosecution of war, according to the law of nations, Congress, under the Constitution, may authorize to be done, and nothing more.

This view accords with that of Marshall who in Brown v. U.S. (William Cranch, *Reports of Cases Argued and Adjudged in the Supreme Court of the United States, 1801-1815,* 9 vols. [Washington, D.C., 1804-17], 8:121-54) appealed to the law of nations to justify the existence of the right of confiscation. Furthermore, the general principle advanced by Mr. Justice Field is, of necessity, also at the basis of all those decisions of our courts in which belligerent rights have been tested and determined by an appeal to and in accordance with the principles of that law of nations.

It is therefore pertinent to inquire what is the rule of international law on this matter.

Rule of International Law Concerning Confiscation after Peace Declared

Hall in his work on International Law states the law of nations thus:

Sec. 202. Acts of war done subsequently to the conclusion of peace, or to the time fixed for the termination of hostilities, although done in ignorance of the existence of peace, are necessarily null. They being so, the effects which they have actually produced must be so far as possible undone, and compensation must be given for the harm suffered through such effects as cannot be undone. Thus territory which has been occupied must be given up; ships which have been captured must be restored; damage from bombardment or from loss of time or market, etc., ought to be compensated for; and it has been held in the English courts, with the general approbation of subsequent writers, that compensation may be recovered by an injured party from the officer through whose operations injury has been suffered, and that it is for the government of the latter to hold him harmless. It is obvious, on the other hand, that acts of hostility done in ignorance of peace entail no criminal responsibility. (William Edward Hall, *A Treatise on International Law*, ed. A. Pearce Higgins, 7th ed. [Oxford, Eng., 1917], 604)

Oppenheim sets out the effects of peace under the law of nations as follows:

On the one hand, all acts legitimate in warfare cease to be legitimate. Neither contributions nor requisitions, nor attacks on members of the armed forces or on fortresses, nor capture of ships, nor occupation of territory, are any longer lawful. If forces, ignorant of the conclusion of peace, commit such hostile acts, the condition of things at the time peace was concluded must as far as possible be restored. Thus, ships captured must be set free, territory occupied must be evacuated, members of armed forces taken prisoners must be liberated, contributions imposed and paid must be repaid. (L. Oppenheim, *International Law: A Treatise*, 2 vols., 3d ed. [London, 1920], 2:367; and see Robert Phillimore, *Commentaries upon International Law*, 4 vols., 3:777 et seq. [publication information for the first edition of this rare book was never found; the second edition was published in London in 1879-89])

Finally our own authority, Kent, speaks very clearly on this point. He says:

A treaty of peace binds the contracting parties from the moment of its conclusion, and that is understood to be from the day it is signed. . . . All that can be required in such cases is, that the government make immediate restitution of things captured after the cessation of hostilities. . . .

Another question arose subsequent to the Treaty of Ghent, of 1814, in one of the British vice-admiralty courts, on the validity of a recapture, by a British ship of war, of a British vessel captured by an American privateer. The capture was made by an American cruiser [and] was valid, being made before the period fixed for the cessation of hostilities, and in ignorance of the fact; but the prize had not been carried into port and condemned, and while at sea she was recaptured by the British cruiser after the period fixed for the cessation of hostilities, but without knowledge of the peace. It was decided that the possession, of the vessel by the American privateer was a lawful possession and that the British cruiser could not, after the peace, lawfully use force to devest this lawful possession. The restoration of peace put an end, from the time limited, to all force, and then the general principle applied, that things acquired in war remain, as to title and possession, precisely as they stood when the peace took place. (James Kent, *Commentaries on American Law*, ed. Oliver Wendell Holmes, Jr., 12th ed. [Boston, 1873], 1:170, 174)

Fully to understand the effect of this principle of international law upon the situation under discussion it must be in mind that property now in the hands of the Alien Property Custodian may not be now treated as property which has been "seized" or "captured" from the enemy with an intent to "confiscate" it as enemy property, as, for example, prizes "seized" or "captured" on the high seas during hostilities which are so seized or captured that they may become the property of the captors under a belligerent right which does not require the payment of compensation for the property seized.

Property in the hands of the Alien Property Custodian was not taken into possession as an act of confiscation, nor with the intention of proceeding to confiscation, as the following will show.

By Section 6 of the Trading with the Enemy Act the President was authorized to appoint an Alien Property Custodian "who shall be empowered *to receive all money and property* in the United States due or belonging to an enemy, or ally of an enemy, which may be paid, conveyed, transferred, assigned, or delivered to said custodian under the provisions of this Act; *and to hold, administer, and account for the same* under the general direction of the President and as provided in this Act." By Section 12 of the Act it was provided that moneys, checks, and drafts received by the Alien Property Custodian should be deposited in the Treasury of the United States, to be "invested and reinvested" by the Secretary of the Treasury in securities specified until the end of the war when such securities should be sold and the proceeds deposited in the Treasury. All other property coming to the Alien Property Custodian was to be "safely held and administered" by him, except as thereafter specifically provided in the Act. In his handling of this property the Alien Property Custodian was to "be vested with all the powers of a common-law trustee." Finally it was provided in the last paragraph of Section 12 of the Act that "after the end of the war any claim of any enemy or of an ally of enemy to any money or other property received and held by the Alien Property Custodian or deposited in the United States Treasury, shall be settled as Congress shall direct" (*United States Statutes at Large,* 40:411, 415, 423, 424; [italics added]. Hereafter referred to as *Statutes*).

There is not in any of these provisions, which are the important ones on the question under discussion, any language which appears even to suggest an intention by Congress to confiscate the properties taken over by the Alien Property Custodian by this mere fact of taking custody and carrying out the provisions of the Act (see in this connection, *inter alia,* Central Union Trust Co. v. Garvan, *U.S. Reports,* 254:554-69; Stoehr v. Wallace, 255:239-51; Commercial Trust Co. v. Miller, 262:51-57). That no such intention to confiscate this property generally did exist, seems conclusively shown by the provision of Section 16 of the Act (*Statutes,* 40:425) which provided as a penalty for any violation of the Act that "any property, funds, securities, papers, or other articles or documents, or any vessel together with her tackle, apparel, furniture, and equipment, concerned in such violation shall be forfeited to the United States." Obviously if all the property was confiscated by its taking over by the Alien Property Custodian, this provision would be both unnecessary and meaningless.

It is true that Section 12 was amended on March 28, 1918 (*Statutes,* 40:459) so as to provide that the Alien Property Custodian should have power to manage and otherwise handle property in his custody "in like manner *as though* he were the absolute owner thereof" [italics added]. But it seems clear that the conferring of power to act "*as though* he were the absolute owner" not only fails to confer ownership, but in terms actually negatives [*sic*] ownership. Furthermore, and this seems conclusive, if this provision is to be regarded as conferring an ownership, then that ownership is vested in the *Alien Property Custodian,* not in the President of the United States in whom the original power of taking over was vested nor in the United States. It is hardly to be assumed that Congress intended to vest in one of the subordinate executive officers by language such as that quoted, a title to the vast property interests which were then in the custody of that subordinate official.

The debates in Congress at the time of the passage of the original Act, and at the time of its amendment show that those in charge of the measures at the time, understood, and so explained to Congress, that the possession of this property by the Alien Property Custodian was to be temporary, that it was to be a custody only with certain powers to change the form of such property so held in custody, and that such property was ultimately to be returned to its owners.

That this was the intention of Congress, is shown by legislation since passed by that body authorizing the return of certain property held by the Custodian. The language of these acts is not that of a grant by Congress to the individuals described, of property belonging to the United States and now to be donated to such individuals. In effect, the language of all these acts merely removes a disability theretofore existing against the real owners of the property and stipulates a procedure by which such owners could recover their property (see Acts of July 11, 1919; June 5, 1920; Feb. 27, 1921; March 4, 1923 [*Statutes,* 41:35, 977, 1147; 42:1511]. See, on effect of these restoration statutes, White v. Mechanics Securities Corporation, decided December 14, 1925 [*U.S. Reports,* lawyers' ed., 2d, 70:275-80]).

That this view as to the nature of the Alien Property Custodian's possession of the property in question is correct, is shown also by the provisions of the Treaty of Berlin which provides (as has been already pointed out) that property in the hands of the Custodian may be "*retained*" by the United States pending certain contingencies. This is not the language which would have been used had it been considered that the United States owned the property. In that event the stipulation would have required a granting or ceding by the United States to the former owners upon the happening of the contingency.

Thus the situation here appears wholly different from that which exists in the case of prizes legally *seized* or *captured* during hostilities with the intention to confiscate or forfeit the same as enemy property pursuant to the laws of war, even where judicial condemnation of such property is not formally completed until after peace is established. To complete the proceedings leading to the forfeiture of such seized or captured property, no further legislative act is necessary; such completion is (as stated) carried out under the rules of the laws of war. But as already pointed out, these same rules of the laws of war do not permit confiscation of property not so *seized* or *captured* during hostilities.

These foregoing authorities and the discussions thereon seem to establish (1) that after peace, ex-enemy (for peace having come, enemies no longer exist) property may by the law of nations, be confiscated, even when actual seizures or captures have been made by those officers (of the ex-belligerent powers) who were ignorant of peace, but who intended that such seizures or captures should be forfeited; and (2) that property not so *seized* or *captured* cannot because of mere possession, be confiscated as an act of war after peace is declared.

If, therefore, the law of nations measures as to confiscations, the war powers of Congress under the Constitution—and to this point the observations of both Marshall and Field directly go—then the confiscation of ex-enemy property after the termination of belligerency cannot be constitutionally carried out as a war power, because the law of nations forbids such confiscation after the termination of war. As Mr. Justice Field said:

> There is a limit to the means of destruction which government, in the prosecution of war, may use, and there is a limit to the subject of capture and confiscation, which government may authorize, imposed by the law of nations, and is no less binding upon Congress than if the limitation were written in the Constitution.

Effect of Treaties of Versailles and Berlin

Nor is the situation changed domestically, it is submitted, by either the Treaty of Versailles or by the Treaty of Berlin, for the following reasons, some of which, though already given, are repeated here for the sake of completeness:

In the first place, being between certain powers for ending war, they could not change the law of nations, which is, in effect, a part of our Constitutional power and limitation in the matter of the war powers.

In the next place the provisions of the Treaty of Versailles are not in language nor in effect (as it is submitted) either *cessions* or *grants* by Germany of property or property rights. Their provisions are at most (a) confirmations by Germany of acts of the Allied and Associated Powers under their "war measures" which were purely domestic legislation—Germany's confirmations amounting merely to certain surrenders ("*estoppels*") already described; and (b) the recognition by Germany that the Allied and Associated Powers "*reserve*" the right "to retain and liquidate" all German owned property, etc., with the stipulation that "the liquidation shall be carried out in accordance with the laws of the Allied or Associated Powers." Here, also, nothing is actually done except to secure from Germany a surrender (already discussed) of rights of objection and interposition which she might otherwise possess. There is nothing here that as to "liquidation" even purports to validate legislation otherwise invalid, or legalize acts otherwise illegal. On the contrary this provision might be interpreted as giving to or as leaving in Germany the right to demand that all "liquidation" must be carried out by constitutional measures.

Nor do the provisions of the Treaty of Berlin increase the extent of the surrenders made by Germany, nor of the powers to be possessed by the United States under the Treaty of Versailles. On the other hand, it is fairly to be argued (as has been already somewhat fully submitted) that the provisions of the Treaty of Berlin distinctly curtail the rights and authorizations granted by the Treaty of Versailles. For while Articles I and II of the Treaty of Berlin stipulate that the United States "shall have and enjoy . . . all the rights and advantages stipulated for the benefit of the United States in the Treaty of Versailles," yet the Joint Resolution of Congress (which was in pertinent part incorporated in the Treaty of Berlin, and by which the "rights, privileges, indemnities, reparations or advantages" specified were "accorded" by Germany to the United States in that Treaty) merely provided that German owned property in the hands of the Alien Property Custodian might be "*retained*" by the United States "and no disposition thereof made *except* as shall have been heretofore or specifically hereafter shall be provided by law until" the German Government "shall have made suitable provision for the satisfaction of all claims against" Germany by persons owing allegiance to the United States. There is here no assertion that such property shall be actually applied to the satisfaction of American claims nor any consent by Germany to any such use of the property.

It seems, therefore, open to Germany to contend that (a) these specific provisions found in a treaty subsequent to the Treaty of

Versailles, supersede the general provisions of that treaty; (b) that by these specific provisions of the Treaty of Berlin the United States undertook merely to *retain* the German owned property until Germany had made "suitable provision" for the payment of American claims; (c) that the power of disposition so *retained* by the United States included neither the "liquidation" nor confiscation of such property, because prior *dispositions* had not been confiscatory and the language of the Resolution does not show an intent to dispose in any other way than that already employed; (d) that the expression "shall have heretofore or specifically hereafter shall be provided by law," meant by a constitutional law, for the United States would not and could not stipulate for approval of an action under an unconstitutional law; (e) that a law confiscating private property in the United States in time of peace would not be constitutional; and (f) that Germany might now interpose upon behalf of her citizens whose property should be seized and confiscated by unconstitutional laws.

Would a law "liquidating," or confiscating private property in time of peace be constitutional? In view of all that has been already said on this point, it is not necessary to belabor the question here. It may be merely observed that having in mind the provisions of the Fifth Amendment that "private property shall not be taken for public use without just compensation," and having in mind the declaration of the Supreme Court in United States v. Russell (Wallace, 13:628-29) that to justify a seizure of a private property, even when just compensation is made therefor, there must be a

public danger . . . immediate, imminent, and impending, and the emergency in the public service must be extreme and imperative, and such as will not admit of delay or a resort to any other source of supply, and the circumstances must be such as imperatively require the exercise of that extreme power in respect to the particular property so impressed, appropriated, or destroyed. . . . If the necessity for the use of the property is imperative and immediate, and the danger as heretofore described, is impending . . . the taking of such property under such circumstances creates an obligation on the part of the Government to reimburse the owner to the full value of the service. Private rights, under such extreme and imperious circumstances, must give way for the time to the public good, but the Government must make full restitution for the sacrifice.

Having in mind, to repeat, the Fifth Amendment and these expressions, it seems clear that a law to be now enacted "liquidating" or confiscating the German owned property at present held by the Alien Property Custodian would be unconstitutional.

Nor is the situation altered (as already indicated) by regarding these Treaties of Versailles and Berlin as themselves the "supreme law of the land." As such law they are domestic law, and as domestic law they are subject to the Constitution, and being subject to the Constitution, the observation just made would apply to them and condemn them as laws sufficient to authorize, under the Constitution, the "liquidation" or confiscation of the property in question. As already intimated above, it cannot be that a treaty, certainly if negotiated without compulsion upon the United States, could change or alter in any way the Constitution, and this would seem obvious where a specific provision of the Constitution specifically prohibits that which is sought to be done by treaty. But an added difficulty may be noted here. As the treaties stand, they could not be self-executory; it would require additional legislation to make operative any provisions they may contain which authorize the "liquidation" or confiscation of this property, and, irrespective of the treaties themselves, it must be that such additional and requisite legislation would fall under the constitutional ban already adverted to.

It is worth while to recall again that the Congressional debates attending the consideration and passage of the Trading with the Enemy Act show that Congress then intended that alien enemy property was to be taken possession of and sequestered with the sole view of holding it during the war and of returning it at the end of the war to its former owners. Indeed from some of the language used in these debates one might almost think that Congress was authorizing a purely philanthropic undertaking.

Property of Non-Resident Alien Enemies

Nor can any point be properly made in this matter that the property now in custody is largely the property of non-resident ex-enemies. Chief Justice Marshall adverted to this phase of the question in Brown v. United States and dismissed the question without discussion on the ground that there existed no reason for treating differently the property of enemy residents and non-residents. He said:

Vattel says, that "the sovereign can neither detain the persons nor the property of those subjects of the enemy who are within his dominions at the time of the declaration."

It is true that this rule is, in terms, applied by Vattel to the property of those only who are personally within the territory at the commencement of hostilities; but it applies equally to things in action and to things in possession; and if war did, of itself, without any further exercise of the sovereign will, vest the property of the enemy in the sovereign, his presence could not exempt it from this operation of war. *Nor can a reason be perceived for maintaining that the public faith is more entirely pledged for the security of property trusted in the territory of the nation in time of peace, if it be accompanied by its owner, than if it be confided to the care of others.* (Cranch, 8:124-25; italics added)

Effect of Germany's Undertaking to Compensate Her Nationals for Property Taken

It has been suggested that since in the Treaty of Versailles (Article 297 (i)) "Germany undertakes to compensate her nationals in respect of the sale or retention of their property, rights or interests in Allied or Associated States," that, therefore, an appropriation by the Federal Government, without compensation, of German owned property now in the hands of the Alien Property Custodian, and the application of the proceeds thereof to the payment of American claims against Germany would not be a legal act and not a confiscation of such property within the meaning of our constitutional inhibitions. Obviously such a contention overlooks or disregards the facts and conclusions already discussed (under the heading "International Status") as to the meaning of the provisions of the Treaty of Berlin and as to the effect thereof on the stipulations of the Treaty of Versailles.

But assuming for the sake of the argument that the pertinent provisions of the Treaty of Versailles are fully operative in this matter, yet there are reasonable, even though technical, answers to such a contention.

Without elaborating any of these, it may be observed that a technical argument, soundly based (as it is submitted) might be made that even under the provisions of the Treaty of Versailles the "*undertaking*" of Germany (involved here and quoted above) related solely to German owned property that might be applied to losses suffered by American citizens on account of the application of German exceptional war measures to the property of such citizens *located in Germany,* and that this is so because the Treaty provisions under consideration specifically and certainly authorize the application of

German owned property to those property losses only which are suffered by American citizens in respect of property located in Germany. As to no other property is there any specific authorization to apply German owned property to losses suffered in respect of such property. Indeed the argument could, with good basis, be carried still further, and the contention could be made that the utmost which the Treaty of Versailles authorizes, is the holding of German owned property as a *pledge* or under a *charge* to guarantee the payment of losses suffered by Americans with respect to their property located in Germany, and that, therefore, even as to these losses there was no authority in the Treaty for applying to losses and in payment thereof the German owned property now in the hands of the Alien Property Custodian.

But whatever the meaning of the provision of the Treaty of Versailles may be in this regard, and however conclusive may be the foregoing submissions, the Treaty of Versailles is subject to the stipulations of the Treaty of Berlin which put the matter beyond doubt.

To recapitulate (for convenience of reference) discussions had and conclusions already reached on this matter,

By Article I of that Treaty, certain provisions of the Joint Resolution of Congress of July 2, 1921, which declared the war with Germany at an end, were adopted and made part of the Treaty. Among those provisions so incorporated into the Treaty was Section 5 of the Joint Resolution which in its pertinent part provided as follows:

> All property of the Imperial German Government, or its successor or successors, and of all German nationals, which was, on April 6, 1917, in, or has since that date come into the possession or under the control of, or has been the subject of a demand by United States of America or of any of its officers, agents, or employees from any source or by any agency whatsoever . . . shall be retained by the United States of America and no disposition thereof made, except as shall have been heretofore or specifically hereafter shall be provided by law until such time as the Imperial German Government . . . (or its successor) . . . shall have made suitable provisions for the satisfaction of all claims against said [German government].

Authority to "retain" property until an obligation is met is obviously not authority to sell the property and apply the proceeds to the liquidation of that obligation. It would require some authority other than the authority to "retain" to accomplish any such purpose.

Since the Treaty of Berlin is subsequent to the Treaty of Versailles, the Treaty of Berlin supersedes the Treaty of Versailles. Therefore, even if the Treaty of Versailles did authorize, as there is ground for contending it does not, the appropriation of German owned property in this country to the payment of the claims of American citizens against Germany, yet by the Treaty of Berlin, the United States in effect surrendered any such right and took in lieu thereof merely the right to "retain" the German owned property *until* Germany "made suitable provision for the satisfaction of all claims against" her.

It is submitted as a result of the foregoing analysis that the United States does not have any undertaking from Germany that Germany will reimburse her own nationals for the property of those nationals which the United States might seize and appropriate to the payment of the claims of American citizens against Germany, and any assertion that now to take German owned property and apply it to the payment of American claims would not actually (for the reason given) constitute confiscation of that property, is not well founded.

But the contention that for the Federal Government now to appropriate to its own uses, without compensation, the German owned property still in the possession of the Alien Property Custodian, would not constitute a confiscation of such property (because of Germany's undertaking), is unsound on constitutional grounds, and this is true even on the assumption that Germany's obligation is real and that she is able and willing to pay.

The Constitutional provisions involved in a decision of the question presented here are to be found in the Fifth Amendment, which reads:

No person shall be held to answer for a capital, or otherwise infamous crime, unless on a presentment or indictment of a Grand Jury, except in cases arising in the land or naval forces, or in the Militia, when in actual service in time of War or public danger; nor shall any person be subject for the same offense to be twice put in jeopardy of life or limb; nor shall be compelled in any criminal case to be a witness against himself, nor be deprived of life, liberty, or property, without due process of law; nor shall private property be taken for public use, without just compensation.

It will be noted that this Amendment covers,—presentment or indictment by Grand Jury, double jeopardy, self crimination, due process of law, and the confiscation of private property.

The protection of the Amendment in these matters is extended to "persons" and to "private property," with no express or implied limitation of any kind as to the sort of person or property falling within its purview. It must, therefore, on reason, apply to any person, whatever his race, nationality, or allegiance, and to all property, whosoever the owner, when such person or such property is within the territory of the United States over which this provision of the Constitution runs. In other words, as to property, the constitutional protection attaches thereto irrespective of the national character of the owner, just as the protection attaches to persons irrespective of their allegiance; or to put it differently again, aliens and citizens appear to stand, as to their person and as to their property, on the same basis under these great, fundamental guarantees.

The foregoing principles are subject to the limitation (as declared by our Supreme Court) that an alien and his property must be legally within the United States in order to be entitled to the protection of these guarantees. An alien who has obtained entrance into the United States in violation of the laws of the United States is treated as if he were not yet within the United States and were applying for entrance thereto, from which considerations it is declared that the guarantees of the Constitution do not run to him nor to his property as they would do if he were legally within the United States.

This limitation seems not, however, applicable to the property under discussion here, at least speaking generally, for this property belongs either to aliens legally domiciled within the United States or to property legally acquired and located in the United States by aliens resident elsewhere. The property in question here is not tainted with any such illegality as would bring it within the limitation above set out.

This being true, the property is to be considered as possessing the full guaranty which would attach to it were it the property of a citizen of the United States.

When private property is taken for public use, it is taken by an exercise of the power of eminent domain, either by the government itself or by an agency of government possessing that power, and there is no other power in the government of the United States by which private property may be taken by government in time of peace.

Since every independent member of the society of nations is sovereign within its own jurisdiction, it is unnecessary to elaborate an argument to show that Germany cannot extend the operations of her laws within the jurisdiction of the United States. Whatever is done in the United States must be done under our laws and subject to our Constitution, and not under and pursuant to the constitution and laws of Germany.

Furthermore, since the Federal Government is a government of delegated power, and so has only those powers conferred upon it by the Constitution, and since the Constitution is the product of the exercise of the sovereign will of the people of the United States, it follows that a foreign state cannot confer upon the Federal Government power or functions which are not conferred by the Constitution, and that the people of the United States, not foreign states, endow our Federal Government with its constitutional powers.

Now the intent of the proposal under consideration is for Germany to apply certain property belonging to her subjects, but located in the United States, to the payment of certain obligations which are due from Germany to American citizens; but such property being outside the jurisdiction of Germany and within the jurisdiction of the United States, the proposal also is that the United States shall condemn for Germany the private property of German subjects in the United States, and shall without the United States itself making compensation for such property to its owners, turn over such private property so condemned to American citizens towards whom Germany has an obligation.

But there is no authority in the Constitution for the United States thus to act as a cat's paw for a foreign state, and under the principle above set out, mere consent by Germany that the United States might so act cannot confer upon it authority so to act.

For the United States to attempt so to act, would be to fly in the teeth of the principle announced by Mr. Justice Strong when he said:

The proper view of the right of eminent domain seems to be, that it is a right belonging to a sovereignty to take private property *for its own public uses, and not for those of another.* Beyond that, there exists no necessity, which alone is the foundation of the right. (Kohl v. U.S., *U.S. Reports,* 91:373-74 [italics added]; and see U.S. v. Jones, 109:51)

Thus reason and authority, and, it is submitted, morality also, forbid the United States to attempt to exercise the power of eminent domain in the United States for the benefit and at the behest of a foreign state.

But there are other considerations equally fatal to this proposal.

It would hardly be contended that government or its agent would undertake to condemn the property of A. and take over that property to its own use upon the mere promise of B. that if the property of A. was so taken, B. would compensate A. therefor. Much less, may the government condemn the property of A. (a private person) to turn over to B. (a private person) upon the mere promise of a foreign state that it will compensate A. Yet this last is precisely the situation which, in the best view, is created by the Treaty of Versailles if its provisions be given the value contended for by the proposers of the contention under discussion.

Now, as stated by Mr. Justice Strong in the passage already quoted, the right of eminent domain can be exercised by a government only *"for its own uses. . . . Beyond that, there exists no necessity, which alone is the foundation of the right."*

Or, as Mr. Justice Story said in his dissenting opinion in Charles River Bridge v. Warren Bridge (Richard Peters, *Reports of Cases Argued and Adjudged in the Supreme Court of the United States,* 16 vols. [Philadelphia, 1839-42], 11:642):

> Although the sovereign power in free governments may appropriate all the property, public as well as private, for public purposes, making compensation therefor; yet it has never been understood, at least never in our Republic, that the sovereign power can take the private property of A and give it to B by the right of "eminent domain;" or, that it can take it at all, except for public purposes; or, that it can take it for public purposes without the duty and responsibility of making compensation for the sacrifice of the private property of one, for the good of the whole. These limitations have been held to be fundamental maxims in free governments like ours; and have accordingly received the sanction of some of our most eminent judges and [lawyers].

Or, as Mr. Justice Swayne said in Township of Pinegrove v. Talcott (Wallace, 19:676): "Private property can be taken for a public purpose only, and not for private gain or benefit."

Now, as pointed out above, the taking which is provided for by the Treaty of Versailles is a taking of the property belonging to one private owner and turning it over to another private owner, to the enrichment of the latter, and this is a proceeding which has been repeatedly pronounced by the Supreme Court of the United States to be contrary to the principles of free, constitutional government, even where compensation for the property taken is certainly paid. Thus in this respect also the proposal under discussion is contrary to sound constitutional principle.

Furthermore, and to restate the principle stated by Mr. Justice Story,—when private property is taken by the Federal Government under the right of eminent domain, compensation therefor must, under the provisions of the Fifth Amendment, be made, otherwise the taking is devoid of that indispensable element which must accompany the exercise of the right at all. Now, it is proposed that the government which shall exercise the right here shall not pay any compensation at all.

Mr. Justice Field said in U.S. v. Jones (*U.S. Reports,* 109:518):

"[Compensation] is no part of the power itself, *but a condition upon which the power may be exercised*" (italics added).

While it is declared by Mr. Justice Harlan in Cherokee Nation v. Kansas Railway Company (*U.S. Reports,* 135:659) that the Fifth Amendment does not require that compensation shall be actually paid in advance of condemnation, yet said Mr. Justice Harlan, "*the owner is entitled to reasonable, certain, and adequate provision for obtaining compensation before his occupancy is disturbed*" (italics added).

The stipulation (already quoted) in the Treaty of Versailles that "Germany undertakes to compensate her nationals in respect of the sale or retention of their property, rights or interests in Allied or Associated States" fails to be a "reasonable, certain, and adequate provision for obtaining compensation before his occupancy is disturbed."

So far as the Treaty itself goes, it does not appear that Germany has made any provision whatsoever to compensate her nationals, yet under the principles announced by Mr. Justice Harlan, such provision is a condition precedent to the taking over of the property. Obviously, if there is no evidence of any provision at all for compensation, there is no evidence that the provision is either reasonable, certain, or adequate. In this connection it is well to have in mind the words of Mr. Justice Gray in Bauman v. Ross (*U.S. Reports,* 167:574) where he said that:

> The just compensation required by the Constitution to be made to the owner is to be measured by the loss caused to him by the appropriation. He is entitled to receive the value of what he has been deprived of, and no more. To award him less would be unjust to him; and to award him more would be unjust to the public.

There is a complete absence of anything in the Treaty to show that Germany is intending or is prepared to make such compensation as is stipulated in these observations by Mr. Justice Gray, and yet such compensation is, to requote Mr. Justice Field, "a condition upon which the power may be exercised," by the United States. Thus in this respect also the proposal under discussion is not in accord with sound constitutional principle.

Finally, it is to be observed that the Fifth Amendment provides that no person shall be deprived of his property without due process of law; and without venturing into a discussion (unnecessary here) of the essential elements of due process, it is sufficient to say that the proposal under discussion seems to contemplate the condemnation of the property concerned without even a semblance of an opportunity for a hearing by those from whom the property is to be taken. In this respect also the proposal under consideration appears constitutionally untenable.

From all the foregoing it is a sound deduction (as it is submitted) that the alleged undertaking by Germany to compensate its nationals for property taken by the United States (without compensation from the United States) and applied by the United States to the payment of claims of American citizens against Germany, does not relieve this proposal under discussion from the operation of the inhibitions of the Fifth Amendment.

CONCLUSION: It is therefore finally submitted that the German owned property still in the hands of the Alien Property Custodian may not, now that peace is established, be "liquidated" or confiscated, but must, when Congress so determines, be returned to those (or their representatives or assigns) from whom it was taken.

American Policy Relative to Alien Enemy Property

1926

Early in 1926, having published the memorandum excerpted in Article Twelve above, JRC prepared the following memorandum and sent it to his friend Warren F. Martin, former secretary to Senator P. C. Knox and former special assistant to the United States attorney general. Through Martin's efforts Senator David A. Reed of Pennsylvania had the memorandum printed as a Senate document. Although the printed document (*American Policy Relative to Alien Enemy Property,* 69th Congress, 2d Sess., S. Doc. 181) bore Martin's name as well as JRC's, on the identification page for this memorandum in the Clark papers there is the note: "JRC prepared this memorandum, Mr. Martin did not write any part of it" (Box 113, N 7, No. 3, JRCP). The last seventeen pages of the Senate document, not included here, discuss "Treaty Provisions Relating to Rights of Resident Alien Enemies on the Outbreak of War," drawn from treaties and conventions between the United States and other powers. Box 113, N 7, JRCP; see also Box 48, Book 1, 1926, Enemy Property, N 7.3, JRCP.

In early human history war was always a question of extermination or slavery. To this even the Holy Writ bears witness, for Saul sinned and was rejected as the King of Israel because he failed to obey the commandment that he should utterly destroy the Amalekites and spare not "but slay both man and woman, infant and suckling, ox and sheep, camel and ass" (1 Sam. 15:3).

Opinions of the Text Writers

Grotius, in his great work—*De Jure Belli ac Pacis*—tells us that—

When the Thracians took Mycalessus they put to death the women and children. So the Macedonians did when they took Thebes; the Romans when they took Ilurgis in Spain; Germanicus ravaged the Marsi with fire and sword without mercy to sex or age. Titus exposed the women and children taken at Jerusalem to fight with wild beasts in the public spectacles. And yet Germanicus and Titus are considered as humane men; so much had that kind of cruelty become customary. (Bk. 3, ch. 4, sec. 9, par. 2)

*   *   *

Nor are those who surrender always received, as in the battle of the Granicus, those were not who were serving under the Persians; and in Tacitus, the Uspenses praying for pardon for the free persons; which prayer, he says, the victors rejected, that they might rather fall by the right of war. . . . Even those who have surrendered unconditionally and been received, you may find, in history, put to death; as the rulers of Pometia by the Romans; the Samnites by Sulla, the Numidians, and Vercingentorix himself, by Caesar. Indeed this was almost the constant practice of the Romans toward the leaders of their enemies, whether taken or surrendered, that they should be put to death on the day of the triumph; as Cicero tells us, and Livy, Tacitus, and others. (Bk. 3, ch. 4, sec. 11–12)

In another part of his work Grotius quotes Celsus as saying:

The things which, belonging to the enemy, are in our hands, are not public property, but the property of those who take possession.

Upon which Grotius comments:

The things which are in our hands; that is, which are found with us when war arises.

In the same paragraph Grotius quotes a passage from Typho, which states that—

Those who in peace come to another nation, if war between the nations suddenly breaks out, become the slaves of those enemies among whom their destiny has thrown them. (Bk. 3, ch. 6, sec. 12, par. 1)

But later Grotius, having commented upon the treatment of captives taken in war, and the peculiar Roman policy which left them with the enemy in order (as Tryphoninus is quoted as saying) "That they might place their hope of returning rather in valor than in peace," states:

But with regard to those that are caught among the enemy when the war broke out, the same could not be said; for they could not be conceived to have done any wrong. Yet to diminish the strength of the enemy, they were retained while the war lasted. These then, by the consent of nations, were to be liberated, on the arrival of peace, as innocent; but other prisoners to be regulated by laws of war, except so far as regulated by compact. And for the same reason, slaves and other property are not restored at peace, except by compact; for they are supposed to be taken by right, and to deny this, would be to make wars grow out of wars. (Bk. 3, ch. 9, sec. 4, par. 3)

And thus the law stood and was understood among the ancient Romans so much so that in the Digests of Justinian it is stated as the settled law—

That the citizens of the country, who had gone to another country in time of peace, became slaves, if war broke out between the two countries and they were seized within the enemy's territory. (Travers Twiss, *The Rights and Duties of Nations in Time of War*, 2d ed., 86 [publication information for the second edition of this rare book was never found; the first edition was published in London in 1863])

This early law so established came on down through the ages until even when our own Kent wrote his lectures "Of the Law of Nations"—the first treatise in English ever written upon the subject—he found himself obliged to declare the law to be that—

When hostilities have commenced, the first objects that naturally present themselves for detention and capture are the persons and property of the enemy found within the territory on the breaking out of the war. According to strict authority, a State has a right to deal as an enemy with persons and property so found within its power, and to confiscate the property, and detain the persons as prisoners of war. (James Kent, *Commentaries on American Law*, ed. Oliver Wendell Holmes, Jr., 12th ed., 4 vols. [Boston, 1873] 1:56)

But while as Kent says, such may have been the law by "strict authority," such had not been the custom of nations for generations prior to the time Kent wrote. Beginning long before the time of Grotius, nations began to have a new conception of the relationship of humans and their rights, and this concept bore particular fruit in the domain of war. The work of amelioration of the savagery of war was greatly accelerated by Grotius, whose work, Ambassador White said, had proved the greatest benefit to humanity of any work not claiming divine inspiration.

Bynkershoek, writing in 1737 upon these rules, denied that notice should be given to enemies to withdraw their property or it would be forfeited, and declared that it was the practice of nations in his time to appropriate it at once, without notice, if there were no special convention to the contrary—

and that wherever there are treaty stipulations, whereby an interval of time is secured to the subjects of a belligerent power to enable them to withdraw themselves and their property in safety out of the enemy's territory, they will rightly be made prisoners of war and their property confiscated, if they should not have withdrawn themselves from the enemy's territory within the time specified by treaty. (Kent, 1:56; Twiss, 87)

[M. D.] Vattel, in his treatise on *The Law of Nations,* first published in 1758, reached a different conclusion upon this matter. In commenting on the declaration of war and its effects, he says:

The sovereign declaring war can neither detain the persons nor the property of those subjects of the enemy who are within his dominions at the time of the declaration. They came into his country under the public faith. By permitting them to enter and reside in his territories he tacitly promised them full liberty and security for their return. He is, therefore, bound to allow them a reasonable time for withdrawing with their effects; and, if they stay beyond the term prescribed, he has a right to treat them as enemies—as unarmed enemies, however. But if they are detained by an insurmountable impediment, as by sickness, he must necessarily, and for the same reasons, grant them a sufficient extension of time. (Bk. 3, ch. 4, par. 63)

So much for the practice of ancient nations and for the theories of the continental text writers down to the middle of the eighteenth century.

Practice of Nations

But to the glory of Anglo-Saxon law be it said that way back, almost at its beginning, a different rule was established.

One of the provisions wrung by the Barons from King John and incorporated in Magna Charta (June 15, 1215) provided that—

All merchants (unless publicly prohibited beforehand) might have safe conduct to depart from, to come into, to tarry in, and go through England for the exercise of merchandise, without any unreasonable impost, except in time of war; and that upon the breaking out of war with their nation they should be attached (if in England) without harm of body or goods, until the king or his great justiciary be informed how English merchants are treated in the enemy's country; and if English merchants are secure, then the enemy merchants should have the same security. (Twiss, 91)

Charles V of France, in an ordinance dated about 100 years after Magna Charta, declared that those foreign merchants who should be in France at the time of a declaration of war had nothing to fear, for they should be allowed to depart freely with their effects (Kent, 1:58; Robert Phillimore, *Commentaries upon International Law,* 4 vols., 3:sec. 53 [publication information for the first edition of this rare book was never found; the second edition was published in London in 1879-89]).

But the Statute of Staples (1354, *Statutes of the Realm,* 27 Edw. 3, c. 17), carried the provisions of Magna Charta still further by stipulating that foreign merchants residing in England at the time war broke out should have notice of 40 days, by proclamation, to depart the realm with their goods; and if within that time, by reason of accident, they were unable to do so, they were to have 40 days more to pass with their merchandise, with the right, in the meantime, to sell the same (Kent, 1:58; Phillimore, 3:sec. 78).

The practice of nations has by no means been uniform. In 1242 Louis IX of France arrested persons and goods of the English merchants trading within the kingdom upon the breaking out of war, whereupon Henry III of England, learning of the action of the French King, retaliated by reprisals against the persons of French merchants resident in England. Louis XI of France (1483) concluded a treaty with Hanse Towns by which merchants of the Hanse Confederation were at liberty to remain in the French dominions for one year after war broke out, with protection of persons and goods (Twiss, 92, 93).

In the sixteenth century, during the time of Henry VIII, the judges of England resolved that if a Frenchman came to England before the war, neither his person nor goods should be seized (Kent, 1:58).

It appears that during the sixteenth century it was commonly stipulated in treaties of commerce that a period of time varying from three months to two or three years after war was declared should be allowed to subjects of the contracting parties, during which time the subjects of one resident within the territories of the other should be allowed to withdraw themselves and their goods and effects from the enemy's country. France is credited with being the nation which, at this particular time, took the lead in the making of this sort of treaty provision.

Induced no doubt by the general principle that led to the making of such treaties, Louis XIV, in the next century, by a proclamation dated February 1, 1666, asserted, in connection with the war which he had declared against Great Britain on January 26, 1666, that—

his declaration of war was not intended to operate against those individuals of the English nation who might be resident in France with peaceful intentions, but that they might withdraw in safety with their goods and effects within three months, saving always to such individuals as might have become naturalized the right to remaining in France as French subjects. (Twiss, 94)

It would appear that the Scandinavian countries followed generally the same course that was followed by Great Britain (Twiss, 92).

In the Russo-Turkish War of 1877, the Czar, by a ukase of May 12, 1877, decreed that the Turkish subjects in Russia should be permitted to continue to reside there and continue their business subject to the laws.

Russia followed a like course in the Russo-Japanese War, when, by an imperial order of February 14, 1904, it was provided:

Japanese subjects are allowed to continue, under the protection of the Russian laws, their sojourn and the exercise of peaceable occupations in the Russian Empire, excepting in the territories which are under the control of the imperial viceroy in the Far East. (John Bassett Moore, *A Digest of International Law*, 8 vols. [Washington, D.C., 1906], 7:192)

Oppenheim, discussing in 1912 the rules applicable to "private and public enemy property, immovable or movable, on each other's territory . . . at the outbreak of war," asserts that—

The last case of confiscation of private property is that of 1793 at the outbreak of war between France and Great Britain. No case of confiscation occurred during the nineteenth century, and although several writers maintain that according to strict law the old rule, in contradistinction to the usage which they do not deny, is still valid, it may safely be maintained that it is obsolete, and that there is now a customary rule of international law in existence prohibiting the confiscation of private enemy property and the annulment of enemy debts on the territory of the belligerent. (L. Oppenheim, *International Law: A Treatise*, 2d ed. [London, 1912], 139)

Oppenheim had doubtless in mind the practice of the great powers, as to which it would appear he is entirely accurate. However, it seems that in the war between Peru and Bolivia on the one side and Chile on the other, Bolivia in 1879 expelled all Chileans from Bolivia and confiscated their goods (Moore, 7:192).

Doctrine of Chief Justice Marshall

No nation has done more during the period of its existence than has the United States in breaking away from the old strict rule which sanctioned the confiscation of enemy property found within its jurisdiction at the outbreak of war. The spirit which has actuated the United States in this matter was well declared by Chief Justice Marshall in the great case of Brown v. United States (William Cranch, *Reports of Cases Argued and Adjudged in the Supreme Court of the United States, 1801-1815*, 9 vols. [Washington, D.C., 1804-17], 8:123), where he said:

The universal practice of forbearing to seize and confiscate debts and credits, the principle universally received, that the right to them revives on the restoration of peace, would seem to prove that war is not an absolute confiscation of this property, but simply confers the right of confiscation. Between debts contracted under the faith of laws, and property acquired in the course of trade, on the faith of the same laws, reason draws no distinction; and although, in practice, vessels, with their cargoes, found in port, at the declaration of war, may have been seized, it is not believed that modern usage would sanction the seizure of the goods of an enemy on land, which were acquired in peace, in the course of trade.

It should be observed in this connection that further on in his opinion, Mr. Chief Justice Marshall, after calling attention to the fact that the rule laid down by Vattel covered, as expressed, the property of those only who are personally within the territory at the commencement of hostilities, yet the great Chief Justice declared that no reason can "be perceived, for maintaining that the public faith is more entirely pledged for the security of property trusted in the territory of a nation in time of peace, if it be accompanied by its owner, than if it be confided to the care of others" (Cranch, 8:125).

Policy of United States

Yielding to national impulses which finally led to the crystallization of the principles and policies so stated by Marshall, the United States by the very first treaty which it ever made with any foreign power, the treaty of February 6, 1778, between "The Most Christian King" of France, and "The Thirteen United States of North America," provided in its Article XX—

For the better promoting of commerce on both sides, it is agreed that if a war shall break out between the said two nations, six months after the proclamation of war shall be allowed to the merchants in the cities and towns where they live for selling and transporting their goods and merchandise; and if anything be taken from them, or any injury be done them within that term by either party, or the people or subjects of either, full satisfaction shall be made for the same. (U.S. Department of State, *Treaties and Conventions between the United States and Other Powers since July 4, 1776* [Washington, D.C., 1889], 302)

From time to time during the next full century following this first treaty—indeed, down to a time when apparently it was no longer considered necessary to embody such a provision in separate treaties, because the principle was presumed to be an established part of the law of nations—the United States continued to make treaties stipulating the safety of private property of the nationals of the one party in the territories of the other party in times of war.

It is interesting to note the periods during which the United

States seemingly either made effort to negotiate treaties of this sort or yielded to the desires of other powers to make such treaties.

Prior to 1780 we made but one treaty of this sort, namely, that with France in 1778. During the period 1780 to 1790 we made three such treaties—one with the Netherlands in 1782, one with Sweden in 1783, and one with Prussia in 1785. This treaty with Prussia, as embodied in the treaty of 1799 with that same power, will be considered in extenso later.

During the period 1790 to 1800 the United States negotiated five treaties of this kind, as follows: With Great Britain in 1794, with Spain and Algiers in 1795, with Tunis in 1797, and with Prussia in 1799.

It is of interest to observe that during this period, that is, on July 6, 1798 (*Statutes at Large of the United States of America, 1789-1873,* 17 vols., 1:577; hereafter referred to as *Statutes*), Congress passed an act embodying these general principles. The provisions of this act will be discussed later.

No further treaties of this sort appear to have been made by the United States for the next 20 years, but from 1820 to 1830 two such treaties were made, one with Central America in 1825 and one with Brazil in 1828. The following decade, 1830 to 1840, saw five such treaties negotiated and ratified, namely, that with Mexico of 1831; with Morocco, with Venezuela, with Peru-Bolivia in 1836; and with Ecuador in 1839. The next 10 years—1840 to 1849—saw the negotiation of three treaties with such provisions, as follows: With New Granada in 1846, with Mexico in 1848, and with Guatemala in 1849. During the next 10-year period, the United States negotiated more of such treaties than it has ever negotiated in any equal period of its history, provisions of this sort being negotiated in seven treaties as follows: With Salvador in 1850, with Peru and with Costa Rica in 1851, with Argentina in 1853, with the two Sicilies in 1855, with Bolivia in 1858, and with Paraguay in 1859.

In the next decade (1860 to 1870), a period which covered our own Civil War—during the operations of which it was found necessary to provide some restraints upon aliens, but with reference rather to their persons than to their property—four treaties were negotiated containing stipulations governing this general matter—with Haiti and with Honduras in 1864, and with Nicaragua and San Domingo in 1867.

In the period 1870 to 1880 three treaties embodying such provisions were negotiated, one each with Salvador and with Peru in 1870 and one with Italy in 1871.

It would appear that the last treaty containing a provision of this sort which has been negotiated by the United States was that negotiated in 1887 with Peru.

Certain broad aspects of these treaty provisions are worthy of consideration as showing the trend of modern thought and practice on this general subject prior to the great reversion to earlier practices during the World War.

It may be stated in a preliminary way that the provisions of practically all the treaties to which reference has been made covered not only the disposition of property owned by enemy aliens and found within our jurisdiction but also the consideration and treatment to be given to enemy persons who might be within our territory during times of war. For present purposes, however, we may disregard those provisions which have to do solely with the treatment of enemy persons found in our jurisdiction at the outbreak of war, because the treatment of enemy persons is not involved in the present discussion.

Certain features of the stipulation in our treaty with France in 1778 are worthy of note. In the first place, the privileges stipulated for by its provisions related only to merchants, and of all merchants it covered only those who lived in "cities and towns." The treaty stipulation did not protect merchants, if any there were, who might live in places other than cities or towns; nor did it protect any persons whoever or wherever they might be and whatsoever their vocation or occupation who were not merchants.

In the next place, the undertaking did not cover property of all sorts and descriptions, but only "goods and merchandises." For example, it did not cover debts nor moneys nor securities; that is, shares of stock and like intangibles. It will, moreover, be recalled that only six months "after the proclamation of war" were allowed for the "selling and transporting" of the goods and merchandises covered by the treaty. Furthermore, while the treaty stipulation provides "for full satisfaction" for any injury done to the merchants who fall within the purview of the treaty, yet there is no express stipulation that such merchants might themselves retire from the country, and obviously there is no stipulation either for retirement or for protection of persons or their property other than those who fall within the limited class described.

However, later treaties tended to correct these defects. The privileges and protection guaranteed by these treaties were variously expressed as to verbiage. A rough analysis and classification of these pertinent provisions will be of some value as showing the scope and character of the stipulations.

Sometimes the privilege was, as with France, for selling and transporting goods and merchandises (France, 1778); or it was to transport or sell effects and goods (Netherlands, 1782); or to carry off or sell effects or movables (Sweden, 1783); or to carry off all their effects (Prussia, 1785); or to collect and transport goods and merchandise (Spain, 1795); or to arrange affairs and withdraw themselves and property (Tunis, 1797); or to arrange their business and transport their effects (Central America, 1825; Brazil, 1828; Ecuador, 1839; Guatemala, 1849; Salvador, 1850; Italy, 1871); or to arrange their business, dispose of their effects, and transport them wherever they please (Mexico, 1831); or to dispose of their effects and retire with their property (Morocco, 1836); or to wind up accounts and dispose of their property (Costa Rica, 1851); or to arrange and settle their affairs and remove with their families, effects, and property (Peru, 1851; Peru, 1887); or to withdraw with all their effects and to carry away, send away, or sell them (two Sicilies, 1855; Haiti, 1864; San Domingo, 1867); or to liquidate accounts and dispose of goods (Paraguay, 1859); or to wind up accounts and dispose of properties (Honduras, 1864; Nicaragua, 1867).

It will be noted that many of these treaty provisions appear to cover personal property only, while others are sufficiently broad to cover real property. An examination of the treaties will also show that these provisions were not generally intended to embrace money, shares of stock, bonds, and other securities which were frequently covered by a further specific treaty provision, or else left without special consideration.

The time after which these operations might be carried out was variously stated. Sometimes the period began with the proclamation of war (France, 1778; Sweden, 1783; Tunis, 1797; San Domingo, 1867); or with the breaking out of war (Netherlands, 1782; Spain, 1795; Algiers, 1795; Mexico, 1831; Morocco, 1836; Mexico, 1858; Argentina, 1853); or when war should arise (Prussia, 1799); or when the countries should be engaged in war with each other (Central America, 1825; Brazil, 1828; Venezuela, 1836; Peru-

243

Bolivia, 1836; Ecuador, 1839; New Granada, 1846; Guatemala, 1849; Salvador, 1850; Peru, 1851; Sicilies, 1855; Bolivia, 1858; Haiti, 1864; Peru, 1870; Italy, 1871; Peru, 1887); or when any rupture should unfortunately take place between the two high contracting parties (Costa Rica, 1851; Paraguay, 1859; Honduras, 1864; Nicaragua, 1867; Salvador, 1870).

Various periods of time within which the privileges stipulated might be exercised were provided for. Frequently the same treaty would stipulate different periods for different individuals, depending upon the place of residence or business of such individuals.

At times it would be six months from the time specified for those living in the coasts and parts (Brazil, 1828; Venezuela, 1836; Ecuador, 1839; New Granada, 1846; Guatemala, 1849; Salvador, 1850; Bolivia, 1858; Italy, 1871), or six months from the coasts (Mexico, 1831; Mexico, 1848; Costa Rica, 1851; Honduras, 1864; Nicaragua, 1867; Salvador, 1870).

Sometimes nine months were given (Sweden, 1783; Prussia, 1785; and Morocco, 1836). Sometimes it was stated in the alternative as nine months from the declaration of war or the date of rupture (Netherlands, 1782); or one year from the declaration of war (Spain, 1795; Tunis, 1797). Where a distinction was made between withdrawal or removal from coasts and ports on the one side and the interior of the country on the other, a period of one year was usually given for removal from the interior places (Brazil, 1828; Mexico, 1831; Venezuela, 1836; Ecuador, 1839; New Granada, 1846; Mexico, 1848; Guatemala, 1849; Salvador, 1850; Costa Rica, 1851; Bolivia, 1858; Honduras, 1864; Nicaragua, 1867; Salvador, 1870; and Italy, 1871).

As already pointed out, the earliest treaty of this kind which the United States made related only to merchants; other citizens were left unprotected. But the inclusion of others than merchants within the privileged classes began very early. In the second treaty of this sort which we negotiated—that with the Netherlands of 1782—the provisions covered "the subjects on each side;" that is, all of them, and that stipulation was followed in our treaties with Sweden, 1783; Tunis, 1797; and Morocco, 1836. The same result was reached under the description "citizens" in the treaty with Algiers in 1795; with Peru-Bolivia, 1836; with Costa Rica, 1851; with Honduras, 1864; with Nicaragua, 1867; and with Salvador, 1870. Sometimes the language used was merchants and other inhabitants (two Sicilies, 1855), or merchants and other citizens and inhabitants (San Domingo, 1867). But in many treaties the stipulation was made to refer to merchants only (Prussia, 1785, 1799; Spain, 1795; Central America, 1825; Mexico, 1831; Venezuela, 1836; Ecuador, 1839; New Granada, 1846; Mexico, 1848; Guatemala, 1849; Salvador, 1850; Bolivia, 1858; and Italy, 1871).

With reference to those who were withdrawing, it was sometimes stipulated that they should have passports for the time necessary to return to their own country, which passports were to serve as safe-conducts (Sweden, 1783; two Sicilies, 1855; Haiti, 1864; San Domingo, 1867). In the second treaty of this sort which we negotiated (Netherlands, 1782) it was stipulated that there should be given to the persons affected and to their vessels and to their effects which they were carrying away, passports and safe-conducts for the nearest ports (Netherlands, 1782); and it is a very general provision of these treaties that those departing shall have for themselves and for their goods, safe-conduct (Central America, 1825; Brazil, 1828; Mexico, 1831; Venezuela, 1836; Salvador, 1850; Costa Rica, 1851; Bolivia, 1858; Paraguay, 1859; Honduras, 1864; Nicaragua, 1867; Salvador, 1870; Peru, 1870; and Italy, 1871).

Some treaties contain specific provision that there should be no arrest of the persons nor property of these enemy aliens during the period of grace allotted to them (Netherlands, 1782). At other times it has been stipulated that no property should be confiscated or sequestered during this period of grace (two Sicilies, 1855).

But all the foregoing relates to the right of enemy aliens to withdraw with their property after war has begun between the United States and the other contracting power. This in itself was a real advance over the strict rigor of the early law. But the great gain which was made by this whole series of treaties consisted not in these stipulations for a period of grace during which time the specified classes of enemy aliens might retire with their property and effects. The great gain is to be found in the stipulations of these treaties which provided that certain enemy aliens might remain in the country during the war and carry on their business as usual. Sometimes the provision was that all but merchants might so remain (Central America, 1825; Brazil, 1828; Mexico, 1831; Venezuela, 1836; Ecuador, 1839; New Granada, 1846; Guatemala, 1849; Bolivia, 1858). At other times certain specified classes—which frequently included as a practical matter all but merchants—were to be permitted to remain and carry on their ordinary affairs (Prussia, 1785, 1799; Italy, 1871).

In some cases the security of the property of enemy aliens was provided for, whether such property was in the hands of the aliens themselves or had been entrusted to others (Paraguay, 1859; Honduras, 1864; Nicaragua, 1867; and Salvador, 1870).

In the great majority of cases, however, it was provided that enemy aliens might remain in the country and carry on their business until "their particular conduct shall cause them to forfeit this protection" (Central America, 1825); or, as it came to be later expressed, "so long as they conduct themselves peaceably and properly, and commit no offense against the laws" (Peru, 1851, 1870, 1887; Peru-Bolivia, 1836); or "so long as they behave peacefully and commit no offense against the laws" (Costa Rica, 1851; Argentina, 1853; Paraguay, 1859; Honduras, 1864; Nicaragua, 1867; Salvador, 1870); or "so long as they conduct themselves peaceably and do not commit any offense against the laws" (Mexico, 1831); or "unless their particular conduct shall cause them to forfeit this protection" (Venezuela, 1836; Ecuador, 1839; New Granada, 1846; Guatemala, 1849).

Thus in a considerable proportion of the treaties it was provided that all enemy aliens might remain in the country and continue their business as usual in times of war, so long as they observed the laws of the country, or in other words rendered to the local sovereign that temporary allegiance to which he was entitled.

The foregoing provisions covered property generally, but in many of these treaties special provisions were inserted specifically covering debts, moneys, and securities. One of the first of these treaties was the Jay treaty with Great Britain of 1794, which stipulated in Article X that—

Neither the debts due from individuals of the one nation to individuals of the other, nor shares, nor moneys, which they may have in the public funds, or in the public or private banks, shall ever in any event of war or national differences be sequestered or confiscated.

It is significant that this treaty also stated the reason for this stipulation. It declared it was "unjust and impolitic that debts and engagements contracted and made by individuals, having confidence in each other and in their respective governments, should ever be destroyed or impaired by national authority on account of national differences and discontent." That reason is as sound to-day as it was the day it was written; and it has been sound ever since the day it was penned.

Similar undertakings as to debts, shares, and public moneys are to be found in very many other treaties (Brazil, 1828; Venezuela, 1836; Peru-Bolivia, 1836; Ecuador, 1839; New Granada, 1846; Guatemala, 1849; Salvador, 1850; Peru, 1851; Costa Rica, 1851; Bolivia, 1858; Haiti, 1864; Honduras, 1864; Nicaragua, 1867; Salvador, 1870; Peru, 1870; and Peru, 1887).

It must not be overlooked that all these provisions related to the alien property itself, and they were in no way limited with reference to the domicile of the alien owner. Indeed it is evident from the nature of the property described, particularly when the incidents of trade and commerce are considered, that its alien owners of this property would, in many cases at least, be domiciled in a foreign country.

It is curious to observe that, aside from "shares in the public fund," the treaty of San Domingo of 1867 did not apparently cover ordinary securities such as shares of stock in corporations.

Another curious variation of the rule of the treaties above enumerated as to debts, etc., is to be found in the treaty of 1855 with the two Sicilies, which merely relieved from sequestration or confiscation during the period of grace allowed for removal.

Another provision of far-reaching importance in certain of these treaties was a blanket stipulation which provided that no property whatsoever should be sequestered or confiscated (Peru, 1851; Costa Rica, 1851; Argentina, 1853; Haiti, 1864; Peru, 1870). And this provision was found in treaties which in other articles provided for the withdrawal of enemy persons and the removal of their property.

Thus for a period of more than 100 years—the great formative period of our history—and beginning with the first treaty this people ever made, the treaty-making power of the United States—the President and the Senate—have carried out a policy that the property of enemy aliens should be safeguarded and protected, whether belonging to enemy aliens domiciled in this country or in a foreign country. We stood in this respect, as in many others, in the vanguard of the nations in the conduct of our international relations.

So much for the policy of this Nation as it was expressed in treaties, a policy which for more than 100 years found expression in the work of the treaty-making power—the Federal Executive and the Senate of the United States.

Legislative Policy of the United States

But, as already indicated, Congress itself took occasion also, at a very early date, to commit itself by statute to the same general principles, and that, too, at a time when war appeared imminent between ourselves and that nation, towards whom we had theretofore looked as our closest friend and with whom we had made our earliest treaty. The incident is worth narrating in some detail.

France was in the midst of the great Napoleonic wars, with almost all Europe arrayed against her. The decrees of Napoleon and the orders in council of Great Britain had resulted in great injury to our commerce. France had sought to make use of our ports in connection with her prizes taken on the high seas. The United States had announced the great fundamentals of the doctrines of neutrality which in the years to come were to be not only our safety but also our glory. France regarded these rules of neutrality and the practices thereunder as violative of her treaty rights and privileges. By a decree of March 2, 1797, the French Directory declared that all enemies' property and all property "not sufficiently ascertained to be neutral, conveyed under neutral flags, shall be confiscated;" that the contraband list should be increased by adding articles used in arming and equipping vessels; that Americans accepting commissions from the enemies of France or serving as seamen in enemies' vessels should be treated as pirates; and that every American vessel should be deemed good prize which should not have on board a crew list in the form prescribed by the model annexed to the treaty of amity and commerce between the United States and France of 1778.

When this decree came into effect, American vessels had for years been carrying documents in the form prescribed by Congress, and no other documents had been required by France, though the war had been in progress for four years. This decree, with other regulations put into force, amounted, when carried out, to a general and summary confiscation of all American vessels. It was at this time that the X, Y, Z correspondence took place between our plenipotentiaries in France and French agents, a correspondence that carried insulting suggestions that we purchase peace with France by making to her a loan and by providing 1,200,000 livres as a douceur—a sweetener of the wounded sensibilities of two members of the French Directory.

Later, in the early part of 1798, new decrees were issued by the Directory which provided that "all vessels found at sea loaded in whole or in part with merchandise produced in England or her possessions should be good prize," irrespective of the nationality of the owner of the goods or the merchandise.

Meanwhile the representatives of the United States at Paris had been refused recognition by the French Directory. They had been treated with such scant courtesy as to amount to insult. They had been forced, by virtue of the indirect negotiations which were attempted with them, to inform the French intermediaries that they considered it degrading to their country to carry on further indirect intercourse. Finally driven to the step by the suggestion from the Directory that it was disposed to deal only with one of the representatives whom they regarded as more amenable than the others, two of the representatives, Pinckney and Marshall, the latter afterwards our great Chief Justice, left Paris, and Marshall returned to the United States. It was in this situation that the Congress of the United States began to prepare for war with France by passing measures providing for the suspension of commercial intercourse between the United States and France, for increasing the naval armament, for the raising of a provisional army, for the defending of commercial vessels of the United States against French depredations, for the protection of commerce and coasts of the United States, and for enabling the President to borrow money. Finally, on the 7th of July, 1798, an act was passed which declared our treaties with France to be no longer obligatory on the Government or citizens of the United States. This statute reads:

Whereas the treaties concluded between the United States and France have been repeatedly violated on the part of the French Government; and the just claims of the United States for reparation of the injuries so committed have been refused, and their attempts to negotiate an amicable adjustment of all complaints between the two nations, have been repelled with indignity; and

Whereas under authority of the French Government, there is yet pursued against the United States a system of predatory violence, infracting the said treaties, and hostile to the rights of a free and independent nation:

Be it enacted by the Senate and House of Representatives of the United States of America

in Congress assembled, That the United States are of right freed and exonerated from the stipulations of the treaties, and of the consular convention, heretofore concluded between the United States and France; and that the same shall not henceforth be regarded as legally obligatory on the Government or citizens of the United States. (*Statutes,* 1:578)

But Congress was not forgetful at that time of stress of the great fundamental principles which it considered essential to obtain between nations in time of war. Accordingly, pursuant to the humane policies which up to that time had been incorporated in treaties with France (1778), Netherlands (1782), Sweden (1783), Prussia (1785), Great Britain (1794), Spain (1795), Algiers (1795), and Tunis (1797), Congress, on the day preceding the passage of this law, had, in anticipation of this action, passed another act which provided that in case of war or actual or threatened invasion, the President should make a proclamation thereof whereupon "all natives, citizens, denizens, or subjects of the hostile nation or government, being males of the age of 14 years and upwards, who shall be within the United States, and not actually naturalized, shall be liable to be apprehended, restrained, secured and removed, as alien enemies (*Statutes,* 1:577).

Then for the very purpose of giving to the French who might be resident in this country the protection to which they were entitled under the treaty which Congress was intending to abrogate, a proviso was inserted in the act which stipulated—

That aliens resident within the United States, who shall become liable as enemies, in the manner aforesaid, and who shall not be chargeable with actual hostility, or other crime against the public safety, shall be allowed, for the recovery, disposal, and removal of their goods and effects, and for their departure, the full time which is, or shall be stipulated by any treaty, where any shall have been between the United States and the hostile nation or government of which they shall be natives, citizens, denizens, or subjects; and where no such treaty shall have existed, the President of the United States may ascertain and declare such reasonable time as may be consistent with the public safety, and according to the dictates of humanity and national hospitality. (*Statutes,* 1:577)

Thus, even though the action of France compelled us to declare as of no further force the treaties between the two countries, yet the people of the United States by their Congress declared that Frenchmen in the United States should have the rights specified for them by treaty in this respect.

These provisions, both for the removal of alien enemies and specifying the time for removal, were carried down through our laws and finally appeared as sections 4067 and 4068 of the Revised Statutes of the United States. These provisions were the law of the land when we declared war against Germany on April 6, 1917, and continued to be the law until October 6, 1917, when the trading with the enemy act was passed.

With the foregoing facts in mind, we are in a position to consider a little more in detail the rights which the Germans in this country had at the outbreak of the war, and, indeed, at the time of the passage of the trading with the enemy act, on the assumption that the treaty with Prussia of 1799 was operative as between the United States and Prussia. It is worth while to look briefly at the negotiations attending the making of that treaty, as showing the extent to which we were responsible for the policy which it embodied.

American-Prussian Treaty

On February 19, 1784, Baron de Thulemeier, envoy extraordinary of Frederick the Great of Prussia to the Netherlands sovereigns, called upon John Adams, then residing at The Hague and informed Adams (as Adams reported to his Government)—

That the King, (that is, Frederick the Great), who honored him with a personal correspondence and was acquainted with my character, had directed him to make me a visit, and to say to me that as his subjects had occasion for our tobacco and some other things, and as we had occasion for Silesia linens and some other productions of his dominions, he thought an arrangement might be made between his crown and the United States which would be beneficial to both. (U.S. Department of State, *Papers Relating to Foreign Affairs (Diplomatic Correspondence)* [Washington, D.C., 1861-68], 1:435; hereafter referred to as *Dip. Cor.*)

Adams replied that he "could do nothing but in concurrence with Mr. Franklin and Mr. Jay, who were at Paris," but that he thought he "could answer for the good disposition of those ministers as well as my own, for forming an arrangement between the two powers which might be beneficial to both" (*Dip. Cor.*, 1:435, 436).

On March 14, Adams, in the meanwhile having taken the matter up with Franklin and Jay, and having communicated to Baron de Thulemeier the expressed disposition of those gentlemen to negotiate a draft of a treaty, received from Thulemeier a letter in which it was stated that Frederick acquiesced in the suggestion made by Adams that they take the treaty with Sweden of 1783 as a basis for discussion.

Some time in April (prior to April 10) Thulemeier transmitted "in original" a "Project of a treaty of amity and commerce between His Majesty the King of Prussia, and the United States of North America" (*Dip. Cor.*, 1:443).

On June 7, John Adams returned to Baron de Thulemeier some observations upon this "project" which the baron had sent to him (*Dip. Cor.*, 1:458).

It is to be noted for our present purposes that while the "project" contained many suggestions as to the conduct of the parties in case of war between either of them and another party, it contained no stipulations relating to the situation which should arise in case of war between the signatories themselves.

On June 3, 1784, Congress issued a joint commission to John Adams, Benjamin Franklin, and Thomas Jefferson, granting to them, or a majority of them, plenary power to negotiate and conclude treaties with various European courts, among them that of His Prussian Majesty (*Dip. Cor.*, 1:501).

On September 9, Messrs. Adams, Franklin, and Jefferson addressed to Baron de Thulemeier at The Hague a communication in which they advised him of the receipt of their commission in due form and notifying him that they were "ready to enter on the negotiations, and to reconsider and complete the plan of a treaty which has already been transmitted by your excellency to your court, whenever a full power from His Prussian Majesty shall appear for that purpose" (*Dip. Cor.*, 1:505).

On October 5, Baron de Thulemeier transmitted to the American commissioners a copy of the full powers which had been sent to him by his sovereign, stated his preparedness to enter immediately upon negotiations, and asked that the commissioners communicate to him their ideas on the manner in which they desired to proceed (*Dip. Cor.*, 1:518).

On November 10, the commissioners forwarded to Baron de Thulemeier a "counter project of a treaty of amity and commerce between His Majesty the King of Prussia and the United States of America." Article XXIII of which and the last sentence of Article XXIV of which read as follows:

Article XXIII. If war should arise between the two contracting parties, the merchants of either country then residing in the other shall be allowed to remain nine months to collect their debts and settle their affairs, and may depart freely, carrying all of their effects without molestation or hindrance; and all women and children, scholars of every faculty, cultivators of the earth, artisans, manufacturers, and fishermen, unarmed and inhabiting unfortified towns, villages, or places, whose occupations are for the common subsistence and benefit of mankind, shall be allowed to continue their respective employments, and shall not be molested in their persons, nor shall their houses or goods be burnt or otherwise destroyed, nor their fields wasted by the armed force of the enemy, into whose power, by the events of war, they may happen to fall; but if anything is necessary to be taken from them for the use of such armed force, the same shall be paid for at a reasonable price; and all merchant and trading vessels employed in exchanging the products of different places, and thereby rendering the necessaries, conveniences, and comforts of human life more easy to be obtained and more general, shall be allowed to pass free and unmolested; and neither of the contracting powers shall grant or issue any commission to any private armed vessels empowering them to take or destroy such trading vessels, or interrupt such commerce.

* * *

And it is declared that neither the pretense that war dissolves all treaties, nor any other whatever shall be considered as annulling or suspending this and the next preceding article, but, on the contrary, that the state of war is precisely that for which they are provided, and during which they are to be as sacredly observed as the most acknowledged articles in the law of nature and nations. (*Dip. Cor.*, 1:520, 526-28)

In the commissioners' letter (*Dip. Cor.*, 1:531) submitting this "counter project," they noted that they added two new articles, the XIII and the XXIII. They seem also to have added a new article numbered XXIV. With reference to Article XXIII, they submitted a supporting memorandum giving the reasons why the article was suggested. This memorandum contains so much of sound sense, of vision, and of far-reaching statesmanlike policy, that it is worth quoting here in full:

By the original law of nations, war and extirpation were the punishment of injury; humanizing by degrees, it admitted slavery instead of death; a further step was the exchange of prisoners instead of slavery; another to respect more the property of private persons under conquest and be content with acquired dominion. Why should not this law of nations go on improving? Ages have intervened between its several steps; but as knowledge of late increases rapidly, why should not those steps be quickened? Why should it not be agreed to as the future law of nations that in any war hereafter the following descriptions of men should be undisturbed, have the protection of both sides, and be permitted to follow their employments in surety, viz.:

First. Cultivators of the earth, because they labor for the subsistence of mankind.

Second. Fishermen, for the same reason.

Third. Merchants and traders in unarmed ships, who accommodate different nations by communicating and exchanging the necessaries and conveniences of life.

Fourth. Artists and mechanics inhabiting and working in open towns.

It is hardly necessary to add that the hospitals of enemies should be unmolested; they ought to be assisted.

It is for the interest of humanity in general that the occasions of war, and the inducements to it, should be diminished.

If rapine is abolished, one of the encouragements to war is taken away, and peace therefore more likely to continue and be lasting.

The practice of robbing merchants on the high seas, a remnant of the ancient piracy, though it may be accidentally beneficial to particular persons, is far from being profitable to all engaged in it or to the nation that authorizes it. In the beginning of a war some rich ships, not upon their guard, are surprised and taken. This encourages the first adventurers to fit out more armed vessels, and many others to do the same, but the enemy, at the same time, become more careful, arm their merchant ships better, and render them not so easy to be taken; they go also more under the protection of convoys. Thus, while the privateers to take them are multiplied, the vessels subject to be taken and the chances of profit are diminished, so that many others are made wherein the expenses overgo the gains, as it is the case in other lotteries; though individuals have got the prizes, the mass of adventurers are losers, the whole expense of fitting out all the privateers during a war being much greater than the whole amount of goods taken. Then there is the national loss of all the labor of so many men, during the time they have been employed in robbing, who, besides, spend what they get in riot, drunkenness, debauchery, lose their habits of industry, and rarely fit for any sober business after a peace, and serve only to increase the number of highwaymen and housebreakers. Even the undertakers who have been fortunate are, by sudden wealth, led into expensive living, the habit of which continues when the means of supporting it cease, and finally ruins them. A just punishment for their having wantonly and unfeelingly ruined many honest, innocent traders and their families, whose substance was employed in serving the common interests of mankind. (*Dip. Cor.*, 1:532)

These articles from the counter project which are quoted above were embodied with slight verbal alterations (which somewhat enlarge their meaning and scope) in the final treaty which was put into force and effect by the exchange of ratification in October, 1786.

This treaty expired by its own limitations in October, 1796. The two countries, however, concluded a new treaty on July 11, 1799 (proclaimed and effective November 4, 1800), which reembodied as Article XXIII the stipulations of Article XXIII of the treaty of 1785, omitting the last sentence of that article. This new treaty also reembodied the provisions of Article XXIV which have been quoted.

This treaty of 1799 expired by its own limitations on June 22, 1810, but a new treaty of commerce and navigation was concluded May 1, 1828 (proclaimed and effective March 14, 1829), by Article XII, of which article the XIII to XXIV, inclusive, of the treaty of 1799 (with certain exceptions not necessary here to note) were revived "with the same force and virtue as if they made part of the text of the present treaty."

This was the treaty in force and these were the stipulations which we were under treaty obligation to observe in our dealings with German subjects and their property resident in the United States at the outbreak of our war with Germany on April 6, 1917.

It is true that, prior to our entry into the war, certain differences had arisen between the United States and Germany regarding the interpretation of other articles of the treaty of 1799, particularly in connection with the William Fry and Appam cases, but so far as the accessible public records go it does not appear that the disputes which the two countries had regarding differences of interpretation of certain provisions of the treaty had ever been considered to abrogate or annul the treaty.

Thus we entered the war with Germany with a distinct and positive agreement that—

the merchants of either country then residing in the other shall be allowed to remain nine months to collect their debts and settle their affairs, and may depart freely, carrying off all their effects without molestation or hindrance; and all women and children, scholars of every faculty, cultivators of the earth, artisans, manufacturers, and fishermen, unarmed and inhabiting unfortified towns, villages, or places, and in general all others whose occupations are for the common subsistence and benefit of mankind, shall be allowed to continue their respective employments, and shall not be molested in their persons, nor shall their houses or goods be burnt or otherwise destroyed, nor their fields wasted by the armed force of the enemy, into whose power by the events of war they may happen to fall; but if anything is necessary to be taken from them for the use of such armed force, the same shall be paid for at a reasonable price. (William M. Malloy, *Treaties, Conventions, International Acts, Protocols, and Agreements between the United States of America and Other Powers, 1776-1909*, 2 vols. [Washington, D.C., 1910], 2:1494)

To make the meaning of this provision and its permanency perfectly clear, it was provided in Article XXIV of the same treaty, which article dealt generally with the treatment which should be accorded to the respective prisoners of war, that—

> And it is declared, that neither the pretense that war dissolves all treaties, nor any other whatever, shall be considered as annulling or suspending this and the next preceding article; but, on the contrary, that the state of war is precisely that for which they are provided, and during which they are to be as sacredly observed as the most acknowledged article in the law of nature and nations. (Malloy, 2:1495)

American Action in World War

In the face of these provisions and in direct opposition thereto—unexcused, as it seems, by any previous legislation on the part of Germany against American citizens resident in Germany that might justify our own action as a matter of retaliation—Congress passed on October 6, 1917, the trading with the enemy act, which provided for the taking over of all German-owned property in the United States.

Looking at that action of ours in the perspective of almost a decade, and having in mind the situation in which Germany was at that time placed—her navy ineffective and largely inoperative, her coasts in a condition equal to that which would have resulted from a wholly and legally effective blockade, she at war with practically all of the great powers of the earth with whom she was not allied, with, therefore, no neutral markets which could have absorbed the great German investments in the United States in any such way as would have made those investments available to Germany—it is difficult to perceive the sound, justifying reasons which actuated Congress in adopting such a course. Many supported the measure, not because they believed either in its wisdom or in its efficacy but because they were unwilling to deny to those responsible for the conduct of the war any power such persons deemed necessary to win the war. The American people accepted the measure in the same spirit. It may conceivably be that the explanation of the state of mind which lay behind the proposal for the action is to be found in a contagious European hysteria with which we had become infected, as well as in that curious psychological phenomenon which also infected many in the Nation and which, by a half-conscious, self-deprecating admission of inexperience and inferiority, led to the doing in the United States of many things merely because they were done in Europe, sight being entirely lost of the great and fundamental difference which existed between the position of the United States in this conflict and the position of France, Italy, and Great Britain, who were really within the zone of actual military operation. Thus, in what might be termed a national brainstorm, we abandoned a century and a third of active policy and practice, and joined with war-ridden Europe in turning back for almost a third of a millennium the clock of progress towards humanizing the savagery and suffering of war.

How firmly fixed the great nations of the earth supposed the principle to be that resident alien enemies should not be molested in their persons or in their property at the outbreak of war may be gauged by the fact that neither in the First Hague Conference of 1899, nor in the Second Hague Conference of 1907 did this question appear for serious discussion, notwithstanding both conferences considered and drafted conventions dealing with the opening of hostilities and respecting the laws of customs of war on land. It is a curious fact that seemingly the necessity of making provision covering this subject did not enter the minds of the statesmen of any of the powers, great or small, present at these conferences. There is not one stipulation in either of the conventions mentioned which covers this subject either in the high-sounding preambles of these conventions or in the positive prescriptions thereof. That they were not, however, overlooking the rights of noncombatant enemies is abundantly evidenced by the provisions which provide, in section 3 of Chapter V of the conventions respecting the laws and customs of war on land (art. 46), that—

Family honor and rights, the lives of persons, and private property, as well as religious convictions and practice, must be respected.

Private property can not be confiscated.

Furthermore, this feeling had gone so far that private enemy property within the jurisdiction of the other belligerent should not be confiscated at the outbreak of hostilities, that the sixth convention signed at The Hague in 1907—relating to the status of enemy merchant ships at the outbreak of hostilities—provided that enemy merchant ships in enemy ports at the commencement of hostilities—

should be allowed to depart freely, either immediately, or after a reasonable number of days of grace, and to proceed, after being furnished with a pass, direct to its port of destination or any other port indicated. The same rule should apply in the case of a ship which has left its last port of departure before the commencement of the war and entered a port belonging to the enemy while still ignorant that hostilities had broken out.

This same convention contained other provisions mitigating the rigor of the strict laws of war as those laws had come down to us from earlier centuries.

This was the state of international law and custom, the condition of mind of the nations of the earth, when the World War began its course of devastation and ruin. It would be a profitless task to attempt to trace out the causes which led Europe to retreat from the advanced ground of humanity and Christianity which it then occupied, and to fall back upon the outgrown, almost forgotten, barbarism of past centuries. The wisest thought to-day appears to recognize that the retreat was an irreparable error. One may be reasonably confident that history will censure it without measure. There came from it no gain, even temporary, that was in any proper degree commensurate with the loss.

But for us in America, unthreatened as was Europe, this retreat without justifiable cause approached the proportions of a national disaster. It falsified a century and a third of unvarying policy, it repudiated a principle which we announced in our very first contact with foreign nations, and which we embodied in congressional act at the very first opportunity that presented.

This retreat showed the ease with which private property might be seized in times of trouble; it carried with it the sinister suggestion that confiscation might, if desired, be readily accomplished. These are dangerous ideas in the present state of world thought.

Looking in retrospect, there is no obvious reason for our action beyond the mental panic into which we were thrown by the threat of German militarism, and the further reason, already suggested, of an unexplainable disposition slavishly and childishly to imitate every measure taken by our associates in arms.

But now that recovery has come from the panic, now that we can once more measurably act and do as we feel our own welfare demands, it seems time to about face and reoccupy the ground we needlessly forsook. The United States ought in all propriety immediately to return this property to those from whom we took it and from whom we have already withheld it far, far too long.

The United States ought again to make operative in our dealings with aliens the principles announced by Hamilton, when, discussing the provision of the Jay treaty of 1794 with reference to the property of enemy aliens—a provision already quoted—he said:

No power of language at my command can express the abhorrence I feel at the idea of violating the property of individuals, which, in an authorized intercourse, in time of peace, had been confided to the faith of our Government and laws, on account of controversies between nation and nation. In my view, every moral and every political sentiment unite to consign it to execration. [source not found]

The Atomic Bomb: "With What Measure—"

8 August 1945

On 6 August 1945 the atomic bomb was dropped on Hiroshima; two days later JRC drafted this brief memorandum. How he planned to use it is unknown, but at the top of both the original and carbon typed copies is the note, "Not Used." Box 232, Folder 1, JRCP.

If the press reports may be relied upon, then we have reached another level in the eternal progress of man. The controlled freeing of the energy bound up in the atom constitutes a great, possibly an unequalled achievement. To the layman, at least, the possibilities envisaged by the discovery seem all but infinite. We appear to be entering a new era of development in the history of mankind. The divinity of the mind and soul of man is more and more unfolded as he goes forward and upward. God is permitting man more and more to conquer and make useful the great forces that operate and control the universe. As we reach in our march ahead, the outer boundary of things known, we push outward the horizon of human knowledge, and bring into view new landscapes with their fields of beauty and mystery and power. As we reach the farther sides of these, again the horizon will be pushed out, again new fields will greet our gaze,— and so on until we shall "become perfect even as our Father in Heaven is perfect" [*sic*—see Matt. 5:48].

But God reveals the truths of nature—His truths—that they

may be used for man's good and advancement. He has declared how precious are His children in His sight; He has said: "For behold, this is my work and my glory—to bring to pass the immortality and eternal life of man" (Pearl of Great Price; Moses 1:39).

He holds men responsible for the use they make of His truth. What he so gives for the good, the upbuilding, the salvation of men, is not intended for use in their destruction. His mercy, His kindness, His love for His children are infinite. "For God so loved the world, that he gave his only begotten Son, that whosoever believeth in him should not perish, but have everlasting life" (John 3:16).

Now, betraying the trust that God places in us when He gives us truth, we first use the great new discovery for maiming, killing, perhaps annihilating our fellowmen on a scale and in a manner never before witnessed among men. The awfulness of it so appalls us that we stand mute, all but paralyzed in the presence of our beginning conquest of one ultimate force of the universe.

The arguments invoked to justify us in this monumental perversion of this great new truth, are specious. We have refrained, obedient to the dictates of humanity and the laws of God, from poisoning wells and streams, from sowing bacteria to bring plagues, from using (it seems) dum-dum bullets, and from employing poison gas,—this latter restraint (it is said) by the direct command of the late President Roosevelt, who in this matter refused to follow the course suggested by his military advisers. The considerations which brought about the non-use of those weapons of destruction are equally potent against the atom bomb. There should be some things which human beings would not do to their fellows.

It will be said,—but this weapon will shorten the war and save the lives of our sons. So be it. But while we of this generation shall die, and our children, and so perhaps escape retribution, our posterity and the nation will live. This great discovery will become the common property of the world's peoples. Our allies probably already know it. Its use to kill will become the aim and practice of all nations. Sometime our children's children will have it turned against them, that they, too, may be exterminated, annihilated. When that time comes they will have no moral weapon against it, for we, their ancestors, will have cursed humanity by its first use; they may have no physical weapon to combat it. And humanity may be as depraved and Christian virtue as dead then as now. Our posterity must pay the penalty, to the last farthing.

Is it not time in the world for a curb to be placed upon the narrow, fiendish concepts of militarists, and their evil lusts and passions by which they are constantly driven to plan and carry out ever increasing woe, misery, destruction, and slaughter of the aged, the infirm, the sick, the crippled, of children, youth, and mothers, of babes at the breast? There are elements of good that must control the base in men, even in war. How long will their ears be deaf to the cries of the Christian conscience of the world, and to their own better instincts as men? How long will they challenge the eternal principle voiced by the Master two millenniums ago: "with what measure ye mete, it shall be measured to you again"? (Matt. 7:2). And again: "Put up again thy sword into his place: for all they that take the sword shall perish with the sword" (Matt. 26:52).

"Let Us Have Peace"

14 November 1947

JRC delivered this address at the annual meeting of the Life Insurance Agency Management Association, held at the Edgewater Beach Hotel in Chicago, Illinois. Box 237, Folder 2, JRCP.

Mr. Chairman, Gentlemen of the Convention:

You confer upon me a great honor by inviting me to speak before this great convention, which represents a vast body of missionaries preaching to the people of this country the gospel of caring for the bereaved widows and orphans who are amongst us. I cannot put out of my mind the words of the ancient apostle:

"Pure religion and undefiled before God and the Father is this, To visit the fatherless and widows in their affliction, and to keep himself unspotted from the world" (James 1:27).

Because what you need most for the success of your great missionary labor, what the nation and the whole world needs more than anything else, is peace, I have taken as my text today the famous dictum of General Grant: "Let us have peace." Whether our free enterprise and our constitutional government can survive another modern global war, no human mind can by itself, tell.

Appomattox came four years almost to the day from the fall of Fort Sumter. It marked the end of one of the bloodiest fratricidal wars of history. As always in such cases, passions had run high on both sides; both sides had been guilty of excesses; great amounts of property had been destroyed; the war cost a million men; there was mourning and suffering throughout the land. A seedbed had been prepared where hate could have been sown for recurring crops of war and misery during long generations to come.

Surrender at Appomattox

Having surrounded Lee's army, Grant, moved by lofty motives of humanity, opened negotiations to stop "further effusion of blood." Lee, moved with a like motive, accepted the approach. Grant suggested a desire for peace stating the one condition he would insist upon,—"that the men and officers surrendered shall be disqualified for taking up arms against the United States until properly exchanged." Lee responded stating his earnest desire for peace and asked if Grant's proposals would lead to that end. Grant answered he lacked authority for such negotiations, but assured Lee that he was equally desirous with Lee for peace, and so was the whole North.

Lee then proposed the surrender of his army. Grant, the victor, asked Lee, the vanquished, where he would like the interview between them to take place. Lee chose the house of McLean, in the village of Appomattox. Grant appeared dressed as were his private soldiers, save for shoulder straps that indicated his rank. Grant, seeking to cause as little humiliation as possible, began the interview with Lee by recalling their joint service in Mexico. They so conversed pleasantly for a short time, when Lee brought up the subject of their meeting, asking Grant for his terms. Grant repeated those he had already given, adding that all arms, ammunition, and supplies were to be treated as captured property.

Grant, still anxious to avoid Lee's unnecessary humiliation, began to talk in a pleasant vein about the prospects of peace; Lee again returned to the subject of the meeting and suggested the terms be submitted.

Grant then wrote out the formal proposals. As he came to the term covering arms, ammunition, and supplies, he glanced at the handsome sword Lee carried, and still urged by the desire to cause as little humiliation as possible, he added a provision that officers should retain their side arms, horses, and baggage. Grant finished the terms with the provision as to the parole of officers and men.

Lee read the terms and observed, "This will have a very happy effect upon my army."

Grant asked if Lee had any suggestions to offer as to the form of the terms. Lee observed that in his army cavalry men and artillerists owned their own horses and asked if they would be permitted to retain their horses. Grant said the terms did not cover this. Lee's face showing some anxiety, Grant said the subject was new to him, but, while the terms would stand as written, he would give orders that all men claiming horses would be permitted to take the animals to be used on their farms. To this generous, unrequested kindness by Grant, Lee observed: "This will have the best possible effect upon the men. It will be very gratifying and will do much towards conciliating our people."

Lee informed Grant that he had no food either for his own men or for his prisoners. He asked Grant if he might return the prisoners. Grant said yes, and asked Lee how much food he needed for his own men. Lee did not know. Grant asked if 25,000 rations would help. Lee replied that this "would be a great relief." Meanwhile, news of the surrender reached the Union army, who began firing salutes. Grant ordered these stopped at once, declaring: "The war is over, the rebels are our countrymen again, and the best sign of rejoicing after the victory will be to abstain from all demonstrations in the field." The men in blue mingled together around common camp fires with the men in gray, often eating from a common mess. The war was actually over.

Grant and Lee met as gentlemen; they negotiated as gentlemen; they parted as gentlemen. The next day Grant made a formal call upon Lee and they visited together for half an hour. There was no bitterness, no hatred. They, for themselves, buried the past.

Grant's terms for Lee's surrender became the terms for the surrender of all the Southern armies.

There was no indemnity. While under the law, the war was rebellion and its wagers traitors, no one suffered a traitor's punishment.

At his last Cabinet meeting, held on the morning of the day of his assassination, Lincoln (as reported by his Secretary of Navy, Welles) said: " 'No one need expect he would take any part in hanging or killing these men, even the worst of them. Frighten them out of the country, open the gates, let down the bars, scare them off,' said he, throwing up his hands as if scaring sheep. 'Enough lives have been sacrificed; we must extinguish our resentments if we expect harmony and union' " (See John G. Nicolay and John Hay, *Abraham Lincoln: A History*, 10 vols. [New York, 1886], 10:283–84).

I believe that God's mercy and love brooded over that meeting of Grant and Lee, victor and vanquished; that He manifested His design and purpose that, the Union preserved and slavery blotted out, this nation should not be cursed with a blight of hate, but that it should feel and live the divine principle voiced by Jesus Himself,—"Thou shalt love the Lord thy God with all thy heart, and with all thy soul, and with all thy strength, and with all thy mind; and thy neighbor as thyself" (Luke 10:27); and that Lincoln came near the divine standard of loving your enemies when he declared "he would [not] take any part in hanging or killing these men, even the worst of them."

A few years later, in accepting the nomination for the presidency, Grant, returning to the spirit of Appomattox, exhorted his fellow countrymen: "Let us have peace" (*New York Herald*, 30 May 1868).

Peace has been the pearl of great price, coveted, searched for, by man during all the ages.

Appomattox showed the temper of this people of ours, not in the course of a long period of growth, advancement, and peace, but at the close of a bloody, fratricidal war, where literally father fought son, and son father, and brother fought brother,—a kind of war that makes more and deeper wounds than any other kind of conflict. Yet this temper and concept, this high idealism and lofty purpose of Grant and Lincoln, seemingly fostered by the tragedies of the war, followed us for a half a century thereafter.

International Relations

With the only great trained military force in the world at the end of the war, and able to work out our will, we patiently dealt with England and France in the matter of their invasion of Mexico, and the French attempt to set up a Mexican monarchy under the Austrian Maximilian. We might then, with comparative ease and complete success, have waged war, driven out the invaders, conquered Mexico itself, and annexed it. There were none in the world then ready to say to us nay. But we forbore. We loved peace.

Britain during the Civil War, had aided the South, in sympathy not only, but by credits and the building of Confederate cruisers and furnishing of armaments. The war was taxing our strength. The Confederate cruisers—Laird's Ironclads—built at Birkenhead, were about to take to sea. Adams, our Minister to Great Britain, renewed at this point his representations against this violation of neutrality, and solemnly declared, "It would be superfluous in me to point out to your Lordship that this is war" [dispatch to Earl Russell, 5 September 1863]. His lordship stopped the sailing, but this, with the depredations of the Alabama and other British built and outfitted Confederate cruisers, left us with a feeling of deep injury. Our property loss had been enormous.

Yet, when the war was over and we were where we could speak boldly and use, if need be, the strong arm, we patiently dealt with England for a peaceful adjustment of our claims. We went to arbitration and won. And let it always be said to Britain's credit, and to ours, that the then two strongest nations in the world solved their differences by the friendly method of arbitration instead of by war, even though the vital interests and honor of each were involved. Again we sought peace.

In the 1860's we forbore war with Spain, declaring her intentions to annex San Domingo, and to repossess certain Peruvian islands.

We were equally restrained in 1895 in the boundary dispute between Venezuela and Great Britain, which threatened a violation of the Monroe Doctrine. It was in the course of his great discussion with Lord Salisbury, that Secretary Olney voiced his striking dictum: "Today the United States is practically sovereign on this continent, and its fiat is law upon the subjects to which it confines its interposition." This boundary was peacefully adjusted.

A like restraint marked our course in 1903 when France, Germany, and Great Britain instituted a pacific blockade against Venezuela. The injuries of which the powers complained were settled by peaceful means.

Peaceful Settlement of International Disputes

From the Jay treaty with Great Britain of 1793, until the recent past, we have encouraged and sought to secure the settlement of international difficulties and disputes by friendly means,—by arbitration where we were concerned, and by arbitration and mediation where others only were involved.

Beginning with arbitrations under the Jay treaty between ourselves and Great Britain, where we adjusted claims arising out of our Revolution, we have entered into numerous treaties, conventions, and protocols for the adjustment of our disputes with other nations, involving indemnities for injuries arising out of wars, involving sovereign rights and title to our national territory, damages for outrages to our citizens and for the despoliation of their property, our rights in the Northeastern Coast fisheries, and to the fur seals of Alaska, our rights under the laws of neutrality.

The three great exceptions to the peaceful adjustment of our international disputes, prior to World War I, were the War of 1812 with Britain, which was the culmination of a long series of injuries and treaty violations that did not yield to friendly solution; our War with Mexico of the 1840's, where we were the aggressor—our motives for waging that war will scarcely stand objective scrutiny, either as to altruism or unselfishness; and our War with Spain of 1898, where we intervened to stop further oppression and bloodshed, really to abate an international nuisance. Except for these wars, we settled by peaceful means every controversy we had with foreign nations from 1793 to World War I, and we had some disputes that took great skill and a will to peace to avoid war.

Mediation

We have more than once mediated to stop wars between other countries; the outstanding example of this is our mediation under President Theodore Roosevelt of the war between Russia and Japan. We have repeatedly exercised our good offices to adjust differences between other countries, particularly in the Latin Americas. In these the peace motive guided our course.

In the two Hague Conferences of 1899 and 1907, while other nations busied themselves mostly with conventions dealing with war, our emphasis was placed on perfecting conventions for the pacific settlement of international disputes. This was in line with the lofty purpose of our national diplomacy until after the last Hague Conference. In all these, peace with other members of the society of nations motivated our course.

Nor should we overlook the special efforts of Secretaries Olney, Hay, Knox, and Bryan to negotiate both general and special treaties to promote peace, nor the Kellogg-Briand Pact for the Outlawry of War.

Nor should we end this brief catalogue of some of our efforts without calling attention to the Rush-Bagot notes by which the United States and Great Britain accomplished the limitation of armament on the Great Lakes, an informal agreement that has robbed our Canadian border question of all threat of trouble for more than 130 years.

That, gentlemen, is America's record, the greatest record for peace made thus far by any nation in the world. Future generations will so appraise it. It is a record that made every man, woman, and child proud of his American citizenship and heritage.

Changing Our Course

But it seems to us of the common people that all this is about to change. Uninformed, we know we must appraise our condition with caution and reserve, we must recognize we may be wrong. Yet the facts we are permitted to know, shock us with their threat of world-wide disaster through another gigantic global war. It seems clear to us that we have forsaken or are ignoring the ideals and concepts of the past; that we are neither planning nor seeking peace; that our actions and policies will not lead to peace, but, on the contrary, they are breeding and fostering that hate, suspicion, and fear which are always the begetters of war, near or remote.

We are not unaware that this estimate will be denied. We shall be assured that what is really sought is peace, and that nothing is done or planned that has not peace for its ultimate aim and end. But we may properly look at the facts we have, and reach our own conclusions thereon, faulty though they may be. Our lack of full information leaves us no other course.

It looks to us as if in our dealing with our conquered foes, we of America have forgotten Appomattox; we have turned our backs on the idealism and lofty conduct and purpose of our whole history; we have with us neither the vision nor the humanity that were the controlling elements of our past. We seem to have turned back the hearts of men more than two thousand years, and to be back into paganism.

Lessons of Appomattox

Since our action at Appomattox was the embodiment of our lofty concepts and high idealism, let us contrast its essentials with those of the course we have pursued and are now pursuing, to see how far afield we have gone.

Effusion of Blood

Grant's first concern at Appomattox was to stop the shedding of blood. Lee was equally concerned.

How have we acted?

It has been affirmed since the war that the "underground" party in Germany offered to cooperate with us to stop the further shedding of blood and to end the war, and that we refused to follow. I do not know the influence that led us to refuse that humane offer, if it was made, and so save further slaughter of our own sons; but when the curtains are drawn back and the whole picture is shown, I shall not be surprised if we shall see that our bloody course was inspired by the German political refugees and their American friends, who, safe on our shores and behind our defenses, were quite willing that American blood should be shed till their thirst for revenge for ills they had suffered, but for which we had not even a shadow of responsibility, was slaked.

During the war, the slightest hint that we should treat with the German "underground" always called forth a tirade of scorn, ridicule, and defamation, poured out to a credulous public by the "smearers" and passed from mouth to mouth by the communists, the "fellow travellers" and their sympathizers, and political emigrés. These war mongers built such an odium about the word "appeasement," that men shrank from doing or saying anything that might draw upon themselves that opprobrious epithet. So thousands upon thousands of our boys were sacrificed.

Stopping the effusion of blood is one element of Appomattox that has had no place in this World War II. Never forget Nagasaki and Hiroshima.

Relieving Sufferings of War

You will recall that at Appomattox, dealing with a foe he could easily and quickly have crushed to the point of extermination, Grant was most careful and solicitous. He let the Confederate officers and soldiers retain their private property; he immediately provided Lee's army with food; the men immediately fraternized together, often eating at the same messes; he paroled all officers and men.

What have we done and what are we doing?

First, it may be said that apparently many, many enemy troops, it may be as many as 2,500,000, are still in detention camps, probably at forced labor.

The reports that appear in the press and that come from observers, leave no alternative but to conclude that we, to some extent, and some of our allies to greater extent, are deliberately following a course that will lead to the starving of great numbers of people, perhaps nations; that we allies are robbing them of the means of recovery not only, but of indispensable sustenance; and that we are not letting them produce the food, fuel, shelter, clothing, necessary to preserve life. We are destroying their industrial plants. A credible source charges "it is mainly American policies that have made mendicants and parasites of the peoples of Europe."

All this may be pursuant to a policy and plan we years ago announced, the Morgenthau plan, not yet, I believe, repudiated, for destroying a whole national life, and remaking it to suit the plan said by some to have been devised under the influence of political emigrés who think their best selfish interests will be best served thereby, and their revenge satisfied. All this makes for hate, and peace and hate never live together.

Conduct of Our Troops

Private reports too numerous to ignore and too constant to admit of real doubt, affirm that our occupying forces are quartered under luxurious conditions that are breeding an intense hatred against us. Certainly not discouraged, and some say encouraged, very many of our own men are reported to be living lives of debauchery of which American troops, *en masse,* have never before been guilty, and which some of us think are unworthy of, and indeed disgraceful to, American citizenship. Some of our allies are accused, without successful contradiction, of deliberately and designedly violating every woman, young and old, maid and wife, within their occupied areas. This means more and more hate, with peace in hiding.

For all this we are at least partly to blame. In the estimation of the oppressed peoples, we shall be held most to blame, first, because we are co-participants in the imposition of the oppressions, and, next, because they believe we could prevent it if we would. And they are right as to the planning and beginning of it, for if, during the war, our own spokesman had said *no* at the right moment, most, if not all, of this would never have happened.

I note all this here because all the cruelty and mistreatment we visit upon the peoples of Europe, in whatever form, builds a hate and a fear which will not bring peace, and which, the tables turning, will bring swift retaliation upon ourselves.

United States versus Russia

Thus far I have spoken of our late enemies. It may be said, probably justly, that they are so thoroughly beaten, so nearly destroyed, that they are no longer a threat, but we must not forget they recovered and returned in one generation after World War I. But grant their impotency for generations to come, yet are we faced with the gravest danger in our history.

Between ourselves and our late ally Russia, we are building a jealousy, a fear, a rivalry, and a hatred that unless halted will take us into the direst tragedy in the history of the world, in its magnitude, in its physical destructive force, and in its intellectual and spiritual degradation, and possibly even to our annihilation. Russia is powerful, largely unimpaired by the recent war. Under her present leaders, she is aggressive, militant, seemingly fearless. Her course compels the conclusion that she deliberately plans and plots world conquest. The ideology for which she fights is polar to ours. Fascism in Italy was never the shadow of a threat; Nazism in Germany was a world-old malady showing some new symptoms; we knew its cure. Communism in Russia is a new poison-plague for which we of the modern world have yet developed neither antidote nor cure. But in world history it is old. There is this difference between Nazism and Communism—the first leaves private property and individualism, however much appropriated and curtailed to meet the immediate crisis; the second destroys both private property and individualism, making the state all-pervading, all-absorbing, a god of human mind.

We alone in all the world challenge Russia's aims. She hates and fears us. We hate and are fearful of her. Thus far the two powers seem to plan and scheme only in terms of force. Battles on land, on sea, in air, are to settle the matter. So far as we of the public know, the two sides have never worked together honestly trying by peaceful means to reach a mutual live-and-let-live understanding. We do not know of even an effort on the part of both parties together, mutually to concede, mutually to put out of view the intent to use force to gain the end sought. Such an effort may have been made, but we do not have the facts. Indeed, we must regretfully admit that our own military establishment seem to be now deliberately planning and preparing for another great war, it must be with Russia, since of the whole world she alone has the power and resource to challenge us, which war both sides plan, it is said, to make the most terrible and destructive of all recorded time.

Our Military Establishment

Furthermore, I regret to say, indeed I am almost ashamed to say, that at the moment, our military branches seem in almost complete control of our own government. They appear to dominate Congress, and under the circumstances, we may assume they are in sufficient control of our foreign relations to be able to set the international scene. To us who do not know, it looks clear that we are today getting the same sort of propaganda of half-truths, told in the same evasive ways, with equivalent hints and dark forebodings that preceded the last war. We are not justified in doubting, on the facts we have, that we of the United States are, for the first time in our history, under a real threat from our military arm, and that if the plans of the militarists carry, we shall become as thoroughly militarized as was Germany at her best, or worst. Certain it is we are being generously dosed with that sovereign narcotic, which designing militarists have in the past always administered to their peoples, the doctrine that to ensure peace we must maintain a great army and gigantic armaments. But this ignores, indeed conceals, the unvarying historical fact that big armies have always brought, not peace, but war which has ended in a hate that in due course brings another war.

Our militarists will no more be able to let a great army lie unused than they were able to withhold the use of the atom bomb once they had it, even though some military men are now quoted as saying the war was won before the bombs were dropped on Nagasaki and Hiroshima. Under the threat that Germany was perfecting such a bomb, we were justified in perfecting ours. But it may well be a disaster to civilization for us unnecessarily to have initiated its use. Some of us think it was shameful.

All this is not the way to peace, but to war.

Lincoln and Nuremberg

How far indeed have we travelled from the gentle spirit, the humanity, indeed the brotherly love of Grant at Appomattox, and of Lincoln in the Cabinet meeting. That spirit brought a peace that has lasted for 85 years, with yet no signs of war. And may we not here place on one side Lincoln's declaration at the Cabinet meeting—" 'no one need expect he would take any part in hanging or killing these men, even the worst of them,' " and on the other side place Nuremberg, where report says men were tried and convicted for acts which, when committed, were not contrary to the law of nations, but declared so after they were committed, thus violating one of our fundamental constitutional concepts that *ex post facto* laws are not tolerable. If we shall ever be the underdog, which pray God we never shall be, Nuremberg will rise to condemn us, and to argue justification for the same procedure against us.

Thus we have wandered far from the ideals, the concepts, the faith, and the works of our fathers, and from the international gospel which guided them. We are the center of a great balance of power operation, a principle in the condemnation of which in the not too distant past some of our ranking officers exhausted their full lurid vocabulary. We no longer may move as seems to us best for our interests and safety, but must join in measures that our partners think are for their interests and their safety, and they are not without ambition, and greed is not wholly absent. How true this is may be learned from a glance at the scheming, brawling, word-mauling United Nations, which seems now to be worth no further consideration than mere mention.

The Policy of the Fathers

The international gospel of the Founding Fathers was forecast by Jefferson in 1793. It was voiced by Washington in his Farewell Address in 1796, when he declared we should have "as little *political* connexion as possible" with Europe, because Europe had a "set of primary interests" with which we had "none, or a very remote relation," wherefore

she must be engaged in frequent controversies, the causes of which are essentially foreign to our concerns . . .

. . . Why, by interweaving our destiny with that of any part of Europe, entangle our peace and prosperity in the toils of European ambition, rivalship, interest, humor, or caprice?

It is our true policy to steer clear of permanent alliances with any portion of the foreign world.

The Monroe Doctrine declaring against the future colonization of the American continent by Europeans, against the extension therein of their political system, against interposition by European powers to control the destinies of the Latin Americas, implemented the principles of the Address. And Jefferson, commenting in 1823 on the Monroe Doctrine, and the complete political separation of Europe and the Americas, solemnly affirmed: "Our first and fundamental maxim should be, never to entangle ourselves in the broils of Europe; our second, never to suffer Europe to intermeddle with cis-Atlantic affairs (quoted in J. Reuben Clark, *Memorandum on the Monroe Doctrine,* State Department Pub. no. 37 [Washington, D.C., 1930], xiv).

Nor may we overlook that great doctrine of neutrality set up under Washington himself and Jefferson and Hamilton, which was aimed at and brought about the localizing of international armed conflicts, and the preservation, under prescribed rules, of peacetime intercourse between belligerents and nonbelligerents. War was to curse as few people as possible. This has been jettisoned for the concept that every war should involve all nations, making all suffer the ravages of a global war.

Until the last quarter of a century, this gospel of the Fathers was the polar star by which we set our international course. In the first hundred thirty years of our constitutional existence, we had three foreign wars, the first merely the final effort of our Revolution, which made good our independence. During the century that followed we had two foreign wars, neither of considerable magnitude. During the next twenty-three years, we had two global wars. While the gospel of the Fathers guided us we had peace. When we forsook it, two great wars engulfed us.

It is not clear when we began our wandering, nor is it necessary to determine the time. President Theodore Roosevelt was hinting our straying when he uttered the dictum "Speak softly and carry a big stick." We were to force others to do our bidding. President Wilson had the full departure in mind when he declared: "Everybody's business is our business." Since then we have leaped ahead along the anciently forbidden path.

In our course under the new gospel of interference with everything we do not like, we have gone forward and are going forward, as if we possessed all the good of human government, of human economic concept, of human comfort, and of human welfare, all of which we are to impose on the balance of the world,—a concept born of the grossest national egotism. In human affairs no nation can say that all it practices and believes is right, and that all that others have that differs from what it has is wrong. Men inflict an unholy tragedy when they proceed on that basis. No man, no society, no people, no nation is wholly right in human affairs; and none is wholly wrong. A fundamental principle of the operation of human society is to live and let live.

Yet, to repeat, we have entered into new fields to impose our will and concepts on others. This means we must use force, and force means war, not peace.

Cost of Our Apostasy

What has our apostasy from peace cost us?

In men, our two recent adventures have cost in casualties, dead, wounded, and missing, 1,402,600, with almost as many saddened and crippled homes.

In money it has cost, in World War I, some $60 odd billions; and World War II cost us some $400 odd billions, including increased civilian help, in total, almost a half a trillion, the great bulk of which we still owe.

In spiritual values it has brought great numbers of our youth and older men to the very depths of desponding atheism. Our whole social structure seems undermined. We are becoming a blaspheming, unchaste, non-Christian, God-less race. Spiritually we seem ripe for another war.

In values of government and law, these wars and the interminglings of men of different concepts of freedom and human rights, have brought into our own system, the despotic principles of

European systems, against which the Fathers warned, though they came to us through doors the Fathers did not see. Many and influential persons amongst us, of alien concepts and sometimes of alien birth, no longer admit that man possesses the inalienable rights of the Declaration of Independence and the fundamental precepts of the Constitution. Our courts no longer guarantee these rights and enforce these principles. We have and are aping and adopting the policies and the legal theories of Europe. Colonel House records that when President Wilson hesitated to launch us into the first World War, because he did not know what measures to take to wage the war, he, Colonel House, assured the President that it was simple, all he had to do, said Colonel House, was to do the things Europe had already done. And so we proceeded, and from then till now, we have constantly and more and more adopted European governmental concepts and laws, to the loss of liberty and of the happiness and security of our people.

All this takes us into a situation that places our destinies largely in the hands of those who appear to be urging us towards war, not peace.

Return to the Faith of the Fathers

It is time we returned to the political faith and work of the Fathers. It is indispensable that we do so if we are to have peace. I believe in the old faith and the old works, under which we had so much of peace. I am a political isolationist in the full sense of the term and am not fearful in declaring it.

I am a political isolationist because:

I fully believe in the wisdom of the course defined by Washington, Jefferson, and other ancient statesmen. The whole history of America before and since the Revolution proves the truthfulness of their assertions. All during our pre-Revolutionary history we were at war, we were robbed, plundered, and massacred because of European wars, in the issues and causes of which we had no concern. History is repeating itself.

I believe American manhood is too valuable to be sacrificed on foreign soil for foreign issues and causes.

I believe that permanent peace will never come into the world from the muzzle of a gun. Guns and bayonets will, in the future as in the past, bring truces, long or short, but never peace that endures.

279

I believe President Wilson had the true principle when he spoke of the strength and power of the moral force of the world. Moral force in a nation fructifies industry, thrift, good will, neighborliness, the friendly intercourse of nations, the peace that all men seek; whereas force is barren.

I believe America's role in the world is not one of force, but is of that same peaceful intent and act that has characterized the history of the country from its birth till the last third of a century.

I believe that moral force is far more potent than physical force in international relations.

I believe that America should again turn to the promotion of the peaceful adjustment of international disputes, which will help us regain the measureless moral force we once possessed, to the regeneration and salvation of the world. We now speak with the strong arm of physical force only; we have no moral force left.

I believe we should once more turn our brains and our resources to the problem, not of killing men, women, and children, combatant and noncombatant, but of bringing to them more of good living and high thinking.

I believe political isolation will bring to us the greatest happiness and prosperity, the greatest temporal achievement not only, but the highest intellectual and spiritual achievement also, the greatest power for good, the strongest force for peace, the greatest blessing to the world.

The Same Old World

I am not shaken in my convictions nor frightened by the assertion of many good people and fostered by the communists and "new thoughters," that the doctrine of the Fathers is outmoded, and that we are in a new world. All the age-old forces are still peering out at us,—greed, avarice, ambition, selfishness, the passion to rule, the desire to enslave for the sordid advantage of the enslaver. Not a single wanton face is missing and the visages of some are more hideous than ever. While radar, the radio, the telephone, the airplane have facilitated our talking and visiting with our neighbors, they have not made new beings out of us nor out of them, nor changed either our characters or theirs. We are just as we were, with the possibility of a little more back-fence gossiping and quarreling, and a little more brawling among the children. But the households remain essentially as they were. We still have oceans between us; we live on different continents, under different conditions. We can and should mind our own business and let others do the same.

In my view, our whole international course and policy is basically wrong, and must be changed if peace is to come. Our policy has brought us, and pursued, will continue to bring us, only the hatred of nations now—and we cannot thrive on that, financially or spiritually—and certain war hereafter, with a list of horrors and woes we do not now even surmise. If we really want peace, we must change our course to get it. We must honestly strive for peace and quit sparring for military advantage. We must learn and practice, as a nation and as a world, the divine principles of the Sermon on the Mount. There is no other way.

What Would You Do?

Someone will, at this point, play the ace question, with that smug finality that always accompanies it,—What would you do?

I frankly answer, I do not know, for I do not know the facts. Furthermore, a critic with no authority or power in a situation, and from whom is withheld a knowledge of the facts, is under no obligation to propose an alternative. He may rest by pointing out defects in policy.

On the other hand, I say, give us the facts, all of them, hiding nothing, and we shall tell you what to do. As one American citizen, I dare government to give us the facts, all the facts, including what kind of war they think the next war will be, what kind they intend to wage, and how many lives it will cost, including the aged, the infirm, and women and children.

We, the common people, have not been told the facts for years, since long before the last war broke. We are not now being told the facts. We can only surmise. But give us the facts and we will answer. And in our multitude of counsel you will find wisdom.

One Suggestion

In conclusion, I will hazard one suggestion:

Unless all history is reversed and its lessons and principles all blotted out, it is inconceivable that any system can be set up by a personal despot or by an oligarchy either of intellectuals or of cruel, heartless, ambitious men, that can permanently rob men of their

281

freedom and put them in slavery. This never has been done. Sooner or later such a system has always broken down; it always will break down, because, despite what atheists and scoffers say or think, man is the child of God, who planted in man's soul certain eternal concepts and urges that are stronger than mortal life or any of the intellectual or physical incidents of mortality.

Among these elemental concepts is the love of freedom; it is found in man not only, but even in the brutes. Man and beast rebel against slavery. They yield to it only under compelling force.

Another elemental eternal concept is belief in God, which may ripen into a knowledge of God. Normal man ultimately demands this belief to make mortality tolerable.

Modern communism as explained by communists who are in places where they speak their real minds, deny God, declare that other men are beasts that must be tamed and worked as beasts. This is an enemy that threatens us within and without. This is not a God-less world.

But men cannot be led indefinitely, nor driven by a savage despotism, down this road to an intellectual and moral abyss. They may follow along for a generation or two. But they will one day rebel against the rule of liquidation. No group can permanently maintain itself by murder, as history proves from the days of the hideous proscription lists of Sulla till now. Fear and ruthless cruelty can rule for a time, but the spirit of liberty ultimately breaks forth and sweeps away everything that lies in its path.

So it will be with communism, which now on a world scale may well be only doing the work of the Paris mobs in the French Revolution, for there are fields of human endeavor where the power of birth and station still afflict man's growth and development.

But the great truth announced by the Prince of Peace, "I am the light, the life, and the way" [*sic*—see John 14:6] ultimately reaches the mind and heart of men, and then they demand freedom. It was so planned in the creation. God gave to ancient Israel a law under which there came at regular intervals, a year of jubilee and freedom, when men were freed of bondage, financial and physical. Paul told the Corinthians, "Where the spirit of the Lord is, there is liberty" (2 Cor. 3:17).

So the light of the Master will ultimately break through the darkness of the infidel, and all men will return to freedom and free institutions and to the worship of Almighty God, for such has been the course of man since he came to this earth, and ultimately every knee will bow and every tongue confess that Jesus is the Christ, and then will come the peace of the world.

Meanwhile, if we shall follow our own destiny, America will work for peace by peaceful means, not by force. We Americans should meet our present problems not as if we are to inflict the punishment that Samuel commanded Saul to inflict upon the Amalekites—we have no such commission—but we should solve our present problems as a developing, but passing phase, still pending a final solution. In our dealing with our international challenge we should adopt the tactics of Washington in the Revolution, which he took from the old Roman, Fabian. We must be alert, make no false moves, take no position we cannot hold, and await the internal solution which history assures us will come to enslaving groups of great peoples. The spirit of liberty will ultimately break forth among them and will sweep away everything that lies in its path.

Meanwhile, let us each set his own house in order. Let us each do a little repenting of our common sins. Let us each recast his own life to fit the example and teachings of the Master. We stand today not too far from the moral and spiritual peace where Lincoln stood during some of the darkest days of the Civil War, when in a Thanksgiving proclamation he said:

We have been the recipients of the choicest bounties of heaven. We have been preserved, these many years, in peace and prosperity. We have grown in numbers, wealth, and power as no other nation has ever grown; but we have forgotten God. We have forgotten the gracious hand which preserved us in peace, and multiplied and enriched and strengthened us; and we have vainly imagined, in the deceitfulness of our hearts, that all these blessings were produced by some superior wisdom and virtue of our own. Intoxicated with unbroken success, we have become too self-sufficient to feel the necessity of redeeming and preserving grace, too proud to pray to the God that made us. (John G. Nicolay and John Hay, eds., *The Complete Works of Abraham Lincoln*, 12 vols. [New York, 1905], 8:235–36)

How terrible that arraignment! How well it fits us today? Let us not forget God, nor forget that remembering him means worshiping Him and keeping His commandments.

That we may hereafter live a free people and in peace, let us return to the basic principles that we observed in the first century and a quarter of our existence. But above and beyond that, I again say, that if we want peace, we must return to the faith and principles of Him who alone can give peace, we must return to the worship of Christ and to the life He marked for us. If you will bring the world to Christ, you will have peace, and it will come in no other way. If you unify the intellectual and spiritual forces of the world, the political forces of the world will become one.

In closing, I return again to the high calling you have as missionaries preaching the gospel of caring for the bereaved widows and orphans of the people. This great labor will prosper or decline depending upon how many people you reach and convert. There are now in the United States more than seventy million life insurance policyholders, whose policies amount to over one hundred seventy-four billions of dollars. One-half the people of the United States have life insurance policies. In the great economic factors of our civilization no other body gives a more important service, indeed, having in mind the nature of your work, no other economic body equals yourselves in the spiritualizing influence your service spreads among the people. You are the corner stone of the whole insurance edifice. You have the greatest stake in our peace and welfare of any group in the world. If you shall weaken, the whole structure will fall. These are not mere words, but solemn truths.

I am sure you appreciate that every time you sell a policy you not only give explanations, but you make promises; you become a moral guarantor of your promises.

To make good your guaranty, the country must prosper, and for the country to prosper we must have peace. No human mind can fathom the abyss into which another war will plunge us. The communists plan that they will be down in the bottom, organized to exploit and enslave us. None of us must leave any act undone that could avert this.

Tens of millions of dependents the country over, look for their sustenance to the promises you made. You are the benefactors of all these. Your benefactions come to them when the need for food, clothing, and shelter is most pressing. Your help eases the heavy load of sorrow that burdens their hearts and that saps the clarity of their minds. They call down upon your heads blessings that only the Almighty can bestow. Thus you may be the instruments that, in God's wisdom, shall help to keep this nation a body of free men.

With Grant, in his reverent petition of three quarters of a century ago, we common people, we who bear the burden of war, cry out to our leaders, "Let us have peace!"

PART THREE

Mexico

The Oil Settlement with Mexico

July 1928

While serving as legal adviser to Dwight W. Morrow, who was United States ambassador to Mexico, JRC wrote two articles on the problems "between the United States and Mexico concerning the rights of American citizens to oil properties in Mexico." The following is the first statement, which he considered a popular treatment—hence the lack of scholarly documentation. It was published in the July 1928 issue of *Foreign Affairs*.

The following September the article was severely criticized in a series of articles in the *Wall Street Journal*. But JRC had realized that his ideas would be disputed and had written to the *Foreign Affairs* editor even before the article was printed, ". . . [this] . . . has been written with *caution,* but you must understand that I must write as a lawyer, upon questions of law as to which there is a very sharp difference of opinion, even among Mexican lawyers, and as to which there has been and will perhaps continue to be a great deal of controversy" (J. Reuben Clark, Jr., to Hamilton Fish Armstrong, 11 May 1928).

Typical of JRC's loyalty and respect for protocol, he concluded his article with two quotations, one from Ambassador Morrow and the other from the Department of State. The editor of the quarterly asked him to prepare "a concluding paragraph of some sort summing up what . . . [had] been accomplished," suggesting that the article stopped rather abruptly (Armstrong to Clark, 1 May 1928). In response JRC wrote: "The significance and value of the adjustment depends not upon what I say, but upon the view which is taken of the matter by the American Ambassador and by the Department of State. I therefore regard it as very important that their words shall be the final words of the article" (Clark to Armstrong, 11 May 1928). The correspondence quoted above may be found in Box 126, P 6, vol. 5, JRCP; the article comes from Box 48, Book 2, 1928, Oil, JRCP.

The controversy between the United States and Mexico concerning the rights of American citizens to oil properties in Mexico acquired prior to May 1, 1917 (the date the new Constitution became operative), began with the representations made by the Department of State regarding the Carranza decree of September 19, 1914. There had been some earlier decrees that were the subject of comment by the United States, notably those issued in 1914 by General Candido Aguilar, as Governor and Military Commandant of Vera Cruz, and that issued by Carranza on June 24, 1913, (amending the petroleum tax law of Madero of June 24, 1912), but action by the Department of State was more by way of enquiry than representation.

The decree of September 19 stipulated, in order that the Government might "know exactly the true wealth of the country and so may rationally and equitably distribute the taxes on the taxpayers," that all property owners and industries should present on a prescribed form, a detailed, signed statement of all their properties, with the value thereof. This valuation was to be made with "the understanding that the Government shall have the right, in case of expropriation for the sake of the public service, to pay to the interested parties as indemnity the value which is definitely fixed in the tax list." Those failing to furnish the list within the time fixed were to be subject to a fine of "five percent of the value of the property they keep secret."

Six months later, the American Vice Consul at Tampico reported that enforcement of the decree was contemplated and that oil men were unable to appraise accurately the value of their unproved land "which was purchased years ago for insignificant amounts, on which taxes have been paid in proportion to the agricultural value up to the present time," and which "may be valueless or worth millions of dollars." Upon the receipt of this information, Secretary Bryan, on March 5, 1915, instructed the Vice Consul that "if authorities attempt enforce decree mentioned, immediately inform Department and strongly protest on grounds confiscatory provisions, apparent injustice oil companies and lack sufficient notice."

From that date to October 30, 1926—a period of eleven and a half years—the government of the United States has made representations to Mexico. At one time—August, 1918—these became so urgent that Mexico understood them to constitute an actual threat of war or intervention.

The Historical Background of the Controversy

In 1783, Charles III of Spain issued a mining code (*Reales Ordinanzas*) for New Spain, including Mexico. In the light of the earlier Spanish mining laws applicable to Spain and the Indias [Indies], it would appear that this law reserved title to mineral substances (including gas and petroleum) in the Sovereign, who, for the exploitation thereof, might grant, in private lands or otherwise, such rights as the Sovereign pleasure willed. The rights so granted might, it seems, be changed or abolished. The two important provisions of this Code were: "The mines are the property of my royal crown, as well by their nature and origin as by their reunion" as declared in the law of 1559; and "without separating them from my royal patrimony I grant them to my subjects in property and possession."

This law drew, as to all minerals, the same sharp distinction between rights to the surface and rights to minerals under the surface that is now found in the law of the United States governing the exploitation or deposits of coal, phosphate, sodium, oil, oil shale, and gas in lands valuable for such minerals and forming part of our public domain.

These *Reales Ordinanzas* remained in force in Mexico until 1884, when the Mexican National Congress passed the first mining code enacted after the achievement of independence. This Code was interpreted by some as divesting the Sovereign (the nation) of its title to gas and petroleum on privately owned lands, and as lodging such title in the private owners of the soil.

The statute of 1884 (with some amendments, the principal one in 1887) remained in force until 1892, when a second general mining code was enacted by the Mexican Congress. This new law was open to the construction that it repealed the Code of 1884, and replaced in the Sovereign (the nation) the title it had under the law of 1783. In this view the nationals of Mexico (and aliens so far as permitted) were again authorized to acquire mining rights in gas and oil deposits in accordance with the principles operative prior to 1884. It has been said that certain provisions of a law of 1901 gave support to such a construction.

The Code of 1892 remained in force until 1909, when a third mining law was enacted which substantially returned (as to gas and petroleum) to the language of the law of 1884.

The Code of 1909, with some modifications, principally by means of Revolutionary decrees, was still on the statute books when the Constitution of 1917 came into force. This seems framed to re-invest the nation with all the sovereign rights and powers possessed by it prior to 1884. The Carranza decrees and the laws and regulations enacted subsequent to May 1, 1917, were drawn to implement this construction of the Constitution.

Subsequently to 1884, and, as it seems, in considerable part subsequently to 1909, large petroleum holdings in Mexico were acquired by American citizens (individuals and corporations), either directly or by stockownership in Mexican or other foreign corporations. The contention of such American interests as to their properties acquired prior to May 1, 1917, has been, in rough, that where they were the owners of the surface, they had the same rights to the oil thereunder that the owner of a fee simple in the United States would have; and that where they held "leaseholds" from native owners, then, since such owners had that same "fee simple" ownership, such "leaseholds" carried with them, for the term thereof, the full "fee simple" rights of the owners.

The United States Government made its representations in substantial accord with the views of the American oil interests on these questions.

The Mexican position, which seems never to have been succinctly or categorically stated, may be summarized in the form in which it finally developed somewhat as follows: The nation never intended to vest and never did vest, by any of its laws, ownership of gas and petroleum in the surface owners; the utmost effect of its laws was to give the owners of the surface the exclusive right to exploit their properties for oil; therefore, no surface owner had an actual ownership of gas and petroleum under his soil, unless and until some act was done by him looking to the exploitation of such materials; and, since the surface owners who had performed no such acts thus had no actual ownership in the gas and petroleum underlying their properties, the Mexican Government might, in accordance with its "juridical traditions" (as Lic. Gonzalez Roa put it in 1923 at the Bucareli Conference) change the rules under which the mining title to such substances might be obtained by such surface owners or their lessees.

The Mexican people adopted a new Constitution, and the Mexican Government thereafter issued decrees, enacted laws, and promulgated regulations, for the development and control of the petroleum industry in conformity with their conception of their sovereign rights.

These differences of view gave rise to discussions between the United States and Mexico, which may be grouped into three periods.

The Pre-Constitutional Period: 1914 to May 1, 1917

During this period representations were made regarding and against decrees which provided for the reporting of properties for taxation purposes and which the United States characterized as confiscatory; against a ruling that drilling permits would only be granted to companies agreeing to obey a law not yet framed and of the purport of which the companies had no knowledge; against a rumored "nationalization of petroleum," which the United States also characterized as confiscatory; and against the requirement of a Calvo clause (an undertaking by the one making it not to invoke the diplomatic protection of his government) in titles, contracts, and concessions, for individuals, stockholders, and companies. Representations were also made against certain provisions of the Constitution of 1917, but not those particular ones which later were involved in the controversy between the two countries regarding petroleum properties; and against a proposed bill providing for a concession for oil exploitation with a period of preference for the present owners to obtain such concession.

None of the matters complained of appear to have been carried to the point where American property was actually taken (except by way of taxation); and all seem, in effect, merged in the difficulties which arose during the next periods.

The First Period after the Constitution: May 1, 1917, to December 20, 1925

During this period representations were made by the United States concerning and against the "nationalization" of petroleum by the Mexican constitution and decrees, on the ground that the same were confiscatory; against the reported refusal to grant drilling permits (the Mexican Government asked for concrete cases of injury resulting from any action by it in this respect); against the Carranza decrees of February 19, May 18, July 8, July 31, August 8, and August 12, 1918, which provided *inter alia* for the payment of taxes regarded as onerous, and for the forfeiture of all rights in and to petroleum in lands not "manifested" (registered) as provided in the decrees; and against the approval by Congress of the foregoing Carranza decrees. Representations were also made against the collection of royalties and other taxes from American companies; against the refusal to permit continued exploitation of lands because of non-manifestation; against the stopping of oil exploitation actually under way; against the "denouncement" by other parties of American properties which had not been "manifested" as required by the Carranza decrees; and against the requirement that to obtain drilling permits, companies must agree to obey a law not yet framed and of the purpose of which they had no knowledge.

When the proposed legislation of 1925 was introduced into the Mexican Congress, the Secretary of State called attention, by an *Aide Mémoire,* to the provisions which would prove objectionable if enacted into law; and the correspondence which followed this initial communication discussed the distinction drawn between "tagged" and "untagged" lands—"tagged" lands being those as to which some "positive act" (an actual act looking to the exploitation of oil) had been performed prior to May 1, 1917, and "untagged" lands being those as to which no such act had been performed prior to that date.

Certain broad questions which arose during this second period require special consideration.

Not a little criticism has been aimed at certain words—*dominio, dominio directo* and *propiedad*—used in the Constitution of 1917. It appears to have been assumed that they are used as terms of art (words expressing a limited and precise legal or juristic concept); however, an examination seems to show the opposite.

For example, the word *dominio* is used with at least two meanings in Article 27 of the Constitution—as describing that title or interest in property which the nation grants to individuals to constitute private property (*propiedad privada*), and as describing that title or interest which the nation reserves always in itself and which is declared to be "inalienable and imprescriptible." Further, it appears that *dominio directo* is used in the same article with at least three meanings—the title or interest which the nation reserves in mineral substances; the title or interest which aliens may not, but which Mexicans by implication may, acquire over lands and waters within a prescribed zone along frontiers and coasts; and the title or interest which the nation has in churches and auxiliary buildings already built, though of "temples" hereafter erected for public worship the nation has *propiedad*. Moreover, *propiedad* has been used in the Article with at least four meanings,—the ultimate interest or ownership which the nation has in all property; the title or interest which the nation grants to private individuals; the sovereign right in territorial waters and in waters generally; and the title or interest (already mentioned) which the nation has in "temples" hereafter constructed for public worship.

It would appear from the foregoing that criticism founded upon the theory that these Constitutional expressions were in fact used as terms of art, might go wide of the mark. The meaning of Article 27 of the Constitution must be gathered from a consideration of the article as a whole.

Two provisions of the Constitution have been pointed to as embodying principles which, if applied, would violate the rights enjoyed by foreign oil interests in Mexico. The first is that found in the opening paragraph of Article 27, which declares:

> The ownership (*propiedad*) of lands and waters comprised within the limits of the national territory originally pertains to the nation, which has had and has the right to transmit the dominion (*dominio*) thereof to private parties constituting private property (*propiedad privada*).

Certainly there has been no doubt since the time of Coke, that, as Kent puts it,

> It is a fundamental principle in the English law, derived from the maxims of the feudal tenures, that the king was the original proprietor or lord paramount of all the land in the kingdom and the true and only source of title. In this country

we have accepted the same principle, and applied it to our republican governments; and it is a settled and fundamental doctrine with us, that all valid
individual title to land within the United States is derived from the grant of our
local governments, or from that of the United States, or from the Crown, or royal
chartered governments established here prior to the Revolution.

Kent calls attention to the Constitution of the State of New
York (1846), which affirmed,

The people of this State, in their right of sovereignty, are deemed to possess
the original and ultimate property in and to all lands within the jurisdiction of
the State; and all lands the title to which shall fail, from a defect of heirs, shall
revert or escheat to the people.

Both in the Philippine Islands and in Puerto Rico, since their
acquisition by the United States, laws have been adopted which
appear specifically to incorporate the same doctrine.

In view of these principles of American law there would appear
to be no well-founded objection to be urged against this provision of
the Mexican Constitution.

Another provision of that Constitution to which objection has
been made in connection with the oil controversy, is that found in
the fourth paragraph of Article 27 which declares that to the nation
belongs (*corresponde*) the *dominio directo* over all mineral substances
including petroleum.

Again, it has been good law, certainly since the time of Coke,
that as to the soil and all its contents "a subject hath not properly
directum, yet he hath *utile dominium,*" or as Blackstone paraphrases it,
"he hath *dominium utile,* but not *dominium directum,*" the latter being
vested in the Sovereign. The decisions of the Courts in the United
States are in accord with this principle, which would appear in
essence to be not essentially dissimilar from the principle embodied
in the Mexican Constitution.

A second matter arising during this second period that deserves
special consideration is the famous "Texas Case," decided on April
30, 1921. In this case the Mexican Supreme Court declared that the
Constitution of 1917 was not retroactive as to oil rights acquired
prior to its coming into operation. The precise question in the case
was whether or not land which had been leased by the owner for oil
exploitation purposes prior to May 1, 1917, was open to denouncement by other parties under the Carranza decree of August 8, 1918.

The court held the land could not be so denounced, because the owners had the right, under the 1909 statute, to explore and exploit the land for oil, and that they had the power to transfer such rights "in the exercise of this faculty, as they did . . . by means of the contract contained in the deed of April 28, 1917, in which it appears that the grantors fixed and received a price higher than would have been paid them for the surface of the land because it was not sought to cultivate such surface or to build upon it, but to look for oil and exploit the same if found. So that the rights granted to the owners of the land by Article 2 of the said law of November 25, 1909, were converted into positive acts, and we therefore are treating of vested rights acquired by the lessee from the date of the oil contract."

A third matter falling within this second period and to be specially noted was the Bucareli Conference. The purpose of this Conference—as afterwards declared by the United States—was to find a basis upon which recognition might be accorded to the Mexican Government. The American Commissioners to this Conference were Messrs. Charles Beecher Warren and John Barton Payne. In the course of this Conference the Mexican Commissioners developed with some fullness their theory of subsurface rights and the doctrine of "positive acts." Those "positive acts," which, if performed prior to May 1, 1917, with reference to any given area of land, would give to the owner of that land or his lessee an "acquired right" to the oil in the subsurface, they described as,

some positive act which would manifest the intention of the owner of the surface or of the persons entitled to exercise his rights to the oil under the surface to make use of or obtain the oil under the surface; such as drilling, leasing, entering into any contract relative to the subsoil, making investments of capital in lands for the purpose of obtaining the oil in the subsoil, carrying out works of exploitation and exploration of the subsoil and in cases where from the contract relative to the subsoil it appears that the grantors fixed and received a price higher than would have been paid for the surface of the land because it was purchased for the purpose of looking for oil and exploiting same if found; and, in general, performing or doing any other positive act, or manifesting an intention of a character similar to those heretofore described.

The lands as to which any of these acts had been performed prior to May 1, 1917, became, in the vernacular of oil men, "tagged" lands; lands as to which no such "act" had been performed were called "untagged" lands.

Shortly after the Bucareli Conference closed on August 15, 1923, recognition was accorded the Obregon Government, and from then until October of 1925 little was said by the two Governments about the rights of American Oil operators in Mexico. However, during the fall of 1925 the introduction into the Mexican Congress of an Alien Land Law bill and a Petroleum Law bill, brought from the Secretary of State the *Aide Mémoire* to which reference has already been made. This initiated a correspondence that did not end till November 1926. The discussion was almost wholly legal in its character and, while it was at times conducted with earnestness and spirit, it seems never to have actually threatened the peaceful relations of the two countries.

The Period from December 1925 to November 1926

The two articles of the Petroleum Law (promulgated December 31, 1925) to which the most serious objection was made by the United States were articles 14 and 15. They seemed to provide, as to "tagged" lands, for the granting of a new right in the form of a concession for fifty years, instead of confirming in perpetuity rights already "vested;" and they narrowed, as it was apprehended, the definition of "positive acts" given by the Mexican Commissioners during the Bucareli Conference.

The provisions of the Petroleum Regulations (promulgated April 8, 1926) to which particular objection attached were Articles 147-59, and Transitory Articles 2, 3, 4, and 6. These articles, being regulatory of the objectionable articles of the law, were likewise unsatisfactory and for the same reasons.

The particular matters which crystallized out of the diplomatic controversy during this period were as follows:

1. Those provisions of the Petroleum Law and Regulations which seemed to provide for the granting of a new right for 50 years, instead of confirming an acquired right in perpetuity.
2. The possible legal inability of American companies to secure confirmatory concessions for lands lying within prohibited zones.
3. The curtailment of the "positive acts" as defined by the Mexican Commissioners at the Bucareli Conference on August 2, 1923.
4. The requirement of a Calvo clause from American Citizens (individuals and corporations).

296

5. The operation, as a "positive act," of the "manifesting" of lands under Circular 11 of January 15, 1915, thus "tagging" such lands.
6. The exact character of the rights and titles possessed by aliens (individuals and corporations) holding interests in lands—"fee or leasehold"—which were acquired prior to May 1, 1917, both when the lands are "tagged" and when they are "untagged."

The correspondence closed with Secretary Kellogg's statement in his note of October 30, 1926, that the United States

expects the Mexican Government not to take any action under the laws in question and the regulations issued in pursuance thereto, which would operate, either directly or indirectly, to deprive American citizens of the full ownership, use and enjoyment of their said property and property rights.

To this the Mexican Government, through Minister Saenz, replied under date of November 17, 1926:

My Government expects on its part that that of Your Excellency will indicate the concrete cases in which recognized principles of international law may have been violated or may be violated in disregard of legitimate interests of American citizens since in such cases it will be disposed to repair such violations.

This was the state of the controversy when Ambassador Morrow presented his credentials on October 29, 1927.

The Ambassadorship of Mr. Morrow

On November 17, 1927, the entire matter assumed a new aspect through a decision by the Supreme Court of Mexico of a case involving the question whether the Department of Industry might properly cancel drilling permits for "tagged" lands because the owner had failed to apply for a fifty-year concession within the year prescribed by Article 15 of the Petroleum Law. The Court, affirming the opinion of the lower Court, held that such drilling permits could not be so cancelled.

The *ratio decidendi* of the opinion seems to be that the company, being the owner of "tagged" lands, possessed oil *rights*, not mere *expectancies;* that rights could not be subjected to restriction in part nor loss in part; that confirmation for fifty years was restriction upon, and a loss of, the rights possessed by the Company which were without limitation of time; that "it is evident that said application could not have been made by the complainant without curtailment of something which belongs to its estate;" wherefore, "it is indisputable that the protested ruling violates in this respect the guarantees afforded the complainant by Articles 14, 16, and 27 of the Federal Constitution." The Court during the course of its opinion categorically stated that a *confirmation* of rights "does not modify them, but . . . recognizes them;" it is a "*recognition of acquired rights.*"

Thus the Supreme Court of Mexico laid down basic principles in harmony with the declarations made by it in the "Texas Case" in 1921.

It may at this point be observed that the constitutional position of the Federal Supreme Court under the Mexican system of Government appears to be essentially different from the constitutional position of our Supreme Court under our system. With us a decision by the Supreme Court of the United States that a law or part of a law is unconstitutional renders the same null, void, and of no effect. This seems not to be the effect of such a decision under the Mexican system. Under that system a decision apparently has no effect whatever upon the law itself, which remains operative upon the statute books until changed by the legislature; and so long as it is upon the statute books, the Executive is bound to enforce it irrespective of the opinions expressed about it by the Supreme Court. Therefore, it seems, the Executive may apply the principle announced in a decision of the Supreme Court only in that case in which the decision is rendered.

A provision of the Amparo law provides that if the Supreme Court makes the same interpretation of the law in five successive cases, that interpretation must be followed by the lower courts, until the Supreme Court modifies its view or reverses itself, or until the legislature changes the law. This seems to be the full meaning of the *jurisprudencia* of which not a little has been said. The Executive appears to be still bound to enforce the law as it stands on the statute books, except as to the cases actually decided.

President Calles on December 26, 1927, sent a message to Congress in which he pointed out that the Supreme Court had held the Petroleum Law unconstitutional in certain parts, and he recommended that the Petroleum Law be amended to conform to the Supreme Court decision. In the course of his message he declared (seemingly in strict accord with the Constitutional principle governing the force and effect of a decision by the Supreme Court) that the Federal Executive "finds it impossible after the decision of the Supreme Court, to carry forward the uniform application of the said law; in view of which it should insofar, as it is able, secure an immediate solution to the conflict existing between a law in force, and the interpretation of its anti-constitutionality"; and he asked for the amendment so that "the effects of the decision . . . should benefit not only those included within its scope, but also those who complied with Articles 14 and 15 of the law . . . for if such were not the case an unequal juridical and material status would be produced—one in addition unjust."

On December 27, 1926, a Committee of the Chamber of Deputies reported favorably the bill of President Calles with some amendments, and stated in part,

the confirmation of a right is its express recognition in all its extent and with such conditions as are inherent therein, so that no restriction can be established in regard to length of term or conditions (imposed) upon the right which is being confirmed, for any restriction in these respects implies a modification of the right confirmed and a retroactive application of the law.

On January 3, 1928, President Calles approved a bill which amended Articles 14 and 15 of the Petroleum Law by providing that pre-constitutional rights should be confirmed without cost by the *issuance* (*not the granting*) of confirmatory concessions "without limitation of time."

Thus the Executive and Congress, responsive to the ruling of the Supreme Court, have made it clear that no new right is to be *granted* for a limited time by the concessions provided for in the Law, but that such concessions are to *issue* as a confirmation of "acquired rights" ("vested rights") and "without limitation of time."

This disposes of the controversy between the two Governments on these two points, insofar as the provisions of the Law can do so.

The task remained for the Mexican authorities to readjust the Petroleum Regulations in harmony with the law.

As already pointed out, one of the matters causing anxiety among the oil companies was whether or not an alien company could apply for and secure a confirmatory concession on its "pre-constitution" properties without forfeiting its rights, particularly where the properties lay within the prohibited zones—"a strip of 100 kilometers along the borders and 50 along the coasts." Apparently the Attorney General of Mexico had on December 3, 1917, given an opinion that under the Constitution (Article 27, Fraction I, Paragraph 7) alien companies could in no event acquire "lands, waters, and their appurtenances in the Republic."

Accordingly, on January 9, 1928, Mr. H. N. Branch, representing the Huasteca Petroleum Company, enquired of the Secretary of Industry, Commerce and Labor, Sr. Morones, "whether an application for confirmatory concession by a foreign company involves surrender of any rights held prior to May 1, 1917." On the same day, January 9, 1928, Minister Morones replied, after quoting that part of the Report of the Committee of the Chamber of Deputies quoted above, that "this Department believes that the petition for confirmatory concession on the part of a national or foreign company does not imply the renunciation of rights acquired before May 1, 1917, such confirmatory concession operating as the recognition of rights which will continue in force subject only to police regulations." This exchange of letters would seem to meet the doubt which had arisen as to whether American companies might apply for confirmatory concessions without forfeiting any of their rights.

Early in February a Committee of the oil companies (American and foreign) submitted to the Ministry of Industry, Commerce and Labor, a draft of proposed amendments to the Petroleum Regulations. Conferences followed, and the proposals were taken under consideration by the Ministry, but they were not found to be satisfactory.

So soon as this fact was learned, informal conferences were undertaken between Ambassador Morrow and his representatives, on the one side, and Minister Morones and his representatives, on the other side, with a view to framing amendments to the Petroleum Regulations that would place them in harmony with the amended Law.

There ensued several weeks of negotiations, which were characterized by the utmost friendliness on both sides, and during all of which Ambassador Morrow kept in the closest touch with the local representatives of the leading American oil companies. At the end of these negotiations the Mexican authorities framed amendments to the Petroleum Regulations which in the opinion of Ambassador Morrow and the local representatives of the leading American oil companies did harmonize the Regulations with the Law and did eliminate the substantial objections made to the old Regulations. The amended regulations were signed by President Calles on March 27, 1928, and promulgated the following day.

Since a doubt had existed as to whether the provisions of the old Regulations relating to "positive acts" (Articles 152 and 153) were as broad as the definition given by the Mexican Commissioners on August 2, 1923, at the Bucareli Conference, the Mexican Government incorporated in the amended regulations (Article 152) the exact language used by the Mexican Commissioners. This was in accord with the statements made by Minister Saenz in his note to Secretary Kellogg of January 26, 1926, and reaffirmed in his note of October 7, 1926. This disposes of the doubt regarding the equivalency of the declaration of the Commissioners and of the provisions of the Regulations on this point.

In order that the oil companies might know just what sort of concession they might expect in case they made application under the amended law and regulations, a draft concession is attached to the amended Regulations which is to be followed "except where the circumstances attending any particular application require the addition of special provisions." This draft contains no Calvo clause, and in place thereof a clause provides that any attempt to transfer the concession to an alien or to a foreign government shall be null and of no effect. This provision is less harsh than those provisions of certain American statutes that any attempt by one alien to transfer land to another alien who has not capacity to take, shall forfeit such land to the State.

The question whether or not the "manifesting" of lands under Circular 11 of January 15, 1915, constituted a "positive act" remains where the formal correspondence left it. It was first specifically raised by Secretary Kellogg's note of July 31, 1926, the next to the last note written by him during the controversy. In his answering note of October 7, 1926, Minister Saenz did not seriously contest the position of Secretary Kellogg, and calling attention to the declarations of the Mexican Commissioners at the Bucareli Conference, he affirmed "that what the Supreme Court and the Mexican Commissioners consider as an act disclosing the intention [a 'positive act'] is the investment of money or effort intended to obtain petroleum." As a matter of the normal evidencing of a fact, it would seem that a formal, bona fide declaration that property had been acquired and was held for the purpose of oil exploitation, would constitute all but conclusive evidence of the "investment of money or effort intended to obtain petroleum." The incorporation in the Regulations of the exact definition of "positive acts" given by the Mexican Commissioners offers a reasonable promise that no difficulty will be experienced in this matter.

We come now to the question of titles. The decision of the Supreme Court, the formal declarations of President Calles, the Report of the Committee of the Chamber of Deputies, the express provisions of the amendments to the Petroleum Law, the formal assurances of the Ministry of Industry, Commerce and Labor, the language of the amended Petroleum Regulations, the draft form of confirmatory concession appended to the Regulations,—all these agree that whatever rights the holders of "tagged" lands had on May 1, 1917, they still have; they are entitled to them and they hold them, as the Supreme Court affirmed, without restriction or loss. The confirmatory concession which is issuing declares "there are confirmed . . . the rights to effect works of petroleum exploration and exploitation" in the properties designated; the confirmation "operates as a recognition of rights acquired which shall continue in force, legal possession of which it confers administratively;" and "this confirmatory concession is not subject to forfeiture, and only obligates the concessionaire to comply with all regulations covering police and safety in the works."

Thus the law, the regulations, and the form of confirmatory concession attached to the regulations appear substantially and satisfactorily to cover the various matters which have been in dispute between the two Governments for more than thirteen years. The confirmatory documents to be issued by the Mexican Government will be a recognition of old acquired rights which continue without change, not the grant of new rights; these confirmations are without limitation of time, instead of for fifty years. The documents will contain no Calvo clause; they will be issued to American individuals and corporations who held rights prior to May 1, 1917, the Mexican Government taking the view that the inhibitory provisions of the Constitution as affecting the acquisition of properties by alien corporations do not apply to such corporations with respect to their properties acquired prior to May 1, 1917. As to the "tagging" of the lands, the exact language of the Bucareli Conference has been incorporated in the regulations, so that the contentions of the United States on this point have been fully met.

Ambassador Morrow made a statement on the foregoing situation, on March 28, 1928, the day on which the Regulations were promulgated. His opening paragraph reads:

These Regulations when taken with the Supreme Court decision handed down November 17, 1927, the legislation passed by the Mexican Congress on December 26, 1927, and promulgated on January 10, 1928, and the letter of Minister Morones issued on January 9, 1928, evidence the determination by the judicial, the executive, the legislative, and the administrative departments of the Mexican Government to recognize all rights held by foreigners in oil properties prior to the adoption of the 1917 Constitution.

On the same day, the Department of State issued a statement which said:

The Petroleum Regulations just promulgated by President Calles constitute executive action which completes the process beginning with the decision made by the judicial branch of the Mexican Government on November 17, 1927, and followed by the enactment of the new Petroleum Law by the legislative branch on December 26th last. Together, these steps, voluntarily taken by the Mexican Government, would appear to bring to a practical conclusion discussions which began ten years ago with reference to the effect of the Mexican Constitution and laws upon foreign oil companies. The Department feels, as does Ambassador Morrow, that such questions, if any, as may hereafter arise can be settled through the due operation of the Mexican administrative departments and the Mexican courts.

The Petroleum Controversy in Mexico

1928–1936

This second of two articles on the oil controversy with Mexico was also written while JRC was legal adviser to Dwight W. Morrow, United States ambassador to Mexico. The first (Article One above) was a popular treatment; the other, from which the following excerpt comes, deals with the strictly legal questions and, after serving its initial confidential purpose, was published in 1936 by the Deseret News Press in Salt Lake City. In its published form, *The Petroleum Controversy in Mexico* is forty-eight pages in length; only the last two and one-half pages, identified simply as "Recapitulation," are reproduced here. Box 48, Book 2, 1928, Oil, JRCP.

In recapitulation, the following points should be in mind:

The fundamental principle of the Spanish mining law, announced definitely at least as early as 1383—that "all mines of silver, and gold, and lead, and of any other metal whatever, of whatsoever kind it may be, in our Royal Seignory, shall belong to us," the sovereign; that mines might only be worked by royal permission, apparently (in the earlier times) specifically given; that all such special rights given by the Sovereign of Spain during a century and three-quarters were, by the edict of Don Philip II in 1559, revoked, annulled, and made void, except only those special gifts upon which work had begun and was then continuing; that notwithstanding such earlier gifts the Sovereign by this edict, "re-

claimed, resumed, and incorporated" into his "crown and patrimony" all the mines of gold and silver and quicksilver whether
found on private lands or elsewhere; that the edict of 1559 destroyed
without compensation the virtually exclusive privileges given under
the edict of 1383 to private individuals for the exploitation of mines
on their own properties; that under this edict of 1559, the only
thing which gave the actual rights which the Sovereign provided to
be granted, was the discovery of a mine, accompanied by the actual
exhibition of ore; that apparently the Sovereign changed at will the
burdens imposed—the royalty exacted—for working mines, both
those already discovered and operated under earlier laws and those
which might be thereafter discovered; that by the edict of 1563
owners of land were given a participation in the proceeds of mines
thereon discovered, which participation was, without compensation, taken away by the law of 1584; that this latter law gave
"propias, en posesion y propiedad" to those who should discover
mines; that Gamboa declared that this "dominio y propiedad de los
vassallos," the "dominio directo, o propiedad . . . el util por virtud
de la merced y concesion de la soberno" which the edict granted to
vassals, were consistent with the claimed royal rights and titles; that
Gamboa further said that while such right—"propias, en posesion y
propiedad"—(which Gamboa characterized as a "concession")—had
been bestowed, yet the "property of the mines remains vested in the
crown;" that notwithstanding this bestowal of property and possession by the edict of 1584 which for 200 years was the law operative
in Mexico and under which mining rights were during all this
period acquired in Mexico, the crown in 1783 made a law for New
Spain (including Mexico) which—in spite of or consistent with the
rights already acquired—again declared the Sovereign to be the
owner of the mines "as well by their nature and origin as by their
reunion declared in the law" of 1559; that the law of 1783 again
granted ("concedo") to his subjects "propiedad y posesion" in mines
so that they might alienate or devise them as they wished; that this
law seems without doubt to have included petroleum within its
provisions; that, as stated by the Supreme Court of the United
States, under this law mining rights are "regarded as severed from
private land and also from public land when granted by the usual
forms of conveyance for agricultural or other ordinary purposes;"
that this law of 1783 giving "propiedad y posesion" to all who

operated mines (which rights were granted by a Sovereign who at the same time declared "the mines are the property of my royal crown" and who gave to his subjects their rights "without separating them—the mines—from my royal patrimony") remained in force in Mexico until 1884, when Mexico, which it would seem had succeeded to the rights of the Spanish crown, enacted its first mining code; that this code gave to the owners of the surface, "exclusiva propiedad" of certain substances under the surface, including petroleum; that this code contains nothing which indicates that the "propiedad" granted by it is different from the "propiedad" granted by the edicts of 1584 and 1783, which left the ownership of the mines in the sovereign; that in 1892, Mexico passed a second mining code which made no mention of bestowing a "propiedad" upon the owners of the surface, but gave to them merely a right to exploit their land without securing from the government a license therefor; that therefore the 1892 law can be construed as taking away the "propiedad" given by the statute of 1884; that in 1905 a discussion took place by the Mexican bar, in which a majority of those recording their opinions took the view that owners acquired no rights to oil (and other minerals) in their lands merely by force of the laws of 1884 and 1892 unless and until they had made discovery; that in 1909 another law was passed which returned to the language of 1884, but again without indicating that the "propiedad" it gave was different from the "propiedad" given in the edicts of 1584 and 1783.

Of all these facts and considerations, purchasers of oil properties must be regarded as legally on notice; they were equally on legal notice (and as a part of the foregoing) that as to the underlying principle of Spanish law there were two opposing views, either of which might prevail, and either of which, if adopted at one time, might be abandoned later—the whole history of Spanish mining law seems to show this. They were likewise on notice that the view which was held by the majority of the bar in 1905, and which was later incorporated into the new Constitution (1917) and the implementing decrees and laws, was the view which was consistent, indeed practically identical, with the view which had obtained in the Spanish mining law from earliest times—a view which, of all, seems among the most elemental of the principles of that law. Under these circumstances, it can hardly be said that purchasers of

307

oil lands did not know, as a matter of law, of the possibilities in the situation, or that they did not assume the risk of the adoption of a less favorable principle than they might wish for.

With the foregoing in mind, it can hardly be said that the doctrine incorporated in the new Constitution, and expressed by their Executive, their legislature, and their Supreme Court, that in order for rights to the oil to vest in the owner there must be some "positive act" performed by such owner, is a doctrine which falls below the minimum standard as to investors who made their investments under legal notice of the existence of the principle. Furthermore, it is submitted that Mexico having declared, by her duly constituted and appropriate governmental organs, that under Mexican law no right to oil is acquired by the owner of the surface unless and until he has performed a "positive act," the United States, in view of the history behind the situation, is not in a position to contest that declaration, nor to say that such declaration, when enforced, deprives any owner of any "acquired right" which he theretofore possessed.

Nor does the fact that the Constitution provides that no private property shall be taken without compensation, change the situation, for the question is not the protection of a right but the existence of a right; and under the law as declared by Mexico, no right exists, upon which the Constitutional guarantees can act, until the performance of a "positive act;" and under the law and regulations as amended, the rights possessed by owners who have performed "positive acts" are recognized and protected.

Official Farewell to Mexico

10 February 1933

On the evening when Mexico officially bade farewell to Ambassador JRC and his family, a banquet at the foreign office was followed by a reception described by Arthur Bliss Lane, counselor of the embassy and chargé d'affaires, as "unique," "an extraordinary demonstration," even "brilliant." The event was reported by many to be "the most brilliant affair" ever given at the foreign office in their memory.

Speaking on behalf of Mexico, Dr. Puig Casauranc expressed his regret at the coming departure of JRC and his appreciation for the work he had done. Then, referring to the policies Ambassadors Morrow and Clark had followed, he said, "These policies are the only ones that can secure that at the time of separation or return of a diplomatic agent to his native land, official expressions and observances of protocol be made in a spirit of sincerity and real cordiality until they become—as is my expression of today in the name of the Government of Mexico—a living manifestation of sympathy and affection, rather than an official act and a ceremonial protocol." He concluded his remarks with a toast in which he said of JRC, "Mexico will always greet [him] with open arms, in whatever capacity, official or private, he may return to us" (*El Universal,* 11 February 1933). JRC replied with the following brief remarks. Box 49, Folder 33, "Reading copy of farewell speech made at banquet in honor of Mrs. C and self at For. Office before leaving Mexico."

It is a distinguished honor which you confer tonight, an honor to my illustrious predecessor Ambassador Morrow, and to President Hoover and his administration of the Foreign Affairs of the United States. For this honor I extend my deep and sincere thanks. It will not pass unnoticed by the Government and people of the United States. For such small part as I dare to assume to myself, I ask you to accept my profound gratitude. Whatever virtue has flowed from the work of Ambassador Morrow and myself, has come because we have represented, as best we might, the mind and heart of the American people.

Mr. Minister, to no one could come a greater honor than the assurance you give me of the sympathy and affection of the Mexican people. To possess a place in the hearts of a people is the most priceless heritage that can come to any man, however high may be his degree and however lowly may be his station. The hearts of the people make the holiest shrine in which mortals may be placed.

Mr. Minister, the old diplomacy, representing intercourse between personal sovereigns and not peoples, was supposed to have two fundamental precepts: that an Ambassador should despise the Minister of Foreign Affairs of the country to which he was accredited, and should hate the people to whom he was sent. Both of these precepts I have grossly violated.

For you, Mr. Minister, and for your predecessors in high office, I have affectionate esteem and a deep respect. From each of you I have received that courteous treatment and kindly consideration which always obtains between the representatives of friendly and equal sovereign States. We have been able to adjust questions pending between our Governments and reach understandings that must cement the friendships of our two great peoples whom we represented. It has been not only a pleasure but an honor to know and work with you.

Moreover, I hope I may venture to say that, also violating the old rule, I have found for the people of Mexico a genuine love, which shall never forsake me.

Mr. Minister, the mists that obscure the history of the past of your people hang very near and very heavy, but through them we dimly perceive civilization after civilization rise, flourish, and decay. We glimpse monuments of civilizations greater than any heretofore known; we hear echoes of desperate conflicts in which were forged the iron qualities that characterize the race.

History records a patient, indomitable racial will to hold the heritage of this past, a heritage of culture, of character, of experience, and of wisdom, which is a graven record upon the mind and heart of those remnants of former peoples that make the present race.

It has seemed to me, Mr. Minister, that all this past is an integral and vital part of the present, and that, therefore, to understand the present we must comprehend something at least of the past.

It is in this view and in this spirit that I have approached my work in Mexico; and this view and this spirit have given me a tolerance for the ardent zeal with which at times the race has surged to and fro; they have given me a sympathy with the aspirations and ideals proclaimed in your revolution; they have accounted, and have given excuse, if not reason, for the measures which always mark a rebellion, when a people, downtrodden for generations, grope upwards for the light of the sun. This view and this spirit have given me the faith that, coming down through the generations, there lies somewhere in the deep recesses of the racial mind of Mexico, a spark of that cumulated wisdom and experience, descended from former ages and greatness, that shall in due time blaze forth and light the race along a new path, leading to greater glories.

Mr. Minister, my leaving Mexico would be an intolerable grief, did I not have your generous assurance that I am welcome to return, and did I not take with me cherished memories, never to be forgotten, of the courtesy and kindness, the care and solicitude, the affectionate interest, the hospitality, you have so bounteously shown me.

Mr. Minister, our two nations must always be friends; they must never be enemies. Common interest, the considerations of propinquity, the requirements of human brotherhood, imperatively demand this. Our paths of progress lie parallel. We must live together. We have no problems which mutual forbearance, mutual understanding, mutual respect, mutual tolerance, mutual will to do justice and equity as between equals, will not solve. As someone has said: God made us neighbors; we must make ourselves friends.

Ladies and Gentlemen, join me in a toast to His Excellency the President of Mexico, to His Excellency the Minister for Foreign Affairs, and to beautiful Mexico and her people, their peace, their prosperity, and their happiness.

PART FOUR

Miscellany

The Nature and Definition of Political Offense in International Extradition

April 1909

JRC's responsibilities as assistant solicitor in the Department of State in 1909 included being in charge of matters concerning extradition. One of the major cases he handled was that of Jan Janoff Pouren. The Russian government had applied for Pouren's extradition upon the charges of murder, arson, burglary, and attempt to commit murder. The case gave rise to a number of issues to which JRC responded with memoranda. As a consequence of his work on the Pouren case and other extradition matters, he was invited to present a major address at the Annual Meeting of the American Society of International Law held in Washington, D.C., on 23 and 24 April 1909. It was the first major public address in his legal career and was reprinted in the proceedings of the society for the year 1909, beginning on page one. See also Box 46, Book 1, 1909, Extradition, E 9.1, JRCP.

JRC began by stating that the questions that would arise in connection with his subject could be divided roughly into two classes: first, those "relating to the international aspect of extradition," and secondly, "those which have their source in the general principles of our constitutional law and concern only or chiefly the rights of civil liberty guaranteed by the Constitution:" His paper, he said, would "confine itself to a brief sketch dealing with certain phases of the second division named." Near the outset of his remarks, JRC said:

315

Congress appears neither to have seen fit, not deemed it necessary to lay down any statutory rules or regulations regarding this matter. . . . The sources, therefore, to which one must look for the principles governing this question are the extradition treaties themselves, the decisions of the judiciary, and the determinations of the executive.

After remarking on the paucity of political refugee cases upon which either the courts or the executive had been called to pass judgment and indicating that the conclusions suggested must be regarded as tentative, he said:

The particular subject selected for present treatment may be appropriately dealt with under four heads: *first,* the nature of the defense raised when the fugitive pleads that the crime with which he is charged is political; *second,* the tribunal, judicial or executive, to which such a defense should be addressed; *third,* the tribunal, judicial or executive, by which the sufficiency of this defense must be finally judged and determined; and *fourth,* a consideration of some of the essential elements which go to make up a political offense as those elements may be drawn from the language of the treaties, the decisions of the courts, and the determinations of the executive.

JRC divided the first heading into three subdivisions. The first began:

[I.] (a) At the outset of the discussion I venture to suggest, merely, a question which perhaps lies at the base of this branch of the subject: "Is the so-called 'political crime or offense' (in the sense in which the term is here used) to be regarded as properly a crime at all, from the point of view of international extradition?" In other words, is not the so-called political crime internationally a neutral or colorless act to which no criminality does or can attach, and for this reason an act which is outside the purview of extradition treaties?

After discussion, he concluded:

It is therefore believed that a political crime or offense may perhaps be considered as not in any real sense a crime, within the meaning of international agreements for extradition.

He then posed another question:

(b) A second question arising in connection with this branch of the subject may be stated as follows: "Is the defense that the crime charged is political in its character, a plea to the jurisdiction of the court or should it be classed as a plea to the merits?"

Again, after discussion, he concluded:

In the light of these various considerations it would appear not unreasonable to regard the plea that the crime charged is a political act as a plea not to the merits but to the jurisdiction.

Of the third subdivision he said:

(c) A third phase . . . relates to the burden of proof and the amount of evidence necessary, under the plea that the act charged is political.

[The courts] now uniformly hold that it is only necessary for the demanding government to show probable cause to believe the fugitive guilty of the crime charged in order to be entitled to his surrender. The meaning of probable cause in this connection has been defined by Judge Morrow to be "such evidence of guilt as would furnish good reason to a cautious man, and warrant him in the belief, that the person accused is guilty of the offense with which he is charged" (*Federal Reporter*, 62:982), and this view of the law was expressly approved by the Supreme Court in *Ornelas v. Ruiz.*

It seems sufficiently apparent from these observations that the burden of proof—that is, the burden of establishing all necessary allegations—rests *as to the merits* upon the demanding government, which must make out a *prima facie* case against the accused. However, inasmuch as under the principle just stated, the proceeding before the commissioner is not a trial, but is a mere preliminary examination to determine whether or not the accused shall be surrendered to be placed upon trial, it is not necessary for the demanding government to establish the guilt of the accused and the burden placed upon the government is satisfied when it has shown that there is probable cause to believe that an extraditable crime has been committed and that the accused has committed it.

. . . The problem is difficult indeed, and . . . the question of the burden of proof, in the sense . . . of establishing the political or nonpolitical nature of the crime, becomes fundamental.

This question may be appropriately considered, *first,* with reference to the general rules of practice that govern in matters of pleas running to the jurisdiction; and *secondly,* with reference to the rules that may be deduced from the language of the treaties.

First, concerning the general rules of practice . . . the burden of establishing the plea will always rest where it first lies, upon the party making the positive averment that the crime is political. . . .

Secondly, the rule as it may be deduced from the treaty provisions . . . is a thoroughly established doctrine of our courts that extradition treaties are to be interpreted broadly and liberally, rather than narrowly and technically.

. . . The general purpose of the political clause in extradition treaties appears to be to provide against the surrender of political refugees for punishment for political crimes.

These considerations would seem to establish that the fugitive, in order to be entitled to his discharge from custody, must do more than merely raise a doubt as to the political character of the offense . . . but [the rule] should provide that his discharge is due when he has a preponderance of the evidence in his favor. This seems to be the general rule governing pleas running to the jurisdiction.

In conclusion to heading one, JRC said:

If the conclusions above set forth upon this branch of our discussion are sound, it would appear (1) that the plea that the crimes or offenses charged are political in their nature, is a plea to the jurisdiction and not to the merits; (2) that the fugitive pleading to the jurisdiction has the burden of establishing it by a preponderance of evidence; (3) and that the commissioner's findings upon this question are subject to review by the courts under writ of *certiorari* and *habeas corpus*.

II. *The second branch of the subject as outlined deals with the question of the tribunal before which the defense of the political character of the act should be pleaded.*

At the end of his discussion of this branch of the subject, he said:

It would seem a necessary conclusion that such evidence as the fugitive may have tending to establish that the crime for which he is demanded is in reality a political offense should be offered to the committing magistrate. As a practical matter, it may be said that so long as the present practice is maintained in the Department of State, no fugitive would be quite safe in neglecting or refusing to present before the commissioner his defense that the crime with which he is charged is political.

III. *Is the political nature of the act finally passed upon and determined by the courts or by the executive?*

* * *

Under normal conditions it is not possible in any case to deliver up to a demanding government a fugitive from the justice of that government unless the action is concurred in both by the judicial and executive branches of this government. If either of these consider that the fugitive should not return, it is impossible for the demanding government to obtain him through extradition process.

IV. *The final phase of the discussion upon this subject has reference to the elements and characteristics of political crimes and offenses as they may be deduced from the adjudged cases.*

. . . In almost all of the cases of political offenders who have sought refuge in this country and whose surrender has been denied by this government upon extradition proceedings instituted by the government from which they came, there has been no recognition whatsoever of the belligerency of the party to which the fugitive belonged. This is true of the Mexican revolutionists of the 90's, as well as of the recent revolutionary fugitives from Russia. In these cases, therefore, the real question at issue was whether or not, as a historical fact, there existed in the demanding country a revolutionary movement in the general rather than in the technical meaning of that term; if so, whether or not the fugitive was a member of one of the parties; and if he was, whether or not the crime with which he was charged was committed in the course and as a part of the political activities of that party to which he belonged.

* * *

The Russian cases suggested that perhaps the further question may at some time arise as to whether or not a political act may not be carried out with such barbarity or inhumanity as to deprive the offense of immunity under the treaty.

As JRC came to the close of his thirty-printed-page address, he obviously recognized that his talk had taken more time than had been alloted for it; but even so he regarded it as fragmentary and incomplete. This is his concluding paragraph:

But the time allotted for this address has passed some time since, and it is necessary to bring these remarks to a close. What has been said is confessedly fragmentary and incomplete, and many of the most interesting and important phases of the subject have been but touched or suggested. Enough has, however, been said to indicate how few of the principles (even of those that are fundamental) which control the extradition of persons claiming to be political offenders, have been determined. Experience teaches how necessary it is that these principles be sought and applied with greatest care, in order that, on the one hand, no true political refugee shall be deprived of the rights given him by treaty, and, on the other hand, that our body politic shall not be corrupted by the continued presence amongst us of large numbers of criminals who seek to avoid a just punishment for all kinds and degrees of crime, on the ground that they are political offenders.

Right to Protect Citizens in Foreign Countries by Landing Forces

5 October 1912

JRC became solicitor for the Department of State of the United States on 1 July 1910. The following November a revolution commenced in Mexico. JRC was much involved in American-Mexican affairs, and his deep concern for the lives and property of American citizens in Mexico during the period of Mexico's grave internal strife gave rise to this very important memorandum. At its end JRC attached a twenty-eight-page appendix entitled, "Chronological list of Occasions on Which the Government of the United States has taken Action by Force for the Protection of American Interests; Including Certain Instances in which Similar Action has been taken by Other Governments in Behalf of Their Nationals." The following is an abbreviated form of the published memorandum. Box 69, JRCP.

The precise question at issue is whether or not one state may, if necessary, use actual force (i.e., use its army and navy) for and in behalf of and to secure the protection and security of the persons and property of its citizens resident or domiciled in another state in cases of sudden emergency where the other state fails, either through its unwillingness, its impotence, or from any other cause, to protect the citizens of the first state and their property from destruction.

An examination of the authorities appears quite clearly to show that one state may, without giving just cause for offense to another state, thus interpose in favor of its nationals resident in the other state; and there is not a little authority for the proposition that such interposition by the one state as against the other is a matter of right and, indeed, duty.

The whole subject has been clouded by the fact that this interposition has not infrequently been seemingly regarded as actual intervention in the internal political affairs of another state and for that reason has, as a principle, fallen within the severe strictures which various writers have passed upon such intervention.

In order that the question may be properly elucidated and that the distinction between such intervention and mere interposition of the kind under consideration shall be clearly understood and distinguished, it seems desirable first to consider the discussions by international law writers of the subject of intervention.

In the first part of the memorandum JRC devoted twenty pages to a discussion of "Formal Intervention." In the second part, a fourteen-page discussion of "Interposition for the Protection of Citizens," he said:

The general discussion above will serve to illustrate the perplexities, difficulties, and disagreements which exist regarding the general question of intervention. It would, however, appear that not a little of the confusion so aptly pointed out by Lawrence (T. J. Lawrence, *The Principles of International Law* [Boston, 1895], 3) is due, at least in part, to the failure of most writers to appreciate or make the distinction made by Mr. Moore in his *Digest* (John B. Moore, *A Digest of International Law*, 8 vols. [Washington, D.C., 1906]) between political intervention and nonpolitical intervention or, as it may perhaps be otherwise termed, interposition upon behalf of citizens. The result of this has been that the writers have discussed the subject almost uniformly from the standpoint of political intervention—that is, an intervention by one power in the local political affairs of another power—for example, for the purpose of preserving a particular form of government (the Holy Alliance), or for the purpose of assisting a revolutionary government (cf. France in the War of Independence and our intervention in Cuba in 1898), or for the purpose of preventing the accession of a revolutionary government (the intervention of Great Britain in the affairs of Portugal, 1847), or to preserve the *status quo* in the so-called European "balance of power" (the division of Poland by Russia, Austria, and Prussia), and that such writers have applied to the nonpolitical intervention or interposition all the strictures or commendations which they have applied to political intervention. But it is by no means a logical necessity that the rules and purposes underlying political intervention (which has received the animadversion of many international law writers) should be controlling or even applicable to the nonpolitical intervention or interposition which is exercised solely for the protection of the citizens of the intervening state resident or domiciled within the non-protecting state. Nonpolitical intervention or interposition need not have, and as a matter of fact almost never has, so far as our precedents go, any reference to the internal politics of the invaded country in the matter of either supporting or changing the particular form of government. Moreover, not only are considerations of that sort usually absent, but they are impliedly and oftentimes expressly eliminated from consideration (e.g., the intervention of the powers in Mexico, 1861). The sole motive for this nonpolitical intervention or interposition is the protection of citizens or subjects either from the acts of the government itself or from the acts of persons or bodies of persons resident within the jurisdiction of a government which finds itself unable to afford the requisite protection, until the government concerned is willing or able itself to afford the protection. When this is accomplished the interposing state withdraws, leaving the government either as it found it or as it may have been altered or changed by purely internal and local means, with which matters the interposing government has had no interest, concern, or connection. In other words, the distinction must be drawn between an intervention designed to secure a change, or to protect from change, a particular form of government or a dynasty and an intervention having no political purpose whatsoever, being designed merely to protect citizens where the local government is either unable or unwilling to give such protection, the internal policies of the affected government being of no concern whatsoever to the interposing power save as they affect the protection and security of its citizens and their property.

There is considerable authority for the proposition that such interposition by one state in the internal affairs of another state for the purpose of affording adequate protection to the citizens of one resident in the other as well as for the protection of the property of such citizens is not only not improper, but, on the contrary, is based upon, is in accord with, and is the exercise of a right recognized by international law.

In the third and concluding part, ten pages in length and entitled, "Suggestions regarding Certain Considerations of Constitutional Law Involved in and Connected with the Use of American Forces for the Protection of American Citizens on Foreign Soil," JRC began as follows:

Although it is not the purpose of this memorandum to deal with the question of interposition for the purpose of protecting citizens otherwise than from the standpoint of international law, still it may not be amiss to suggest a few points having a bearing upon or concerning questions of American constitutional law, which questions may be involved in the use of American troops for this purpose, and particularly upon the question as to whether or not under the Constitution the President has the right and power to use the forces of the United States for such purposes without authorization by Congress.

The final two paragraphs read:

It is therefore believed, as already stated, that the President may, under his constitutional powers and without the necessity of ancillary legislation, enforce those rules and principles of international law involved in the matter under discussion.

It is again observed that the above observations upon this phase of the subject now being considered are made merely by way of suggestion and with no thought or pretense of more than a cursory consideration. It is entirely possible that a more detailed and careful study would lead to other or modified conclusions.

The Function of the Red Cross in Time of Civil War or Insurrection

11 May 1912

Having been appointed by the chairman of the International Relief Board of the American Red Cross to membership on a committee to study and report on the assistance of Red Cross societies to forces engaged in insurrection, revolution, or any kind of civil disobedience, JRC was asked by the committee to prepare a memorandum on the subject for its use. He obliged with a 110-page memorandum plus a 43-page appendix. Over his signature as chairman, a shorter but more technical report detailing the committee's recommendations was submitted to the American Red Cross. It was not the intent of the committee that the proposals be submitted to the Red Cross organizations of other nations in the form of that report, but in any event the American Red Cross sent out copies of the report for the general information of other Red Cross organizations.

The international conference, with delegates from 31 countries of Europe, Asia, and North and South America, convened on 7 May 1912. On 10 May an international committee of seven, including JRC, met to examine his report; its proposals were rejected by a vote of five to two. The next day, after the conference had heard General Luigi Ferrero di Cavallerleone of Italy present the majority report of the committee, JRC presented his minority report. It reflects his great concern for the sick and wounded in times of armed conflict irrespective of the political status of the victims. Box 68, F 10, vol. 1, F 10.8, JRCP.

As a minority member, dissenting from the views of the majority of the committee as they have been presented, I desire to make a few observations.

In the first place, I wish to make it perfectly clear that I am not here as a representative of the American Government; that I am not here as an official of that Government; but that I stand before you as a private American citizen accredited to this conference by the American Red Cross.

As I explained to the members of the committee on the occasion of its meeting, some misapprehension appears to exist regarding the real situation in this matter. The facts are that in December last the International Board of the American Red Cross appointed a committee to study and prepare a report on the problem of Red Cross assistance in times of insurrection, revolution, or any kind of civil war. This committee made its report on April 1, 1912. At that time I had not had opportunity to prepare the address which it was proposed I should deliver to this Conference. Therefore, the American Red Cross, in order that the general subject matter to be discussed might be before the delegates coming to the Conference, sent out, in place of the address which under ordinary circumstances would have gone, copies of this committee's report. It was not contemplated that this matter should be presented to the Conference in the precise form in which it was stated in the report which was merely a detailed statement by a committee appointed by the International Board of the American Red Cross and which was designed primarily to suggest the difficulties which would have to be met in the premises. It was, however, the intention and is the intention of the American Red Cross, and the address which I had proposed to deliver would have made this point clear, to present for consideration the general proposal of the feasibility and advisability of attempting to provide for Red Cross assistance in time of armed civil disorders.

Moreover, I desire to call to your attention two fundamental and essential elements contained in the report of the American committee which was sent to you. First, it was contemplated that in each case in which the question of rendering the service arose, the established government should have the right to declare whether or not Red Cross assistance should be extended to the disturbers of the government, and that such assistance could not be rendered without the assent of the government. The other point which must be kept carefully in mind and without due consideration and appreciation of which this matter can not be properly understood, is that the offering of assistance by the Red Cross Societies of neutral countries could not constitute and was not intended to constitute a recognition of belligerency, or even a state of actual war, or as a step in the direction of such recognition. It was to be and was to be regarded as an offer of a philanthropic, private, non-official organization desiring to extend its aid to suffering humanity.

In this connection you will permit me to offer the suggestion that all the questions involved will probably become materially simplified if it be clearly kept in mind that the Red Cross is an organization which has and can have obviously no international political status; that its sole reason for existence is the dispensing of aid, relief, and succor to suffering humanity wherever such exists and irrespective of race, creed, or conditions; that its activities where engaged are, as a consequence, wholly devoid of international political significance or effect; and finally that therefore a tender of service by it is not and cannot be construed as an act having any, even the slightest, political color or meaning. The Red Cross is not generally a governmental agency save in a very limited sense and under special conditions, namely, after it has been incorporated as a part of the military sanitary service of a country in time of war. These essential and fundamental considerations will, I feel quite sure, be found to relieve, if not indeed actually demolish many seeming difficulties.

The Conference will, I trust, permit me to make a suggestion pertinent to this point. I observe that my illustrious colleague, General Yermoloff, has made his declaration in the "capacity of delegate of the Imperial Government" of Russia, and he states that "the Imperial Government could not in any case or in any form be a contracting party or even only a discussing party to any agreement or recommendation on this subject." In view of these words, it will not perhaps be amiss in me to suggest that this Conference is not a Conference of the Powers. It is not a Conference of sovereign States. It is wholly and merely a Conference of private, benevolent and philanthropic organizations which have only indirect governmental connections and which have met for the purpose of concerting together regarding ways and means of extending their beneficent work. A little thought will, I am sure, make quite clear the propriety of bearing this fact clearly in mind, since quite obviously States would scarcely care to assume the responsibility for acts done by this Conference composed as it is so largely of people having no governmental connection and whose actions, therefore, they could not control. And, inasmuch, as the Conference is not a Conference of States, but a Conference of unofficial societies, and a Conference whose action in no way, not even the slightest, is binding upon the Powers, it would appear that it may with propriety discuss at least initially projects which the States themselves might not care to enter upon. I can not but feel, therefore, and with due deference, that the reservation made by my illustrious colleague is not entirely consonant with the character of this assemblage.

Recalling, as has already been stated, that the service contemplated in the proposal is merely that of nursing the sick and wounded and relieving human suffering among those afflicted in times of civil disturbance, and remembering that it is the initial and primary duty and purpose of the Red Cross to extend such aid and relief to sick and wounded soldiers in time of armed conflicts, I have to bring to your notice that there is urgent need for the extension of the service as proposed. The whole history of armed and organized insurrections and revolutions with which, unfortunately, all are familiar, amply demonstrates this point. One incident will suffice for illustration.

In a recent civil disturbance with which a State was afflicted, the forces of the contending faction fought two battles. The total number of men engaged on both sides was approximately six thousand. Of these, two thousand—that is, one-third of the entire number— were either killed or wounded. While each faction had some military sanitary organization, it was entirely inefficient both as to numbers and equipment, and most of the wounded lay, after the battles, for days on barren hillsides, exposed, without any care or attention whatsoever, to a burning tropical sun, and literally hundreds (having without avail dragged themselves for protection behind rocks and bushes) needlessly perished, not so much from the effect of their wounds as from exposure, hunger, and thirst. These hundreds died after their cause was lost or won. Their deaths advanced not a whit the principles for which they fought. It was an awful and needless loss of human life which might, it would seem, have been saved by the assistance which the Red Cross could have given, and would have been eager and anxious to give had there been any way in which it could have been accomplished.

Is it necessary to do more than suggest that to deny that the discussion of plans and methods to relieve these soldiers wounded in regular battle is within the province of this Red Cross Conference, would be to stultify the very essence and spirit of the work for which the Red Cross was created?

The proposal made by the American delegation is not a mere dream nor the idle theory of a visionary. We are not driven merely to surmise either as to the propriety, the effectiveness, or the acceptance of such assistance in times of civil disturbances. The American Red Cross, through its regular organization, has over and over again extended assistance in time of insurrectionary disturbances, both to the insurrectionists and the regular forces, and to combatants and non-combatants. It extended such assistance to Cuban non-combatants in Cuba in 1897-98; to the Nicaraguan combatants of both forces in 1909; to the Honduras revolutionists in 1911; and, with the world at large, to China in 1912. But this is not all, the United States Government has itself repeatedly landed portions of its regularly organized military sanitary service sometimes under a Red Cross flag and sometimes apparently without it; and such service so landed has nursed the sick and wounded of both factions of civil disturbances. Such assistance was extended to both factions in San Domingo and in Venezuela in 1903; to the insurrectionists in San Domingo in 1906; to both sides in Nicaragua in 1909; and in Honduras in 1911. In none of these cases, so far as is reported, was there any objection to or resentment at such assistance by the parties concerned, and, on the contrary, there appeared to be an appreciation of the service and of the disinterested motives which prompted it.

Moreover, it may not be amiss to recall to your minds that in the Boer South African war, which by some has been termed a civil war, Red Cross assistance was rendered to the Boer forces by the Red Cross societies of Germany, France, Italy, Spain, Netherlands, Sweden, Norway, Denmark, Greece, and Switzerland, and it would appear that in the recent revolutionary disturbances in China the whole world has extended relief.

I find in the report of the committee the expression "that the Latin Republics are placed in a situation different from that of the others, States of Europe, even different from that of North America." This is no suggestion of mine, nor is it one for which I am in any way responsible. In reply I would say, grant that the situation is different, and grant the seemingly natural implication from this that the necessity for the service does not exist in Europe or in the United States, still I submit with due deference that these are not reasons why we should hold ourselves aloof from a movement contemplating the rendering of assistance in those cases in which it is needed. It is quite true that for a period of fifty years the Government of the United States has enjoyed full stability and tranquility, but we have in the past had our troubles, and if my memory is playing me no tricks there have been within the last half century changes and attempted changes of no small significance in the internal governments of the nations of Europe. And here let me point out that the proposal of the American Red Cross looks to assistance extended by the Red Cross of other countries than that in which the civil disturbance exists and so differs from the proposal of my honorable colleague from Cuba, who suggests that the National Red Cross of a given country extend in time of civil conflict in that country its aid impartially between the regular soldiers and the insurrectionists.

I observe that my esteemed colleague (General Yermoloff) states that insurgents and revolutionists can be considered under the laws of his country only as criminals. I presume that the words "traitor" and "treason" are known to all languages and to all peoples, but I beg to suggest to his attention the fact that the opinion of the world upon matters of this kind has in the recent past made much advance. In early times disposition was not wanting to consider that every soldier before capture and after capture, whether well or wounded, might be treated as an enemy and put to death, but we have outgrown that conception. We now, in times of international conflict, vie one with another in extending assistance to those of the enemy who may happen to fall in our hands. Now the prisoners of war are treated as our own soldiers, they are nursed back to health and strength with the identic care and attention given to our own, and are returned under appropriate conditions to the forces or country from which they came. In this connection I need do [no] more than refer to the reciprocal treatment of Spain and the United States in 1898, and of Russia and Japan in 1904. Shall we say that those who oppose us in civil conflict, those who are kindred to us, our fathers, our sons, and our brothers, ought to receive or shall receive less consideration, less kindness, and less love than our alien enemies?

My colleague has moreover quoted the words of an illustrious American General, who, when speaking in a situation arising out of our great Civil War, said that "On no earthly account can I admit of any thought or act hostile to the old government." I am sure that this is a sentiment which rests in the heart of all of us, and in ordinary times at least he is a traitor indeed who holds a different opinion. But the proposition under discussion is in no wise inconsistent with this. May I direct my colleague's attention to the fact that notwithstanding General Sherman held and with his sword supported "the old government," yet he treated those of his valiant foes whom he captured in a civil war, not as traitors and criminals in the eyes of the law, but as prisoners of war and so entitled to all of the rights and privileges belonging to such a character. Moreover, I must remind my honored colleague that in that great conflict to which he has alluded, the greatest of its kind in history, the military sanitary service of the government of the United States, and the Sanitary Commission, the co-operating volunteer aid society, treated all those coming under their care with absolute impartiality, no matter whether they wore the blue of the Union or the grey of the Confederacy. The wounds of all were dressed, the pains of all were relieved, all were nursed as if they wore one color. In this connection I am reminded of an equally famous remark of the same great General, "War is hell" (William Tecumseh Sherman, 19 June 1879). Laconic as this is, it gives the whole picture of the horrors of war. It is the object of the present proposal to mitigate so far as may be possible the pains and the agonies of that inferno.

It is not improbable that military critics will tell us that the whole proposal will be fundamentally unacceptable because under certain extremities volunteer Red Cross assistance under such an arrangement as is foreshadowed would certainly, perhaps vitally, interfere with effective belligerent operations. Not being a military expert, I am in no position to deny this, but I may be pardoned if I say I doubt it. This thought is an old acquaintance of the workers of the Red Cross. You and I know that this is the same pronouncement formerly used against any participation by volunteer aid societies in recognized war. You and I know that this pronouncement appeared at the framing of the first Geneva Convention and that it continued, in decreasing force, for almost fifty years. We know that the Red Cross had nearly half a century of earnest educational work against this pronouncement, and nearly fifty years of actual and effective participation in hostilities on land and sea without seeming successfully to meet it. But the world moves and the pronouncement is dead. We here have made the beginning in this movement by initiating consideration; others will push the work forward; finally its fullness will come. The Red Cross has done a mighty work. Where fire and flood have devastated, the Red Cross has rebuilt; where sickness and disease have raged, the Red Cross has ministered; where famine has stalked, the Red Cross has furnished food; and where war has scourged, the Red Cross has healed the wounds. But there is yet work to be done and it is my faith that the Red Cross will do it. And so while we may not today or this year see the way of accomplishment of this proposal, yet the way will be opened so that in the not distant future, it will be apparent to all that sickness, pain, and the pangs of death may be as properly relieved in times of revolutionary disturbances as in times of actual war; that the consideration, the care, and the love which we extend to alien enemies may be equalled, let us hope exceeded, by the consideration, care, and love which in times of such disturbances we extend to our fathers, our sons, and our brothers who are differing with us thus vitally.

Mr. President, in view of these considerations, I have the honor to propose that this Conference adopt in lieu of the report submitted by the committee, the following resolution:

WHEREAS, it is the initial and primary duty and purpose of the Red Cross to extend aid and relief to sick and wounded soldiers in times of armed conflicts; and

WHEREAS, it is of the essence of the service that it shall be purely benevolent, philanthropic, and impartial, and without any political status or significance; now therefore be it

Resolved, That it is the wish of this Ninth International Red Cross Conference that there be referred to the International Committee with a request to obtain thereon reports from the various Red Cross organizations, the question of framing some feasible and advisable proposal for extending the activities of Red Cross societies to armed and organized insurrections, revolutions, or other civil disturbances.

The Panama Canal and the Region of the Caribbean

27 September 1915

This article discussing commercial and military aspects of the Canal and the Caribbean seems not to have been published. It is signed "Jay R. Sea, Jr." Box 46, Book 3, 1915, Memo-Notes, J 9.20, JRCP.

It is old and unchallenged wisdom that "a shoemaker should stick to his last." It is equally uncontroverted that a plain man eating his breakfast omelet knows more about the egg than the hen that laid it.

The mean of these two truths is a principle that seems sufficient to justify a few civilian comments and suggestions addressed to our professional diplomatic and military men. Particular point is just now given thereto by the renewed agitation for the acquisition of the Danish West Indies.

Nature has decreed that every living organism, plant, animal and social, must, if it is to live, protect itself, even at the cost of a part of the organism itself; and further, that when such protection ceases, the organism must die. This is the great natural law which seemingly has known and knows no exception. Until the law is changed every man and every state must be prepared to fight and win, if he or it wishes to live.

So, however much we might desire otherwise, we Americans must, if we are to live freemen, and if the United States itself is not to perish, count as a future contingency (however remote) a possible protective war with some first class power of either the West or the East.

It is obvious that in such a war the Panama Canal may be to us a source of strength, of weakness, or even of disaster. It will be a strength in so far as it facilitates the mobilization and movements of our navy, and in a slightly lesser degree the free flow of our commerce during such war; it will be a weakness in so far as its existence has induced us to regard our fleets on our two coasts as actually one fleet on either coast at our option, and in so far as the maintenance of its effectiveness in war times costs an undue price of effort, treasure, and blood. It will be a fatal disaster in so far as it fails to meet in war-time the reliance we place in it as a means of military mobilization and of maintaining free commerce. Indeed viewed from these various angles, there seems, as a matter of fact, to be a fair doubt whether the Canal is, after all is said and done, a military asset or liability. However, that is beside the point, we have the canal and therefore must make the most of it. The great purpose must be to secure the strength and to avoid the weakness and the disaster. To do this measures must be taken now. Preparation after war begins will be monumentally inadequate, and fatal.

An effective wartime use of the Canal requires free access to and control of its entrances, and unhampered and unobstructed passage over its waters. The latter is a question of effective fortification and police—essentially technical military matters to be left to the army and navy. So, in part, is the control of the entrance to the Canal. However, access to and control of the entrance to the Canal involve also certain broad, general questions of geography and policy, which, while intimately related to purely military problems, are of such a character as properly to entitle a civilian to an opinion thereon.

Free access to the Canal in time of war is necessary for two reasons,—first, to enable the proper movement and mobilization of the constituent parts of our fleet and possibly the transfer of our troops from one coast to the other (this is so vitally important as to need no comment); and secondly, to afford an unimpeded movement for our commerce both with foreign countries and between our own east and west.

Now the value of a foreign commerce, both as to markets in which to sell produce and in which to buy supplies of all kinds, including munitions of war, is so fully shown in the present war as to make unnecessary demonstration here. This much may, however, be sketched out:—Should for example our selling markets in Latin America be, as appears possible, considerably extended in the near future, those producing export products in this country will come so to modify and adapt their products to the needs of such markets as to make the goods unsalable in other markets. Thereafter adjustment of trade and commodities to other markets in peaceful time will be slow and expensive, and in war times probably impossible. The same principle will hold as to any other foreign trade we shall build up. Again, we could not now and, to be safe, we must assume we never shall be able to manufacture at the outset sufficient munitions for our indispensable needs in any war with a first class power. We shall be forced to meet this deficiency by importing from foreign countries. It would thus be imperative in case of a great war that our ante-war markets be retained during war, first as a matter of self-preservation, and secondly, in order to minimize, as far as possible, the financial embarrassment and difficulties that inevitably accompany international conflicts. In so far as the Canal can or should be of use in such commerce, it is necessary that it be kept open.

As all of our canal-routed inter-coastwide commerce and a good part of our Latin-American commerce, as also all of our trans-canal movement of vessels of war, troops, and supply ships, must converge to two points, one in the Caribbean and one in the Pacific, both of which we must completely protect, the problem of annihilating all our trans-canal traffic becomes for a belligerent merely a problem of striking either of these points from a secure, accessible base. This in turn reduces itself to a problem of obtaining and maintaining a base, for it is all but a certainty that, in case of war between ourselves and a foreign power possessing such a base, the enemy fleets and forces would be safely at their base before the first war-like blow was struck. With such a base, the enemy could and would virtually take his own time and opportunity to strike us.

The map shows that the coast of southern United States, Mexico, Central America, Colombia, and much of Venezuela are cut off from the Atlantic Ocean by a system of islands that make of the Gulf and Caribbean practically land-locked seas. The present ownership of this land-lock is of interest. At its northern extremity lie the republics of Cuba, San Domingo, and Haiti, no one of which is able to protect its own sovereignty against violations by a first class power, which could at will seize, occupy and use, as a base for operations against us, any desirable harbor possessed by any of them. Moreover, outside all of the above-named lie the engirdling Bahamas (British) which have in the past served as sheltering harbors, if not bases, from which to launch commerce destroying enterprises against the trade of the United States. Lying inside those countries and commanding the windward passage is Jamaica (British), midway between Cuba and Haiti; and farther west, right up under Cuba's southern coast-line, are Grand and Little Cayman (British). To the west of San Domingo is Puerto Rico, undefended and probably undefendable. Next, almost touching Puerto Rico, comes the first of the Lesser Antilles, the Danish island of St. Thomas, with (as it is said) a potentially magnificent harbor. Strewed along thickly from there to Venezuela come the Leeward and Windward Islands, possessions of Denmark, France, and Great Britain. Inside these and close to the Venezuelan coast are the Dutch islands, Curaçao and the Sisters. Possessions of Denmark and Holland are as liable to violation as are Cuba, Haiti, or San Domingo. Any first class power desiring to use any of the Caribbean islands of these nations will do so, irrespective of anything the powers can do by themselves.

With the possible exception of Mexico under normal conditions, there is no country of the mainland, from the Rio Grande to the mouth of the Orinoco, that could even appreciably retard, to say nothing of repel, an attempt by a first class power to secure a lodgement upon and the maintenance of an occupation of any part of its coasts, or to protect itself against any sort of aggression of a great power. And this means that any great power at war with the United States could seize and use as a base any desirable harbor owned by any one of such countries. Each and every [one] of these countries and islands is within striking distance either of the entrances to the canal or of commerce and war vessels and equipment bound for it, and for that matter of the harbors and coasts of the United States itself and of all our commerce.

On the Pacific coast, added to Mexico, the Central Americas, and Colombia, is the Republic of Ecuador and its islands, the Galapagos,—a country within effective striking distance of the canal and its traffic, equally impotent to prevent an infringement of its sovereign rights, therefore subject to violation by having its bays or islands seized for use as bases from which to strike us, and so equally dangerous potentially to the United States in case of war between it and a great power.

To offset all of this Caribbean potentiality for evil, we have on the South Atlantic Coast, two naval stations,—one at Key West and one at Guantanamo Bay on the southern coast of Cuba; and a navy yard at New Orleans, our nearest other navy yard being at Charleston, entirely outside of this zone.

The lay mind puts naval bases into two classes,—those fully prepared, equipped and fortified before a war, such as Portsmouth, and Cuxhaven, and those improvised after war begins, such as Zeebrugge.

It would seem obvious that any proposal by a European power to establish upon this hemisphere a naval base of the first kind, should meet with an emphatic and final veto from this government, backed up, if need be, by force of arms, and this should be so whether the proposal contemplated the use of territory and waters already owned by such power, or the use of territory hereafter acquired for that purpose. Such an act would in itself be a challenge, a slap in the face. The Monroe Doctrine could appropriately be invoked to account for an opposition to at least a part of such a situation. The doctrine of self-preservation would, however, be quite sufficient to justify any objection we might make to part or all of such a plan. And as for precedent, Great Britain's veto upon Germany's acquisition of Agadir as a base, because the latter lay near and upon Great Britain's East India trade routes, is quite ample to cover any action the United States might take. We have said it would seem obvious that such would be the situation, because remarkable to say, a reported intention of Great Britain (announced some time before the outbreak of the present war) to maintain in American waters, a considerably increased naval force, based at the Bahamas, not only met with no protest or remonstrance from our government (so far as is known), but our public press accepted the proposal as a proper and innocent one. Probably a contemplation of the existing war had made us wiser. It is to be hoped so. Great Britain's wisdom long antedated her existing difficulties or she would now be crushed.

It ought to require no argument to show the menace which the establishment of such a base would involve for this country. But some illustrations may serve to visualize the situation. The distances given are merely approximations based either on Atlas statements, or on a landsman's measurements on the map.

Nassau (British Bahamas) is only 300 miles farther away from Colón than is Guantanamo; it is practically as near as Key West; and it is 400 miles nearer than New Orleans. Kingston (Jamaica) is nearer to Colón than New Orleans is to Havana; it is 150 miles nearer to Colón than is Guantanamo; 400 miles nearer than Key West; and 900 miles nearer than New Orleans.

St. Thomas (Danish West Indies) is 375 miles nearer Colón than New Orleans and one half as far again away as is Guantanamo.

Martinique is 400 miles nearer than New Orleans, and the Barbados are approximately the same distance as New Orleans.

Samana Bay, the wonderful harbor of San Domingo, is only a little farther than Guantanamo. The ports of Haiti are about a like distance.

The Dutch islands, are immediately off the coast of South America. Venezuelan and Colombian ports lie almost in the offing of Colón.

On the other hand European ports are from 3000 to 5000 miles from Colón.

On the Pacific coast, Mare Island, San Francisco, the nearest navy yard we have, is 3277 miles from Panama. Magdalena Bay in Mexico is 3000 miles; Fonseca Bay is 900 miles. Going south from Panama, Bahía Bay is 700 miles from Panama; Guayaquil is 850 miles; and the Galapagos are 1200 miles. Japanese ports are 8168 miles away.

A European fleet based upon any American port or harbor named on the Atlantic side of the Continent is not only from 2500 to 4500 miles nearer than the European ports from which such a fleet must operate in the absence of an American base, but as already pointed out above, such an American-based European fleet would be in some cases actually nearer Colón than any port of our fleet could be, if at its own base. The resulting advantages to the preponderant European fleet are too clear to call for enumeration or comment. The situation on the West *vis à vis* Japan speaks for itself.

To the layman, it appears obvious, as already pointed out, that the United States must now take steps which will forestall any attempt to secure or create a permanent base by any foreign power on any of the Americas. Further and moreover, the United States must now take steps and adopt measures that will prevent any other power in war time from acquiring and using as a temporary base any American port or harbor which does not already belong to it.

To meet our needs in the matter, the United States should immediately acquire from the proper countries, rights to establish naval stations or bases that shall enable the United States to meet on an equal footing those countries which now have territory and harbors nearer to the canal than are our own. The treaty with Nicaragua initiated by Mr. Knox, covering certain naval base rights in the Gulf of Fonseca is the beginning of such a policy, but before this treaty can be made effective, supplementary treaties must be negotiated with Honduras and Salvador. Similar treaties as to important harbors or usable outlying islands, should be made with Mexico, Ecuador, Venezuela or Colombia, or both, probably Guatemala, San Domingo, and such of the other countries as a wise naval policy may require. The Danish West Indies must be purchased, whatever they cost.

In addition to the foregoing and in order to forestall the establishment of permanent bases by European powers, the United States must make treaties with all the interested American countries which shall in appropriate form stipulate that such countries shall under no circumstances alienate any territory to a European power, nor grant to any such country any lease of territory, nor any right or concession which would ripen into such a cession of lease, or which could be made to serve as and for such a cession or lease, and to this end the United States must have the right in case of war between one of those countries and a European power (a condition which might be easily forced) to participate in the peace negotiations. Such treaties should also contain provisions providing that the establishment of coaling stations even for vessels of commerce in peace times shall only occur as the result of measures taken in concert with the United States and under an agreement giving to the United States certain protective rights in case of war. The need for this is obvious if we ask ourselves (in the light of the violations of South American territory by the various belligerents during this war) how long a belligerent operating on the Pacific would, for instance, hesitate to coal his fleet, indeed to seize the entire supply for his own use, from a Galapagos island coaling station merely because to do so would be to violate Ecuadorian sovereignty. The pre-prepared apology which would readily come to Ecuador from the violating power, would scarcely compensate us for the loss of a naval battle suffered at the hands of the freshly coaled belligerent. No coaling station of any sort, can be permitted in any of the areas under consideration, unless under the protection of such armament and fortifications (controlled by the United States) as will render its violation too hazardous to be attempted.

In addition to these treaties or as parts of them, there must also be agreements between the United States and these various American countries giving to the United States the right to cooperate with those countries for the protection of their sovereignty from violation in case of a war between one of the Great powers and the United States. That is to say, the United States must have the right upon the outbreak of a war with one of the Great Powers and without the delay incident to haggling out a treaty covering it, immediately to cooperate with these countries, by landing and using troops or what not, in order to prevent the establishment of a temporary base for naval or land operations. A few thousand men at the right place at the right time, might save hundreds of thousands later on. Such agreements might also appropriately cover the making with these countries of plans, and possibly the partial execution thereof, for fortifying their strategic points and potential naval bases suitable either for permanent or temporary use.

It will not do to assume that these things will not happen and therefore treaties covering them are unnecessary. The advantages of such bases are so obvious and the necessity therefore so imperative in case of war with the United States that great powers will inevitably seek to secure them. The principle of the ounce of prevention and the pound of cure is nowhere of greater force in our whole national life, than when applied to this situation.

While the foregoing discussion has been bottomed upon the necessity for protecting the Canal, each and every [one] of the considerations are just as pertinent to a proper and judicious handling of our protective policy without the canal. The canal and its uses merely emphasize our pre- and ever existing situation and condition.

General Political Principles
from "The Mexican Situation"

6 March 1920

On 6 March 1920 JRC delivered a very long address on "The Mexican Situation" in the Salt Lake Theater. He gave it again on 28 October of that year in Richfield, Utah. It was his purpose in this address to discuss "the policy of the United States in Mexico" from "the beginning of that revolution which led finally to the resignation of Díaz and the succession of Madero."

He spoke on the Madero revolution, Huerta and Mexico, then Carranza and Mexico. He addressed President Woodrow Wilson's policies of tolerating a steady stream of humiliations to the United States in a variety of forms, including the loss of lives and property. Taking Wilson's claimed rationale of service to mankind, JRC examined the effects of Wilson's policies on the people of Mexico, and then their effects upon the people of the United States.

The preface to his conclusion stated his position succinctly: "But after all Mexico is not the disease from which we suffer, but only one of the symptoms. The disease lies deeper and is to be found in those disintegrating forces which now stalk through our land seeking to destroy our government."

After a few introductory paragraphs JRC devoted several pages to what he called general principles. He discussed those principles first as they concerned individual persons in relation to their body politic, or nation, then as they concerned individual nations in relation to the family of nations. It is only this portion of the long

341

address that is given here. Box 47, Book 1, 1920, Mexican Situation, SL Theater, J 10.14, JRCP.

In discussing any problem, it is always well to get first in mind the general principles which must be applied in solving it. Indeed there is no other way in which an accurate solution of a problem can be reached, except by the merest chance. And the chances of solving a problem by mere guess work without knowing the facts with which you deal, or the principles which should control, are sufficiently disastrous, as indicated in the failure of the Administration so far to solve the Mexican problem, to make us wary of any such course. We may, therefore, I think spend to advantage a little of our time in determining the elements involved in the question we are now considering.

If a half hundred men were to be placed together upon an island which belonged to no nation and over which therefore no law extended and to which the law of no nation applied; where there was no law, custom, or precedent restraining any of them; each one of these men would be a law unto himself. The only sanction, the only compelling mandate which any of them would obey would be the law and the mandate of physical force. Each man would be a sovereign, unhampered, unrestrained. But this elemental natural law of physical force is so destructive of the peace, the happiness, and the prosperity of man, who normally is peaceful and not warlike, that immediately and inevitably these men would come together and frame some plan, some system of rules, regulations, and laws to govern their intercourse with [one] another, so that they might live and prosper.

This body when so organized would constitute a society of men welded together into a body politic. Obviously in such a situation, the fundamental thought in the mind of every sovereign man who met to frame this government would be,—how much of my full, complete, absolute liberty and license which I now possess as a sovereign man am I willing to give up in the making of this new government? And the test he would apply before acceptance to each and every proposition which might be made would be,—is this necessary to protect me in my legitimate rights both as to my person and as to my property?

Of course, it would not be possible for these men at the beginning to frame up a system of laws which would last them for all time. As they settled down on the land and their interests began to increase and their work to diversify, as they began to develop special industries, new rules and new regulations would be necessary to accomplish their protection in their new rights. But for every change or development, the test would be always the same, what must I have and what must my neighbor have in order to protect him and me in our legitimate rights as to both our persons and our property?

Now all of these rules and regulations would take the form of restraints on prior liberties and licenses, for law, both human and divine, is largely made up of "thou shalt nots." But there would be in any organization set up by the members of our little society a recognition that there were certain things as to which they wished to be wholly unrestrained. First of all each must be equal before the law. There must be no ruling of the many by the few; there could be no aristocracy, no small group of self-seekers possessing exceptional powers and privileges before the law that enabled them to dictate to and oppress the great body of citizenry. Then they must be free to think as they wished, to worship as they wished, to speak their own minds, to express any views which they might hold without question or challenge, save only that by their actions they should not infringe upon the rights of others or cause others injury. That is to say they would want freedom of speech, freedom of the press, freedom of religion. In these matters each would retain his own complete sovereignty. And one other thing would come home early to these men of our society, their own house as well as their own persons must be inviolate save under stringent and far reaching safeguards. In other words they would early come to see that a man's home is his castle. As a great English jurist said, "all the powers of the Crown may not enter the poor man's home; it may be frail, its roof may shake, the winds of Heaven may enter, but the King himself may not put a foot across the lowly threshold" without warrant and due process of law.

Lastly the members of our society would wish to regulate their own methods of life, to regulate their own households in the way that should seem to them most meet and fittest, without restraint or interference. In other words, here would be a part of their sovereignty which they would retain in themselves absolutely, complete and unrestrained. As to this part they would be absolute anarchists living without law of any sort; and you will long since have recalled to your minds that under our Constitution we have the very realm of anarchy which I have described.

There are in the World some fifty sovereign and independent nations, each a complete and absolute law unto itself save in these matters only in which it has voluntarily or by force of arms surrendered some of that independence. But these nations very early found, as the members of our little society found, that absolute freedom of action was incompatible with peace, development, and prosperity. It was early apparent that the strong preyed upon the weak, that the strong growing stronger preyed upon others slightly less strong, with the result that woe and misery, not peace, liberty, and happiness would be the rule of the earth. And so, generations and generations ago, the nations came together and formed a society of nations; and out of their contact of peace and their combats of war came a body of laws and regulations, self-imposed, by which these sovereign nations regulated their intercourse one with another. Each nation gave up under these rules something of its full sovereignty, something of its absolute independence. But on the other hand, each sovereign nation recognized, just as the member of our little society recognized, that if they were to remain essentially free and independent, if they were to enjoy peace, prosperity and happiness, if they were to be permitted to work out their own art, culture, and civilization, their own political and economic systems, there were certain things as to which they must maintain their complete, undefiled sovereignty. And the things they retained are curiously like the things retained by the individuals of our little society,— each nation must be free to think as it wished, to speak as it wished; it must be free to worship God as it wished; the homes of its nationals, that is its territory, must be its castle, not to be entered save in accordance with prescribed rules and regulations; it must be free to regulate its own internal affairs in a way that would permit it to work out fully its own destiny. And lastly, just as in our little society it was of the absolute essence that every member of the society should be equal before the law, so it is of the essence, in this society of nations, which was formed so long ago, that every nation shall be equal to every other nation. Or to use the words of the great Marshall, "Russia and Geneva are equal."

The Society of nations thus formed has made its rules and regulations by the free consent of all. No member has been bound or restrained contrary to its will; it owed obedience to no rule to which it did not itself consent. There is in this society no such thing as a council of the League behind the cloak of which a small minority of the members may hide in ruling the balance of the world. There is and could be no autocracy of nations if human progress and civilization are to flow on unhindered, any more than there could be an autocracy in our little society of men.

It necessarily follows from these principles that the people of each of the nations have the absolute, complete, and uncontrolled right to have that form of government which they wish, whether it was monarchy, absolute or limited, autocracy, or republic. No other single nation and no combination of nations have the right to lay a hand with compelling force upon any nation in respect of these matters, and it follows further from this latter principle that the personnel of the government set up by a people is a matter of no concern whatsoever to any of the rest of the world. It is not the business of one nation to say when the people of another nation are or should be satisfied with these matters. These are things which the people concerned must decide for themselves. All that the other members of the society have is a right to insist that that government and its personnel should observe the rules and the regulations established by common consent for the government of the intercourse between the nations, and this is a paramount right, to be exercised against the nation violating it by any or all of the other nations. Indeed the observance of these rules and regulations was a condition precedent to the nations becoming a member of the society of nations and the maintenance of such observance is a condition precedent to remaining in that society.

It also follows from the general principle that the form of government and the personnel thereof are to be settled by the people of the nation; that the manner in which that personnel acquire position in the government is not a matter of international concern. As to these matters the only thing which other nations have to consider is whether those claiming to be the officers of the government actually are exercising governmental authority. It is a matter of no international concern whatsoever whether such officers are holding their positions *de facto* or *de jure*,—that is whether they were officers merely by the fact that they are exercising the authority of officers, or whether they are officers because they have legally been placed by the nation in the position which they held.

It is imperative that this should be the law of nations, otherwise there could be no independence of nations. What, for example, would be our position, if any nation or group of nations had the right to come in and question the result of our presidential elections? Could we lay claim to freedom and independence if, for example the nations or any of them had a right to come and sit in judgment on the contested election between Mr. Tilden and Mr. Hayes? Could we lay claim to be a sovereign nation if other powers had the right to come in and investigate as to whether or not Mr. Roosevelt had been in league with the assassin of President McKinley? Could we rightfully claim independent existence if it had been possible for some intellectually perverted rule of Europe rightfully and legally to deny recognition to our government and to refuse to have intercourse with this people on the ground that Mr. Roosevelt was responsible for the death of Mr. McKinley? No, these things could not be, and it has been the unquestioned law of ages that such things were not matters of international concern, save only between those effete nations of Europe where the selfish interests of royalty required dynastic families to maintain one another, where royal incompetents must "hang together in order that they might not hang separately." Except where despotism and autocracy were threatened, even autocratic nations have not dreamed of such interference.

From the time that Washington took his first oath of office, we had not till in the last decade questioned the legitimacy, the legality of the means by which a ruler had become ruler. It was enough for us that the ruler occupied the seat of government, that he was maintaining government over the people of his nation, and that he was able and willing to perform his international obligations. So firmly had we adhered to this principle of conduct, so imperative did we consider its mandate, that when in 1903 a palace revolution resulted in the wanton and savage murder of the rulers of Serbia for the express and vowed purpose, and with none other in mind, of putting a new ruler on the Serbian throne, we recognized without question and without hesitation the beneficiary, if not co-conspirator in that murder. In other words, with the moralities of other nations we are not as a nation concerned. Equally it is not a matter of international concern as to the means taken by a people to work out the form of government the people desire. If they can and are willing to work it out by a method of balloting, all well and good; but if on the contrary their ballots cannot procure for them what they wish and they thereupon resort to revolution, that is their concern alone, and no other nation has a right either to interfere or even to complain, except only first to secure their own safety from the effect of such a revolution, or second, to take necessary steps and measures to protect its own nationals in the disturbed areas.

And who are we to presume to challenge this right of a people to adjust its wrongs by revolution? Who are we to say that someone else may dictate when we are or should be satisfied with our internal conditions? It would be idle for me to recount to you the history of our own revolution; it would waste your time and mine for me to explain to you how legal means may at times prove wholly inadequate to adjust wrongs and overthrow tyranny; or to explain to you how liberty and freedom rarely come save by a vast expenditure of treasure and blood,—so unwilling is despotism to die. Except for our exercise of this Divine Right of revolution, we should to-day be England's colony cheering for its royal master, instead of a great free independent people cheering for the flag only, and for the eternal principles of right and justice for which it stands. Nor is this all. When revolution threatened the destruction of this Union, when the British Government, threw all its sympathy and all the resources it dared in the balance against your freedom, against the preservation of the Union, when they sought to intervene in the great conflict between the North and the South by [lacuna in text] it remained only for Mr. Adams our Minister to St. James, upon being advised by [Earl Russell] that he intended so to intervene and so to take sides against the Union in this struggle, to make cause against the duly constituted officers of this Government and so to express an opinion as to when we were or should be satisfied with our government or its forms, calmly and with the dignity of a citizen of this Great Republic, to remark, "It would be superfluous in me to point out to Your Lordship that this is war" (dispatch to Russell, 5 September 1863). That was our answer to a great people that sought to decide for us our internal questions; that sought to tell us the right kind of government we should have; that sought to advise us how we should conduct our affairs. And shall we the great, the mighty, the powerful one of all the nations of the world deny to others the right which we claimed for ourselves?

But as I have already intimated above, interposition on behalf of a nation's citizens when they are threatened either by unsettled conditions or otherwise in another country, is entirely permissible. This government has repeatedly, both alone and jointly with others, landed forces both in times of revolution in foreign countries and in order adequately to protect American citizens and their property when no such revolution existed. We initiated this practice certainly as early as 1811 when President Madison occupied Amelia Island off the coast of Florida and we have continued the practice until the present time. A compilation of instances made in 1912 showed that we had landed troops, generally marines, or had used the navy to protect our interests on at least a half a hundred occasions and in no case had such protection of American interests been construed as an act of war. Because under the accepted principles of international law it does not lie in the mouth of any nation which fails adequately to protect foreigners within its jurisdiction to deny to the powers to which such foreigners owe allegiance the right to interpose and if necessary land forces for the protection of their own threatened nationals.

The full legal and moral answer to any nation complaining of such an act of interposition is,—"Set your house in order and protect our citizens, and we shall immediately withdraw." But you cannot cloak injustice, persecution, and atrocities against our citizens, by invoking the inviolability of territorial sovereignty recognized by the society of nations. Because by permitting such conduct and conditions to exist, you virtually place yourself outside the pale of civilized nations, and you may no longer invoke those salutary rules of conduct by which such nations are controlled in their intercourse one with another.

The foregoing are the general principles so far as they affect the situation we are to discuss, by which nations are governed.

Some Elements of an American Foreign Policy

4 April 1925

This memorandum was prepared at the request of Judge Salmon O. Levinson, chairman of the American Committee for the Outlawry of War, for use in appointments he and a friend had with Senator William E. Borah and President Calvin Coolidge to discuss an American foreign policy toward the outlawry of war. The request was made at short notice, and JRC responded with this message: "Your telegram received your order rather large one for the house but as we make it a point to fill all orders will do the best we can." In his cover letter JRC said:

I am accordingly enclosing a very "rough and ready" memorandum in which I have tried to deal with some of the fundamentals of what I regard as a true foreign policy. A good deal of it is trite and more or less obvious, but for my own use (at any rate) I wished to get it down. I understand you want now a discussion rather than a formula. At any rate, I had personally to elaborate a general outline before I could frame a formula. I, therefore, send the enclosed rough memorandum which is in two main parts. The first part contains a general statement of the basic premises upon which the others are based, including a discussion of the "Outlawry of War." The second part is made up of several parts, one deals with our policy towards the Americas; another with our policy towards Europe; a third with our policy towards Australasia and South Africa; and a fourth with our policy towards the Far East. The Near East has not been separately considered, but for now may be regarded as part of Europe. This all sounds much more ambitious than I intend. All of them have been dictated since Wednesday morning, with interruptions for pressing regular work. They were prepared without notes, and developed as I went along. There are many omissions I am conscious of, many I am sure that I know nothing about. I have had no time to polish. So you take them in the rough.

* * *

I am aware that the material which I am sending is not so wholly and completely altruistic as you might like it; but altruism like charity begins at home. Moreover, I am so convinced that the world without the steadying physical, moral, and spiritual influence of America would stand in grave danger or reverting to a second Dark Ages, that I am perfectly sure in my own mind that the first duty of any foreign policy upon which we enter is the preservation of the United States and its form of Government with its free institutions. This to the end that this steadying influence to which I have referred shall be indefinitely perpetuated for the world's good. I do not believe this estimate is inspired either by national egotism, jingoism, or ignorance, but that it is a fair appraisal of the world's condition.

I hope the material I am sending will not be without value to you, rough though it is. *Moreover, I reserve the right to change any and all views therein expressed, after more mature reflection.* In view of the stress under which it was made (with this lack of mature reflection and consideration) . . . I will ask you to confine the use of this memo to yourself and Colonel Robins.

Trusting that you will be able with Senator Borah to work out some sort of real constructive policy that will be based upon adequate protection of our own civilization and institutions, and that you will be able to persuade the President to adopt and follow such a policy, I [make] every wish for your success in the undertaking.

Only part one of the large memorandum is given here. Box 48, Book 1, 1925, Outlawry War, J 11.16; see also Box 92, J 11, No. 17, JRCP.

Some Basic Premises

No foreign policy is a national end in itself. It is but a means to an end, and that end is the growth, development, and perpetuation of the nation adopting the policy.

Originally the growth and development of nations were viewed in terms of most narrow selfishness, but the modern world has shown that just as with individuals, so with nations,—an "enlightened selfishness" requires that in mutual dealings the other party shall profit also. A nation advances farther and more quickly when it is accompanied by the rest of the world, than when striving to go alone. Thus the measures by which is carried out any foreign policy aimed to foster the growth and development of a country must be so framed, and from time to time so modified as to accommodate themselves to the reciprocal interests of the other nations involved. Live and let live is as sound a precept of conduct for nations as for individuals.

Furthermore, even in those measures which relate to the perpetuation of the nation where, even under modern conditions, the nation must be more narrowly and intensely selfish than in matters affecting its growth and development, there are yet matters of mutual concern and protection in which a nation may well yield something of its complete and unqualified independence or sovereignty for the sake of the advantages of help which it may secure from others.

A few basic elements may be more specifically stated.

The prime purpose of a wise foreign policy for the United States must be the protection of our sovereignty and continental territorial integrity, the perpetuation of the essentials of our Constitutional Government with its free institutions, and the development of the material, intellectual, and spiritual welfare and happiness of our citizens.

The Protection of Our Sovereignty and Continental Territorial Integrity

Concerning our sovereignty it is to be said, as intimated above, that no member of the family of nations is, or can be, fully independent—wholly and completely sovereign. The very fact of membership in the *family* of nations connotes the surrender of some abstract right of sovereignty, for membership in a family must lay limits and bounds to what a member may in custom, in comity, or in law do. Furthermore, the history of nations shows that as nations have come into closer physical, intellectual, and commercial contact they have found it to their mutual advantage to surrender certain rights of sovereignty which when nations were in these respects more isolated they found it desirable, if not necessary, strenuously to preserve and maintain. The further development of nations along the course they are now travelling makes evident that further surrenders of abstract rights must come. It is not necessary here to attempt to guess what the objects of surrender shall be. It is only necessary to recognize that the development of the world will require that such surrenders be made. Perhaps this basic principle may be here laid down on this point; namely,—While the theoretical state is fully independent and sovereign, industrially, economically, and politically, the past has shown such great inroads upon the industrial and economic independence of the nations that no nation can now be said to be even industrially or economically independent; that this industrial and economic dependence has made necessary a relinquishment of the exercise of certain sovereign political powers, for example, the right of prohibiting commercial access to the ports of a foreign nation, the right of forbidding ingress and egress by subjects of a foreign state, the right arbitrarily to deal with the subjects of a foreign state while resident within the state, etc., and that it seems certain a further industrial and economic development will require a further surrender of political sovereignty. The question is merely one of degree. What shall and what shall not be given up is to be determined when the occasion arises.

Concerning Our Continental Territorial Integrity

It is of course imperative that we hold our mainland, self-preservation requires this; but it is open to question whether or not a wise foreign policy requires that we shall determine to hold our insular possessions (including the Canal Zone), and this might even include Hawaii. This question may be looked at from two points of view: *First,* the point of view that the world will move on with its land-grabbing propensities undiminished, or: *Second,* that territorial aggression shall be curtailed if not eliminated.

If the first rule is to continue to govern the world, we must certainly plan to hold Hawaii, the Canal Zone, Puerto Rico, Danish West Indies, and to maintain control of Cuba, meanwhile augmenting our holdings in the Greater and Lesser Antilles as much as possible. These possessions must be held and augmented in order that we may have suitable outposts from which to strike in case aggression is aimed against our mainland. There is a question whether we should make any attempt to hold the Philippines permanently.

If territorial aggression is to be either curtailed or destroyed, some will question whether the United States should attempt to hold any of its insular possessions except perhaps Hawaii, which is now essentially European in civilization, and except the Canal Zone, which should be retained for the benefit of the commerce of the world. In so far as the element of security of the mainland is concerned, it is obvious that with no threat of aggression there is no need for fortified outposts, and, therefore, from the military standpoint our insular possessions need not be retained. However, there are certain raw materials which can be more cheaply produced in the West Indies (for example, sugar) than they can be produced upon the mainland of the United States, and, therefore, a wise foreign policy might require that we keep these sources of supply within our own control and jurisdiction, for, as it may be well to observe here, the elimination from the world of war and of the aggressions of war will not eliminate from the world industrial and commercial competition and the aggressions which result from such competition. A foreign policy which fails to recognize this fact will lamentably lack of wisdom.

There is, however, another consideration making against our retention of these foreign lands,—it is open to question whether we can properly and adequately govern alien peoples. It is true that our parent, Britain, has been eminently successful in this field, but she is an Empire, we are a Democracy; a distinction which may spell the difference between success and failure. This is particularly true as to the Philippines, because of their remoteness, their physical and climatic characteristics, and the uncivilized condition of their inhabitants.

The Perpetuation of the Essentials of Our Constitutional Government with Its Free Institutions

We are a young nation. Compared with Britain's thousand years, with Rome's centuries, and with Egypt's ancient millenniums, we must be considered not only youthful, but immature, yet in a scant century and a third we have moved to a position of primacy amidst a group of world powers, any one of which is greater than the greatest power of antiquity. It is literal fact that no nation within recorded time has progressed as has this nation and no nation within that time has had to face in its growth the competition of powers already great world powers when it was born.

A consideration of these facts can leave no thoughtful man in doubt that our governmental institutions, our civilization, and our citizenry are of extraordinary excellence, vitality, and power. But our achievements have not been alone for ourselves, but have been for the world,—achievements made possible only because of our position of prestige and power, which almost always have been exerted in the world for freedom, for righteousness, and for peace. If doubt be entertained as to the relative value of our achievements of the past or as to the potential value of our worth in the future, let the doubter cast his view to the Republics to the South of us, many of which are almost as old as are we, several of which have the advantage of climate, soil, and natural resources which we possess, and yet which have languished in their progress and development almost immeasurably as compared with us, and whose influence for good in the world is not to be compared at all with ours.

Under these circumstances it is not too much to say that under no circumstances whatsoever must our foreign policy contemplate any essential change or modification in that Constitutional Government of ours under which all this has become fact, and this must be so not alone for the selfish advantage which it may bring to us, but for the good which we shall in the future be able to carry to the world. Among these essentials which we may not change are those involved in the division and mutual independence of our governmental powers (legislative, executive, and judicial), the principle that all governmental powers are limited powers, the rule by and through majorities, the election of the makers and executors of the law, the removal of officers for malconduct, the bill of civil rights putting our civil liberties beyond the reach of government in time of peace, and the power of amendment by majorities. The success of our Constitutional Government has been so overwhelming in the past that we may not with safety trifle with it in the future.

The Development of the Material, Intellectual and Spiritual Welfare and Happiness of Our Citizens

The nation being the sum of its constituent individuals, the nation can be no stronger than its people. Whatever weakens the people weakens and ultimately destroys the nation. Our nation has grown and developed, has augmented its power and prestige in precise ratio and proportion as the peoples themselves have grown and developed materially, intellectually, and spiritually. So the perpetuation of our Constitutional Government with its free institutions, imperatively demands the continued growth, development, and prosperity of its people.

Thus a second *sine qua non* of a wise, far-seeing foreign policy is the development of the material, intellectual, and spiritual welfare and happiness of our citizens, and of these three the last is perhaps the most important, for history records no nation of preeminence among world powers, whose people has not had as the base of its life a deep spirituality that entered into and dominated the lives of its people. The world has yet to see its first enduring and vitalizing nation that was atheistic. Nor may this element be safely disregarded or ignored on the theory that somehow man has changed in the last decade to a different sort of being. The evolution of man is not so easily or so quickly accomplished either physically, mentally, or spiritually. Despite the scientific and materialistic achievements of modern civilization and the veneer of culture which man today possesses, elementally and fundamentally he is what he was when first he came out of the woods and settled upon the plains. He is moved by the same passions, subject to the same stimuli, and acts and reacts from the same motives. Such change as has come during the last half century has been by way of giving to the great mass of mankind a greater love for the material things of life than men theretofore possessed. Heretofore, living on and with but the bare necessities of life they were content with such, but having tasted the luxuries they now demand them. Therefore, a foreign policy which would sacrifice the material welfare of our people or tend to lessen their enjoyment of the luxuries, or that would weaken and disintegrate the spiritual fibre of the people, must either end disastrously as a policy or must involve the people and the nation in disaster, or both.

*   *   *

Since a foreign policy is for the guidance and control of our dealings, intercourse, and relationships with foreign nations and their peoples, and since such dealings, intercourse, and relationships are not confined to the activities of the nation as such, but embrace also dealings, intercourse, and relationships between the nationals of the respective nations, both those that reside within the home state and those which reside in the alien state, it is obvious that a foreign policy involves not only international agreements and contracts, but domestic legislation and conduct as well. That is, there is a subjective and objective side to every foreign policy. It may be observed here that when the society of nations was in process of forming and the needs of the people were simple, indeed elemental, a sufficient foreign policy was found in one which provided for an independent national existence and freedom from belligerent molestation. The task of the Minister of Foreign Affairs at that time was merely the maintenance of unimpaired sovereignty,—the preservation of territorial integrity and political independence; and as nations rarely touched one another save upon and relating to these matters, and as the contact when occurring was usually war-like, such Ministers and their Chancelleries were chiefly concerned with questions connected with what Jomini calls "Statesmanship and its relations to war." Upon this intercourse these Ministers and their Embassies gradually developed the elemental and fundamental principles having to do with sovereignty, and framed the fundamental rules, laws, and customs of war.

But the growth and consequent specialization of civilization, with the resulting complexity of the national, social, and political life greatly multiplied and varied the needs of the individuals, and, therefore, of the nation. New discoveries, new inventions, new industries, new means and methods of communication and intercourse, all combined to draw the world's peoples into closer relationships. Nations no longer primarily interchanged the crushing blows of the field, supplemented by the polite but empty compliments of the court, but they began also to interchange their sciences and their literature, and to trade in what they ate and what they wore. Peace with its concomitants became the normal and more important status of the world.

And so it comes that while we as a nation are still concerned in what other powers are doing in the way of training and equipping their armies and navies, are still interested in the secrets of fortifications, defenses, and mobilization, yet we are equally concerned and interested in what the other nations are inventing, discovering, and writing; and what they are raising, manufacturing, and mining; and what they are exporting and importing; and in their policies as to tariffs and bounties. For if all classes of people of the United States are to maintain their present intellectual standards, they must share in the art, literature, and science of the world; and if they are to continue in their present high standard of living with the comforts and luxuries now enjoyed still remaining within the reach of the man of moderate means and the wage earner, and if they are to secure the same returns for their labor, there are markets to be found for American goods, for the products of American farms and ranches, and for our mineral products; and there are markets to be discovered from which we may secure by barter or by arrangement the things which we do not have and which, being produced and manufactured in other countries, we must secure from them. In securing both selling and purchasing national markets, modern diplomacy plays through a wise foreign policy a most important part. So that while national security and the general welfare are now as ever the ultimate desiderata of a foreign policy, the problems involved in obtaining and securing them are daily becoming more numerous, more complex, and it would be safe to say, more difficult.

A positive foreign policy is far more than the mere observance of the rules and principles of international law and the requirements of comity—these are basic to the barest and simplest intercourse of all nations—such a policy is to be found in aggressive far-seeing domestic legislative enactments and in international agreements that look not to the present alone, but to the future also.

For us the problems inherent in domestic legislation are peculiarly involved and difficult because of the dual character of our government,—state and Federal for while the Federal Government is exclusively charged with the conduct of our foreign affairs and our Federal organization is exclusively responsible to foreign nations for such conduct, yet the State legislatures may by legislation seriously affect, if not indeed interfere with, our most vital relations with foreign countries. A wise foreign policy on our part would, therefore, require as one of its initial steps, Federal legislation under and pursuant to which that provision of our Federal Constitution which provides that the Congress shall have power "to define and punish . . . Offenses against the Law of Nations" shall be made effective, and which shall also enable the Federal Government to enforce the provisions of treaties which are declared to "be the supreme Law of the Land."

Obviously domestic legislation, Federal and State, affects our intercourse with foreign nations through the regulation of commerce—incoming and outgoing, the regulation of immigration and emigration, and the regulation of the rights, duties, privileges and obligations of foreigners resident or cormorant [*sic*—prob. transient] in this country.

Without going into detail here it will perhaps be sufficient to say for present purposes that it is not believed that the requirements of our own people, their welfare and happiness, will permit any essential change in the policies we have heretofore followed in the foregoing matters. Both great political parties now declare for a tariff that shall adequately protect the American working man; no partisan conflict has ever arisen over the exclusion of Asiatics; nor over some restriction upon general immigration; nor over the rights of aliens to travel and reside in the United States; nor over the right of the States to regulate the ownership of real estate within their jurisdiction,—the five great fundamentals of what may be termed our domestic-foreign-policy. These matters have been the basic elements of a policy under which we have grown and prospered. So far as popular expression has gone, they seem to embody the will of the people. We cannot, therefore, assume either the need or demand for a change therein.

But we properly look to international agreements, formal and informal, as embodying the real essentials of a foreign policy. Speaking generally, those agreements which prescribe the rules and regulations and set out the respective rights and duties of the contracting nations as such, are usually political in their character, while those which deal with matters affecting the industrial, commercial, financial, scientific, and literary intercourse of the nationals of the respective countries are non-political, whether (as already intimated) such nationals are domiciled within the territory of their own sovereign or within the territory of the other contracting sovereign. Such political and non-political agreements may be embodied in the same treaty or agreement or in different treaties.

The bulk of our political treaties heretofore made have ended wars or provided for the acquisition of territory, or stipulated boundary adjustments, and set out the rights and duties accruing to each nation in the case, either of war between themselves or in a war in which they were neutrals. Other treaties [are] of a political character [and] such have provided for extraterritorial rights in Japan, China, Siam, Turkey, Egypt, Morocco, and elsewhere.

Speaking generally regarding our political agreements it may be said that our policy heretofore has been strictly to avoid any and all alliances with any and every foreign power. This is the result of a traditional policy as old as our Government itself. So far have we carried this principle of non-entanglement with foreign nations, that it has been only in very recent years that the United States participated in a joint diplomatic representation to an offending power against which the United States with other powers had a grievance; it was the standing practice of the United States to decline to participate in a joint representation, but to make on the contrary an individual representation which might be either identical with or substantially the same as the joint representation. The policy of non-entanglement and non-joint representations, was first seriously breached by our attitude and action during the World War, but even there our status was never definitely that of an ally, and hence it was that in the Treaty of Peace the phrase "Principal Allied and Associated Powers" was used to cover the uncertainty as to whether or not we were an ally or merely an associated power.

Prior to the World War we had joined with Germany and Great Britain in certain international agreements covering the Samoan Islands, in which there was a joint accountability one to the other, if not indeed a joint responsibility. The "Four Power Pact" of December 13, 1921 perhaps comes nearer to an understanding in the nature of an alliance with foreign powers than any treaty which has yet been made by this Government, and that merely provides that in certain contingencies a joint conference of the parties signatory shall be called, to which conference the whole subject of dispute will be referred for consideration and adjustment in order to arrive at an understanding (in case of aggressive actions) as to the most efficient measures to be taken jointly or separately to meet the exigencies of the particular situation.

It will be recalled the Senate of the United States refused to advise and consent to the ratification of the Treaty of Versailles and likewise to the supplemental treaty between the United States, Great Britain, and France, which provided for the guaranteeing of French territorial integrity under certain contingencies named.

But notwithstanding our past policy, there would seem to be little question but that the urge of popular sentiment is now towards some sort of international agreement looking to the prevention of future international wars, and that such an agreement when framed will possess some of the characteristics of at least a defensive alliance. This will be so radical a departure from the hitherto existing policies of this Government as to require the extreme of caution, at least in the early stages of development. Among the matters which may be properly regarded as basic in this connection there may be mentioned these:

National respect and national and international morality require that governments shall enter into no treaty obligation which the peoples of the respective governments will not observe and support when the actual stress comes. An alliance which should last only until the need for action thereunder arose would at this stage of the world's history be calamitous. Better to wait a quarter or a half or even a full century for the consummating of such agreements than now to make them and have them broken. The hope and the faith of the world in the efficacy of united action for peace is now too great and too promising to risk its crushing by repudiated treaties. This fundamental consideration suggests two others.

First: Altruism is an effective motive in times of peace; it has not yet proved its efficacy in times of war. We speak much of love for our fellowmen, but all too few individuals, and no nation, has reached the stage where they will die for pure altruistic motives. Thus it is imperative that our foreign policy shall for the present lay down as an indispensable requisite to any alliance or quasi-alliance which we may make, that the subject matter concerning and over which the alliance shall become operative, shall relate to some subject matter in which we have a present, actual, material interest.

Second: All such alliances or quasi-alliances should be clearly defensive in their character, that is to say, they should provide that our cooperation, whether military, economic, or financial, shall be for the purpose of defense against aggression and under no circumstances for aggressive measures, except upon and after express authorization by Congress. That this will involve difficulty in the matter of determining whether given military operations are offensive or defensive is admitted, but all such questions must be left for determination as they arise, the general principle being as already stated.

As to non-political agreements, they have, as already indicated, covered in the main matters of residence, travel, finance, trade, and commerce, together with the general protection of industrial property.

There seems to be in the world today a quite apparent economic revolution which thus far has found its extreme expression in the Bolshevism of Russia. A less extreme, but none the less certain evidence of such a movement is the International Labor Office set up under the Treaty of Versailles and now functioning. The end aimed at by this general movement appears to be the setting up of a new or modified economic system which shall result in an approximate economic equality among men. Intimations of this movement have been present in international relations for many years, witness the treaties which provided that workmen's compensation acts shall be extended to aliens. Fortunately or unfortunately we in America have been less subject to this movement than has any other country enjoying Western civilization. The reason for this would appear to be that while in this country we do have a relatively few instances of enormous wealth, yet among the great mass of the people there exists an economic equality found nowhere else in the Western world, and that economic equality provides a higher standard of living for the so-called working man than exists in any other country in the world. So long as that condition exists there will probably be no real demand from the American people for any sort of economic or industrial alliance with other peoples. However, there is present among us the same leaven that worked for Bolshevism in Russia, a leaven which seems to aim at the levelling of economic conditions not in one country alone, but throughout the world. Thus it is not difficult to foresee that sometime in the near or distant future there may be a combination among non-American working men of other countries of the world to force those countries to combine in some sort of an economic movement against the United States with designs to compel us to conform our labor standards to theirs. If the mass of the American working people can be brought to see that this means a lowering of their standards of life it will be possible to gain their support to combat this pressure when it is brought. Otherwise, we shall face a readjustment of our existing national industrial and economic life.

In the meanwhile, as already somewhat elaborated upon, it will be the task of our foreign policy while preparing for the contingencies just described to provide markets for our own products, raw and manufactured, and to find markets from which we may get our needed materials.

Moreover, any consideration of problems connected with our foreign trade, particularly our export trade, must not overlook the fact that we are not yet essentially an exporting nation. The great bulk of all we produce in this country is used up in this country, whether it be food stuffs, raw mineral materials, raw cotton, manufactured products of various kinds, steels, or whatnot; nor must it be overlooked that the great bulk of our capital is used in the development of our own country. We have not so far been forced to look for any considerable investments abroad. We are justified in believing that this will continue to be our situation for a good many years to come. Indeed one would expect that until we have reached that degree of saturation as to population, industry, and capital which shall be equal to the great countries of Europe, we shall not be actually driven into competition with them in foreign commercial activities as a matter of existence, such a competition, for example, as exists between France, Great Britain, and Germany. Therefore, our foreign policy will, wherever it touches such matters, differ from the policies of other great world powers, every one of which, except Russia, depends in good part upon its exports for its life. Nevertheless, a wise foreign policy must now concern itself with securing the best markets for our surplus, of which we have some in all our major lines of activity, and the disposition of this surplus should be made, so far as possible, with a view to building up permanent markets to which we may turn when the exporting trade becomes one of our essentials.

One of our time-honored policies in connection with our foreign commercial policy is that of reciprocity, which is, of course, intimately connected with our domestic tariff policy. A reciprocity policy is not without its value, but it will probably become increasingly difficult because of similar policies adopted by other nations, for example, the nations composing the British Empire. They already have arrangements for reciprocal concessions regarding imports and exports and it appears that these arrangements may be extended rather than curtailed. The mid-war period saw similar tendencies towards reciprocal trade arrangements between the powers which had been allies during the War, but it is not believed that this movement will become dangerous to us on account of the jealousies, rivalries, and hostilities which are arising between these powers.

But without entering into further details it is evident that a wise foreign policy must provide for the making of international agreements and arrangements which shall give us markets in which to sell, as also markets in which to buy; not otherwise can we maintain our present standards of living, to say nothing of increasing them.

The foregoing will sufficiently indicate some of the basic premises in the light of which our general foreign policy must be based.

The fundamental principles thus covered, with others not mentioned, may require different application in at least three or four world regions,—the Americas, Europe, the Far East, and Australasia and Africa. From the present outlook the importance of these relations will approximate somewhat the order in which the regions have been named above, the most important being named first: this would seem certainly true if we look ahead a century or more.

But before discussing the regional policies which may be involved in this general suggested world division, it is necessary to consider certain new policies but just now emerging in our own and other countries and applicable to the entire world.

The normal method of crystallizing world sentiment and then reducing that sentiment to an international rule of conduct and action is through world conferences which frame multipartite treaties, which upon due ratification thereafter control the intercourse of states in the matters covered thereby.

Every wise foreign policy for each and every of the individual nations of the world must have as its first and prime object, as already pointed out above, the protection and perpetuation of the individual nation carrying out the policy, and the very statement of this principle connotes the possibility of an annihilating war which may destroy the nation. Therefore, among the fundamental principles of every wise foreign policy must be the dual object, the first, of successfully meeting the various problems of actual war, and second and equally important, of effectively eliminating the causes which produce war.

In so far as the successful meeting of the problems of war are concerned, as that is affected by a foreign policy, the end to be reached is twofold: *First:* the making of such military alliances with strong nations as shall afford the maximum assistance in case of war; and, *Second:* the providing of markets, both selling markets and buying markets, by and through which may be supplied the necessary war time materials for both combatant and non-combatant purposes.

The territorial isolation of the United States, together with its great and growing population and its immeasurable supply of natural resources of all kinds, relieves the foreign policy of the United States from the immediate necessity, at least, of working out either of these sets of problems.

But the very fact of our relative self-sufficiency in these matters intensifies the interest which we have and the influence which we have excited and ought to exert in the direction of the elimination of the causes of war. No nation threatens us; we fear no nation. It has been the conscious or unconscious realization of our uniquely favored position in this matter that has led us during the whole period of our national existence as a nation to stand so firmly and work so ardently for the pacific settlement of international disputes. At both Hague Conferences the American representatives stood for the most extreme proposals looking to this end,—proposals which were in the main defeated on both occasions by the attitude of the War Lords of Germany. The expense, the loss, and the horrors of the World War have, however, brought a change in the attitude of European countries, or at least in peoples of these countries, so that the time seems now most propitious for the working out of a system which shall more effectively provide than any heretofore worked out, for the adjustment of international disputes by non-warlike means.

There has been recently an extraordinary crop of plans for the accomplishment of this purpose; most of these have been characterized either by short-sightedness, by ignorance of world affairs and world problems, or by selfishness upon the part of the nation whose nationals have advanced them. Almost all of them, at least those conceived outside the United States, have had for their fundamental basis the thought of perpetuating the territorial *status quo* created by the Treaty of Versailles and the associated Peace Treaties. It has resulted from this fact that the bulk of these plans have provided somewhere in their machinery for a world military alliance, that is for massing the world's armed physical force behind the Versailles Treaty; and specifically this has meant that France was to be guaranteed in her territorial possessions and protected in her militaristic policies which involved the stabilizing and perpetuation of the various European shadow states set up by the Treaties of Peace. In other words, the plans proposed for the maintenance of peace have for the most part been based upon the creation of such a powerful military machine that war against it would be impossible.

Of such a world organization these things may be said: *First:* It is unnecessary for the keeping of peace among the smaller powers of the world, any one great power can do that: *Second:* These plans have not as yet provided for the participation of all the great powers of the world except upon such terms as to certain of them as were humiliating to such powers and therefore unacceptable to them except under such measures of compulsion—financial, economic, or militaristic—as would make such nations so treated resentful to the point of breaking away and waging war whenever it was felt they had sufficient strength successfully to make the issue. *Third:* It would provide for the establishment of a military machine by every great power, a machine which would be created and maintained on some ratio which would be proportioned to the strength of the nation maintaining it (however that strength might be measured), and, therefore, would not essentially change the present relative strengths of the powers concerned nor tend to lessen their watchfulness and their jealousies. Indeed and on the contrary, to prescribe a fixed and set military strength to each of the great powers would require the setting up of such a system of espionage on the part of each of the other powers as against any and every other power except itself, as has not yet been seen in the world's history; and,

Fourth: All these plans recognize the legality of war as a means of enforcing international rights and obligations not only, but also as to the carrying out of aggressive militaristic and imperialistic plans and designs.

It is more or less futile merely to trace an alleged analogy— which does not in fact exist—between quarrels as among private individuals and quarrels as among nations, and to say that because duelling has been eliminated that therefore war should be exterminated. The abolition of war may, it is believed, be put on surer ground; namely, that the moral concept of the peoples of the world (and the moral concept of any people is always far below the moral concept of the individuals which compose it) is now sufficiently advanced and sufficiently crystallized to enable us to say that the world no longer looks with tolerance upon mere wars of aggression, and that the peoples of the world are prepared to say that hereafter such wars must not be.

It is in this view that the "Outlawry of War" is the only plan now under discussion which adequately meets the present moral concept of the world and which has in it those elements and possibilities that will make most for the peace of the world, establish the principle that aggressive international war is a crime, and that the nation or nations waging [it] are criminals to be internationally punished as such, and that embodies a principle to which no nation of honest intentions can take exceptions,—a principle to which the moral forces of the whole world can be rallied.

But obviously an adequate plan cannot stop with a mere outlawry of war. There must be added instrumentalities for the hearing and peaceful adjustments of disputes between nations, and a further instrumentality by which the nations of the world may meet in conference for the purpose of discussing and crystallizing world opinion. The World Court and the League of Nations will not answer for these instrumentalities because the World Court is indissolubly bound up with the League of Nations, and the League does not embrace all nations, makes discriminations among those which it does include, and is founded upon the recognition of force as a lawful and valid means of settling international disputes irrespective of the rightfulness of the cause for which war is waged.

The writer personally has nothing to add in its broad outline to the plan hitherto proposed by him and printed in "Unity" of October 4, 1923, and in the "Advocate of Peace" of December, 1923 [see Part One, Article Eight, 125–41, this volume]; that is to say, there should be a convention between all the nations of the world outlawing international wars; there should be a second convention or conventions codifying international law; there should be set up an international judicial system with a compulsory jurisdiction, and there should be provided a plan for a world's deliberative Congress. To the observations made in the article referred to regarding the organization of the world for the "Outlawry of War" the following modifications and additions are submitted.

The declaration of the principle of the "Outlawry of War" and the prescribing of the reparations, restitutions, and penalties to be inflicted upon the nation aggressively waging war, should be one single undertaking with all states parties thereto and mutually bound, one to all, and all to one. The sanction should not, however, be equally world-wide,—for the imposition of the sanctions the world should be divided into regions. A more or less obvious and perhaps wise regional division for the imposition of the sanctions, might be this: Europe, including North Africa and the Near East in one division; Asia in a second division; Africa and Australasia in a third division, and the two Americas in a fourth division. The effect of such a regional division would be this: For example,—In case of war between two American countries, all such aid as might be extended to the state attached would be extended by American states, not by the states from any other region; and all reparations, restitutions, and penalties would be imposed by American states and not by the states of any other region. Obviously this would preserve for the Americas the principle of the Monroe Doctrine,—

doctrine which is part of the warp and the woof of our international policy, and which is honored and revered by all our citizens. Such a plan would thus meet the sympathies and prejudices of all Americans, and would beside have a real value in keeping outside of America any international burglars, and certain nations must still be so classed. It would, moreover, as to our participation and to such a plan give us the essential material interest in the particular controversy,—the interest of settling our American disputes without European or other interference.

In case of difficulties between two nations each in different regions, as for example, between the United States and Japan, the matter would involve then all the states of the two regions whose combined duty it would be to join in defensive measures that might either generally or specially be determined upon, as also in any measures designed to compel reparations, restitutions, or measures by way of penalty.

It is obvious that wherever and whenever the Asiatic region became involved it would likewise involve every nation whether located in Asia or not, which had possessions in Asia. Thus in a war between the United States and Japan, there would be involved not only the Asiatic powers, but France, Great Britain, and Portugal in Europe, and if the Asiatic region were defined to include the Philippines, then the United States also, and the Netherlands.

The real problem for all governments, and particularly for the United States, under any convention such as is suggested for "Outlawry of War" is that of the measures which it and all other third parties should be obligated to take in any belligerent operations between belligerents in order to end the state of belligerency and, if necessary, punish the aggressor. It will be here that the principle already suggested, namely, the absence of a material interest in the controversy between the two belligerent powers, will come into full play.

These measures which might become necessary in a given case, might be those of actual military operation or those of a non-military character. As to the latter, there would perhaps be no real difficulty. It could, without real difficulty, be stipulated that financial aid should be furnished, Red Cross assistance rendered, contraband and non-contraband supplies furnished, and any other service rendered except the sacrifice of American lives. The American Government might safely obligate itself to render such non-fighting assistance without any reservation beyond that mentioned below; but when it came to cooperating in belligerent operations with one of the parties, the situation presents more difficulties. These difficulties will not be so great where they merely involve Naval operations such as blockade, transporting troops and supplies as convoys, etc., because our Naval establishment is at all times more or less complete and manned by professional fighters who have adopted the profession or taken their enlistment with the possibility of fighting in view. Furthermore, there would not be an insurmountable difficulty in a commitment providing for the use of the standing Army of the United States and for the same reasons. As a practical matter, of course, if our participation in sanctions were confined to the American region (as above indicated) the foregoing measures would be all that we should ever be required to take, at least for the next few generations.

But a real and perhaps insurmountable difficulty would appear in undertaking to bind this Government beforehand to really employ its man power in belligerent operations, except upon the opportunity of determining by Congressional Act whether or not it should be so employed at the time when the occasion for the employment should arise. When this problem is faced the real wisdom, if not necessity, of regional undertakings as to sanctions becomes strikingly apparent. However, it may be found that the whole plan will fail unless it be possible to provide for the use of the man power of the various nations in belligerent operations in times of stress. In working out a plan for such operations the following considerations must be noted:

First: The use by belligerents of the man power of a third nation—one who under the existing law of nations would be considered as a neutral—must under any and all events be for purely defensive purposes.

Second: These defensive measures should not contemplate any military operations by the cooperating government except within the territorial limits of the government to which the assistance is rendered.

Third: It should not contemplate normally the use of the man power of assisting nations in any real aggressive operations even within the territory of the nation to which the assistance is rendered.

It is thoroughly understood and appreciated that the foregoing suggestions are fine drawn and perhaps impracticable. They are mentioned merely as indicating the line along which thought should be expended in working out the problem.

But speaking broadly of the whole problem, it seems that perhaps the United States could not undertake to do more than the following suggestions indicate, and it may be this is as far as any nation ought in wisdom to go as to sanctions rendered in the interest of a nation repelling an aggressive attack,—

First: To render financial help;

Second: To furnish supplies, contraband, and non-contraband;

Third: To render Red Cross assistance. The foregoing measures might be made, for the United States, automatic, that is operative upon the finding of an aggressive war without requiring further Congressional authority other than appropriations.

Fourth: To furnish its man power up to a number, say equivalent to that put in the field by the power repelling attack, but in no case to exceed a certain specified number, such belligerents to use the man power so furnished to it exclusively in non-belligerent activities behind the lines and outside the zone of military operations, that is, for service on lines of communication, at supply depots, for ambulance and hospital service, etc.

Fifth: To render such aid as the Government of the United States might take pursuant to express Congressional authorization, including in such aid the use of the man power of America, including the Navy, in actual belligerent operations.

Any plan for the "Outlawry of War" must contemplate (as the foregoing discussion has assumed) the legitimate use of force as an act of self-defense upon attack, or as an act of self-preservation either prior to attack or otherwise, or as a means of compelling an aggressive belligerent to desist from his operations. This will necessarily involve in any controversy the question as to which of the two contending contestants is the aggressor, because under the convention aid must be rendered to non-aggressors only. Therefore, any plan for the "Outlawry of War" should provide for a summary conference of all the non-belligerents in the region affected, for determining the question as to which of the belligerents should be regarded as the aggressor, the convention to provide an undertaking by each of the parties to it that pending this determination by the non-belligerents neither belligerent party should conduct any belligerent operations or carry on further belligerent preparations, and that the party violating this undertaking by any belligerent movements or activities whatsoever should be regarded as the aggressor in the conflict, irrespective of the merits of the initial controversy. The general convention should also stipulate (and this is vital) that no power should be under any obligation, moral or conventional, to undertake either the automatic measures provided for in the convention, nor the voluntary measures contemplated by it, in behalf of any nation which it regarded as the aggressor in the controversy.

In cases of interregional disputes the same rules might be worked out and applied through a conference of the non-belligerent members of the two regions.

The foregoing plan has this essential merit, which is the *sine qua non* of any practical plan so far as the United States is concerned, namely, it retains in the executive of the United States the right, when a dispute arises between two other nations, to determine which of the two is in the right with reference to that controversy before even the automatic undertakings with reference to finance, supplies, and Red Cross activities go into operation, and it retains in Congress the right to determine even then the question as to whether or not the United States shall engage the man power of the nation in belligerent operations and the extent to which such power shall be used.

But thoughtful consideration of this subject makes it apparent that no effective plan may be carried out which does not involve some surrender of perfect freedom of action on the part of the non-belligerent nation, some surrender of sovereignty, if it is desired to state the problem in these terms; but it is believed the foregoing suggested plan contemplates the minimum surrender which any effective plan can demand.

Memorandum on the Monroe Doctrine

17 December 1928

This may be the most widely recognized government document associated with JRC. He began preparing it at the request of Secretary of State Frank B. Kellogg, in the fall of 1928, a few weeks after he himself had been sworn in as undersecretary. He submitted it to Kellogg with a letter of transmission on 17 December. As published by the Government Printing Office in 1930, the memorandum is 236 pages long. Four pages are devoted to a "Statement of the Doctrine," 106 pages to the "Historical Background of the Doctrine," 67 pages to "Instances which Might be Considered or Have Been Considered as Falling Within the Purview of the Principles Announced in the Monroe Doctrine," and 57 pages to "announcements and declarations touching matters and incidents which have been said *not* to fall within the Doctrine or its underlying principles." The seventeen-page letter of transmission (ix-xxv) is printed with the memorandum as a sort of introduction. Excerpts from it, along with the complete "Statement of the Doctrine" (3-6), are reprinted here. Box 133, JRCP.

Memorandum to the Secretary of State

The Secretary.

Herewith I transmit a Memorandum on the Monroe Doctrine, prepared by your direction, given a little over two months ago.

371

Voluminous as it is, the Memorandum makes no pretense at being either a treatise or a commentary on the Doctrine; the shortness of time available for the work and the urgency for its completion, coupled with the performance of regular Departmental duties assigned to me, forbade such an undertaking.

Obviously the views set out, both herein and in the Memorandum, are not authoritative statements, but merely personal expressions of the writer.

* * *

The Memorandum deals . . . with such matters and incidents of our history as had a bearing on the Doctrine. . . .

There follows, after this, extracts of the pertinent parts of our diplomatic correspondence which immediately preceded Monroe's declaration, the declaration itself, and then the more important instances, arranged in chronological sequence, in which the principles of the Doctrine or the Doctrine itself has come under consideration and application.

Then follows a collection, under classified headings, of various announcements and declarations touching matters and incidents which have been said *not* to fall within the Doctrine or its underlying principles.

* * *

The Doctrine . . . declared by Monroe, when reduced to its lowest terms, covers—

(1) Future *colonization by any European powers* of the *American continents.*

(2) Any attempt by the *allied powers* to extend their political system *to any portion of this hemisphere,* or (in its second statement) *to any part of either continent.*

(3) Any interposition, *by any European power,* for the purpose of oppressing or controlling in any other manner the destinies of the Latin American Governments "who have declared their independence and maintained it, and whose independence we have, on great consideration and just principles, acknowledged."

(4) Noninterference by the United States with the existing colonies or dependencies of any European power.

(5) Policy of leaving Spanish American colonies and Spain to themselves in the hope that other powers will pursue the same course.

Behind the Doctrine, though not expressly stated in words by President Monroe, is the principle of the complete political separation of Europe and the Americas, or, as Jefferson put it, "Our first and fundamental maxim should be, never to entangle ourselves in the broils of Europe; our second, never to suffer Europe to intermeddle with cis-Atlantic affairs" (October 24, 1823).

* * *

The Memorandum shows that each of these essential principles of the Doctrine had been understood, announced, and invoked as between ourselves and Europe, years before the framing of Monroe's declaration was contemplated.

* * *

The Doctrine states a case of United States *vs.* Europe, not of United States *vs.* Latin America.

* * *

Should it become necessary to apply a sanction for a violation of the Doctrine as declared by Monroe, that sanction would run against the European power offending the policy, and not against the Latin American country which was the object of the European aggression, unless a conspiracy existed between the European and the American states involved.

The Doctrine has been useful, and such indeed was the real motive of its announcement, and it will remain of such use that it should never be abandoned, as a forewarning to European powers as to what this country would regard, in a restricted field, as inimical to its safety. It has been equally useful to the Americas as forecasting our attitude towards certain international problems and relations in which they might be involved.

* * *

It has also been announced that the Monroe Doctrine is not a pledge by the United States to other American states requiring the United States to protect such states, at their behest, against real or fancied wrongs inflicted by European powers, nor does it create an obligation running from the United States to any American state to intervene for its protection.

* * *

The so-called "Roosevelt corollary" was to the effect, as generally understood, that in case of financial or other difficulties in weak Latin American countries, the United States should attempt an adjustment thereof lest European Governments should intervene, and intervening should occupy territory—an act which would be contrary to the principles of the Monroe Doctrine. . . .

As has already been indicated above, it is not believed that this corollary is justified by the terms of the Monroe Doctrine, however much it may be justified by the application of the doctrine of self-preservation.

* * *

Finally, it should not be overlooked that the United States declined the overtures of Great Britain in 1823 to make a joint declaration regarding the principles covered by the Monroe Doctrine, or to enter into a conventional arrangement regarding them. Instead this Government determined to make the declaration of high national policy on its own responsibility and in its own behalf. The Doctrine is thus purely unilateral. The United States determines when and if the principles of the Doctrine are violated, and when and if violation is threatened. We alone determine what measures if any, shall be taken to vindicate the principles of the Doctrine, and we of necessity determine when the principles have been vindicated. No other power of the world has any relationship to, or voice in, the implementing of the principles which the Doctrine contains. It is our Doctrine, to be by us invoked and sustained, held in abeyance, or abandoned as our high international policy or vital national interests shall seem to us, and to us alone, to demand.

It may, in conclusion, be repeated: The Doctrine does not concern itself with purely inter-American relations; it has nothing to do with the relationship between the United States and other American nations, except where other American nations shall become involved with European governments in arrangements which threaten the security of the United States, and even in such cases, the Doctrine runs against the European country, not the American nation, and the United States would primarily deal thereunder with the European country and not with the American nation concerned. The Doctrine states a case of the United States *vs.* Europe, and not of the United States *vs.* Latin America. Furthermore, the fact should never be lost to view that in applying this Doctrine during the period of one hundred years since it was announced, our Government has over and over again driven it in as a shield between Europe and the Americas to protect Latin America from the political and territorial thrusts of Europe; and this was done at times when the American nations were weak and struggling for the establishment of stable, permanent governments; when the political morality of Europe sanctioned, indeed encouraged, the acquisition of territory by force; and when many of the great powers of Europe looked with eager, covetous eyes to the rich, undeveloped areas of the American hemisphere. Nor should another equally vital fact be lost sight of, that the United States has only been able to give this protection against designing European powers because of its known willingness and determination, if and whenever necessary, to expend its treasure and to sacrifice American life to maintain the principles of the Doctrine. So far as Latin America is concerned, the Doctrine is now, and always has been, not an instrument of violence and oppression, but an unbought, freely bestowed, and wholly effective guaranty of their freedom, independence, and territorial integrity against the imperialistic designs of Europe.

J. Reuben Clark

December 17, 1928.

Statement of the Doctrine

The Monroe Doctrine was announced by President Monroe in his annual message of December 2, 1823. The President had two main situations in mind: that which existed on the northwest coast of this continent where Russia was proposing to extend her control; and that which existed with reference to the Spanish colonies in the Western Hemisphere which had thrown off the Spanish yoke and as to which there was some agitation in Europe for cooperation among certain European powers to resubject these Spanish colonies to Spanish or other monarchical rule. But the President seems also to have had in mind, in a relation other than that incident to colonization, the whole Western Hemisphere, outside of the United States.

As to our northwest coast—President Monroe first called attention to the desire of Russia "to arrange by amicable negotiation the respective rights and interests of the two nations on the northwest coast of this continent" as to which she had made a similar proposal to Great Britain and then affirmed the friendly disposition of the United States towards Russia and our solicitude to cultivate "the best understanding" with the Government of the Emperor of Russia. He then declared:

[T]he occasion has been judged proper for asserting, as a principle in which the rights and interests of the United States are involved, that the American continents, by the free and independent condition which they have assumed and maintain, are henceforth not to be considered as subjects for future colonization by any European powers. (James D. Richardson, *A Compilation of the Messages and Papers of the Presidents,* 10 vols. [Washington, D.C., 1896-99], 2:209)

Later in his message, President Monroe called attention to the unsettled condition of European affairs, particularly with reference to Spain and Portugal, where the result which attended an effort to improve the people was not such as had been anticipated; and to the friendly sentiments entertained by the United States towards the liberty and happiness of their fellow men on the European side of the Atlantic, though we have never participated in their wars, "nor does it comport with our policy so to do." President Monroe then continued:

It is only when our rights are invaded or seriously menaced that we resent injuries or make preparation for our defense. With the movements in this hemisphere we are of necessity more immediately connected, and by causes which must be obvious to all enlightened and impartial observers. The political system of the allied powers is essentially different in this respect from that of America. This difference proceeds from that which exists in their respective governments; and to the defense of our own, which has been achieved by the loss of so much blood and treasure, and matured by the wisdom of their most enlightened citizens, and under which we have enjoyed unexampled felicity, this whole nation is devoted. We owe it, therefore, to candor and to the amicable relations existing between the United States and those powers to declare that we should consider any attempt on their part to extend their system to any portion of this hemisphere as dangerous to our peace and safety. With the existing colonies or dependencies of any European power we have not interfered and shall not interfere. But with the governments who have declared their independence and maintained it, and whose independence we have, on great consideration and on just principles, acknowledged, we could not view any interposition for the purpose of oppressing them, or controlling in any other manner their destiny, by any European power in any other light than as the manifestation of an unfriendly disposition toward the United States. (Richardson, 2:218)

Finally, after calling attention to our neutrality in the war between Spain and her colonies, to which we should continue to adhere "provided no change shall occur which, in the judgment of the competent authorities of this Government, shall make a corresponding change on the part of the United States indispensable to their security"; to the interposition "by force" of the allied powers "in the internal concerns of Spain"; to our policy, with reference to European wars, "not to interfere in the internal concerns of any of its powers; to consider the government *de facto* as the legitimate government for us; to cultivate friendly relations with it, and to preserve those relations by a frank, firm, and manly policy, meeting in all instances the just claims of every power, submitting to injuries from none," President Monroe further declared,

But in regard to those continents circumstances are eminently and conspicuously different. It is impossible that the allied powers should extend their political system to any portion of either continent without endangering our peace and happiness; nor can anyone believe that our southern brethren, if left to themselves, would adopt it of their own accord. It is equally impossible, therefore, that we should behold such interposition in any form with indifference. . . . It is still the true policy of the United States to leave the parties to themselves, in the hope that other powers will pursue the same course. (Richardson, 2:219)

The Six Prime Points of the Doctrine

An analysis of these declarations reveals that six prime matters are covered by President Monroe's message.

1. The *"American continents"* were not subject to colonization by *any European power*. This in terms certainly includes North and South America. Impliedly, colonization is considered antagonistic or detrimental to the "free and independent condition which they" (the "American continents") "have assumed and maintain." The "rights and interests" of the United States were involved in this principle.

2. The United States would consider any attempt on the part of the *"allied powers"* to extend their system to any part of *"this hemisphere as dangerous to our peace and safety."*

This in terms covered the "allied powers," at this time, Austria, France, Russia, and Prussia; it covered the whole Western hemisphere, those parts occupied by the Spanish colonies and other parts; it was aimed at the allied "system."

3. "With the existing colonies or dependencies of any European power we have not interfered and shall not interfere."

It would seem, having in mind the sentence following and the expressions of paragraph 49 of the message, that this sentence might be interpreted as indicating we would not have had, at that time, any objection to reconquest by Spain of the colonies which had gained and maintained their independence and which we had recognized. This is not clear beyond doubt, because later in his message, President Monroe declared that while it had become evident, looking at the comparative strength and resources of Spain and those colonial governments and their distance from each other, that Spain could never subdue them, yet we would leave the parties to themselves. (Of course later we took a definite position against reannexation or reconquest by Spain.)

4. With reference to Spanish colonies which had declared and maintained their independence and which we had recognized, the United States "could not view any interposition for the purpose of oppressing them, or controlling in any other manner their destiny, *by any European power* in any other light than as the manifestation of an *unfriendly disposition toward the United States.*"

This declaration related to all European powers, not specifically excluding Spain; it specifically referred to the revolted Spanish colonies; it went beyond the reassumption of control over them by Spain or the extension to them of the allied "system;" it covered interposition in their affairs not only for the purpose of oppressing them, but for the purpose of controlling in any other manner their destiny by *any European power.*

5. Specifically, the United States declared that it was "impossible that the *allied powers* should extend their political *system to any portion of either continent* without *endangering our peace and happiness.*" It was equally impossible that we should behold "such interposition" by the allied powers in any form with indifference.

This being directed against the *allied powers,* did not, *ex vi termini,* include Spain, and at this time Great Britain was not counted within the group that was popularly so designated.

6. It was "still the true policy of the United States" to leave the parties, that is, the revolted colonies and Spain, to themselves to adjust their difficulties as they saw fit.

This was the Monroe Doctrine. Under it future colonization by European powers was to be regarded as antagonistic or detrimental to the free and independent condition of these continents; the extension of the allied "system" to any part of this hemisphere was considered dangerous to our peace and safety; interposition by any European power, for the purpose of oppressing or controlling the destiny of the rebelled Spanish colonies which we had recognized was to be regarded as a manifestation of an unfriendly disposition towards the United States; our peace and happiness would be endangered should the allied powers extend their political system to any part of either continent, and the interposition of those powers in any form could not be viewed with indifference; the true policy of the United States was to leave Spain and her rebelled colonies to adjust their difficulties between themselves.

The Doctrine was thus one of self-preservation for the United States.

The provisions of the declaration fall obviously into two classes: those relating to "future colonization *by any European powers*" on the "American continents;" and those relating to political operations, though the formula "interposition for the purpose of oppressing them, or controlling in any other manner their destiny" seems sufficiently broad to cover other than purely political "interpositions." The distinctly political inhibitions run against the allied powers, and "to any portion of this hemisphere," or, as stated in the second formula, "to any portion of either continent;" the inhibitions as to "interposition" run against "any European powers," and in terms relate to Spanish American "governments who have declared their independence and maintained it, and whose independence we have, on great consideration and on just principles, acknowledged."

In this memorandum no attempt is made to trace separately the development of these different classes of inhibitions, nor to identify, as belonging to the one class or the other, the occasions on which the Doctrine or its underlying principles have been invoked by this Government.

The reason these matters were regarded by President Monroe and his Cabinet as antagonistic and detrimental, as dangerous to our peace and safety, as a manifestation of an unfriendly disposition towards the United States or as endangering our peace and happiness, is best understood when we consider the historical facts—the circumstances which at that time were in the minds of Monroe, Adams, Calhoun, Jefferson, and Madison. For it was the views and discussions of these men which lay behind and which shaped and framed the announcement which President Monroe made to the world, as well as determined the terms in which the declaration was couched. [Ed. note: Beginning with the "Six Prime Points of the Doctrine," p. 377, all italics are JRC's.]

Collecting on Defaulted Foreign Dollar Bonds

January 1940

JRC had been associated with the Foreign Bondholders Protective Council, Inc., almost from its inception and had served both as a director and as its president. In this article, published in the *American Journal of International Law*, 34, no. 1 (January 1940), he described the origin of the Council, its purpose, how it operated, its accomplishments, and some of the principles which controlled its work. Box 219, Folder 11, JRCP.

The Foreign Bondholders Protective Council, Inc., was organized in December, 1933, for the purpose of securing resumption of service—interest and amortization—on defaulted foreign dollar bonds then amounting to about $2,500,000,000 issued by some 23 countries. The Council concluded its first negotiations in February, 1934. Since then there has been actually paid to American bondholders, on account of the interest only of such defaulted bonds, $103,938,000 in cash and $37,204,000 in scrip—a grand total of $141,142,000. This has been done on a total expense account for the Council (covering the whole of the Council's work) of thirty-four hundredths of one per cent (.0034) on the amount of interest so actually paid to bondholders, or of twenty-seven thousandths of one per cent (.00027) on the face value of the bonds concerning which the Council has negotiated. It may be added that of the total sum of $2,500,000,000 of defaulted bonds, the Council has since its organization negotiated regarding the resumption, continuance, or increase of service on over $1,773,000,000. Of this sum, permanent settlements were arranged as to $245,000,000 and temporary settlements covering $1,528,000,000.

The Council was formed by a group of gentlemen who had been personally requested to set it up by the Honorable Cordell Hull, Secretary of State, the Honorable William H. Woodin, Secretary of the Treasury, and the Honorable Charles H. March, Chairman of the Federal Trade Commission. It was created in lieu of the organization of the Corporation of Foreign Security Holders provided in Title 2 of the Securities Act of 1933 (*United States Statutes at Large,* 48:92), after the Administration had determined not to establish that body.

Following a meeting between President Roosevelt and the organizers in October, 1933, the White House issued a formal statement approving the creation of the Council, stating the need therefor, and outlining certain general principles that should govern its work. The Council was not to be a profit organization, was to carry on at the lowest possible expense to the bondholders, was to decide its own affairs independently, and Administration officials were stated to "have no intention, however, of seeking governmental direction or control of the organization, nor will they assume responsibility for its actions." The Council has carried on its work in accordance with these principles.

The Council does not represent the bondholders legally. It cannot negotiate settlements that are binding upon them. It has never called for deposits of bonds. The regular procedure of negotiation by the Council is this: It approaches the defaulting debtor on dollar bonds in an effort to induce it to resume or to increase its interest and sinking fund service on its bonds in accordance with the bond contract. Whenever the defaulting debtor can be so induced, the Council enters into negotiations with the debtor to secure from it the best possible offer of service. When the debtor makes the offer, the Council follows one of three courses: it tells the bondholders the offer is fair and equitable under all the circumstances, if in the Council's judgment such are the facts; or if the Council believes the offer is unfair, it tells the bondholders so, and may recommend against the acceptance of the offer by the bondholders; or the Council may pass the offer on to the bondholders without any expression of opinion. In no event is the bondholder bound either to accept or reject the offer; he is in no way committed either for or against the offer; he makes his own decision about it. The offers arranged for by the Council always run to each and every bondholder, and not to a selected group only.

Believing that the world-wide depression made it undesirable, both for the bondholder and the defaulting debtor, to attempt to make final arrangements on the debt, the Council has endeavored to get the defaulting debtors to offer a temporary service covering a few years, the permanent settlement to come later when the condition of the world became more normal. However, some of the debtors have insisted on permanent arrangements now, seemingly in the belief that the present was their most opportune time for adjustments.

Of the approximately $2,500,000,000 foreign dollar bonds in default when the Council was organized, approximately $1,200,000,000 were Latin American dollar bonds, and $1,300,000,000 were European dollar bonds.

The following table shows the approximate amount of interest service, both cash and bonds (funding) which were offered to holders as the result of either temporary or permanent adjustments negotiated by the Council from the time of its organization up to the end of 1939. These figures do not include sinking fund payments made under any plan, but merely those payments made for interest.

It is of interest to note that on the permanent settlements, the average annual interest rate return (at the lowest rate called for under the adjustment plans) has been approximately 4.3%; the sinking fund arrangement has been approximately 1.2%, or a total service of 5.5% per annum.

To meet the expense of all of this work, the Council has spent approximately $80,000 per year, including rent, clerical help, supplies, preparation and printing of the Annual Report, statistical service, telephone, telegraph, travelling expenses, negotiation expenses, officers' salaries, and all incidental costs whatever.

Being a strictly non-profit organization and having neither capital stock nor assets, the Council has found difficulty in financing itself. Failing to get some sort of endowment, it turned to the issue houses and banks on the theory that as they had profited by the issuance of the bonds they should contribute to the protection of the rights of the bondholders. This plan had the express approval of the Administration. Later the Securities and Exchange Commission condemned this plan, and the Council then turned to the bondholders

	Outstanding When Adjusted*	Period for Which Interest Was Offered	Cash	Bonds
Brazil (temporary)	$ 375,965,035	3-3½ yrs.	$ 32,678,707	
Germany (temporary)	1,066,786,000	1 yr.	32,640,000 (a)	
Germany (temporary)		2½ yrs.	1,759,950 (b)	$29,332,500 (c)
Dominican Republic (permanent)	16,292,500	5½ yrs	4,810,095	
Buenos Aires (permanent)	72,605,424	4 yrs.	10,489,968	
Costa Rica (two temporary)	10,489,351	2-2½ yrs	519,863	
China—Treasury notes (permanent)	5,500,000	2½ yrs.(d)	343,750	1,058,750
China—Hukuang (permanent)	7,500,000	2 yrs.	375,000	...... (e)
Hungary—non-State (temporary)	11,468,000	2-2½ yrs.	436,741	
Cuban Public Works (permanent)	40,000,000	3½ yrs.(f)	4,450,250	3,476,800
Yugoslavia (two temporary)	42,366,300	3-4 yrs.	4,111,594	2,890,000
Poland (two temporary and one permanent), including Silesia and Warsaw	53,851,980 (g)	1 yr. (h)	3,456,475	440,000
		7 mos. (i)		
		1½ yrs.(j)		2,818,879

Uruguay (permanent)	52,947,500	2 yrs.	3,989,125	
Montevideo (permanent)	4,863,500	2 yrs.	360,982	
Mendoza (permanent)	4,327,000	2½ yrs.	342,400	6,443
Santa Fé, Province and City (permanent) ...	8,859,200	1 yr.	354,368	
	$1,773,821,790		$103,938,147	$37,204,493

* Where there are more than one adjustment, the amounts given are for the earliest one.

(a) Based on $1,066,786,000—the figure given in February, 1934, as then outstanding.
(b) Received as 3% interest on $29,332,500 funding bonds.
(c) Amount issued only.
(d) Cash for 2½ yrs.; scrip for short-fall during 2½ yrs. and for 15 yrs. back interest at 1%.
(e) Scrip to be, but not yet, issued. $562,500 for short-fall during 2-yr. period and for 6½ yrs. back interest at 1%.
(f) Cash for 2½ yrs.; bonds for 4 yrs.
(g) Amount outstanding under temporary adjustments; $41,185,400 under permanent adjustment.
(h) 1 yr. under first temporary plan.
(i) 7 mos. under second temporary plan.
(j) 1½ yrs. under permanent plan.

385

(from whom it has asked 1/8 of 1% of the face value of the bonds on which it has arranged permanent settlements), and to the debtor states on the theory that a debtor should bear at least a portion of the costs of refinancing. The bondholders have in largest part generously responded, though some (largely foreign holders, American speculators, and arbitrageurs) have accepted the benefits of the Council's work but have refused to contribute to its support. To remedy this situation the Board of Visitors (named by the Secretary of State and the Chairman of the Securities and Exchange Commission at the request of the Council) have approved a levy (the maximum being 1/8 of 1%) on all bonds participating in any adjustment.

Speaking generally, defaulting debtors on dollar bonds, are defaulting, not because they are unable to pay all or a good part of their debt service, but simply because they do not have the will to pay. For example, one country in total default on its dollar bonds since 1932 and 1935, had, during the seven years of default, a favorable trade balance with the United States of approximately three times the amount of the full contract interest service on their dollar bonds, yet during all this time it refused either to serve its bonds or seriously to discuss service, though paying full service on its total internal debt, even up to 10% per annum. Other cases are almost as flagrant. Six Latin American countries having a favorable balance of trade with the United States in 1938 made no interest payments on their bonds for that year. In contrast with that, four countries—Argentina, Dominican Republic, Haiti, and Uruguay—had unfavorable balances of trade with the United States for 1938, and yet paid full bond interest for that period. There are some defaulting debtors who will make no adequate service, if any at all, upon their defaulted dollar bonds, except under governmental pressure.

In its work the Council has at all times applied certain principles. It has steadily refused to discuss or even listen to arguments to the point that the principal amount of the bonds should be reduced, or that adjustments should be made that would in effect constitute a reduction. The Council's files contain great numbers of letters showing that there are thousands, if not hundreds of thousands, of bondholders who bought their bonds at the original issue prices. These are in great part aged people who invested their life savings in "government gold bonds" frequently under a sales representation that they were "better than money in the bank," because the bonds drew a high interest rate, and bank balances drew a low interest rate. These people write from hospitals, infirmaries, county poor houses, and bare homes. They say these bonds represent all they have in the world. The Council has refused to sacrifice the rights and necessities of these American citizens to the interest of defaulting debtors, able to pay and lacking only the will so to do.

One of the iniquities of the existing condition of foreign dollar bond defaults is this: while governments allege they are unable to find either funds or dollar exchange to pay the interest and sinking fund on their bonds, nevertheless, such governments (many, and indeed most of them) have been able to find both funds and dollar exchange to buy up in our markets their own bonds at the very low prices at which the bonds are selling due to their own wilful default. The Council has complained and inveighed against this in vain. In its 1937 Report the Council said:

> Because of the character of such a transaction as this repatriation of defaulted bonds, the participants therein do not usually disclose the extent of their operation, and it is therefore difficult to obtain accurate figures regarding the extent of the operation. But from such fragmentary information as the Council can secure it would seem that some municipal defaulters have bought up while in continuous default, as much as 83.5% of their indebtedness outstanding at the time of default; one country with an outstanding indebtedness at the time of default of over 850 millions, has repatriated, at default prices, approximately 1/3 of the debt. Thirteen countries in default (on which fairly accurate data have been obtained) had at the time of default approximately $1,815,347,000 of dollar debt outstanding. These countries have in some 7 years repatriated approximately 25% of this debt, though all the time alleging they had not available funds or exchange to serve their bonds.

Government estimates indicate that almost a dozen countries in default in service payments on their dollar bonds, most of them alleging as a reason for their default a lack of dollar exchange, have been able to find enough of that exchange to repatriate from 15% to 50% of their outstanding dollar issues.

Another contention which defaulting debtors frequently make is that their bonds are in the hands of holders who have bought them at the low prices existing since default, and therefore that the interest should be cut to what would be a fair return upon the price actually paid. The Council has refused to yield to this argument because, first, of the great injustice it would work on the original holders (already referred to), and next because it considers dishonest an argument by a debtor which would put a premium upon his own wilful default.

In this connection the Council has had constantly in mind that there is a certain fundamental difference between enterprises and investments made by Americans in the United States and the same sort of operations undertaken by them in foreign countries. Where the enterprise is domestic, the national wealth is not much concerned with who, among the people of the United States, shall gain or lose with reference to that enterprise. If "A" loses to "B" in such an investment, the property being still in the United States, the national wealth is not in any way impaired. However, where the American capital is invested in bonds of a foreign country the situation is wholly different. This bond investment is an outlay of the national wealth which is lodged in the foreign country. If the investment is not returned to the United States, the national wealth has been by that much depleted. For example, a foreign government borrowing a dollar and paying back 20¢(on the theory that since the particular holder of the obligation at the time of payment had paid only 20¢ for it, the debtor should be able to wipe out his obligation by the payment of the 20¢), would deplete the national wealth by 80¢ for every dollar which had been originally invested.

One of the considerations most frequently urged upon the Council in connection with an application to reduce either the principal sum of indebtedness or the service (interest and amortization) thereon, has been that of "capacity to pay" which is, in fact, brought forward rather as *incapacity to pay*. This is frequently urged by debtors whose revenues are approximately at the same height as when the loans were made, but whose expenditures have enormously increased, either for war equipment or for the frills of modern governmental activities. It will be recalled that the phrase originated in a discussion between sovereigns with reference to obligations running between them, and arising out of a joint partnership, political operation, for political purposes, the World War. If these sovereigns, in such a discussion, wished in adjusting their sovereign debts to take account of the relative "capacity to pay" of the sovereign debtors, their partners in the joint enterprise, such was their sovereign privilege. They were dealing as equals about their own debts, and could, with reference thereto, be generous or otherwise as suited their sovereign interests, conveniences, circumstances, or commitments.

The Council has said, however, that neither this phrase, "capacity to pay," nor the principle it formulates has any proper place whatsoever in a discussion between a sovereign and his private foreign creditors. A sovereign must be assumed to know when he borrows from private parties whether or not he will be able to pay, whether or not he is incurring an obligation within his "capacity to pay." The foreign creditor is not able to determine this matter for himself, either at the time of the borrowing or thereafter. Furthermore, whether a sovereign pays, or does not pay, depends in greatest part upon his will to pay. For few, if any, governments have borrowed beyond their *capacity* to pay if they really had a will to make the necessary levy upon the property of their nationals, and to pay. No nation has any right to invoke its lack of "capacity to pay" its obligations to private creditors until it has fully exhausted its taxing powers, and no debtor sovereign now in default, in so far as the Council is advised, has even approached a condition of exhaustion of its taxing powers.

The Council has announced its intention to continue to take advantage of every opportunity that may arise to aid the holders of defaulted foreign dollar bonds.

Some Factors Affecting Trust Investments

15 August 1940

Some fifteen months before the surprise Japanese attack on Pearl Harbor in December 1941, JRC gave this address before trust officers attending the Eighteenth Regional Trust Conference in Salt Lake City, Utah. Their concern for international trade gave them a special interest in the war then raging in Europe, but JRC saw not only the Atlantic but also the Caribbean and the Far East as problem areas. He devoted his speech principally to four issues: government spending, taxation, international finance, and foreign trade. Box 221, Folder 7, JRCP.

I am greatly honored in the invitation to speak to you tonight. But I come clothed in a good deal of embarrassment, because I am neither financier nor economist. However, I am emboldened somewhat and a bit heartened by the principle which lies behind an incident that happened between Andrew Carnegie and Philander C. Knox, one of the greatest statesmen our country has produced. Mr. Knox told me that on one occasion Carnegie was a party to some patent litigation. The case had gone to the Supreme Court of the United States, then a real court. Carnegie was anxious. He asked Mr. Knox to become of counsel in the case and present an argument. Knox protested that he knew nothing about patent law. Carnegie, the wily, shrewd Scotchman, replied, "That is just why I want you. I've got so many patent attorneys to argue about the

patents that I am afraid they will miss the real points in the case."
Knox accepted the employment and won the case.

I am not so vain as to think I can be a Knox for you in your
problems, but perhaps I may give you some suggestion, possibly
helpful, as to how some matters in your field appear to the great
body of us who have little money to place in your care and yet who
are intimately affected, as we believe, by what you think, believe,
and do with the vast funds others put at your disposal.

I think I do not need to belabor to you either your duty, your
responsibility, or your power. These are all so obvious I will not
even mention them further.

To us uninitiated, it does seem as if we are now well within the
threshold of a financial and economic crisis that has no parallel in
our national history since in 1790 it was determined that the Federal Government should assume the debts of the States. Looking
backward, we see now that the issue then was unity and order or
disunion and chaos. We uninitiated have a haunting fear that some
such issue may face us now.

Within the control of you Trust Officers of the United States
lies no small part of its private wealth. How you invest these funds
can have a vital determining force on the economic and financial
welfare of the country.

The problem of investment is today unique in our history.

Heretofore you dealt with and under fixed and accepted principles that gave relatively a "rule o' thumb" to guide you. The occasional financial panic or depression you had to meet operated also
under certain principles which could always be dimly perceived if
not, indeed, actually understood and measurably shaped and brought
under control. You could go forward without its being necessary for
you to give the slightest heed to political considerations, save perhaps
during an occasional presidential campaign when protection or free
trade became an issue. But even then the full success of the one party
or the other brought no disturbance that could not be met without
great difficulty. Certain nation-wide industries were always sound,
were always safe investments at right prices. Your task was more or
less that of buying and selling at the right time. You operated upon a
stable and secure foundation of economics and government.

But now, to us uninitiated, that golden age of relative security
and comfort for the mass of the people seems in danger of passing. It
looks to us that your problem now is not merely that of right buying

and selling in stable and standard industries. We surmise that you must now also try to guess how long that stable and standard industry will so remain; that you must be troubled with the queries: when will government enter the same field, with money on which government usually makes no return, if indeed it ever really seeks to make one, to the destruction of competing private industry; or when will government take over this industry or that, paying therefor in inflated currency or in unstable, depreciating, and insufficiently secured paper—bonds, paper dollars, treasury notes, or what not; or when and how may government take over an exercise of a destructive control of the industry, or levy against it ruinous taxation; or how long will it be the fundamental law that private property, life and liberty may not be taken without due process of law, or how long will the very form and fabric of our Republic remain to prosper and bless us?

As we uninitiated see it, these are some of the major problems you must solve in these fields, if you shall continue wisely to handle the trust funds in your custody.

In other words, you have facing you now not alone the uncertainties of economics and finance—the right time for buying and selling—but you have now a political hazard, and this is the most uncertain and far-reaching of all hazards attending the sale, acquisition and holding of property. Whenever a political hazard appears in an economic and political system, the welfare and prosperity of the people are basically jeopardized. I shall not at this time say anything about the threat of this hazard to the "Life, Liberty, and the pursuit of Happiness" of the Declaration, the most precious political gifts that God has vouchsafed to man.

At the moment you have the added problem in finance and economics of how far will this national paroxysm of unreasoning, hysterical war-fear carry us or warp or change our national life, before the courage and sanity of our people re-assert themselves. On the information we uninitiated have, it seems clear that this fear has been sown by European propagandists and political emigrés and their sympathizers in this country who are urged forward in their cause by hate and selfishness.

To us it looks as if the work of these European propagandists and political emigrés has brought this curious complex amongst our people: We seem now to propose to adopt for ourselves as having the maximum of power and wisdom to save us and this Republic, those very principles of economics and government which we have but recently not only derided as bordering insanity in their concept, but which we have also unreservedly condemned as un-American and destructive of the inalienable rights of men as proclaimed in the Declaration of Independence and guaranteed by our divinely inspired Constitution. We cannot but fear that these panic-stricken officers are now proposing to incorporate into free America all the basic and essential principles and practices that have destroyed liberty and built dictators in Europe, and they propose this upon the pretext that the exercise of these despotic powers in America is necessary to save our liberty and free institutions.

It seems to us uninitiated that this whole pack of arguments is false; that they who propose these measures of dictatorship and tyranny are, if honest, too immature and unwise to be trusted, and, if dishonest, too traitorous to be listened to.

With all the earnestness I possess I urge you to combat this enemy with every means at your command, and particularly that you fight him with that God-given weapon—a free ballot.

You gentlemen must also be interested in taxation, because this bears a close and vital relationship to investment. I am not at the moment referring to taxation because it reduces or destroys profits (that element may be immediately overcome by a mere change in policy). Nor am I now speaking of the principle involved in the aphorism of John Marshall—"The power to tax is the power to destroy" (Henry Wheaton, *Report of Cases . . . in the Supreme Court . . . ,* 11 vols, [New York, 1816–26], 4:431). Taxation can be stopped before it is complete confiscation—maybe.

What I have now in mind seems to us uninitiated much more far-reaching, and is clearly more insidious and less apparent than either of the others, and it is even more destructive than either, for it affects the whole body politic, not merely those taxed—I refer to the use of the people's property—for tax money is property—for wholly non-productive purposes. For whenever a dollar is used for other than to help produce another you have burned it up. You have depleted the national wealth by just that much—making the nation, the people by that much the poorer, for by just that much the sustenance for the whole people has been destroyed, the sustenance from which they get their food, fuel, clothing, and shelter.

Furthermore, it looks to us uninitiated that whatever money—property—is consumed, is put beyond the taxing power, leaving just that much less property to be taxed. So to keep up the pace, taxes must be increased on the property that is left.

Thus, as we see it, constantly increasing taxation takes more and more property out of production, less and less property is left to be taxed and to support the people, until, unless there be a halt, the system finally consumes the whole property of the people it infects. To cure this curse takes generations, and in extreme cases, a whole national life.

No one of us uninitiated will deny that expenses for government are necessary in order that property and human liberty and life may be safe, though in strictness the bulk of all such expenditures are wholly lost to production and therefore lost to the national wealth. However, this expenditure is a necessary economic evil, to be confined to its narrowest feasible limits. But our immense and sumptuous government buildings, some with living quarters so luxurious as to make the palaces of the ancient Roman emperors, even in their greatest heyday, look almost like a chimney sweep's hovel, our pleasing but unnecessary monumental highways, our immense amusement centers and facilities, our multiplicity of scatter-brain projects for so-called public improvements of infinite variety—etc., etc., etc.,—and a great proportion of State and Federal present expenditures are for these purposes, all these are beyond the necessities of government, which can wisely be met only in their full bareness; all these may please our vanity and enhance our pride, but every dollar spent for them makes us that much poorer and reduces by that much the national wealth from which alone can further public funds be gotten, and from which alone the people can be fed, clothed, housed, and warmed.

So to us uninitiated does it likewise seem as to all the enormous sums planned for defense, and I favor a fully adequate defense, for however necessary adequate defense may be as a matter of self-preservation, and self-preservation is an elemental law, it must not be overlooked nor forgotten that every dollar spent thereon goes into non-productive materials and enterprises and by so much reduces the national wealth, and takes away that much from the people.

Furthermore, revenues derived from war-material exported to warring countries, exports which are burned up in war between other countries, seem to us uninitiated to be revenues that really do not enrich us, because for every dollar we now get from these foreign countries for all such supplies, it looks to us we may lose many more after the war, since the conflict will, as matters now look, inevitably bring them to near or utter exhaustion, whereupon their purchasing power will be seriously impaired if not all but destroyed for at least a generation. It seems to us we stand to lose more than we gain by war exports.

To us our present mad government spending orgy of the people's property seems to affect rather more intimately and immediately the poorer of us than the rich, for while taxes as such seem, when superficially considered, to touch mainly the plutocrat, yet the destruction of the national wealth strikes directly the heart of the welfare of the whole people and particularly the poor, who must be fed, clothed and sheltered from and by the national wealth which is being so depleted.

The problems involved in these considerations are not only vital but far-reaching. You must make up your minds whether or not the accumulated wealth of generations being so dissipated, our standards of living must fall, whether the development of the fine arts and sciences must hesitate if not cease, whether education must slow down, whether the work of the people in productive activities—the mill, the farm, the store, the counting house—must become less and less, because fewer and fewer dollars will remain for expansion, depreciation, obsolescence and repairs. You must consider whether it may turn out that only the toil, and thrift, and frugality of many generations to come can build us back to where we were. Thus does it look to us, the uninitiated, who see in all this a possible nightfall; to you initiated, it may be a passing cloud over the sun.

All of this affects intimately and basically the securities you purchase with your trust funds.

But I want to say a few words about that phase of international trade and financing where my opportunities for observation have been a little more intimate. For if our world goes on, we must look more and more to international trade and finance for investment.

Our economic or commercial interest in foreign nations comes primarily from three ways, in so far as our national income is concerned: what we sell to them; what we get from them because of the investment of our funds within their confines; and the returns on what we lend to them. I am not now concerned with the so-called "invisible exports and imports."

As purely preliminary I may say that: our total exports from 1928-1933 were valued at $33.2 billions (there are all kinds of ways of estimating the value of our exports); our total foreign investment in productive enterprises in 1936 was estimated at $6,700,000,000 (it is probably about the same now); our total lendings in 1930 were $10,032,204,000, not including the $10,000,000,000 plus accrued and unpaid interest on the debt owed by the Allies to our people. Thus somewhere around $20,000,000,000 to $25,000,000,000 of the people's savings are bound up in foreign securities and investments, not now yielding adequate return, and on half of this amount the people themselves are meeting the interest out of their own pockets. Our national loss in revenues on this account runs into very large figures.

When wisdom finally returns to our council chambers and with it a return to private financing, you will be expected to do your share in placing the securities.

I need not tell you gentlemen that of course the outstanding obligations of foreign governments are not held in Wall Street, as some propagandizing and not too honest politicians would have us believe. These obligations are mainly held by the moderately-circumstanced people and represent their savings. Nor do I need to repeat that, as to the Allied debt, the people not only furnished the money that was lent to the Allies, but that they are now taxed to pay the interest on that Allied debt.

You know as well as I that these are matters which are not weighing upon the plutocrats solely. We non-plutocrats are all bearing our share. We uninitiated feel that this situation merits more consideration than it has thus far received. The Federal Government instead of aiding and abetting the defaulting debtors in their dishonest niggardliness, should be aiding the holders of these defaulted securities to secure the service thereof. At the present moment this is not being done. On the contrary, Federal loans seem now to be contemplated to the worst offenders among all the defaulters; it seems these new loans are to be made without just and equitable arrangements being made by these defaulters to serve their defaulted debts, notwithstanding the fact that those seemingly now most favored for Federal loans are now and always have been amply able and with sufficient dollar exchange, to serve their obligations in full. The rule of any sound international finance must be that able debtors must pay by their contract; crippled debtors must do something, as much as they can. You Trust Officers are vitally interested in this, because the maxim "false in one, false in all," applies particularly to a dishonest debtor repudiating one debt that he may incur another.

I wish to say a few words now with reference to our foreign trade, not including our actual investments in properties in foreign countries (now in a most precarious condition) and not including our foreign lendings just referred to.

You Trust Officers are vitally interested in foreign trade, for it is such trade that must take our surplus, and the marketing of surplus is necessary to make the wheels go round.

So far as can be now seen, the tempo and character of world trade after the war will be fixed by Europe, no matter who the victor may be. It will almost certainly be so if, as now seems not unlikely, Germany shall win.

Galling as it must be to our pride, we must admit that the financiers and commercial men of Europe are, in matters of world trade, far and away more skilled and experienced than are we, who are, in these things, the rawest of amateurs.

You know as well as I that since the World War, the Allies, in seeking the last cent from Germany, and Germany in searching to avoid the payment of every penny possible, have built up such a system of world trade as modern times have not before seen. Quotas, barters, compulsory clearances, and the infinity of trade barriers and restrictions invented to carry out the purposes and to safeguard the interests of those two groups, have brought a new era in world commerce. To us uninitiated it looks as if we in our unskill and unwisdom have shuffled along, following now one, now the other of these warring systems.

Just a word or two now about money. By speaking I shall prove that I know the meaning of the word *"uninitiated"* which I have used so frequently; and I shall also prove that I have used the word accurately.

Anyone who believes that gold is a holy thing, sacredly necessary to trade and commerce, may not have all the factors of the problem in mind, and might well withhold final judgment for a time.

Our responsible authorities seem to have assumed first that if we had all the gold and silver of the world, the earth and all its riches would be ours. But to us uninitiated it has seemed that the more we got of gold and silver, the more the world learned how to get along without it. It could not be, could it, that we are holding the bag—a bag of gold rocks?

Some of us uninitiated surmise that maybe we bought the gold with the deliberate and malicious thought that we would dominate and control world trade. But this to some of us is a supremacy that would be just as ignoble and oppressive as a political supremacy and so no more to be sought by a high principled, righteous living nation than would be political supremacy, which just now we are condemning with the most virriolic vocabulary we possess.

However, some affirm we cornered the market with the thought and actual intent of bringing about just the result that seems threatening, that is, the destruction of the money system as a step towards wiping out the so-called capitalistic system. Some say that the army of communistically minded who have been lodged in the very highest governmental places, as Congressional investigators affirm, an army that has pushed us about, shoved us out of our accustomed marts, and thrown us into tax-barred commercial prisons, is an army quite capable of such a plot. Could it be as some contend, that there have been in our governmental circles a lot of deceivers, and an equal lot of deceived, poor fellows who were quite unable to match wits with the deceivers, and that some of these deceived seem finally to discern feebly what it all means and, as caught in a trap, are racing round and round trying to find a way out? It is said that just now they seem to think they have found a hole by lending large sums to discredited and unscrupulous borrowers in order to try to keep them on the gold standard, and so make valuable our bag of rocks. But short of a miracle, this particular step will be a vain hope.

May I suggest considerations justifying this conclusion by a few words about the much touted economic and political solidarity of the Americas which is to work such wonders for our trade and seemingly for our defense.

The figures given are taken from the recent study on the Foreign Trade of Latin America by the United States Tariff Commission. Presumably they are as favorable to the solidarity thesis as accuracy would justify.

The total export trade of the United States to all countries in 1938 amounted to $3,094,440,000 of which Latin America took $494,821,000 or 16%. The total import trade of Latin America (same year) amounted to $1,488,500,000 of which the United States furnished $494,821,000 or 33%. Thus the total imports of Latin America for 1938 would lack $1,606,000,000 of our total exports. In other words Latin America's total imports are only 48% of our total exports. Or if we had all the Latin American trade we must still find a market for over 52% of our exports.

Now as to our imports: The total import trade of the United States for 1938 was $1,960,428,000 of which Latin America furnished $453,517,000 or 23.4% out of a total export trade of Latin America of $1,833,700,000 or 24.5%.

Thus the total exports of Latin America would fall short by $127,000,000 of our import requirements.

So if Latin America is to take the place of the rest of the world in our commerce, they must take (based on 1938 figures) from us 84% more of our total exports, and we must take 77% more of their total exports, than now. And for them to take all of our exports (assuming they either need them or want them) they must buy nearly 52% more than they are now buying from the world. Furthermore, since we must buy all they sell, if they shall buy all we sell, we must buy over 93% of our imports from them.

Of course this could not be done if we wanted to do it and for one reason, because the markets simply do not exist in either place for the full products of the other, and certainly Latin America can supply only a fraction of our import needs.

But if we could absorb all this Latin American trade as it now exists we should alienate and irritate the rest of the world to the point of wrecking our friendly relations with all of them, and they probably could not take the other 52% of our export production, and this loss would surely wreck us.

But we cannot get the whole Latin American import trade, or anything like that amount, for a variety of reasons.

First, we cannot get it or keep it away from Europe in peace times because we cannot use all the Latin Americas sell without destroying our own agriculture, and they must sell all if they are to buy fully, and next, because all their national and racial sympathies, all their art and culture, all their juridical and governmental traditions, all their ties of kinship and affection, run to Europe and not to the United States, whom they have always feared, and fearing, they dislike, and so will not deal with us except when it is to their distinct advantage so to do. And please do not assume that debtorship to us for money we now lend them to buy our goods will be sufficiently persuasive to keep them buying from us when the war stops. Their present generally wilful default on honest debts of $1,243,000,000—or 77.2% of bonds outstanding as of December 31, 1939, gives the negative to any such hope as that.*

Furthermore, and this is a vital point in our trade relations, their exports are almost wholly raw materials, the bulk of which, except the purely tropical products such as coffee, bananas, and other tropical fruits, are competitive with us. I refer to sugar, tobacco, cotton, rice, wheat, corn, flaxseed, pelts, hides, meats, and various mineral products. It could only be a phantasy, born of such hysterical fear as now afflicts us, (a dominating fear, real or simulated, born of the unjustifiable apprehension of foreign aggression, plus, it may be, a fear of having the people realize how they have been duped) it could be only such a phantasy that could lead us to think that we could either purchase and consume all these raw materials, except by breaking down our own production, or that could lead us to believe that we could purchase and re-sell them to advantage to Europe or elsewhere, or even give them away except to the ruination of our own production.

For is it not clear, what an attempted purchase and consumption of these cheap-labor produced, foreign food and agricultural staples would do to our own producers? Surely it need not be argued that every pound of meat, and butter, and wheat, and cotton, and all the rest brought in for our use and used, must reduce by that much our use of what we ourselves produce to the detriment of our own producers. Surely it can be seen now, that to subsidize our own farmers not to sow and not to reap, or pay them to kill off their hogs and cattle, so that a market for foreign materials including Argentine beef, can be created here, is a course we cannot indefinitely follow. This, it must certainly be seen, is not the way to create national wealth.

---

*D. W. Ellsworth in a review of the business outlook of the United States in the *Annalist* of July 25, 1940, makes the following statement: "Under all the circumstances the proposed increase in the capital of the Export Import Bank to $500,000,000 seems unwarranted and unwise. Some statisticians have estimated that the loss of our entire export trade to South America would cause a decrease of no more than one point in the Federal Reserve Board of index of industrial production. Hence the only reasons for sending millions of American dollars on credits to Latin America would be of a political or charitable nature."

We ourselves, following Europe's lead, are, in effect, making some excursions into the barter system by our Reciprocal Trade Treaties. But it is one thing to make a barter arrangement with a country to furnish us what we do not produce and to furnish them with what they do not produce, and quite another thing to make a barter arrangement that would only result in buying from them the things which we ourselves produce. Excuse my making the trite observation that this latter system inevitably means that the standard of life of those of us who produce the competitive materials, must sink to the level of the producers in those other countries, or else go out of production to something else, and it is never denied that the living standards of laborers and producers in our country is now about that enjoyed anywhere else in the world. And may I say here that reciprocal trade treaties with countries producing what we produce can be free trade in its most acute form, and means in its final analysis a levelling of all labor to a common base, which will be the lowest base found in any competitive producing country.

The older ones of us recall that during the World War we deliberately tried this same trick, we planned to steal, maybe I should soften it and say absorb, the Latin American trade from Europe. We announced this then with a fan fare of trumpets. While the war lasted we had some measure of success. When the war ended, trade resumed its normal channels. The Latin Americas went back to their first loves. We have no right to think they will not do so again.

Furthermore, is it quite the thing for a real he-man country to pick the pockets of his friend behind his back while the friend is fighting head on for his life with an all but overpowering assailant? This is hardly chivalrous and surely it does not square with the Christian virtues. I would say it is not decent. I assure you that you cannot so build international friendship, nor even a tolerant comity. I tell you you cannot build a permanent trade relation on this basis. I tell you this is war seed.

All these matters are factors in the problems you men must solve.

Before closing I wish to say a very few words about the political, and seemingly military, solidarity of the Americas—alliance is the more accurate and descriptive term—to which we seem to be trying to woo a rather coy, and instinctively cautious if not wise Latin America.

They know, as we know, that as our allies they would be subject to attack and invasion by a foreign foe making war on us, except as we could protect them; and they know and we know that we may be, in such a contingency, too much occupied saving our own hides, to be able to save theirs.

Again they know and we know, by common report and common non-expert knowledge, that none of them, not one, could of itself individually or in any combination of some or all of them together, confidently hope seriously to embarrass or delay, to say nothing of prevent, any first class world power from landing on their shores, any number of troops the invading power might wish to land. If such an operation were to be defeated, the United States must do it. Furthermore, no one of them has a navy that would be a serious problem for one full grown European battleship plus a couple of modern cruisers and a few destroyers.*

Still again and on the information available to us uninitiated: there is not one of them that could by itself fabricate the materials and build even the smallest battleship or an ocean going merchantman, or that could fabricate the materials and build an airplane or a tank, or arm a battleship or other war vessel after it was built; there is not one of them that could by itself fully arm and equip an ordinary division of a modern army with its artillery, tanks, and airplanes; there is not one of them that could against the will of a first class power, send, of its own power, a regiment of soldiers outside of its own boundaries by sea; there is not one of them that could, in the face of a powerful enemy, send to us over seas, one bushel of wheat, one pound of beef, or any other food stuff, nor that

---

*The naval strength of the principal Latin American countries is given as follows in Jones Fighting Ships for 1939.

	Battleships	Cruisers	Coast Defense	Destroyers Old	Destroyers Modern	Submarines	Torpedo Boats
Argentina	2 (27,720 tons each)	3 (modern)	2	4	5 (1928) 7 (1936)	3 (1932)	
Brazil	2 (19,200 tons each)	2			1 (in commission) 9 (building)	4	6
Chile	1 (28,000 tons 1913)	3			6 (fairly modern) 2 (1913)	6 (1928) 3 (1917)	
Peru		2 (old)			2	4 (1928)	1 (old)

could by itself and against such an enemy, send us one pound of necessary raw war materials they might produce, nor that could give us any real aid or succor that we did not ourselves make available. There is not one of them, that could in the face of the opposition of a powerful enemy, send and get for itself one penny's worth of our production. They are not, they never have been maritime nations; they have not, they never have had any real shipping. As pointed out above, they have no protective naval force, even if they had, as they have not, a merchant marine. Yet we talk on about the need and wisdom of an alliance, a solidarity of All the Americas, with them as active partners, able to carry their share of the load.*

But there is a far more ominous element than any reliance for help we might place in these weak nations. Suppose we became allies—do you not see how through their unfortuitous conduct towards other powers, either directly or through measures taken against the nationals of such powers, things not unheard of in the past, these Latin American nations might on their own account involve us in war with a first class power, in a matter of no concern to us at all, or else place us where we must be false to our plighted word?

I am again perhaps inexcusably trite when I say these are perilous times. No nation, including our own, is giving us the full picture, telling the whole truth. I am fully familiar with the stock reasons advanced for such a course, reasons of State is the classic, mystery phrase. There is something to be said for the reasons where nations are actually at war, for not the least important of the weapons of war are falsehood and deceit. But the propaganda we are getting from Europe is calculated to make us think nothing but good of one belligerent, and nothing but bad of the other. We have forgotten who declared this war. We have forgotten how conquest has in the past built the great empires of the present.

We are entitled to our sympathies, but we should as a matter of

---

*Popular articles indicate that Chile and Brazil are making a beginning at acquiring some merchant tonnage and that Argentina has drawn plans to the same end. It is also reported that Argentina and Brazil are being equipped for assembling some small naval vessels. But on the reports, it must be concluded that most of the maritime development is still in the planning, blue-print stage, with perhaps some "on order" added. There is no present merchant tonnage that could be counted on for help now.

intellectual pride try to be just. British ancestored, my sympathies go with Britain; but there are millions of our fellow citizens who wish for the other side. As a nation we should be the great neutral—and when anybody who really knows what he is saying tells you that neutrality is a thing of the past, I tell you that man wishes to get us into this war; he is engaged in the great game of bluff, falsehood and deception. We have not been neutral in this war. If we had been we should now be able to speak in a voice that war-torn Europe would not only hear, but hearken to.

I spoke of the reasons of diplomats for not telling the people the truth, and that there was some cause for this when war is on. I perceive no need for it when war is not on, unless to conceal measures leading us into war, and then there is every reason we should know.

At the moment two sources of trouble should be watched—the Far East, where in a provocative interchange of notes lasting over many months we have apparently repudiated in effect the Lansing-Ishii agreements of President Wilson's time, which formally recognized a sort of Monroe Doctrine in behalf of Japan in the Far East. The other source of trouble is the Atlantic and Caribbean areas, where foreign possessions exist, and where as the recent Havana agreement seems to indicate, we seem to be proposing to take on a duty and responsibility far in excess of any legitimate interpretation of our own Monroe Doctrine. For that was framed to help those American peoples who were trying to throw off European control and domination; it was not framed as a means of enabling certain European powers finally to perpetuate their sovereignty on this hemisphere, and boiled down, the newly negotiated agreements seem to mean just that.

Trouble in the Far East could and probably would bring Britain to our side as an ally, and being allies in the Far East, then, we would be told, we must be allies everywhere. War in the Atlantic and Caribbean to protect French and British possessions against other Europeans would of course take us into the war. Every constitutional lawyer knows that, if so minded, the President as Commander in Chief of the Army and Navy can, without any action by Congress, order such acts by the Army and Navy as shall constitute war in fact and so bring such a pressure to bear on Congress that it would be compelled to follow the President's lead with a formal declaration of war. I repeat these are perilous times.

But I have spoken too long. I will close by bearing my testimony that the Constitution under which we live is God-given; that the liberties and free institutions it guarantees and sets up meet the divine principle that no man's conscience should be compelled, that God intends that men shall worship as they wish, that human slavery shall not exist, that every man shall enjoy the fruits of his labors, that life and property shall be secure, that due process of law shall obtain, that men shall speak and write freely, that "Life, Liberty, and the pursuit of Happiness" shall be the common heritage of man. Any man who would change or destroy these is not only a traitor to his country, but an enemy of mankind.

God bless and preserve our country with its liberties and free institutions.

Some Factors in the Proposed Post-War International Pattern

24 February 1944

Looking toward a just and permanent post-war peace, JRC gave this address at the annual officer-installation dinner meeting of the Los Angeles Bar Association at the Biltmore Hotel. Box 228, Folder 2, JRCP.

You have bestowed upon me a signal honor in asking me to speak on this anniversary occasion. I fully understand that this honor carries with it a grave responsibility, for organizations such as yours have far more significance and far greater obligations than the merely social. I am equally mindful that in speaking to you, I am speaking to a distinguished group of that great body of our citizenry, who, because of their training and experience, must take an important place in the future of this country, whether we shall go left or go right. You who are elevated to the Bench are the dispensers of justice and equity to the people, the guardians of the peace and the order of our society. You who are of the Bar man the watchtowers of the nation that give view far and near. Your eyes must be the first to see and you the first to make ready to meet the oncoming of tyranny. Upon the Bench and the Bar of the country rests the great responsibility of seeing that our liberties and free institutions are preserved. Legislators may be incompetent, executives may be dishonest, but if the Bench and Bar be honest and filled with integrity, then under the Constitution, the people are secure, and free institutions will still live with us. But security and liberty both take flight where the judiciary is corrupt.

The Constitution

We may say a beginning word about the Constitution and the duty thereto of you who are here. From those who should have revered that great document, we have had flippancy and derision. To many of the common people there has come a disrespect for and a desire to rid themselves of what they have been encouraged to think are the shackles of the Constitution. They are saying we should have a modern, an up-to-date Constitution, one suited to our times and conditions.

Knowing something of the sound doctrines regarding the Constitution which my friend, Preston D. Richards, has been teaching in these purlieus, there is no need to belabor here in this presence an argument that the Constitution is, in the matter of fostering and protecting human rights, the inspired crystallization of the wisdom of man and the embodiment of all his experience from the beginning. Being thus engendered of the ages, how idle seriously to think that a mere century and a half could render it obsolete. The matter is brought before you here only to urge upon you the duty which is yours and not to be pushed aside, of losing no chance to teach the people, in season and out of season, the priceless value of the government and free institutions set up under the Constitution. When human freedom is outgrown, the Constitution will be obsolete— but not before.

May I add one thought more: They of the Bench and Bar who for power or place or gain, shall traffic in or prostitute the principles of freedom that are basic to our republican form of government, will violate their solemn oaths, will betray their clients, and will be traitors to a lofty, even holy trust. They should be purged from our midst. Already too many of us have shown an easy willingness to let pass unchallenged encroachment after encroachment upon our liberties. The Bench and Bar of the nation must cease to temporize with tyranny. After quoting the words of the Master to the hypocritical Pharisees, that a "city or house divided against itself shall not stand" (Matt. 12:25), Lincoln added: "I believe this government cannot endure permanently half slave and half free" (John G. Nicolay and John Hay, eds., *The Complete Works of Abraham Lincoln,* 12 vols.

[New York, 1905], 3:2). He spoke of land-spread and government. Living today he might have phrased his principle: There can be no freedom that is half bondage; there can be no law that is half royal favor or half lawless force. There can be no partnership between liberty and slavery.

Strength at Home and Abroad

We have spoken thus because underlying our international relations of the future are our conditions at home. We cannot be weak within our borders, and strong outside them, either as a matter of force or as a matter of moral strength. We have built ourselves to our present rank in both force and morals, because of the form and past policies of our government, because we were a free people, unhampered in thought, in speech, and in action, because we were able to gather and enjoy the fruits of our own labors, unafraid, unspied on, unvictimized by government. If we shall change this now, we shall lose our place, we shall be generations building back to where we were a decade ago. Yet we have already travelled far along a new and evil way.

It has seemed that tonight we might with profit analyze some of the policies now operating in our foreign relations, to see if we can determine where they might lead us and what might be our lot thereunder.

The Four Freedoms

We shall pass over, for this purpose, our diplomacy for the last decade, a diplomacy which it seems has been the most provocative in all our history, with the possible exception of our discussions with Great Britain in the 40's and 50's of the last century over transisthmian communications. But we will make this one comment: It is now clear that our diplomacy during this last decade could lead only to war. Some of us said this at the beginning of the decade as well as now.

Of the things we shall consider tonight we may take first, because it involves principles basic to the Administration's whole foreign policy as now announced, the President's unilateral declaration of the essentials of security as embodied in the Four Freedoms—freedom of speech, freedom of religion, freedom from fear, and freedom from want (White House Release, President's Message,

409

6 January 1941, 7). We shall pass over the additions made by other public and pseudo-public officials.

The first two of the President's freedoms are known to political science and help to spell individual liberty.

Perhaps we may assume that freedom of speech includes freedom of the press. These two run hand in hand. You know that these freedoms are relative terms and that with us there are the limitations of libel and slander. But whose freedoms are to be given in the world setup,—ours, Britain's, Russia's, or some new concept?

Who will determine this standard of freedoms?

The Atlantic Charter

We may at this point profit by reading the Atlantic Charter, signed and issued as you know by President Roosevelt and Prime Minister Churchill (White House Rel., 14 August 1941, 1-2). Its principles are embodied in eight points. Some declared the purposes of the signers; others declared principles for world-wide application among all nations, including ourselves. These points are:

First, their countries seek no aggrandizement, territorial or other;
Second, they desire to see no territorial changes that do not accord with the freely expressed wishes of the peoples concerned.

If the Charter had been signed by Russia, these two announcements would give hope at least to heroic Finland, to Estonia, Latvia, Lithuania, Poland, and it might be, Roumania.

Third, they respect the right of all peoples to choose the form of government under which they will live; and they wish to see sovereign rights and self government restored to those who have been forcibly deprived of them.

This is carefully worded, but the underneath principle might raise some question about India and Puerto Rico, Egypt and the Boer South Africa, the Dutch East Indies, the Philippines, and other countries on the earth's surface not in the possession of the enemy states.

Fourth, they will endeavor, with due respect for their existing obligations, to further the enjoyment by all States, great or small, victor or vanquished, of access, on equal terms, to the trade and to the raw materials of the world which are needed for their economic prosperity.

This seems to forecast a free trade world. It would open up our trade and raw materials on "equal terms" to everyone. If Russia had signed, it would have been supposed to open up her trade and raw materials in like manner. Britain's prime needs, after food, are trade—markets—and raw materials.

Fifth, they desire to bring about the fullest collaboration between all nations in the economic field with the object of securing, for all, improved labor standards, economic advancement and social security.

This seems a pious and praiseworthy hope provided that these things are not to be gained by other nations at the expense of our own, that is, provided it does not mean a levelling downward to a common standard, a procedure which is now openly urged by some who call themselves Americans.

Sixth, after the final destruction of the Nazi tyranny, they hope to see established a peace which will afford to all nations the means of dwelling in safety within their own boundaries, and which will afford assurance that all the men in all the lands may live out their lives in freedom from fear and want.

Here are two of the Four Freedoms; but there is no mention of freedom of speech or of religion. The latter are vital to free peoples; they cannot be granted to a people and still keep them in subjection. But one can think of several countries where these two freedoms of speech and of religion would threaten the existing order. A despot might give freedom from want, and might at least for a time anesthetize them into freedom from fear. Freedom from want for India, China, and Asia, generally, will tax the resources of the world, to say nothing of the task of caring for Europe. Russia appears not to be committed to this plan.

Seventh, such a peace should enable all men to traverse the high seas and oceans without hindrance.

This is not a promise of freedom of the seas, but the statement of a conclusion which might or might not be realized, and might not mean at all what is meant by freedom of the seas.

Eighth, they believe that all of the nations of the world, for realistic as well as spiritual reasons must come to the abandonment of the use of force. Since no future peace can be maintained if land, sea or air armaments continue to be employed by nations which threaten, or may threaten, aggression outside of their frontiers, they believe, pending the establishment of a wider and permanent system of general security, that the disarmament of such nations is essential. They will likewise aid and encourage all other practicable measures which will lighten for peace-loving peoples the crushing burden of armaments.

These are the lofty aspirations and the tried, and failed, machinery of the Treaty of Versailles.

The Charter was not incorporated in or referred to in the Four-Nation Declaration at Moscow (State Department Release, 1 November 1943; *New York Times,* 2 November 1943), nor were the Four Freedoms, nor was the Charter referred to in the Declaration of Teheran (White House Rel., 6 December 1943; *New York Herald Tribune,* 7 December 1943), nor in the Allied-Turkish Statement at Cairo (*New York Herald Tribune,* 8 December 1943), nor the Cairo Communiqué by the United States, Great Britain, and China (White House Rel., 1 December 1943). It was mentioned in the Declaration on Iran (*New York Herald Tribune,* 7 December 1943).

Russia has apparently joined in no agreement or declaration on policy that embraced the Four Freedoms, except that freedom of speech, of the press, and of public worship were mentioned in the Moscow Declaration Regarding Italy (State Dept. Rel., 1 November 1943; *New York Times,* 2 November 1943).

With the President's interest in the Charter and the Freedoms in mind, the omissions noted could hardly have been a matter of chance, and if the omissions were by design, they could suggest a deep-seated cleavage on the whole program. If Russia is not willing to move forward on those principles of self-restraint that are embodied in the Charter, we may expect trouble ahead.

We must not overlook that the principles of self-restraint and of altruistic aspiration embodied in the Charter are as applicable to and against us as to and against any other nation. They are not something we are graciously to bestow or impose upon others, we remaining free to follow our own bent. What we do to others, we must permit others to do to us.

I need only suggest here that to make effective these freedoms of speech, of the press (if it be included) and of religion, there must be complete cooperation thereto among the executive, the judicial, and the legislative branches of a government. The freedoms fail if any one branch is unwilling. Thus there must be control over the whole

government to make them effective, and if there be any unwillingness, as there will be somewhere, say in Timbuktu or somewhere
else, this control must be from some outside source to bring these
freedoms to the people; and of course, in the last analysis such
outside control must be by force. Lincoln said: "No man is good
enough to govern another man without the other's consent"
(Nicolay and Hay, 2:228).

We are reported to be training men to head up our occupying
forces in some foreign country; it may be they are to see that the
freedoms are given to the people thereof. Who is going to occupy us
to see that we keep the standards? And when we shall finish shortly
our consideration of the freedom from want and fear you will appreciate that there could be excuse for some outside power to come in and
make us meet our professions and promises on those accounts too.

Freedom From Want and Fear

Freedom from want and fear are not terms of art either in
domestic political science, or in international relations. We must
get their meaning elsewhere.

As defined by the President when he announced them, freedom
from want meant "economic understandings which will secure to
every nation a healthy peace time life for its inhabitants" (White
House Rel., 6 January 1941, 7). This is not too definite or clear.
But explanations since made by him as well as the actions of the 44
United Nations Food Conference and of the since organized United
Nations Relief and Rehabilitation Administration, have made clear
that it is in the international mind to do what the President states
has never been done before in all history, that is, "feed all the
peoples of the world as we now know human beings should be fed"
(White House Rel., 7 June 1943, President's Address, 1). That is a
great concept, but a rather large order, having in mind India's
nearly 400,000,000, China's 450,000,000, to say nothing of the
suffering millions in the rest of Asia, in Europe, in Africa, in the
Latin Americas, in the continents and islands of the seas, and then
our own 130 odd millions.

As first defined by the President, freedom from fear meant "a
world-wide reduction of armaments to such a point and in such
thorough fashion that no nation will be in a position to commit an
act of physical aggression against any neighbor" (White House Rel.,

413

6 January 1941, 7). This is a great concept also, but by no means a new one, either in theory or practice. Some of you will recall that the Central Powers in World War I were disarmed by the Armistice and the Treaty of Versailles, and that for the rest of the world of strong powers, President Harding called a Limitation of Arms Conference in Washington which entered into formal treaties providing for reduction of the naval armament of the great powers. The result of that plan we all now know.

But the Atlantic Charter, signed by President Roosevelt and Prime Minister Churchill, gave another, and I think the true and originally intended meaning to the phrase freedom from *fear* and *want.* This Charter, as you will recall, provides in its paragraph Sixth, and I repeat the essential parts here, that the "national policies of their respective countries" would be that, after the "final destruction" of Nazi tyranny, a peace shall be established "which will afford to all nations the means of dwelling in safety within their own boundaries, and which will afford assurance that *all* the men in *all* the lands may live out their lives in freedom from fear and want." The Atlantic Charter was incorporated by reference into our understanding with Greece (White House Rel., 9 July 1942) and Yugoslavia (White House Rel., 24 July 1942), and was noted in the Declaration on Iran (*New York Herald Tribune,* 7 December 1943), while freedom of speech, of the press, of political belief, and of religion were mentioned in the Moscow Declaration Regarding Italy (State Dept. Rel., 1 November 1943; *New York Times,* 2 November 1943).

Obviously, the Charter's declaration that a peace shall be established that will assure that "*all* the men in *all* the lands may live out their lives in freedom from fear and want," supplemented by the President's measure of feeding all the peoples of the world "as we now know human beings should be fed" and as they never have been fed before (Final Act, United Nations Conference on Food and Agriculture, 1943, cited hereinafter as Final Act, 11, 36), to which may be added the statements of the Food Conference that each government accepts the responsibility of making it possible, so far as within their power, of providing each person with "adequate social-security measures, such as family allowances, social insurance, and minimum wages" (Final Act, 26), all these aspirations and purposes take the principle out from a normal international operation between States themselves, and make it into a domestic

414

operation for every country,—Germany, Japan, Italy, Holland, Great Britain, China, the United States, and all down the list. Furthermore, the thought behind it all seems to be that it is every nation's business to see that the stated standards are reached and maintained among all the other nations.

Now the Charter also affirmed, as we have seen, that the declaring powers "respect the right of all peoples to choose the form of government under which they will live," and the Teheran Declaration affirmed (Russia was here) that the negotiators "look with confidence to the day when all peoples of the world may live free lives, untouched by tyranny, and according to their varying desires and their own consciences" (White House Rel., 6 December 1943). But a free government is a government by uncontrolled majorities. I think the world has never seen any other kind of *free* government. Suppose a majority government in any State,—Germany, Holland, Poland, Russia, Great Britain, or the United States, sets up a government which fails to operate so that "*all* the men" in that country are able to "live out their lives in freedom from fear and want" as finally defined. What then? As the President declared, no nation ever yet had such a government (White House Rel., 7 June 1943, 1). Are any of us to be brought under compulsion to maintain the standards? If not, the standards will not be maintained. If so, then you have a military occupation and war.

A plan for providing this freedom from want has been already outlined in some fullness. We shall now deal with that plan.

Freedom from Want

You will recall that in May-June of last year a 44 United Nations Conference on Food and Agriculture was held at Hot Springs, Virginia, at a nominal cost for the foreign delegates.

The work of this Conference has not by any means received the attention it so richly deserves. I urge you gentlemen to study it, for a plan was there outlined for the regimentation of the world in the production and distribution of foodstuffs, with aside observations on world finance and industry. We will sketch a few only of the major conclusions of the Conference as embodied in its Final Act.

These conclusions may be gathered into two groups: the scientific and the political. The first, while wordy, repetitious, and pretentious sometimes to the point of being almost smile provoking, contains many admirable and desirable things. Perhaps it is not really a fault they are unreachably altruistic. The Final Act incorporates and reincorporates advanced theories on foods and food values. It plans to meet the dietary problems and necessities of the entire world, as seen by the experts met at the Conference. (It has nothing to say about the curse of alcohol, nor of the poison of nicotine, nor of caffeine, nor opium and all its derivatives, nor of any deleterious drugs.) The documents annexed to the Final Act pointed out the dietary needs and diseases of our own South, of India's 400 millions, of China's 450 millions, of the peoples of tropical Africa, of Egypt, of Mexico, Chile, Bolivia, and elsewhere. Great Britain stood out as the only country mentioned and receiving only commendation. Russia escaped all mention (36ff). But the purpose of it all is good, just as ethical and philosophical standards are good.

However, I wish to say a few words about the political phases of the plan.

The underlying principle is that the establishing of "freedom from want for all people in all lands" is the "mutual responsibility" of all the nations, as likewise "coordinated action to establish such conditions of international security as will make possible an expanding and balanced world economy" (24).

In summary, the plan provides for a control and regimentation of the production and distribution of foodstuffs throughout the world and among the nations of the world. The organization is not a magnified Red Cross to administer help to stricken areas throughout the earth, but a sort of superstate to supervise and direct the food resources of all peoples.

The aim is that in every country "each person" who is "without an adequate diet" shall have his diet improved "in the direction of obtaining the physiological requirements of health," with "adequate social-security measures, such as family allowances, social insurance, and minimum wages." Furthermore, (and the phrases may be ominous) there is to be "some form of *direct* action to make protective foods available free, or at low prices, to groups with inadequate diets" (26). That is, if you need food, find it, and take it.

The plan contemplates the allocation of the production of particular foodstuffs to particular areas. For example, the increasing of herds in certain parts of Europe, and the holding back of the rebuilding of depleted livestock herds in other countries (this probably refers to us), and also a holding back of the production of any crops "which compete for acreage with essential foods" (16, 18).

A system of price control measures are to be set up upon "the principle of mutual responsibility" (24) to prevent "fluctuations in the prices of food, the instruments of production" (described in another place as "fertilizers and machinery") and also "other necessities, including industrial goods" (17, 25).

The plan is to aim at a "world-wide policy of industrial and agricultural expansion," which will require "reorientation in agriculture" (18).

Plans are to be devised "to ensure an adequate supply of credit to agriculture," at low rates of interest; aid is particularly for the small farmer (20).

Wages and hours are to come under consideration as to farm labor and industrial workers (20).

Land tenures likewise are to be studied "to promote the productivity and efficiency of agriculture and the welfare of its workers, with a view to possible changes in existing systems" (20). Could this mean that the State is to take over the ownership of the land?

Agricultural populations are to be moved from overcrowded agricultural areas, both "intranational" and "international" and in such cases the organization is to support arrangements "to provide adequate safeguards for the settlers" (23-24).

International commodity arrangements are to be made, involving "changes in the scale and character of production" of farm products in the one country or the other; "adequate reserves will be maintained" (25).

There is to be brought about "an equilibrium in balances of payments" and an "orderly management of currencies and exchange" (25).

International grade standards are to be established, containers are to be standardized (27); transportation charges are to be controlled; middlemen are to be eliminated; and marketing, processing, storage, and distribution costs, and margins between producers and consumers are to be reduced (30).

To reach "an economy of abundance" (24), it is declared to be "an integral part of this program, to reduce barriers of every kind to international trade and to eliminate all forms of discriminatory restrictions thereon, including inequitable policies in international transportation, as effectively and as rapidly as possible" (25).

One provision more—I quote it in full:

> The democratic control and educational programs, which are features of the cooperative movement, can play a vital part in the training of good democratic citizens, and assist in inducing a sound conception of economic matters. (20)

Now, gentlemen, please understand: All this is on a world-wide basis; each and every nation is involved; it is a two-way street; it is not alone what we are going to do for and to the others; it is what they are going to do for and to us. For we are only one out of a present 44 members of the organization (now raised by Russia to 59 or 60), and we are the one with the greatest present power of production, of diversification, of transportation, of available natural resources, and of financial power. We are the Santa Claus. But remember also, we have considerable numbers amongst our 130 millions who do not enjoy the affluence measured out by this document for the Australian bushmen, or the headhunters of Borneo.

And speaking of finances, our present ante to sit in on this gigantic game of strip resources and well-being and just for immediate war relief in stricken trans-Atlantic areas,—not counting the Grand Design of relief from want in all the world—is "one percent of the national income of the country for the year ending June 30, 1943" (Selected Documents, United Nations Relief and Rehabilitation Administration, 1943, cited hereinafter as Sel. Doc., 45) or as fixed by a resolution in Congress, one billion three hundred and fifty million dollars annually. (U.S. Congress, House Committee on Foreign Affairs, H. J. Res. 192, 78th Cong., 1st Sess., 28 March 1944). But as time goes on and we begin our relief to all the world, we shall have to put far greater sums in the pot, by loans or otherwise to our less opulent and wiser members, to keep the game going.

The Final Act of the Food Conference provided for the establishment of an Interim Commission and a Permanent Organization (Final Act, 12-13). Only one seems to have been established to date (Sel. Doc., 32). Instead there has been established the United Nations Relief and Rehabilitation Administration under an Agreement signed in Washington, November 9, 1943, by the representatives of 44 nations (Sel. Doc., 1). While designated as an *agreement,* it is in form a treaty under the tests heretofore applied in our constitutional law. However, it is to be treated, it is understood, as an

Executive Agreement and so not requiring the treaty action of the Senate, though imposing obligations upon us and upon all the other signatory States, including the payment of monies from public funds. Fourteen of the nations realizing its character signed with reservations, making it subject to ratification in accordance with their constitutional procedures. For us, the agreement was signed by the President, himself, and without reservation or reference to constitutional procedure (Sel. Doc., 16-20).

Protection of Minorities

Having all the circumstances and conditions in mind, and taking into consideration certain minority influences that have been operative in the framing of all this, it is difficult indeed to escape the conclusion that these principles were invented and are fostered for the prime purpose of protecting the minority groups of Europe who have fled their native countries but wish to return thereto after the war,—a purpose to make Germany, and Austria, and Poland, and the Balkan States, and perhaps Russia a safe place in which they may live "in freedom from fear and want."

This fact becomes clear when we note the provisions of the international Agreement covering primarily war relief, which stipulates "for the return to their homes of prisoners, exiles, and other displaced persons" (Sel. Doc., 37), and also properly lays it down that relief shall be distributed fairly, "without discrimination because of race, creed, or political belief," but adds that account shall be taken however of "needs caused by discriminatory treatment by the enemy during its occupation of the area" (Sel. Doc., 31).

Looking to the post-war period, and remembering that the fear and want concept is intended for permanent application, not temporary, we must not overlook that we, ourselves, have minority problems as old as the nation. We have the colored minority, we shall have a Japanese minority, and we have other minority groups that bid fair to bring trouble. We have always had some want amongst us. Who will bell this cat of America?

International Police

I suppose this is where this much touted international police force appears. A few airplanes, we are told, will be able to persuade the majority to treat the minority as someone else outside the country believes they should be treated. Since fear and want are to be eliminated, this airplane persuasion must of course not use fear. (Perhaps the airplanes are to be used merely to drop educational pamphlets.) But who will lay down and who will apply the rule as to fear or want—either for Russia or for us? Whose airplanes are going to bomb us into subjection without fear, so that the minority, not the majority, shall rule as somebody else thinks they should rule? Britain also has some minority problems in India, in Africa; the Netherlands have them in the Dutch East Indies, and other nations have them elsewhere.

I trust you will pardon my giving my own formula for international rule: It fits this situation: You never complain that some other power does what you do, unless he violates his own law by so doing. You never ask another power to do what you do not do, unless his own laws entitle you to ask for it. That is a sort of living-in-glasshouses formula.

Liberty, freedom, is the right of the majority to rule. The love of liberty is a fairly universal passion of humanity when free to express itself. But liberty was never implanted in the hearts of a people from the point of a bayonet, nor will it ever be from the nose of an airbomb. Can we keep a straight face and say that bombers and occupying armies are to bring subjection without fear,—that they will give freedom from fear through fear?

Our Finances

Having in mind the meeting of all these obligations incident to bringing the Four Freedoms to the peoples of the world, as well as the cost of maintaining our own homes and feeding and clothing and housing and educating our own children,—with all this in mind we may give brief notice to our own financial situation. I believe I am reasonably accurate in these astronomical calculations.

With a gross public Federal debt, direct and guaranteed, of approximately 170.6 billions of dollars; with a projected expenditure for the future of 8 billions of dollars per month, of which 3 billions are to be raised by taxation and 5 billions by deficit financing, or a total of 60 billions of debt for the year, making a total debt of, say, 230 billions by December 31, 1944; with a total war program authorized since July, 1940, of 344 billions; with a request

for an additional 100 billions, making a total on this count of 444
billions; with constantly rising taxes and cost of living; with drastically and increasingly curtailed production of foodstuffs; with a
reported almost saturated but still accumulating stock pile of ships,
steel, copper, aluminum, small arms ammunition, and apparently
other armaments, to say nothing of the still unused stock piles of
aluminum cooking utensils and used rubber tires we collected with
brass bands and uninformed hysterical enthusiasm; with a national
spending philosophy which is described as holding "that public
finance is really only a matter of bookkeeping, that a rising debt has
no adverse consequences, and that without a constantly increasing
debt we cannot have full employment and prosperity" (*Washington
Close-Up*, August 1943, 5); with the knowledge that Britain's total
expenditures during the war period July 1, 1940 to June 30, 1943,
was only 60.9 billions of dollars, and Canada's only 9.8 billions of
dollars, while our expenditures were 125.2 billions, and that apparently we have not lessened that ratio to date; with the forecast that
our ante into the overhead cost of the game of the United Nations
Relief and Rehabilitation Administration is to be 40% of the total
(the United Kingdom gives 15% and Russia 15% with driblets
handed out to the other nations, the total for the whole British
Empire being only 24.8% against our 40%) (Sel. Doc., 67); with
our initial commitment for immediate war relief approximating
1.35 billions of dollars; with the recollection of the principle that
sent millions of yards of our rayon to clothe the dusky beauties of
North Africa while our own women folk went without; with a
recollection of the shiploads of wheat we sent to the same place to
feed starving natives, only to find these same natives with large
stores of home-grown wheat, the export of which we had prevented
and which we had to buy from them at fancy prices; with a partial
knowledge of the billions we have virtually forced on Latin America
who are reported now to fear more our economic dominance than
they formerly feared our supposed armed imperialism; with an indisputable knowledge that we are bringing the whole world into a state
of mind where they expect from America every conceivable help in
any dreamed of amounts, by money and other assistance without
any thought of the slightest responsibility on their part that they are
ever expected to pay any considerable part of it back to us; with a
monumental Santa Claus-minded control here, giving gratuities,
not as the real Santa Claus, out of their own pockets, but on the

contrary, out of your pockets and my pockets,—with all this in mind it would be superfluous in me to say anything about our future finances. He who would discover them, must fathom the deepest abysses of the lowest financial hell. I have no desire to make the trip, but we may all have to make it together.

But let us assume we get the money somehow,—that we discover a gold mine, or strike an oil well, or that Britain and France pay their first world war debt, or that Britain and Russia compensate for their lend-lease aid, or that the Latin Americas repay to us the great advances we have made to them, or that Britain says you go ahead and recoup from world trade, or that the nations pass the hat for us, or that everybody burns up the Government bonds he owns, so that somehow we come into funds,—still it will take more than money to work out this plan. It will take grit and work and sacrifice from all of us, not merely the few; it will spell scant rations, long and longer hours, fewer comforts, cheerless days; it will demand of all, not the few, the highest order of patriotic devotion, civic virtue, moral courage, intense industry, and complete unity to a single purpose. And not only must we here in America have these things, but they must be the common possession of the peoples of the world.

Do you believe we and the world have the civic virtue, the moral force, the honesty, the spirituality, the brotherhood of man in our hearts, enough to carry all this through?

National Deficiencies

Where do we, ourselves, stand in these necessary qualities?

You know how near we are to Cleveland's dictum: "Public officers are the servants and agents of the people." You know that now we sometimes have a shamelessness that shocks. So also you know that great groups of our people expect to live without work as of right, and intend so to live; that our children, who tomorrow must carry on, are being corrupted by false economic, social, governmental, and religious doctrines, even in our public schools; that we are oppressed by a great mass of rules, regulations, and directives that are unconstitutional, that are the off-scourings of legally dissolute bureaucracies, and that are making of us a lawless people, both by omission and commission; that we are unbelievably wasteful in food, materials, machinery, transportation, manpower, and above and beyond all, wasteful of the virtues that go to make character; that we are increasingly careless of our word and our promises, a carelessness that affects all classes and all vocations; that the Government has lost all sense of balance between taxation and successful business, and that business has lost its sense of proportion between wise and unwise expenditures because government is supposed to be paying such a large part of the expense; that never before have the people been so divided into classes as now, ready and of a temper to fly at one another's throats.

But I need name no more—though there are many—of the things that now hamper us, and will do so more and more, in our effort to get back to sound thinking and right living, to wise national growth and to the upbuilding of the prosperity and welfare of all of the people. Yet I wish clearly to make the point that, unless corrected, these matters I have touched upon will not only retard, if not make impossible, our national recovery, but are likely to stand as a bulwark against our successfully meeting any great international burden after the war.

If we are to be the savior of the world we must come to our task with the spirit and the virtues of a savior.

International Handicaps

We may now say something about the international moral fiber that the world has for use in coming to this task of world salvation.

We may say to begin with that the world has gone back a half a millennium in its conduct of international relations in time of war, and may we say further that no nation has to bear a greater blame for this than our own.

Lessening the Horrors of War

Three and a quarter centuries ago the great Dutch publicist, diplomat, theologian, and litterateur, Hugo Grotius, brought forth his work *De Jure Belli ac Pacis*. This work has deeply influenced the conduct of nations at war from his time on until the opening of World War I. Grotius stated these reasons for writing the treatise:

I saw prevailing throughout the Christian world a license in making war of which even barbarous nations would have been ashamed; recourse being had to arms for slight reasons or no reason; and when arms were once taken up, all reverence for divine and human law was thrown away, just as if men were thenceforth authorized to commit all crimes without restraint. (Prolegomena [preface], sec. 28)

From the time of Grotius until World War I, men had consciously tried ever to lessen the ills of war, and especially to relieve non-combatants—old men, women, and children, the sick and the wounded—from the ravages of war. Nations had sought to find ways to restrict as much as might be the theater of war, and to recognize and protect neutrals in their normal trade and travel. War was held a curse whose evils should be kept, so far as might be done, within the smallest limits and affecting the fewest number.

In this great march of humanity for a higher level of international life and relations among the peoples of the earth, this great country of ours took a leading and glorious part.

The first body of rules ever issued by any power for the control and guidance of its armies in the field, was that prepared by Dr. Francis Lieber and promulgated by Lincoln in 1863 for the use of the Union Armies in the Civil War. It went beyond the usual war practice of nations in protecting the weak and innocent. These rules are said to have been largely followed by the armies of France and Germany in the Franco-Prussian War of 1870, and to have been basic to all codes since drawn covering the laws and customs of war (James Brown Scott, *The Hague Peace Conferences of 1899 and 1907,* 2 vols. [Baltimore, 1909], 1:525-27). This advanced code prohibited the use of poison in wells, in food, or on arms; forbade inflicting of additional wounds upon a disabled enemy; declared that commanders should, as a rule, give notice of bombardments "so that non-combatants, and especially the women and children may be removed before the bombardment commences;" it stipulated the sanctity of protective flags or signals for buildings containing works of art, scientific museums, astronomical observatories, precious libraries, so that they might be preserved; and so on with like protection for non-combatant life and non-military private property (John Bassett Moore, *A Digest of International Law,* 8 vols. [Washington, D.C., 1906], 7:178-80). This was in 1863, in a code made of our own volition. Holland, an unsympathetic British authority, characterizes the rules "as certainly more severe (that is, against the belligerents) than the rules which would be generally enforced in a war between two independent states" (Thomas Erskine Holland, *Studies in International Law* [Oxford, Eng., 1898], 85).

The Hague Conferences of 1899 and of 1907 embodied in formal multi-partite conventions, all these principles, extending them in some instances, as for example, by specifically prohibiting in the First Conference the dropping of projectiles and explosives from balloons, and by inferentially doing so in the Second Conference (Scott, 1:649-54).

The Convention on the Laws and Customs of War on Land of the Second Hague Conference 1907, had provisions: Forbidding the use of poison or poisoned weapons; the killing or wounding treacherously of individuals belonging to the hostile nation or army; the killing or wounding of an enemy who, having laid down his arms, or having no longer means of defense, had surrendered at discretion; it forbade any rule or practice that no quarter would be given, and likewise the employment of arms, projectiles, or material calculated to cause unnecessary suffering; enemy property was not to be destroyed or seized unless such destruction or seizure be imperatively demanded by the necessities of war; family honor and rights, the lives of persons, and private property, as well as religious convictions and practices, were to be respected; and pillage was formally forbidden. This provision must obviously be taken as calling for the sparing of women and children upon considerations pointed out by Grotius nearly 300 years before (Grotius, bk. 3, ch. 11, sec. 9). It was also provided that: "In sieges and bombardments all necessary steps must be taken to spare, as far as possible, buildings dedicated to religion, art, science, or charitable purposes, historic monuments, hospitals, and places where the sick and wounded are collected, provided they are not used at the time for military purposes" (Art. 27), all which were to be properly marked and notified to the enemy.

This summary survey has been given in order that you might gather, more or less clearly, the advance which humanity had made towards curtailing the horrors and suffering of war.

Our Backsliding

Now let us be unflinchingly honest with ourselves and then ask whether there is any one essential thing that was forbidden by these ameliorating codes that has not been practiced in this present war, and the most of them in World War I. The things over which we professed horror at the beginning of the war—the bombardment from the air of cities, towns, and villages, the wholesale destruction of property, the indiscriminate killing, including the aged, the infirm, the women and children—do we not now hail all these as achievements deserving highest praise?

It will not do to pass off all these operations and others as being merely a matter of retaliation on our part. We as well as the enemy have been aggressors, both in the last war and in this. Furthermore, that one nation violates a law is no proper justification for another nation to do so. Remember the old dictum: "Two wrongs do not make a right." Our love for peace, our actual record for peace, our boasted concern for humanity, should have led us to seek some arrangement with our enemies to curtail barbarous methods, rather than to try to outdo them. There is, moreover, the strongest reason for believing that the General Staff of every first class power in the world, including our own, spent their full effort between World Wars first and second in trying to develop methods and weapons that would wipe out peoples, not merely destroy armies and navies. All planned for a war of extermination. They will be at it again after this war, unless curbed.

Having in mind the day by day plan and effort to instill hate in the hearts of the peoples of one warring group against the peoples of other warring groups; having in mind the suffering, the indignities, the sickness, the woes and misery, the starvation which the one or the other side has inflicted on the other; remembering the loss of husbands, sons, and kin, and the grief and anger this has built in the hearts of all peoples,—having all this in mind, and this may be the worst curse of the war, can we not see how difficult it will be, after the war is over, for the nations to settle down to rebuilding the world even on the basis of brotherly love? Yet, if the rebuilding is on any other basis than kindness and brotherly love, it will be merely another chapter in the rule of force and hate, a precursor for another war. Our peace will be but another armistice of Versailles.

Union Now

There is one matter we might mention here as an incident to the post-war world,—the propaganda now waging for our "union now" with Britain in a world super-state.

Some facts should be in mind. For hundreds of years, western Europe has feared and sought to make herself secure against the Russian Bear. This was one prime consideration of the great plan of Henry IV conceived in the brain of Elizabeth [I] of England. This fear was one of the causes that wrecked the Holy Alliance. With Germany defeated and a prostrate France, there will be nothing between Russia and the Atlantic. The United Kingdom will be without her usual European protection worked out through alliances and balance of power arrangements. She now seeks aid to this end from beyond the Atlantic. It would hardly do to form an open alliance against Russia; and both Britain and ourselves should be wary of an alliance with her. So the device is conceived of a "union" of states, which, however, would tie the nations together more securely than an alliance and be a greater threat to Russia.

But such an alliance would lead, and such a "union" will lead, sooner or later, to a counter-alliance by the other nations that would challenge the power of such a "union," so meaning either constant war for supremacy or a war of absolute conquest by the one or the other and a consequent enslavement of the conquered. Peace without liberty spells a stalemate in civilization and spiritual development. "Union now" has far more ill than good in it. Nor must America ever become a party to an attempted military domination of the world.

The propagandists for the "union now" plan, are trying to build a sentiment therefor by telling us how interested Britain is and always has been in our welfare, prosperity, and security; that she has been during the whole history of the Republic a sort of guardian angel watching over us; and that during the century and a half of our national existence we have been the hapless and helpless beneficiaries of British land and sea power.

Of course, this is not fact. We have grown and prospered in spite of, not because of Britain's power.

There have been occasions when the United States and Great Britain have risen to heights of forbearance and tolerance and peaceful intent, one towards the other, unequalled in the history of great nations. We may recall to our minds two of them,—the Rush-Bagot Agreement for the limitation of armaments on the Great Lakes and the arbitration of the questions involved in the British construction and outfitting of Confederate raiders. We have also settled by equally peaceful means our northern and Alaskan bound-

427

ary between Canada and ourselves. We began this peaceful course under the Jay Treaty of 1794. There was another incident, a gesture, with Dewey at Manila Bay, but in appraising this we should not forget that Germany was then fast growing in power, that she was threatening in North Africa, and that Britain needed a friend then too.

But there is another side to the picture. We will sketch it out briefly.

British Guardianship Over Us

In appraising this guardianship we are entitled to remember that as we tottered forward after Yorktown, Britain refused to surrender forts and territory coming to us under the treaty of peace, driving us to the threat of war measurably to obtain our rights; so with the harassment of American commerce almost to destruction during the period of the British Orders in Council and the French decrees, including the Berlin and Milan decrees; so when Britain, still clinging to our territory, incited the Indians on our borders to all the horrors and savagery of Indian warfare against our defenseless settlers, fired upon our vessels, stopped American vessels on the high seas, impressed American seamen, and then waged with us the War of 1812; so with her challenge with France of the Monroe Doctrine, of which they now erroneously claim authorship, in La Plata (1846) with armed force; so we may remember when, the North and South being locked in a death struggle, Britain joined with France and Spain in an armed invasion and occupation of Mexico, contrary to the Monroe Doctrine, though, be it said to her credit, Britain retired from this venture when the imperialistic aims behind it became clear; we may remember, too, when during that same struggle of our Civil War, Britain permitted the outfitting of Confederate raiders to such an extent and in such manner, that our Minister, Charles Francis Adams, was forced to point out to Earl Russell, the British Foreign Secretary, "It would be superfluous in me to point out to your Lordship that this is war" (dispatch to Russell, 5 September 1863); nor may we forget the long disputes over our rights in the Northeastern Coast fisheries, which more than once brought us to the brink of war because of measures of exclusion visited against us by the Canadian Government; we may recall the British boundary dispute with Venezuela when we again had to threaten in order to bring about the observance of the Monroe Doctrine, and so also in the matter of the Pacific blockade of Vene- zuelan ports in 1903 by Great Britain and other European powers. We may not forget either the trade rivalries that have gone on since the beginning, and particularly when after the Civil War, our ships and commerce driven from the seas by Confederate raiders, built and fitted out in British shipyards, Britain seized the shipping of the world while we staggered forward again in an effort to regain our place. Nor may we forget that in the present British War Parliament already they are complaining about us and our possible interference with unhampered British trade after the war, notwith- standing the enormous vital contributions we are making to her under lend-lease.

Let us be just to Britain, but not unhistorically maudlin.

World Organization

We may now touch one point only about a world organization.

In the eighth paragraph of the Atlantic charter, the disarma- ment of certain nations is affirmed as necessary "pending the estab- lishment of a wider and permanent system of general security."

In the Moscow Declaration, it was asserted by the four signa- tories:

4. That they recognize the necessity of establishing at the earliest practicable date a general international organization, based on the principle of the sovereign equality of all peace-loving states, and open to membership by all such states, large and small, for the maintenance of international peace and security. (State Dept. Rel., 1 November 1943, 1-2; *New York Times,* 2 November 1943)

This was signed by Secretaries of State, not by the heads of States. Sometime some point may be made of that fact.

In the three power Declaration of Teheran—signed by President Roosevelt, Premier Stalin, and Prime Minister Churchill, the most powerful triumvirate in all history—the post-war setup was stated with greatest caution,—indeed the whole Declaration is a model of care and circumspection. Here they said:

Emerging from these cordial conferences we look with confidence to the day when all peoples of the world may live free lives, untouched by tyranny, and according to their varying desires and their own consciences. (White House Rel., 6 December 1943; *New York Herald Tribune,* 7 December 1943)

A number of interesting questions "emerge," like the negotiators, from these various statements and others made by one or more of the signers, but we shall consider now but one,—that which declares for "a general international organization, based on the principle of the sovereign equality of all peace-loving states, and open to membership by all such states, large and small."

The principle of the equality of sovereign States "large and small" is as old as the modern "society of nations," now renamed to meet the spirit of the times, "the community of nations."

The principle was announced 120 years ago by Chief Justice Marshall in these words:

> No principle of general law is more universally acknowledged than the perfect equality of nations. Russia and Geneva have equal rights. It results from this equality that no one can rightfully impose a rule on another. Each legislates for itself, but its legislation can operate on itself alone. A right, then, which is vested in all by the consent of all, can be divested only by consent. . . . As no nation can prescribe a rule for others, none can make a law of nations. (The Antelope, Henry Wheaton, *Reports of Cases Argued and Adjudged in the Supreme Court of the United States,* 11 vols. [New York, 1816-26], 10:122)

In this statement also are announced a number of principles that are basic to our whole existing world status and the status proposed in the post-war pattern. We will use only the dictum: "Russia and Geneva have equal rights."

Applied to a world organization which is based on the "sovereign equality of all peace-loving states . . . large and small," the principle means that in such an organization the vote of Panama would equal the vote of the United States, the vote of Salvador would equal the vote of England, and the vote of Haiti, the vote of Russia, that is, this would have been true of Russia prior to her action on the 2nd of this month, when apparently she so divided herself up as to give her sixteen or seventeen votes.

If the vote of Russia shall be increased by this new move, then Russia will have 16 or 17 times as many votes as we have, nearly 3 times as many as Britain and her dependencies, within 1 vote of all the countries in continental Latin America, and within 10 votes of all the rest of Europe combined as of 1929. In any conference with only the United States and the British Empire, Russia will outvote us more than 2 to 1, and in a conference just with ourselves 16 or 17 to 1, as stated.

In the Council created by the food Agreement (U. N. R. R. A.) 44 nations are represented (Sel. Doc., 3), Russia counting as one. In the new arrangement, there will be 59 or 60 nations, out of which we shall have one vote, and Russia 16 or 17.

The Council for Europe set up under the food Agreement (U. N. R. R. A.) is made up of eleven countries of Europe besides Russia, and in addition Brazil, Canada, and the United States (Sel. Doc., 53). Russia under the new setup, will outvote all the others combined. Russia will likewise dominate the Committee on Supplies, and the Committee on Financial Control (Sel. Doc., 10, 55, 57).

In any final permanent arrangement effort will no doubt be made, under some such pattern as the League of Nations Assembly and Council, to give to a few great powers the control of the organization. But, for rather obvious reasons, that refinement will not be given out just yet. We must not discourage or throw suspicion in the minds of the small powers.

It is not necessary to point out to your members of the Bar, just what could happen to us in any world organization where we are 1 out of 59 or 60 in all matters of voting; nor how hazardous our situation could be if the organization should put us by its votes under any obligation as to military expeditions against recalcitrant members or as to financial aid and assistance to the indigents.

What Might Be Done

Some one will ask,—What may we do to solve this situation?

First, this is a problem for all citizens, and not for a few interested and revolutionary bureaucrats. It is the problem of every industry, of every farm, of every profession, of every household, of every man and woman of the nation, for if the present plans shall carry through they will want our money to pay their bills, and want us and our sons to police the world. The problem is not insoluble, taken over the years. With courage and unselfishness we shall work it out. But it will not be solved by wistful thinking or by revolutionary design. It calls for common council, not for dictatorial decree; it calls for a united purpose of a united people, not for selfish design fathered by an alien minority. The wisdom of the mass is always greater than the thinking of the few, however able the few may be.

Certain things may be mentioned as the *sine qua non*'s of any permanent solution of the world disease:

Peace Based on Justice

We must have a peace based on justice rather than might, that is, it must be a peace upon terms that will leave all peoples willing if not anxious to carry them out, because that is a peace that is clearly an alternative to another war. No permanent peace will come unless this be done. The men who are fighting and their families want peace now and hereafter; they of America are not primarily concerned with questions of empire holding or empire building.

Along with this peace should come a will to increase the spirituality of the earth's peoples and a building up of a true spirit of the brotherhood of man by treating all men as brothers, not as enemies nor as menials or inferior orders of creation. Real peace will never come till the Gospel of Christ rules the hearts of men, until we shall yield obedience to the great commandment drawn from the statutes of Israel's Law-Giver: "Thou shalt love the Lord thy God with all thy heart, and with all thy soul, and with all thy mind. This is the first and great commandment. And the second is like unto it, Thou shalt love thy neighbor as thyself. On these two commandments hang all the law and the prophets." So spake the Master to the quibbling Pharisee (Matt. 22:37-40).

And after the Christ had gone to the Father, James rephrased the principle: "If ye fulfil the royal law according to the scripture, Thou shalt love thy neighbor as thyself" (James 2:8).

When this time comes, then shall the world have peace from arms, and that higher peace promised by Him who alone can give it, for He said: "Peace I leave with you, my peace I give unto you. . . . Let not your heart be troubled, neither let it be afraid" (John 14:27).

Such a peace would eliminate at once all armed force, because a rule of force is always a rule of hate on both sides, and peace will never be born of hate. This would dispose of international police forces, occupying armies, and all the impossible tasks incident to alien domination. Since war lords know only armies and guns and brute force, none of them of the victor nations would like this, but we their peoples would welcome it as our redemption from bloodshed. For the people love the paths of peace and quiet and the orderly progress of an ever-increasing culture and advancing civilization and a constantly growing spirituality.

A solution by a rule of brute force would discard all the wisdom of the ages and take us clear back to the dawn of civilization. Surely we have grown too much through the generations to make this the best answer we can now make. Surely we shall not try to live through again the whole history of human kind, again using all the devices of armed peace and selfish power that have failed from the beginning.

World Disarmament

To bring us to our peace, we should have total, not partial world disarmament as the Atlantic Charter suggests. The reasons may be given in a sentence. You will no more have a world society of law and order by taking away the guns from a part of the gang and letting the others tote theirs, than you will by having all of them tote all the guns they can carry,—and all history shows this last will not bring peace.

Moral Force

We must have a world organization for purposes of deliberation, but not for the purpose of waging wars and imposing sanctions. We must bring to bear in the solution of matters of world concern, that moral force of the world of which President Wilson rightly thought so highly. As the situation stands today, we of America have lost our own moral force in world affairs,—a force which was once very great; we speak now only as our brute force may sustain us. There is indeed no moral force left in all the world to whose voice the warring nations are as yet willing to harken. We are now living under the law of the jungle where in cataclysms every beast fights to the death for his own life.

Are we Christians? We act like pagans.

Peaceful Adjustment of International Disputes

One other element I will name, that is, the peaceful adjustment of international disputes.

We, ourselves, have a great record for the adjustment of our

international disputes by peaceful means, instead of by war or force-
ful compulsion. No nation has had a more effective or glorious past
in developing the system than ourselves. We cannot even catalogue
our achievements tonight,—they are too numerous; but this much
may be said:

By the first treaty (Jay treaty, 1794) between ourselves and the
Mother Country after our treaty of peace, we set up the system of
arbitration of international difficulties, instead of settlement thereof
by war. From then till now we have so worked out peaceably,
literally hundreds of cases that were possible causes of armed conflict. We have, over and over again, arbitrated boundary disputes—
that ever-fruitful source of war. We have so settled many scores of
claims of our citizens for injuries suffered at the hands of other
countries. We have so adjusted questions touching rights of fishery
in coastal waters recognized and secured to us by treaty, as well as
questions touching invasions of our sovereignty, our rights as neutrals, our rights as a belligerent, our rights and duties on the high
seas, the rightfulness of the decisions of our Supreme Court. We
have even arbitrated the rightfulness of acts of war committed
against us. Futhermore, where we have been convinced that judgments rendered by arbitral courts in our favor have gone beyond the
demands of justice and equity, we have refunded the excess to the
injured country. The record is a glorious one. It has helped to make
of us a heretofore peaceful nation. It has been a strong bulwark
against our shedding the blood of weaker nations and of our own
sons. Yet in spite of this record of a hundred and fifty years, in spite
of this custom or tradition we had built, I recall no announcement
of any effort so peaceably to adjust the difficulties that lie behind the
present holocaust. We have lost, at least for the moment, the temper to live at peace with our brethren of the world, our fellow
Children of God.

But I must close.

I have touched tonight upon many matters and many incidents
and principles. I have perhaps left you with few concrete, definite
concepts or conclusions in your minds. This was inevitable, insofar
as my abilities are concerned, for the field of enquiry was very broad
and none I have named might wisely go unmentioned. But if I shall
have left you with the conviction that the matter is too complicated
to be settled by some rule o' thumb, or by some fireside chat, or by
the *ipse dixit* of some ambitious, interested, would-be world leader;

if I shall have left you with the conviction that great issues and basic human urges and passions are involved which could preserve or could ruin our system of society and government, even our civilization, all depending upon how the urges and passions shall be directed and used; if I shall have left you with the determination to know more about all this before you give your approval or disapproval of any plan that may be proposed; if I shall have left you with the knowledge that the situation in which we find ourselves is one of dire distress, and must be considered and solved without heat or rancor or partisanship, upon the utmost wisdom and highest patriotism,—if I have been able to do this, my purpose in speaking to you shall be fully met. It has not been my purpose to try to tell you what to think or what to do.

Members of the Los Angeles County Bar: this future of ours is a matter of concern for every citizen, for the task that lies ahead will rest with a heavy hand upon each of us. But the burden is yours, each of you, and yours not only, but the burden of your sons and your daughters, your grandsons and granddaughters, even for generations to come. For we may not waste away our strength, our civic virtue, our inheritance of free institutions, and recover them in a day. They were built by the generations of illustrious, patriotic ancestors who preceded us; they must be saved from destruction by ourselves, then rebuilt to even greater perfection by those who follow us. We can do it if we shall have the will to do it; our children can do it if we shall inspire them to its accomplishment.

We must come to the task of decision that now faces us, with the purest motives. Avarice, greed, selfish ambition, the thirst for power and place and dominion, must all be thrust from our hearts. We must come with the loftiest patriotism, with a single allegiance, undivided, unshared, undefiled, for the Constitution under which we live—so in effect runs the oath of office of each of you who grace the Bar of this commonwealth. Our hearts and hands must be clean of all foreign *isms* and alien political cults. The Constitution and its free institutions must be our ensign.

For America has a destiny—a destiny to conquer the world—not by force of arms, not by purchase and favor, for these conquests wash away, but by high purpose, by unselfish effort, by uplifting achievement, by a course of Christian living; a conquest that shall leave every nation free to move out to its own destiny; a conquest that shall bring, through the workings of our own example, the blessings of freedom and liberty to every people, without restraint or imposition or compulsion from us; a conquest that shall weld the whole earth together in one great brotherhood in a reign of mutual patience, forbearance, and charity, in a reign of peace to which we shall lead all others by the persuasion of our own righteous example.

This, gentlemen, is the destiny of our America. May God give us citizens strength to live for it, and the moral power to achieve it.

The San Francisco Charter

1945

A penciled note at the top of the draft of this paper reads, "Begun in June-July 1945." In 1961, when President Ernest L. Wilkinson of Brigham Young University was permitted to read a copy of the draft, JRC's secretary, Rowena J. Miller, made this note regarding the paper, "This is a rough draft of a memorandum which he wrote at the time the United Nations was forming back in 1945 and was never really finished." Also, a note attached to the back of the front fiberback cover containing the draft reads, "If published at all—to be published as unfinished manuscript as of the date it was written—1945." One final note was written by JRC to his secretary on 18 February 1961, eight months before his death: "Not to be released to anyone prior to publication, if any." This is the initial publication of this document, and so far as possible it has been reproduced in the form in which JRC left it. Handwritten insertions have been included in the text, as also the one marginal note. Box 231, Folder 4, "United Nations Charter, Study of San Francisco Charter, June-August, 1945," JRCP.

To the Editor of the Deseret News:

Acceding to your request I am submitting to you a few general observations upon some of the more obvious and important factors of the San Francisco Charter. I have not attempted to make anything

437

but a more or less cursory analysis. [Marginal note: Roosevelt died April 12, 1945.]

The opening session of the Conference was on April 25, 1945. Two months later almost to the day the Charter was signed (June 26, 1945). It was submitted to the Senate on July 2, 1945, with a letter from the Secretary of State urging prompt ratification. The Senate opened its hearings on the treaty on July 9th; it closed them on July 13th. The Senate gave its advice and consent to ratification on July 28th. Thus we were launched into a world organization involving us in relationships and obligations, new not only to ourselves but to the other nations of the world, after a consideration of less than a month by the Senate of the United States, after four days hearings by the Senate Committee, and before the people generally had opportunity to study and consider this basic departure from all the traditions and practices of our country over the more than a century and a half of its existence. The old saw about marriages between individuals—and this professes to be a sure-enough marriage between nations—carries a lesson to us now: "Marry in haste and repent at leisure."

The overwhelming vote for the Charter by the members of both parties in the Senate is conclusive evidence that the Senators thought their respective constituencies were for the Charter. But their haste suggests they were not anxious to put it to the test by debate and consideration. The hearings, as reported in the press, were in the main, a travesty on exhaustive consideration. It may be the people of the country are as strongly for the Charter as the Senatorial weathervanes indicated. If so, one comes back to the dictum of Lincoln: "You can fool all the people some of the time and some of the people all of the time—but you cannot fool all the people all of the time." There is a day of reckoning coming for those who either wittingly or unwittingly betray the hopes and aspirations of the people.

1. The Charter Versus the League Covenant

Aged, faltering, dim-eyed Isaac, groping to probe the mother-inspired deceit of Jacob, plaintively, complainingly said: "The voice is Jacob's voice, but the hands are the hands of Esau" (Gen. 27:22).

The Charter has some, not many, new words, a few new phrases, there has been some regrouping of materials and some changes of emphasis, but, in all essentials, it bears a remarkable, indeed unmistakable, family likeness to its father, the Covenant of the League of Nations (in essential features it is a counterpart); in declared purpose it resembles its grandfather, the Holy Alliance; and both in framework and purpose its features are unmistakably those of its great grandfather, the Grand Design of Henry IV, and of its remote founding ancestor, the Amphictyonic Council that was evolved fourteen centuries before Christ. There is nothing really new in the San Francisco Charter, except those terms that build a new military alliance and these are old in principle. It is the same old body dressed in some patched up clothing.

The League Covenant had an assembly made up of representatives of all members of the League; so has the Charter for Charter members; under neither plan has this popular body any real determinative powers in vital matters.

The Covenant had a Council with a backbone of five permanent members, the then most powerful nations of the world,—the United States, the British Empire, France, Italy, and Japan, and four members from the smaller powers to be chosen from time to time; the Charter has a "Security Council" with five permanent members, presently the now most powerful nations of the world,— the United States, the United Kingdom of Great Britain and Northern Ireland, the Union of Soviet Socialist Republics, the Republic of China, and France, with six non-permanent members to be elected by the Assembly. While as a matter of voting this puts the control of the Security Council into the hands of the smaller powers which could thus determine what the large powers must do in waging war, this is not the way it will work, because no important action can be taken without the consent of the Permanent Members, that is the five great powers. The Security Council is in fact the governing body of this new world organization. There is no essential difference between the League Council and the Charter's "Security Council," the word "security" adding nothing in fact.

The League Covenant provided for a Permanent Court of International Justice; the Charter provides for a like Court, and adopts as the Constitution for that Court the essentials of the Statute framed to govern the operation of the League Court.

Each plan provides for a permanent secretariat, with very considerable powers, which in fact looks after all the details of operation of the Organization.

These are the essentials of both plans.

439

There are certain auxiliary organizations in both.

The Covenant had provision for a labor organization "to secure and maintain fair and humane conditions of labor for men, women, and children, both in their own countries and in all countries to which their commercial and industrial relations extend;" the Charter provides for an economic and social council for securing "higher standards of living, full employment, conditions of social and economic progress and development," with some details as to the operation of the Council.

Both the Covenant and the Charter provide for a world military commission which shall have large advisory and controlling powers over the joint military forces—the "international police force" of the Charter that under certain conditions could grow into armies of millions of men—that are to be created for enforcing peace. The army we might contribute to any military expedition to enforce the Charter would pass from our control to that of the "Security Council" and the "Military Committee," once it became part of the "international police force."

The Covenant provided for granting "mandates" to picked, favored nations over various countries and islands. The Charter recognizes these mandates, and also sets up (1) a plan for administering "territories whose people have not yet attained a full measure of self-government" (these non-self-governing territories are not named), and (2) a further plan for the establishment of "an international trusteeship system" over "such territories in the following categories as may be placed thereunder by means of trusteeship agreements: (a) territories now held under mandate; (b) territories which may be detached from enemy states as a result of the second world war; and (c) territories voluntarily placed under the system by states responsible for their administration." A Trusteeship Council is to be set up to assist in the administration of trusteed territories. Apparently the trusteed states have no voice in any matter touching themselves.

The Covenant contemplated the establishment of regional understandings among contiguous states; the Charter specifically provides for such regional arrangements.

The Covenant provided for and required world disarmament "to the lowest point consistent with national safety and the enforcement by common action of international obligations." The Charter has no equivalent provisions. In fact it seems to contemplate no limitation upon the military establishments of any of the United Nations, for our national administration is urging an expansion in our own military organizations that will not only be the greatest in our own history, but the greatest in the world.

The Covenant provided that international treaties made by members of the League must be registered to be effective. The Charter also provides for such registration but provides further that every treaty must conform to the Charter provisions, and this seems to apply both to existing treaties and future treaties. We are to give up our sovereign power to make treaties.

Just as the plan of Henry IV was in essence and purpose a military alliance against Austria and the Hapsburgs; just as the Holy Alliance was in fact a military alliance against France; just as the League Covenant was an alliance against Germany and her allies in World War One,—so the Charter strips down to a military alliance against the enemy states in World War II. If this element of the Charter is eliminated, including the provisions for the imposition of armed and economic sanctions, and if the provision for territorial aggrandizement by the big powers, through mandates, through the administration of non-self-governing peoples, and through trusteed territories, be stricken out, there is not left enough peace mechanism to make an equivalent for the Hague Convention of 1907 for the Pacific Settlement of International Disputes. "The voice is Jacob's voice, but the hands are the hands of Esau."

Perhaps the most striking feature of the Charter is the plainly discernible track of the Great Bear, either by way of express grants of power available and advantageous to him or by limitations against the exercise of powers by the Charter members,—all for the benefit of the Bear.

2. Underlying Principles

There are certain underlying principles that should be in mind in considering the wisdom of the organization to be set up by the Charter.

Foremost among these principles is this: The Charter must be weighed and measured not solely by the advantages, even the blessings, it might give if it worked—and this is the point of view most frequently urged—but it must on the contrary also be weighed and measured by the disadvantages, the ills which it could bring if it did not work. For the ills might far outweigh the blessings so that we might find ourselves "paying too dearly for our whistles." Or in other words we should ask ourselves,—if it works what will we get; if it fails what will we suffer.

In the next place we should appreciate that the Charter is to make its try in a world of stern, even brutal realities, not in a Utopia nor in a millennium. Never before in the history of the world have so many people and nations, numerically, come under the influence of hate and carnage with the whole evil brood of passions that trail after them. We have been so intrigued by the concept and phrase that godless men coined—"total war"—that we not only tolerate, but take pride in boasting about, butcheries of peoples that a generation ago would have shocked to the very core all but the most depraved. The old, the infirm, the sick, the helpless, the women, the children, all are gleefully murdered in mass, and the more we slaughter the greater we proclaim our glory in arms.

The honor and chivalry of our fathers, that at least shed some respectability and even charity over the horrors of war, are dead. All this does not bespeak an atmosphere into which we may let fly a dove of peace, even if wearing a coat of armor, with any hope that it can live. Men's hearts must change and righteousness must rule their lives before peace will come.

In the third place, so far as we are concerned, the Charter is launched upon a public sentiment that has been wind-whipped into a toleration and unresistant acceptance of about anything the Executive proposes. One directive after another has been proclaimed, one failure has trod upon the heels of another "so fast they follow," and time and again we have weathered successive failures, so that we have come to feel maybe we can weather them all. So let us try another, is the thought.

But this is not just another directive. It is an international agreement. If we ratify it we shall pledge our words not only but our national good faith and honor to live up to the Charter promises. We cannot assume them today and cast them off tomorrow because we find them too burdensome, *except* we are willing to abide the penalty which would surely mean loss of respect and confidence, and also of prestige (whatever that may be worth), and which could mean a "total war" against us by all the powers who are parties to the Charter. Mr. Stettinius was quoted as saying we might leave the Charter organization if we wished, but the printed copies of the Charter, including the official Senate print, contain no escape clause. If we join we must expect to stick, and in the language of the street (not inappropriate in this relation), if we stick we are stuck.

Another point: If we shall join in this organization we shall enter under such an unsettled world condition as has not been seen before on this earth save in great social, economic, and governmental cataclysms. We must consider what would be our situation if we incurred, deliberately (as we might) or inadvertently (as we may) the penalty of "total war" against us by the other Charter members, embracing all the nations of the earth except of course ourselves and the humbled and crippled enemy states. Recalling that Russia would be our enemy, would anyone doubt the extent of the measures of sabotage with which we would be victimized by the communists of this country in favor of Russia? But if we remained in the organization and kept our good standing, how shall we get along with communist Russia with her own particular aims and ambitions, that are not the same as ours.

Furthermore we have accustomed ourselves, many of us, to regard Britain as a friend upon whom we might rely in any contingency or emergency. As a matter of fact we have, in the last years, trailed her ambitions and her diplomacy, disregarding our interests where they clashed with hers. But whatever her friendship for us may have been in the past, what of the future with her communistically veering government? Will she walk with us or with the Bear?

This international mess should be shunned, not married.

Again looking to the Charter itself, it is in drafting, in provision, and in plan but a weak imitation of the League of Nations Covenant. One cannot escape the comparison of a sophomoric essay with a dissertation for a doctorate. The League failed, not because America was not a party but because that plan and no such plan can succeed until men shall be changed in their ambitions, greed, and thirst for power and dominion over their fellowmen. And it may be added that now and for the next period—however short or long—we shall have added to the other factors of the situation just named, the struggle between opposing ideologies that are at one another's throats in a life and death struggle.

Someday, when men have repented and gone to righteous living—it may be not until He shall come to reign whose right it is to reign—we shall have a world of peace, but not until then.

But on no account should we have gone forward on the theory

that *maybe* the Charter Organization will work and so let us make a try, unless we are ready to plumb the depths of sorrow and ill that can come from a failure.

Furthermore, if we are going forward on the theory that we can try it and abandon it if we do not like it, have we any reason to suppose and any right to expect that any of the others are going forward except on the same theory and intention; and if all are going forward on that thesis what reason have we for any real belief that the Charter organization will or can succeed. In this view, it is bound to strain, if not indeed to break on the first real vital issue that arises, for if there is no real will to make it succeed, it becomes only a makeshift to enable us temporarily to bridge over a threatening present crisis.

It is of interest to note that the "Four Freedoms,"—freedom of speech, freedom of religion, freedom from fear, and freedom from want, are not [states] specifically mentioned in the Charter; nor, it may be observed in passing, are certain important provisions of the Atlantic Charter to be found in the San Francisco Charter, for example, the provision that we desire to see no territorial changes that do not accord with the freely expressed wishes of the people concerned; that we recognize the right of all peoples to choose the form of government under which they will live; and the provision that sovereign rights and self-government should be restored to those who have been forcibly deprived of them, and the provision for the abandonment of the use of force. These provisions were lost somewhere in the shuffle, a term particularly apt in this situation.

3. The Good Things

The Charter has elements that make for the peace of the world.

The Making of the Charter Itself

In the first place, as making for peace, there is the simple fact of the making of the Charter setting up the organization of the United Nations, for the people believe this organization is calculated to bring peace into the world. Thus the Charter crystallizes in the popular mind the desire for peace and by that much promotes peace. That the sponsors of the Charter—those of the inner circle behind the scenes, the diplomatists, the militarists, the heads of states—

know that in all probability in the present outlook and perhaps by the plan of some of them, it is merely another truce while the worn-out peoples of the world gird themselves for another conflict which shall be more terrible and destructive than the one we are ending,— this fact for the moment does not matter. When the disillusion comes, all of the inner circle may be dead; one can only wonder whether those who are alive when the time comes will be thought by some to be fit subjects for trial as war criminals. The next world war will be even more than the present one, a life and death struggle between ideologies, between truth and error. If the militarists have their way it will be the most fiendish war of all time. Already we have ourselves contributed the atom bomb.

But, as stated, the Charter makes for peace by crystallizing for the moment the peace yearning of the peoples of the world.

Peaceful Adjustment of International Disputes

In the next place, the Charter contains an outline for the peaceful adjustment of international disputes. The Charter plan is not as complete as the League Covenant plan (Covenant, Art. 11ff), and there is nothing new in the Charter over the Covenant. The Charter names merely and adopts, but without any rules or regulations for their use, long-ago-developed agencies for the peaceful adjustment of international disputes: negotiation, enquiry, mediation, conciliation, arbitration, and judicial settlement (Charter, Art. 33). These come into the Charter, through the League Covenant, from the Hague Conventions of 1899 and 1907, and they came into the Hague Conventions from the earlier practices and customs of the nations.

The distinction envisaged in the Charter between *arbitration* and *judicial settlement* is not a healthful one, nor is it a forward step.

The Charter is deficient in not setting up any machinery for the operation of these methods of peaceful adjustment. Even mediation between two contending states by a third disinterested state may be most difficult. We refused, during the Civil War, to permit Great Britain and France even to make an offer of mediation between the North and the South (John Bassett Moore, *A Digest of International Law,* 8 vols. [Washington, D.C., 1906], 7:9).

The Statute of the International Court of Justice (annexed to the Charter and based upon the Statute of the League Court) contains a provision, under conditions named, for *compulsory arbitration* (Statute, Art. 36), which is analogous to our domestic procedure by which we hale into court any one against whom we have a grievance whether he wishes it or not. This, when it operates, makes for peace. But in the past normal arbitration has always been by agreement of the parties. Yet compulsory arbitration is really the only procedure that can reasonably promise an effective peaceful settlement of international disputes. But it is so serious for a nation to undertake to be haled into an international court to be tried for some act or failure to act and to abide the judgment of the Court no matter what it may be, that nations hesitate to agree to the procedure unless they know by what rules or standard their conduct is to be judged by the Court, because up to now international law in many fields is so meager and unsettled that nations do not know how they should shape their conduct in order to be blameless or by what rules and principles their conduct, if questioned, will be judged by the Court. This makes the nations generally unwilling to agree to compulsory arbitration, except under reservations as to the matters covered by their agreement.

I have said there is nothing really new in the Charter, but this statement must be qualified. As will be pointed out later, the Security Council—the over-governing body of the United Nations—has tremendous powers and among them is a power to intervene "in any stage of a dispute" and "recommend appropriate procedures or methods of adjustment" (Charter, Art. 36). This provision could be interpreted to authorize the Security Council to intervene even in a case pending before the International Court and "recommend" the decision to be made by it. While this would not shock the judicial consciences or sensibilities of the countries that are governed by the Civil Law (for with them such interference with judicial processes by the head of the state is recognized), yet for countries living under Anglo-Saxon-American jurisprudence this would constitute a travesty on justice. In fact, to follow such a procedure would tend to destroy in the minds of all peoples, respect for the Court and an unwillingness to resort thereto, to a point which would likely forestall any appeal to it. This would be a great blow to the peaceful adjustment of international disputes.

As has been intimated above, this whole peaceful adjustment machinery must be considered a step backward from the development therein reached by nations of the world prior to the negotiation of the Charter. This might at first sight seem to make sure that the Charter provisions, going only part of the way, would be lived up to, but the obvious military power established by the Charter, and put behind its instrumentalities is such a threat as is not healthful for the peaceful adjustment of disputes.

The Assembly

The creation of a popular Assembly in which the affairs affecting the nations of the world can be more or less freely discussed, definitely makes for peace. Nefarious schemes, individual, national, or international, do not prosper under publicity. Such a body has been a part of every world-peace plan, since the Amphictyonic Council, fourteen hundred years before Christ. In early plans the Assembly was the real governing body of the system. This gave a voice to each member in all decisions affecting world peace. This in turn gave a strength to the early organizations which of necessity is denied to the later plans where the Assembly becomes largely a debating forum. Unfortunately, it would seem that under the Charter even the full right of debate may be curtailed once the Security Council has taken jurisdiction of a dispute (Charter, Arts. 12, 36.1). Nevertheless, the safety-valve element involved in the public discussion in an international gathering of a threat to the peace of the world, is not to be either ignored or belittled, providing, of course, the discussion is free. However, it is not to be overlooked that under the Charter the Great Triumvirate—Russia, Great Britain, and the United States—sit in the Assembly along with the little states, and it will be a courageous, even foolhardy, little state that will brave the frown of only one of these by urging, even in debate, a cause which is disapproved. We are still in a world of realities.

Economic Factors

It is difficult to appraise the value of the economic factors of the Charter, though they are couched in high sounding phrases. They could make for peace if they work out as happily and generously as the fine words promise; but if they do not work satisfactorily and breed jealousy, discontent, and charges of favoritism, they could stir up more trouble than almost anything else.

The League Covenant in its day (Covenant, Art. 23) provided

for organizations to secure and maintain fair and humane conditions of labor for men, women, and children, both in the member countries and in all countries to which their commercial and industrial relations extend; it was planned to secure just treatment for native inhabitants, to control traffic in women and children, as also in opium and other dangerous drugs; to supervise trade in arms and ammunition; to secure and maintain freedom of communications and of transit and equitable treatment for the commerce of all League members, particularly in devastated areas, and to take measures to control disease. These were all great ideals and history tells us what was done, or not done, to carry them out.

The Charter sets up a special organization with prescribed duties, to carry out its economic provisions (Charter, chap. X), and it uses many more words in telling what shall be done. But the essential factors in the Charter are the same as those in the League Covenant, with additional particularizations, one of which is interesting as showing the influence on the San Francisco Conference of minority groups, particularly emigré European groups. It is provided (Charter, Art. 35): "with a view to the creation of conditions of stability and well-being, which are necessary for peaceful and friendly relations among nations based on respect for the principle of equal rights and self-determination of peoples, the United Nations shall promote: . . . universal respect for, and observance of, human rights and fundamental freedoms for all without distinction as to race, sex, language, or religion."

This "race, sex, language, or religion" language is also used in declaring the purposes of the Organization (Charter, Art. 1), in declaring what the Assembly shall study and make recommendations about (Charter, Art. 13), and in stating the basic objectives in the Trusteeship System (Charter, Art. 76, c).

The terms "human rights and fundamental freedoms" are not defined, and may mean much or nothing. However, the intent of the proponents may be gathered when it is remembered that there may be placed under trusteeship agreements, portions of ex-enemy territory (Charter, Art. 77), that these provisions apply to such territory, and that European emigré groups are said to be planning to return to their homeland in ex-enemy territory for permanent residence.

Obviously, no one would wish to quarrel with any sound, practicable plan to uplift humanity in economic matters. This is a part of the Christianity we all profess. Whether our standards and methods of living and livelihood are either desired by or suitable for all peoples, is at least questionable. Many races and peoples doubtless believe their way is better than ours. The Arab would probably no more wish to live as we live, than we would wish to live as he lives. But we should have a kindly concern to lift every man's standard of living to the level which suits him best, and when his ways are too primitive, to teach him better ways. The Charter provisions, if carried out, could help to better the living of peoples in the world.

But one gets the impression from the elaborate provisions of the Charter that some smaller nations and backward peoples may have accepted the inequalities, even discriminations, of the Charter Organization in the belief that they were, in compensation, to be the recipient of great masses of money and materials, — food, clothing, fuel, luxuries of all sorts—far beyond the capacity of the United States (and we are to be the principal Santa Claus) to provide. We must not overlook the undertakings we made in the United Nations Relief and Rehabilitation Administration (UNRRA) nor President Roosevelt's dictum that we are to do what never before has been done in history, "feed all the peoples of the world as we now know human beings should be fed" (White House Release, 7 June 1943, President's Address, 1)—India's 400,000,000, China's 450,000,000, Russia's (say) 170,000,000, all of Europe, the British Isles, Latin America, and, last but not least, the United States, for our food supply has been curtailed as never before in our generation, and still greater curtailment is promised us. It looks as if we are to try to bring men to a common level in the only way men have ever been brought to a common level, by reducing all men to the lowest or near lowest level, because as a matter of character, intellect, capabilities, and spirituality all men cannot be brought to the highest levels. The Lord Himself has not been able to bring the peoples of the world to this condition.

4. Will the Charter Organization Certainly End War

There seems no reason to doubt that such real approval as the Charter has among the people is based upon the belief that if the Charter is put into effect, wars will end. The mothers, wives, and sweethearts probably feel that hereafter, with the Charter in operation, their loved ones will not be sent to foreign countries to give their lives for some cause that only indirectly, if at all, affects our

449

vital interests or security. In this thought they are deceived. The Charter will not certainly end war. Some will ask,—why not?

In the first place, there is no provision in the Charter itself that contemplates ending war. It is true the Charter provides for force to bring peace, but such use of force is itself war. Secretary Stettinius in his radio broadcast of May 28, 1945, frankly affirmed this when he said:

> But, it is objected, what happens if one of the five permanent members embarks upon a course of aggression and refuses to recognize the machinery of the World Organization? How can the aggressor be restrained if his own contrary vote prevents the Council from invoking force against him? In such an event the answer is simple. Another world war has come, vote or no vote, and the world organization has failed.

It is further true that the Charter contemplates and measurably provides for certain organizations and also announces certain formulas for action, that if taken advantage of, would work out peaceful adjustment of international disputes. But more efficient plans and better formulas therefor have been in existence as and connected with world organizations since the first Hague Conventions of 1899, provisions which were amplified and perfected in the Hague Conventions of 1907; yet in spite of these, World War I came.

Then in certain respects the Hague Convention plans were amplified by the League of Nations Covenant, though the Covenant provisions fell short of the Hague Conventions in other respects. But notwithstanding the Hague Conventions and the Covenant we are just now finishing World War II,—the most devastating war of all time judged by the numbers of peoples involved and the fiendish means of destruction.

We now come to the San Francisco Charter with yet inferior instrumentalities and less perfected procedure than have for almost a half century been available and partly operative among the nations, with a blind hope—induced by unjustified, even false, representations—that somehow, though nations still are sinful, terribly sinful, greedy, thirsty for dominion and power, and driven forward by opposing ideologies for which they are willing to fight and die, yet somehow a miracle will happen and less perfected means will succeed where better ones failed, and so we shall have peace. But we have no real, sound reason to believe it will be so.

Furthermore, our military establishment and their civilian militarist followers, are using all means at their command, fair and unfair, to maintain a great standing army, by keeping indefinitely (as it appears) in the service the bulk of the men now in the service, and constantly adding thereto by large monthly inductions. The militarists are supplementing this plan with a peace-time military conscription plan that will maintain a huge army, even, it may be, to the increasing of the one we have. If peace is here, why these plans? Quite clearly, the militarists not only expect war, but plan for it.

The only real accomplishment of the Charter for peace (and when all is said and done it comes to this) is the setting up of an alliance between Russia, Great Britain, and the United States, so that we, the three great powers of the world, shall all be on the same side when the next world war envisaged by Secretary Stettinius, shall come. To make sure that we shall then be on the same side, each of us is to arm himself fully so that, such would seem to be the argument, any two of us can by force compel any recalcitrant amongst us to be good. That is, we are, in fact, each arming against the others. Hardly could a more fatuous plan be conceived. This means another world war so surely as we go forward under it, and if Britain continues along her new and present domestic political policy, we must contemplate the possibility, in sometime to come, probably not too far distant, of having to stand against Russia and Great Britain, probably with most of Europe with them, if the Potsdam plan is carried through, and no one can foresee who, if any one, will be with us.

The Charter is built to prepare for war, not to promote peace.

In the second place, the Charter, unlike the League Covenant, contemplates the building and maintaining of large military establishments, as has just been pointed out.

In the League of Nations Covenant there were distinct provisions providing and announcing principles for the reduction of armament among the nations (Covenant, Art. 8ff), and for the curtailment of the manufacture of munitions of war. Not only were these provisions definite and positive, but the whole spirit of the instrument was in the same direction. Disarmament of the whole world was to be brought about.

On the other hand the Charter merely provides that the Assembly "*may consider* . . . the principles governing disarmament and the regulation of armaments" and "*may make*" recommendations to the members of the Security Council (Charter, Arts. 11, 26), for the *"regulation"* of armament rather than for *disarmament*.

Under the Covenant, a Limitation of Arms Conference was held and a certain degree of limitation on naval armament was secured. The United States initiated this Conference. When the term of the Conventions neared the end, we seemingly took no steps whatever to renew them, nor to see that during the last years of their existence, they were observed. Our militarists never really wanted the limitations; they always wanted the maximum military establishment. So they systematically over the years torpedoed the Conventions, building up a sentiment and belief among the people that somehow we had been betrayed. Nevertheless, it must not be forgotten that the limitation of armament agreed to at the Conference was in accordance with, though not pursuant to, the mandates of the League Covenant to which we were not parties. Nor should it be overlooked:

That the strength of nations is relative, not absolute; we are weak or strong as compared with other nations.

That at the Limitation of Arms Conference it was agreed that the relative strength of the Navies of the United States, Great Britain, and Japan should in that order be as 50-50-30.

That battleships and auxiliary craft were so limited in size and construction as to maintain the above ratio.

That our own experts at that time regarded this ratio as giving us adequate protection and security.

That to add to our security the Conference treaties forbade fortifications in certain areas, and specified the non-fortifiable areas for Japan.

That the treaty provided: "The maintenance of the *status quo* under the foregoing provisions implies that no new fortifications or naval bases shall be established in the territories and possessions specified; that no measures shall be taken to increase the existing naval facilities for the repair and maintenance of naval forces, and that no increase shall be made in the coast defenses of the territories and possessions above specified."

That so far as Japan was concerned this treaty not alone protected us in matters of naval strength, but it gave us national security in matters of the fortifications of insular possessions.

That this treaty, so affording protection, did not expire until December 31, 1936.

That apparently no effort was made while it was in force to ensure its observance and no effective effort was put forth to extend it beyond the expiration date.

That if this treaty had been maintained in full force and effect, the present war in the Pacific would not have come, first because Japan would not have challenged our superior naval strength—five to three, and second because she would not have had the heavily fortified approaches in the isles of the Pacific which have cost so much blood and treasure to reduce and occupy.

Disarmament is one of the surest and greatest elements in a world peace, and our experience proves only that when disarmament arrangements are made we must see to it that they are lived up to, before strength is built up to challenge the treaty obligation.

In the third place the Charter specifically provides for the waging of wars and for our participation therein. The stipulation is that if economic sanctions prove ineffective to bring a recalcitrant state to time, armed force shall be brought against her, that is, war will be waged (Charter, Arts. 41ff) The Charter members, including ourselves, agree to furnish air, sea, and land forces (in numbers not specified or suggested in the Charter) upon call of the Security Council. We are to make special agreements covering this matter, which agreements "shall govern the numbers and types of forces, their degree of readiness and general location, and the nature of the facilities and assistance to be provided" (Charter, Art. 43). Congress has surrendered its constitutional powers in this vital activity. These agreements we make are to cover total forces—with us whether 1,000,000 or 2,000,000 men, or 10,000 or 20,000 airplanes, or 10 or 20 battleships; the number of lesser fighting craft is not indicated, to say nothing about supplies and equipment. But the number of troops or military equipment of any kind that we are to furnish for any particular war or campaign is to be determined, it seems, by the Security Council and Military Staff Committee. We have no controlling voice in that; nor do we control the occasion on which we furnish the men (Charter, Art. 43ff). Since these operations involve war, one would naturally suppose Congress would have protected its constitutional war making powers, but it did not. Some will hope the members of Congress and the Senators will have opportunity to explain to their constituency why they did not.

Under the Charter a Military Staff Committee is to be created to consist of the Chiefs of Staff of the permanent members of the Security Council (that is, the United States, the United Kingdom of Great Britain and Northern Ireland, Russia, China, and France), the United States having one vote. "The Military Staff Committee shall be responsible under the Security Council for the strategic direction of any armed forces" furnished by the powers. Questions about who commands such forces in the field are to be settled later (Charter, Art. 47). The Security Council decides, in any situation, what nations are to furnish troops and how many and the quantity of other military equipment for handling the international problem (Charter, Art. 48). Congress and the Executive have surrendered their constitutional power here, and the nation has lost its power to control its war making, which is one of, if not the most, essential elements of sovereignty.

The Charter further provides that "in order to enable the United Nations to take urgent military measures, members shall hold immediately available national air force contingents for combined international enforcement action" (Charter, Art. 45). The strength of these units is to be determined by special agreements, but after we supply them we lose sovereign control over them. This is a war operation.

Under the Charter members may declare war in "self-defense," but the Security Council may adopt any measures it thinks necessary "to maintain or restore international peace and security" (Charter, Art. 51). This again is war on another account. How far the excuse "self-defense" can be carried in declaring and waging war, is a matter of history.

In the Charter regional arrangements for using force in settling international disputes are sympathetically countenanced with the provision that before action is taken the authorization of the Security Council must be obtained, *except* action taken against enemy states, for example, Finland or the Baltic States, that may "renew their aggressive policy" (Charter, Art. 53). In these excepted cases there seem to be no restrictions. The further rape of Finland is here made possible. This is another occasion for war.

Before force can be applied all the permanent members of the Security Council must vote *aye* (Charter, Art. 27). By voting *no,* we could stop measures of force; so could Russia. But if the international force were not used in a war to stop a war, then of course the unstopped war would continue. So that war would not end by waging a new one. War is inevitable on either score.

The Charter is a war document not a peace document, and, as already pointed out, is drawn primarily to try to keep such an alliance among the great powers as will forestall war among them. But Secretary Stettinius frankly admitted the weakness of the Charter on this point.

Now Charter proponents are going to try to explain all this by saying that all that is contemplated is an international police force. But an international police force drawn from standing armies big enough in each country to ensure that the country maintaining them could successfully wage another world war on its own account (and this is obviously what is planned), is merely a token of a thoroughly militarized world with its weight of military burden that, if carried forward and maintained, will finally crush every nation that persists in such a course. The people will first groan under the bankrupting tax exactions that must be imposed upon them to carry the load and then moan and weep over the loss of sons that will come when the war machine gets under way, as get under way it must in order to preserve itself. For, as every McCauley school boy knows, history proves nothing more clearly than that large armies always breed wars. Give a military man a great army and he sets about to prove he is an Alexander, a Hannibal, a Caesar, a Napoleon, or all of them rolled together in one. His glory, not the lives of men, becomes the dominating motive.

With sincere apologies for the coarse, gutter vulgarity of the phrase, this is the "blood and guts" type. As the boys say: "Our blood and his guts." Contrast with this the sensitive conduct of Lee at Gettysburg over Pickett's charge.

5. The Administrative Agencies of the Charter

There are two superior administrative agencies,—the Assembly, the popular body which is little more than a glorified debating society, with few real powers and those relatively unimportant, and second, the Security Council which has all the real power in the whole organization, legislative, executive, and judicial. This is a civil law organization, not a common law nor American constitutional law body. Some of our alphabetical bureaus have given us some experience in this un-American system because they usurped and brought within their scope the same powers.

455

The Assembly

The Assembly *"may consider . . . and may make recommenda-tions"* to the Security Council; it "may call to the attention of the security council" certain matters concerning international peace and security (Charter, Art. 11); but the Assembly may not make recommendations as to any matter concerning which the Security Council is exercising its function as bestowed upon it by the Charter, that is, when the Security Council steps in, the Assembly steps out (Charter, Art. 12); the Assembly "shall initiate studies and make recommendations" for "promoting international cooperation in the political field" and encouraging the "progressive development of international law and its codification," and also "for promoting international cooperation in the economic, social, cultural, educational, and health fields, and assisting in the realization of human rights and fundamental freedoms for all without distinction as to race, sex, language, or religion," and in this connection the Assembly, to further the principle "of equal rights and self determination of peoples" (Charter, Art. 13), can recommend measures for the peaceful adjustment of international situations (Charter, Art. 14), and even the Security Council is to make reports to the Assembly about its work (Charter, Art. 15). But the Assembly can actually do little about these various matters, except talk about them.

The United Nations, presumably through the Assembly and its auxiliaries, are to promote among the United Nations "higher standards of living, full employment, and conditions of social and economic progress and development; promote solutions of international economic, social, health and related problems; and international cultural and educational cooperation; and universal respect for and observance of human rights, and fundamental freedoms for all without distinction as to race, sex, language, or religion" (Charter, Art. 55), and to assist in all this the Assembly is to set up from among its members an Economic and Social Security Council with a wide field of investigation (Charter, Art. 61ff), the results to be reported with recommendations to the Assembly (Charter, Art. 62), which in turn may make report and recommendations to the Security Council (Charter, Arts. 10, 13, Chaps. IX and X). The Assembly also elects some members, but not all, of the Trusteeship Council (Charter, Art. 86 c). But in all this there is neither legislative decision and action nor executive administration. It is all just investigation, report, and recommendation. The "Security Council" is the real power.

The Assembly also has certain powers (noted later) in connection with the functions and powers of the "Organization."

The Assembly approves the budget of the Organization (Charter, Art. 17), but it does not apparently initiate it; it also "considers and approves" the budgetary arrangements for the specialized social agencies it may create to make studies and recommendations for report to the Assembly, to be by it reported to the Security Council (see supra).

The Assembly "shall receive and consider, annual and special reports from the Security Council" (Charter, Art. 15), but it is not authorized to take any action with reference thereto.

The Assembly may admit new members, suspend members, expel members upon the recommendation of the Security Council (Charter, Chap. II, and Art. 19), and exercise certain advisory functions in relation to trusteeships, as well as carrying out the functions of the Organization as to trusteeships, international social and economic problems (Charter, Arts. 16, 60, 85).

It may perhaps be conveniently pointed out here, that the Charter is unfortunately hazy in some provisions.

The Preamble to the Charter (which obviously and for obvious reasons is cast in the form of the Preamble to the Constitution of the United States) affirms that the nations constituting the San Francisco Conference "do hereby establish an international *organization* to be known as the *United Nations*."

Thereafter the two terms "Organization" and "United Nations" are used in the Charter in provisions which often are obscure as to their real meaning and operation. We should expect that all actions and functions under the Charter would be taken and exercised by instrumentalities set up by the Charter. But this is not so. Certain things are prescribed for and powers given to the "Organization" or the "United Nations" with no statement as to the agency to carry them out, and there appears to be no central or general organization set up by the Charter.

For instance, there is the most important provision in Article 2.7 (inserted, the press reports, upon the urgent insistence of John Foster Dulles) which greatly helps in preserving us from some of the dangers of the Charter. It reads:

Nothing contained in the present Charter shall authorize the United Nations to intervene in matters which are essentially within the domestic jurisdiction of any state or shall require the Members to submit such matters to settlement under the present Charter; but this principle shall not prejudice the application of enforcement measures under Chapter VII.

Presumably "United Nations" as here used would embrace all the agencies set up under the Charter, but it does not say so. Furthermore, the term "enforcement measures" is indefinite. Does it mean the raising of the international peace force, the use of that force, the use of any territory (country) and its facilities, or the application of force? There is room here for dispute. One thing seems clear: this provision should exclude the United Nations from interfering with the handling of minority groups by their own country. We have minority groups amongst us that promise future trouble for us. If they could bring the armies of the world against us to compel us to do what they want, we should be in an unhappy condition.

By Article 8 the "United Nations" are to place no restrictions on the eligibility of men and women for any service in "the principal and subsidiary organs." Does this prevent the organs themselves from placing such restrictions?

By Article 2.6 the "Organization" is to ensure that non-member states act in accordance with the principles of the Charter, but it is not stated whose job it is to carry this out. By Article 4, the "Organization" is to determine whether states seeking membership "are able and willing to carry out these obligations." What body or organ of the "Organization" shall do this, but probably the Assembly (Charter, Art. 4.2). By Charter Article 17.2 "expenses of the organization" are to be borne by the Members as apportioned by the Assembly, but there is no statement as to what these "organization" expenses cover. Moreover, the "Organization" is to make "recommendation for the coordination of the policies and activities of the specialized agencies," and may initiate negotiations for the creation of new agencies (Charter, Arts. 58, 59), but responsibility for the exercise of these functions is lodged in the Assembly (Charter, Art. 60). Provision is made (Charter, Art. 105) for necessary privileges and immunities, in the territory of each member, for the "Organization," and for officials of the "Organization," concerning which the Assembly may make representations. This provision is not clear.

All the foregoing shows either carelessness or haste, or both in drafting. Under the stress of operation many other points will arise resulting from infelicities of draftsmanship.

The Security Council

This body, which is the ruling body of the Charter organization, with the full legislative, executive, and judicial powers for the entire organization, is composed of China, France, Great Britain and Northern Ireland, Russia, and the United States, who are permanent members, and six others elected for two years from among the other members of the United Nations (Charter, Art. 23).

The members confer on the Security Council primary responsibility for the maintenance of international peace and security, and agree that in carrying out its duties under this responsibility the Security Council acts on their behalf. . . . The members of the United Nations agree to accept and carry out the decisions of the Security Council in accordance with the present charter. (Charter, Arts. 24, 25)

The Council with the assistance of the Military Staff Committee is *responsible* for submitting to the members plans "for the establishment of a system for the *regulation* of armaments," not for *disarmament* (Charter, Art. 26).

The Council is to function continuously. It may establish "such subsidiary organs as it deems necessary for the performance of its functions" (Charter, Art. 29).

Non-members of the Council may participate in its proceedings when the Council believes that the non-member's interests are involved, but seemingly not otherwise (Charter, Art. 31). The Council shall invite both members and non-members, who are parties to a dispute under consideration, to its meetings to participate, without vote, in its discussions, the Council laying down controlling rules for such participation by non-members (Charter, Art. 32).

On all matters other than procedural, the Council must reach its decisions by the affirmative vote of seven of the eleven Council members, including the affirmative vote of all the permanent members (Charter, Art. 27). The negative vote of either China, France, Great Britain, Russia, or the United States will defeat any proposal, other than procedural. This gives a veto power to every permanent member of the Council; and that negative vote will doubtless be cast when any one of them thinks its vital interests are to be injuriously affected. This means either that, in such case, nothing will be done to control or solve any dispute, even a war, which will then continue, or it means the situation will arise of which Secretary Stettinius spoke, and another world war will come.

The Council "shall, when it deems necessary, call upon the parties to settle their dispute," by "negotiation, enquiry, mediation, conciliation, arbitration, judicial settlement" (Charter, Art. 33), (all of which were developed at the Hague Conferences of 1899 and 1907 and before) or by resort to regional agencies or arrangements, or other peaceful means of their own choice (Charter, Art. 52).

The Council can interfere at any time, in any of these peaceful procedures, at its discretion, even, it would seem, in an arbitration or judicial procedure (Charter, Art. 36).

If the parties fail to compose their differences by any of the peaceful means named, they "shall refer it to the Council," which decides the matter (Charter, Art. 37). This is a practically unlimited authority and power over the international relationships of all the peoples of the world.

The Council determines whether any situation contains a threat to the peace of the world or constitutes an act of aggression, it then makes suggestions of a provisional nature (Charter, Art. 40), decides on what measures less than armed force may be used to settle the dispute (Charter, Art. 41), or "may take such action by air, sea, or land forces as may be necessary to maintain or restore international peace and security" (Charter, Art. 42). This gives plenary powers as to the use of force against any nation in the world.

The measures less than force "may include complete or partial interruption of economic relations and of rail, sea, air, postal, telegraphic, radio, and other means of communication, and the severance of diplomatic relations" (Charter, Art. 41).

The obligation of members to furnish these armed forces has been already noted (Charter, Art. 43).

Each member is obligated to "hold immediately available national air-force contingents for combined international enforcement action," the strength of the various units to be determined by the Council and the Military Staff (Charter, Art. 45).

Plans for the "application of armed force" are to be "*made by the Security Council* with the assistance of the Military Staff Committee" (Charter, Art. 46).

The Security Council determines the action required by the members to carry out its decisions, and the United Nations are to join in carrying out their decisions (Charter, Art. 48).

Pending action by the Council, members may undertake individual or collective measures of self-defense, but such measures of self-defense in no way affect the right or responsibility of the Security Council to take such action as it deems necessary in the premises (Charter, Art. 51).

Regional arrangements, apparently among neighborhood powers, are encouraged for dealing with appropriate matters relating to international peace and security, and the Council in proper cases is to make use of all of such arrangements, but no enforcement action shall be taken by such organizations without the consent of the Security Council, except measures against enemy states (Charter, Chap. VIII).

It is not clear that the Security Council has any definite functions with reference to non-self-governing territories and the Charter provisions with reference thereto are very sketchy (Charter, Chap. XI).

As to the Trusteeship territories the Security Council has, as to strategic areas therein, all the functions of the United Nations, including approval of the terms of trusteeship (Charter, Arts. 82, 83), and the Council shall use the Trusteeship Council to assist in the performance of the functions of the United Nations in matters relating "to political, social, and educational matters in the strategic areas" (Charter, Art. 83.3).

The mere narration of these powers suggests how much the Charter impairs our sovereignty in that most vital element of sovereignty, the waging of war.

6. Subsidiary Agencies

As to governing functions under the Charter, the foregoing are the essential agencies. But there are other "organs" that fit in the picture, one of them being the seeming bait that induced the smaller powers to accept world dominance by five powers. These are:

a. Military Staff Committee

This Committee and its functions have been already treated in the paragraphs on "Will the Charter End War." The Committee has immediate charge of the armed sanction of the United Nations.

461

Under the Charter it will conduct the wars which the Charter obligates the United States to wage. It will have command of our troops and direct their operations (Charter, Chap. VII, Arts. 46, 47).

b. Pacific Settlements Organization

Repeating the substance of what has been already said: This is but a continuation of the organization set up under the League of Nations Covenant, including the International Court of Justice, which is to function under a Statute based on the existing Statute of the International Court of Justice. There are no new essential elements in the plan. The inefficacy of this organization to prevent war, even among the smallest nations, is the distressing and discouraging history of the last twenty odd years. Too much hope may not now be placed in it. There is this retrograde step in the present plan,—the Security Council seemingly has the power to intrude itself into the proceedings, apparently either to stop them or to give a desired direction to them, in the Council's discretion (Charter, Art. 36). Such a power robs the plan of any true semblance of a judicial organization where law and justice, not power or politics, should control.

c. Regional Arrangements

These have been already referred to in the sketch on the Security Council. They may be made by members for dealing "with such matters relating to the maintenance of international peace and security as are appropriate for regional action" (Charter, Art. 52). The Charter does not specify what these matters are, and the regional action can not under any circumstances interfere with the powers and functions of the Security Council (Charter, Arts. 52, 34, 35).

The Charter contains no indications as to where these regions are to be set up, nor as to their constituent membership. The press (whether inspired or not, is not clear) has heretofore suggested an American region, composed of the two Americas; there have been suggestions that Russia would set up some kind of an Eastern and South Central European region (The Potsdam Communiqué gives some substance to this); and recently the press has talked about a new and enlarged British role in the Far East and Malaysia.

Such an American Region might include, as the Covenant included [*sic*—this may mean "indicated"] a treaty recognition of the principles of the Monroe Doctrine, which would mean the virtual destruction of the Doctrine by giving other powers a voice in its operation, whereas now we ourselves decide the occasion and the time when we shall employ it.

One would expect a Russian Region to include states controlling free access to the Mediterranean and as near as possible to the North Sea, both of which build troubles for Britain. But if such a region is made then Britain must have a counterpoise region in Western and West Southern Europe, a balance of power arrangement with all the troubles and problems which that would envisage, vis-a-vis the Russian Region on the East and South East.

The Malaysian, Indian, Australian Region, British dominated, would give monopolistic control over some essential raw products, such as rubber, unless our industrial chemists are permitted to develop a fully serviceable synthetic rubber.

The interplay of political interests in all these fields will worry the earth not a little.

d. International Economic and Social Cooperation and the Economic Security Council

This could have been the bait that lured the small powers into a recognition of the practically suzerain power over them by the "big three," Russia, Great Britain, and the United States, for the two other permanent members of the Security Council—France and China—are at present, negligible as military powers in world politics.

We repeat the declared purposes of these organizations:

To create conditions of stability and well-being which are necessary

for peaceful and friendly relations among nations based on respect for the principle of equal rights and self-determination of peoples, the United Nations shall promote:

a. higher standards of living, full employment, and conditions of economic and social progress and development;

b. solutions of international economic, social, health, and related problems; and international cultural and educational cooperation; and

c. universal respect for, and observance of, human rights and fundamental freedoms for all without distinction as to race, sex, language, or religion.

All members pledge themselves to take joint and separate action in cooperation with the Organization for the achievement of the purposes [as above set out]. (Charter, Arts. 55, 56).

Specialized agencies for these purposes already set up, may be brought into a working relationship with the "Organization" (Charter, Art. 57). This would seem to cover such agencies as the UNRRA, which, report has it, is not going too well, except in paying large salaries to its official staff. The "Organization" has recommendatory supervision over these specialized agencies, and may set up new specialized agencies if and as desired (Charter, Arts. 58, 59). One can visualize a world order of specialized alphabetical agencies with everybody on the pay roll. We know something about that.

The Charter Organization has set up its own special agency to carry out its declared purposes,—the Economic and Social Council, consisting of eighteen members, elected by the General Assembly from the members of the United Nations (Charter, Chap. X).

This Economic and Social Council (as already stated) "may make or initiate studies and reports with respect to international economic, social, cultural, educational, health, and related matters and may make recommendations with respect to any such matters to the General Assembly," to the Members, and to the specialized agencies. "It may make recommendations for the purpose of promoting respect for, and observance of, human rights and fundamental freedoms for all." It may prepare draft conventions on matters within its fields and submit same to the Assembly, and under prescribed rules may call international conferences "on matters falling within its competence" (Charter, Art. 62). This Council may enter into agreements with specialized agencies, subject to the approval of the General Assembly, for bringing such agencies into relationship with the United Nations. It may arrange for reports from the specialized agents, and make recommendations for coordinating their activities (Charter, Art. 63). This Council may furnish information to the Security Council and shall assist that Council upon its request (Charter, Art. 65). It may, as directed by the General Assembly, perform designated functions in carrying out recommendations of the Assembly, and, with the approval of the Assembly, perform services for the members. It shall set up Commissions "in economic and social fields and for the promotion of human rights," as well as Commissions required for the performance of its functions (Charter, Arts. 66, 68).

e. Declaration Regarding Non-Self-Governing Territories

As already noted, the provisions of this Declaration are sketchy. The opening paragraph reads:

> Members of the United Nations which have or assume responsibility for the administration of territories whose peoples have not yet attained a full measure of self-government recognize the principle that the interests of the inhabitants of these territories are paramount, and accept as a sacred trust the obligation to promote to the utmost, within the system of international peace and security, established by the present charter, the well being of the inhabitants of these territories. (Charter, Art. 73)

The Charter adds some details as to what the dominant state must do to bring this about.

The non-self-governing peoples are not named, but we may assume they could include India, and Egypt, the Dominions and Crown Colonies of Britain, our own territories, and The Netherlands' possessions in Malaysia, with other peoples the world over who are not now self-governing. As the Charter contemplates that other peoples not now under a dominant state may be brought thereunder, Russia must get her share.

f. International Trusteeship System and the Trusteeship Council

The Charter provides: "The United Nations shall establish under its authority an international trusteeship system for the administration and supervision of such territories as may be placed thereunder by subsequent individual agreements. These territories are hereinafter referred to as trust territories" (Charter, Art. 75).

The Charter article next following this, sets out the objectives of this system conformably to prescriptions in Article 1 of the Charter. They read:

a. to further international peace and security.

b. to promote the political, economic, social, and educational advancement of the inhabitants of the trust territories, and their progressive development towards self-government or independence as may be appropriate to the particular circumstances of each territory and its peoples and the freely expressed wishes of the people concerned, and as may be provided by the terms of each trusteeship agreement.

    c. to encourage respect for human rights and for fundamental freedoms for all without distinction as to race, sex, language, or religion, and to encourage recognition of the interdependence of the peoples of the world; and

    d. to ensure equal treatment in social, economic, and commercial matters for all members of the United Nations and their nationals and also equal treatment for the latter in the administration of justice, without prejudice to attainment of the foregoing objectives and subject to the provisions of Article 80 (Charter, Art. 76)

This Article 80 referred to reserves from the effects of these trusteeship agreements, except insofar as recognized in the agreements themselves, the "rights whatsoever of any states or any peoples or the terms of existing international instruments to which Members of the United Nations may respectively be parties."

The purposes set out in these provisions are on their face such as would generally command the respect of all men. But clearly they envisage special consideration for European political emigrés. Furthermore, it is clear that some minority group is trying to force itself upon other and more or less socially or economically unwilling groups by again demanding the elimination of distinctions based upon "race, sex, language, or religion," as was done also in the economic and social provisions and in the provisions laying down the duties of the Assembly.

The Charter further provides:

    1. The trusteeship system shall apply to such territories in the following categories as may be placed thereunder by means of trusteeship agreements:
        a. territories now held under mandates;
        b. territories which may be detached from enemy states as the result of the Second World War; and,
        c. territories voluntarily placed under the system by states responsible for their administration.
    2. It will be a matter for subsequent agreement as to which territories in the foregoing categories will be brought under the trusteeship system and upon what terms. (Charter, Art. 77)

Territories "which have become Members of the United Nations" are not subject to trusteeships, "relationship among which shall be based on respect for the principle of sovereign equality" (Charter, Art. 78).

The trusteeship agreement shall include the terms of the trusteeship, and designate the administering agency, whether one state, or the Organization (Charter, Art. 81).

"Strategic areas" may be designated in trusteeship agreements, these areas to come under the Security Council which may avail itself of the services of the Trusteeship Council (Charter, Art. 82).

One Charter provision regarding trust territories may have special significance:

> It shall be the duty of the administering authority to ensure that the trust territory shall play its part in the maintenance of international peace and security. To this end the administering authority may make use of volunteer forces, facilities, and assistance from the trust territory in carrying out the obligations towards the Security Council undertaken in this regard by the administering authority, as well as for local defense and the maintenance of law and order within the trust territory. (Charter, Art. 84)

The Trusteeship Council is composed of those administering trust territories, the permanent members of the Security Council who do not have trusteeships, and enough other members to make equal in the Trusteeship Council, those administering trusteeships and those not (Charter, Art. 86).

The Trusteeship Council investigates and reports upon the conduct of the administering agent of the trust territory, using for this purpose as may be desired the Economic and Social Council (Charter, Art. 88).

g. The Secretariat

The Secretariat for the Organization has no special provisions or functions that require notice.

h. Miscellaneous Provisions

There are some very important "Miscellaneous Provisions"—one relates to treaties, and provides that every treaty or international agreement, entered into after the Charter comes into effect, by any Member of the Organization shall be registered, and if not registered it may not be invoked "before any organ of the United Nations." Should there be any conflict between the prescriptions of treaties and the Charter, the Charter shall prevail.

i. Transitional Security Arrangements

Among the "transitional Security Arrangements" may be noted that which stipulates that pending the making and coming into force of such of the special arrangements setting up the international armed force already referred to as the Security Council shall deem adequate for the purpose, the four powers that are parties to the Moscow Declaration (Russia, Britain, China, and the United States) "shall consult with one another and as occasion requires with other Members of the United Nations with a view to such joint action on behalf of the Organization as may be necessary for the purpose of maintaining international peace and security."

This significant fact should be noted here. It has been already referred to in the section discussing "underlying principles."

The Charter does not anywhere provide that freedom and liberty shall come to any state or to any people in the world that are not free. On the contrary it recognizes and in so far as possible, legalizes every political dominance now existing on the earth and specifically provides for the establishment of others, disregarding those heretofore held by "enemy states."

The Atlantic Charter, whether signed or unsigned, purported to express the views of two great theretofore liberty-loving nations. The peoples of the earth so believed and still refuse to accept pettyfogging explanations to the contrary.

That Charter (as already recited) declared that the conferees, "speaking for their respective governments," first "desire to see no territorial changes that do not accord with the freely expressed wishes of the people concerned," and next, they "respect the right of all peoples to choose the form of government under which they will live; and they wish to see sovereign rights and self-government restored to those who have been forcibly deprived of them."

These things were declared in a solemn and critical moment in world history and were supposed to be responsibly and soberly said.

Yet now, under a plan which it is desired should be regarded as set up under a great peace document establishing a world peace organization that is to bring "equal rights and self-determination of peoples" and "universal respect for, and observance of human rights and fundamental freedoms" (Charter, Art. 55), it is formally declared that some peoples of the earth are to remain as they are under mandates, which as history shows is a polite term to designate the holding of a people under subjection without freedom or liberty; other peoples described as non-self-governing territories are to be held under subjection because—this is not stated in the Charter—some powerful state wishes them and their territory; while still another group of peoples are to be trusteed to some power or powers and obviously for the purpose of some sort of exploitation, these latter peoples to be either presently mandated peoples, or peoples detached from enemy states, or peoples "voluntarily placed under the system by states responsible for their administration" (Charter, Art. 77). None of these peoples are to have, so far as the Charter provision goes, anything to say regarding their fates, the pious provisions of the Atlantic Charter and the San Francisco Charter to the contrary notwithstanding.

As among individuals all this misrepresentation and shifting would make a case of outrageous fraud and deceit. As among nations it spells a lack of elementary integrity which in turn bespeaks an absence of honor, and when honor among nations goes, international chaos follows.

Finally, we may note this provision:

Nothing in the present Charter shall invalidate or preclude action, in relation to any state which during the Second World War has been an enemy of any signatory to the present Charter, taken or authorized as a result of that war by the governments having responsibility for such action.

So far as ex-enemy states are concerned, they are outlawed; it is open season on them.

Concluding Observations

The Charter makes us a party to every international dispute arising anywhere in the world, and puts upon us a high moral and internationally legal obligation to support our decision by sending our sons to fight to support, even (as Secretary Stettinius said) if it involves us in another world war.

In this connection it should be in mind, that the "peace" arrangements we are making in Europe seem to put our boys along side the Russian and British soldiers in every tinder box that lies along side every powder keg in Europe. Knowing that this intimate relationship in Australia has led, in Australia, to actual armed rioting between Australian and American troops with actual deaths resulting, it takes little imagination to visualize what will probably happen as among our men and the Russians and British soldiers in Berlin, Vienna, or wherever else they may be thrown intimately together. Nor does it take much wisdom to foresee the serious international complications that can arise therefrom. Truculent military officers representing each of three mighty nations, each officer believing that his is the mightiest and best nation and so destined to rule the world, can touch off a world conflagration merely because he feels insulted over some trivial matter of protocol.

Not only does the Charter Organization not prevent future wars, but it makes it practically certain that we shall have future wars, and as to such wars it takes from us the power to declare them, to choose the side on which we shall fight, to determine what forces and military equipment we shall use in the war, and to control and command our sons who do the fighting.

Public Loans to Foreign Countries

20 November 1945

JRC delivered this address at the 273rd Meeting of the National Industrial Conference Board, Inc., at the Waldorf-Astoria Hotel in New York City. Box 233, Folder 6, JRCP.

Musicians like new arrangements of old melodies. I give my arrangement of a well known story.

Way out on the prairies, where you travel on and on, and still on the prairies, a farmer was resting his mules in the corner of the field. It was near sundown. The mules dropped their long necks till their noses almost touched the ground. They were tired; so was their driver. One of the great state highways came down alongside the field, and just at the corner where he had stopped to rest, the highway forked in several directions. A great limousine, painted red, very red, came swaying down the road as the driver broke all speed limits. He was hurrying to get to his destination before night came. Belatedly seeing the forks of the road, he jammed on his brakes and brought the car to a stop, with screeches and moans from brakes and tires. He was just opposite the tired man and the tired mules.

He looked for road signs, but none was standing, all had been hacked down and burned by someone who thought the old signboards were out of date, obsolete.

Finally, after vainly looking about for some guidepost, he asked the farmer if he knew whether the road to the extreme left would take him to Loafhaven. The farmer answered:

"Ah don't know."

"Will the road in the center take me there?"

"Ah don't know."

"Will the road to the right get me there?"

"Ah don't know."

"Which way is Loafhaven?"

"Ah don't know."

Temper lost, the driver said, "You don't know much, do you?"

"Nope," was the prompt reply, "Ah don't. But Ah ain't lost. Ah work."

Our national drivers are pitching forward at breakneck speed; they are searching for a dream—Utopia; they do not know in what direction it lies, nor do they know which road to take to get there. But they are almost at the forks of the road.

But we farmers, and merchants, and mill hands, and white collar men, and bankers, and professional men, "us of the run of the flock"—"we ain't lost"—yet.

We are regimented to work, and we are still thinking and working, on the old rules of debit and credit,—we have to if our drivers are to have money to pay their hotel bills, and to buy gas and tires to get them to their Utopia,—Loafhaven.

Aid to the Needy and Suffering

We "run of the flock" know we must help, and are willing and anxious to help, the poor of the world, with food and clothing and shelter. We want nobody to starve or freeze or die from exposure or disease or plague. We do not want any of these things for our wives and children, and we know that disease and plagues anywhere in the world threaten us. We are all willing and anxious to cooperate with appropriate agencies set up to extend all necessary help to suffering humanity everywhere. Some of us believe the Red Cross could do the job if we all fell in and helped. But of course we are aware this method might not be politically expedient, it would not supply lame-duck ex-officeholders with fat jobs, nor give high salaries to key politicians or to their friends, nor enable any group to wreak vengeance on those they hate. So the Red Cross is probably out.

Santa Claus to the World

But there is much more in the air than I have suggested. First, we are to "feed all the peoples of the world as we know human beings should be fed" (White House Release, President's Address, 1). Then, plans are forming to supply to other countries funds for rehabilitation, for reconstruction, for currency stabilization, for industrial restoration, for new industries, for raising standards of living, for educational and cultural progress and development, for more and better poor houses, general housing, jails, insane asylums, for universal social and economic security, and public insurance, and a hundred other like purposes.

Some feel that behind this plan with its sheep-clothing, outward humanitarianism, is a subversive plot to make the whole world communistic, on the Soviet plan. If this is the conspiracy, it could hardly be better planned.

All this will take a lot of money, and the world plans that we shall furnish most of it. They expect to get it either from our government or from us individuals. They do not care which. Either way, we citizens pay the bill.

As I have just said, to keep the government going we citizens must operate on the old debit and credit plan. Not for us is this luxurious adventure into deficit spending. We must be solvent to buy bonds to keep up the government house, for a bankrupt people means a bankrupt nation. We at the crossroads must have real values.

Let me say to begin with that I cannot guarantee the figures I shall use. I have taken them from government sources or from tables and compilations based (so they say) on government sources. Published tables are frequently not in agreement. I have done the best I could.

Our National Capacity to Finance the World

First: I wish to say something about our national capacity to take on this load our Utopian dreamers propose.

In his statement before the Committee on Finance of the Senate, Secretary Vinson told us that by June 30, 1946, our public debt outstanding would be $273 billions; that our expenditures for 1945 were $100 billions, and that for 1946 (year ending June 30, 1946) the expenditure would be $66.4 billions (of which $50.5 would

473

represent war activities). Combining these figures with others furnished by the government it would appear that since and including 1932 up to June 30, 1946, the Federal Government will have spent $459.258 billions, of which $205.758 billions were raised by taxing the people. During the period 1932 to 1943, inclusive (figures for 1944-1946 were not available to me), the States spent approximately $39.4 billions, and the local governments in the States approximately $63.5 billions, or a total for States and local governments of $102.9 billions. This makes a grand total for Federal, State, and local governments (with years 1944-1946 lacking for State and local governments) of $562.158 billions,—more than half a trillion dollars.

War Expenditures

According to Treasury figures, submitted by Secretary Vinson, the "war expenditures" for the years 1941-1946 were: munitions $219.7 billions; pay and subsistence $72.5 billions; miscellaneous $48.7 billions,—a total "war expenditure" of $340.9 billions. To this should be added $1.7 billions for 1940 (the Treasury says of this, "breakdown not available"). (I wonder where this went.) This makes a total "war expenditure" for 1940-1946 of $342.6 billions, which approaches the equivalent of one estimate of our national wealth, and is $33.2 billions more than our 1938 national wealth. The bulk of this huge sum is as completely lost to our economy as if the money had been burned up.

Ancient and Modern War Concepts

Perhaps this is the point where we might reflect that waging wars in earlier days had this advantage: The sovereign waging the war must always remember that he wanted still to be king, win or lose, after the war was over, so he had to be careful of his men and frugal with the money he exacted from his subjects. In our day and here amongst ourselves, our militarists have no such relationship to us; under our system they hold their jobs, win or lose; so personally they are not so intimately concerned with the wastage of men and the burning up of money, as was the old king. I appreciate this is not a pleasant, even as it is not an easy thing to say. But it is a truth, with far-reaching consequences.

I wish to make this further unpleasant and unpopular observation: If our militarists, in and out of the army and navy, continue to exercise a dominating influence in our foreign relations, particularly *vis à vis* our recent allies, if they continue to exercise an equal influence over our domestic policies relating to armament and military training, I venture the opinion that we shall hardly escape, within the life time of any of us but the oldest, the most terrible war of all time. Gossip has it that some are now talking about that war. What they think we will use for money in such a war, is not clear,—probably their thinking has not gone that far.

Our Expenditures vs. Our National Wealth

Referring to the question of the effect of this vast expenditure on our national wealth: As just stated $342.6 billions were "war expenditures." Now, while a part of this sum was reinvested by the people receiving it, in houses and furnishings, so adding to the national wealth, we are obliged to consider that the bulk of it that was expended in wages, was eaten and drunk up by those receiving it. Waste and extravagance was everywhere to the last degree. This same observation will apply to the non-war expenditures, some $86.431 billions. It is almost certain that enough of this latter sum was wasted to offset the "war expenditures" that were saved by investment to increase the national wealth. Thus it is believed we may truthfully say that the "war expenditures" reached a total waste and loss of $342.6 billions, or, say, approximately 90% of one estimate of our national wealth, and again I say, $33.2 billions more than our national wealth in 1938.

I will not belabor the point that when our national wealth—our capital account—is gone, we are bankrupt; we will be "a busted community."

Nature of Our Bond Indebtedness

I suppose none of us here have any illusions about the $273 billions of bonds. We can all appraise in part at least, our true relationship to them. The government has our money, we have its promise to pay back. It is the old operation of taking cash from the till and dropping in I.O.U.'s.

Who Owns the Bonds

Who holds these securities of ours?

It is a difficult thing for one of us common folk to understand the figures which economists, governments and private expert accountants, bankers, brokers, etc., put out, particularly when each set seems built on a different system. But I will try to indicate how it looks to some of us.

It is said the deposits in all banks in the United States and its possessions total roughly $152 billions. As we understand, very little of this money belongs to the banks, and what there is could be wiped out by a very small drop in their government holdings. These bank funds belong principally to the depositors, to us.

As we have gone along, we depositors have individually put into bonds what we thought we could spare from living necessities, which amount it was said totaled in December 1944 (it will be more now) $52.2 billions. But that is not our total contribution, for the banks have invested in bonds a large proportion of our deposits with them,—commercial banks $84.1 billions, and mutual savings banks $9.6 billions. Our insurance companies have put into bonds, of the money we have given them to protect our families after we have gone, the sum of $21.7 billions, out of a total of $38.2 billions of assets. There are millions of bank depositors, there are some 67 millions carrying life insurance policies, with an average of $2200 to each policy. These bank depositors, policyholders, and members of loan associations and like institutions, and the owners of the stocks, common and preferred, of our great industrial enterprises, which likewise hold large quantities of government securities, comprise the financial middle class of the country. Thank God we have in America no other kind of middle class; in everything else we are all one class, with the topmost achievement open to all of us, indeed even in finance.

War Waste and Financial Middle Class

But by our individual purchases and by our participation in the purchases of these institutions I have named, we, the financial middle class, carry the bulk of this government load. These funds represent our life's savings. If they were to go, we would be ruined, and with us the nation. We middle class cannot go on much further.

All this money represented by government bonds, and much more, has been burned up. In fact, nationally we are, as already stated, the poorer by an amount equal to somewhere near 90% of our total wealth, and $33.2 billions more than our national wealth in 1938. It seems to me that no argument is needed to show that we are not in the same position to go forward in public financing that we were at the beginning of the war. Our assets have been depleted by virtually the "war expenditure,"—approximately $342.6 billions. We cannot pass this off with a mere wave of the hand or a laugh; it is a reality. A national financial mishap can and would wipe out this whole financial middle class, and if they go down our whole economic structure goes with them. We cannot afford to blink our eyes at this.

What We Should Do

We have no business to be undertaking anything in the matter of world economics and financing except the relief of actual suffering a tremendous load—and that should be left in largest part to the regular relief organizations, such as the Red Cross, drawing upon the well known sympathy and generosity of the American people. We can be of no help if we permit ourselves to get into the same desperate straits as those whom we wish to help. You do not get into bed with a smallpox patient in order to be sure you can nurse him to health.

Tax Reduction

There is another matter I wish to refer to.

We have made a beginning in the reduction of taxes. We should all like to see taxes reduced. But the tax reduction should so far as possible be divorced from mere political considerations. No tax plan is sound, as a matter of political science, which does not apply to all the citizens. Every citizen should have a personal dollar-interest in how all the tax money is spent.

It is likely that most of us think of a post-war tax burden, that at the worst shall not be greater than the immediate prewar level.

But that is not the proposed pattern. Secretary Vinson in his statement before the Senate Finance Committee spoke of a non-war-activity expenditure load of 1946, and inferentially thereafter, of

$15.9 billions. But his itemization of such expenditures totals $21.1 billions. But the Secretary apparently did not include any estimates for amortization on the public debt of $273 billions, nor for tax refunds now running about $2.9 billions for 1946, nor for unemployment relief on the new proposed plan (though he did include the 1940 load of $2.2 billions spent largely for W.P.A. projects); nothing was included for military expenditures (except veterans relief), notwithstanding we still have a staggering military establishment which must be maintained till demobilized, which in itself is a costly undertaking, placed at $270 per man discharged; nothing for liquidating war contracts, though the Treasury estimates that this will require $4 to $5 billions; nothing for the large military establishment our military leaders expect to retain, nor for the cost of training the huge reserve army the militarists are now planning; and nothing apparently for the uncompleted lend-lease commitments we seem to have still outstanding of perhaps $20 billions; nothing for the international loans that are now projecting,—all which unestimated items must inevitably run into several billions of dollars.

The prewar tax collections, 1932-1941 inclusive, rose in a steady curve from $1.788 billions in 1932 to $7.67 billions in 1941, with a yearly average for the period of $4.346 billions.

The Treasury's estimates for the coming year (minus the unestimated items I have named), are five times the average for the ten years preceding the war, and three times the actual for the last year before the war.

The Federal tax collections during the war are given: 1942, $13.2 billions; 1943, $22.3 billions; 1944, $44.1 billions; 1945, $46.5 billions; 1946 (estimated) $36 billions.

Apparently we have reduced the tax load by recent legislation by $6 billions, leaving our tax load under the present setup at apparently $30 billions, on our present tax base setup. These are the best figures I can get.

If they are accurate, then our present proposed tax load after the tax reduction just made, is nearly seven times our average prewar tax burden (1932-1941), and more than four times our last prewar year tax load. The non-war estimated budget for 1946 is $15.9 billions; the itemized budget is over $20 billions, with a leeway of some $10 billions (on the $30 billion estimated tax) to meet the unestimated items, which, having in mind the loans foreign governments are seeking, seems far too low.

Reduction of Tax Base

Now, we should not overlook that our tax base has been drastically reduced, how much I cannot estimate. But we shall lose all of the taxes we collected on the proceeds of war contracts. They were enormous. One incident: a friend of mine had a government building project involving the expenditure of $7,800,000. His fees before taxes were $125,000 (they would not give him the regular fee); after he had paid all his taxes he had left to put into his capital account $3200 on a 40% total interest in the proceeds of a $7,800,000 contract.

Our total national income for 1944 (1945 figures were not available to me) is given at $160 billions, of which $80.8 billions paid normal tax and $55.7 billions paid surtaxes, and on an estimated $125 billion postwar national income which some have suggested, $44.7 billions would be taxable. Our total national income for 1940 has been given at $77.8. I have no taxable breakdown for this year.

In 1944 more than half the total income was taxed. In the estimated postwar income I just gave of $125 billions, a little more than a third would be taxed. Obviously, if the income were reduced to the 1940 level, $77.8 billions, very much less actually and in proportion would be taxed, and of course our tax income would be correspondingly reduced.

Balancing Budget vs. Reducing Taxation

The balancing of the budget has been touched lightly and very delicately, but with no real suggestion that it was to be sought. But clearly you cannot reduce taxes even to approach prewar levels and balance the budget, while at the same time carrying on such prodigious non-revenue producing schemes, for ourselves and for the world, as are being projected. Indeed, we cannot make real our domestic dreams, unless we either continue peace-time deficit financing, or increase our taxes, or both. This seems clear to a demonstration.

I believe that our planners know all this and that they have no real intention or expectation of either balancing the budget or of giving up deficit financing or of giving up their schemes which would make attainable one or both of these desirable ends. They must contemplate increasing taxes. Their course is understandable to me on no other premise than that they deliberately plan a continuous policy of enormous taxes and deficit peace spending which shall finally end in debt repudiation, by one device or another, with its resulting chaos.

No Capacity to Make Foreign Loans

With all the foregoing in mind, I am sure this government and our people are in no position to undertake a world-wide policy of public international financing by the national Treasury, because we do not have the funds therefor, and they are not obtainable under any safe financial policy.

* * *

Now so much for governmental wisdom and ability to make further loans to "gimme" governments.

Collection of Foreign Loans

But, however much one might disagree with what I have said regarding our real ability to make and the wisdom of making new loans, I would assume all would agree that our situation is such that we cannot ignore the question of the repayment of the loans. We surely need the tens of billions of dollars we could loan. While some of us do not realize it, a billion dollars is still a lot of money.

Experience shows very clearly that the most important factor in securing the repayment of loans made to foreign governments, is the *will to pay* on the part of those governments. Capacity to pay and lack of foreign exchange to make payment is really not often involved, notwithstanding the whimpering of foreign governments on these grounds.

We Have No Foreign Obligations

I begin with the premise that we do not owe anybody anything anywhere in the world, on any account. A "war expenditure" of 342.6 billions of dollars, with over a million casualties, and a quarter of a million of them dead, mostly on foreign battle fields, and not on American soil to repel an invasion against our own shores, make this clear. Moreover, we must be observant of the implications of the President's phrase in his Central Park speech, where speaking of our Navy, its record, and its purpose, said: "We cannot reach out to help stop and defeat an aggressor without crossing the sea." This obviously contemplates more foreign wars.

Possible Foreign Obligations

I have said we owed nobody anything on any account. Perhaps there should be an exception to this, for we may not yet have settled for camp sites and army transportation and other incidentals in Great Britain while our boys trained and waited there to furnish seventy percent of the force that invaded the continent to make sure Germany would not invade Great Britain. It may be, too, we owe something to France on the same account, for saving her hide, and Belgium, on the same score.

Obligations of Foreign Governments to Ours

When we entered the war in 1941, European governments owed the United States nearly $14 billions, which was the hang over from the First World War and which those governments were making no real effort to pay.

You will recall that this vast fund was the result of funding operations which our fiscal experts at the time declared were most magnanimous towards our debtors.

Our Private Loans to Foreign Governments

Much has been said, in criticism, in derision, even in contempt of the lendings by citizens of this country to foreign countries from 1919 to 1930. Those initiating the loans have been accused of all the financial crimes in the full category. The bankers and issue houses have largely taken all this "lying down." I should like to say here and now that from the information coming to the Foreign Bondholders Protective Council from defaulting foreign governments, it is my opinion that very few of the loans made are properly subject to the charge of corrupt negotiation. As to some loans, concerning which such charges have been hurled most urgently, the record shows that the lenders made every effort and took every precaution to see that no corruption attached to the making and approval of the borrowing.

Just a few figures.

During the period 1919-1930 foreign governments (for themselves and for political subdivisions thereof, and for government guaranteed private loans) made borrowings from private sources in this country of slightly over ten billions of dollars, at that time thought to be an extravagantly large sum, but now hardly more than the largesse distributed among the powers at a Yalta Conference.

On December 31, 1941, on an issued $7 billion indebtedness, made up of 1009 issues, $5.195 billions were still outstanding, of which 327 issues were in default upon a principal amount of $2.3 billions. That is, 44.4% of the total amount outstanding was in default. On that date, of the 41 countries in the world owing us money, every debtor except 4 in Europe (small states all of them) and two in the balance of the world, was in default either as to interest or sinking fund or both, upon one or more issues of government or state or municipal or government guaranteed corporate bonds. On December 31, 1944, there were still 6 countries of the 41 debtors that were not so in default on some issue of bonds put out for which the governments were responsible for service.

Now, all of these defaults were in addition to the defaults on the debts owed to the Government of the United States.

Advances to Foreign Governments during War

It appears that to many of these countries so in default, we have during the war and while they were still in default, and apparently without asking them to make any payment on account of their default, made lend-lease payments totaling some $41.208 billions, up to May 31, 1945, and we had received back $5.5 billions, leaving us a net-giver in the amount of $35.708 billions. To this should be added the $2.8 billions the Export-Import Bank has agreed to loan (also apparently without any commitment from the debtors to pay anything on account), which makes a total advance to governments under these two headings of $38.508 billions.

Moreover, it is understood that very large sums have been invested in some of these countries by military authorities for military purposes, but which are of a character of permanent peace-time use and benefit, for which these countries cannot pay, and which we must either give to them or take bonds therefor.

Critics of the 1919-1930 private lendings have stressed the importunate approaches for loans made by American lenders during the period. But it is reported that some Latin-Americans are now saying that the importunities of the private lenders of those lush days were as a gentle zephyr to the tornado in comparison with the high-pressure methods of our war-time operating government lenders.

It is also reported—I believe accurately—that the government importuned loans were accepted by the foreign governments concerned with no idea or intent on their part (which was more or less openly expressed) of ever repaying them and, it is said, that frame of mind still continues.

Amount of Our Money in Foreign Countries

To recapitulate: foreign countries now have of our money more than $14 billions they owed us at the beginning of the war, the approximately $7 billions they still owe us on account of borrowings from our private citizens, the $35.708 billions we have given them on lend-lease, and the $2.8 Export-Import Bank lendings, or a total sum of our money they have had from us, of over $59 billions, not to count the hundreds of millions for U.N.R.R.A. and public relief, the large Red Cross funds we have given them, the war materials they will be given, the permanent improvements and industries we have made and built on their territories, and many other money and other gifts of which I know nothing whatever.

Risking the Taxpayers' Money

Foreign countries are not at this time good credit risks. The "gimme" spirit is too strong and too universal.

Surely it would be wrong to risk the American taxpayers' money in any such wild-scheme public international financing as is projected so long as we are as we are and the world is as it is. We should leave the making of further loans to foreign countries to private investors who think they have money to lose, or who wish to gamble. Equally, it is sure there is no justification for further mulcting the taxpayers of the nation to carry the financial burdens of the world, when private individuals are prepared to do it.

Can Defaulted Foreign Loans Be Collected

I wish now to make a few concluding observations over the collection of loans made to foreign governments, because obviously a bond or other security is no whit better than the amount you can certainly collect on it, which depends (as to all debtors without the will to pay) upon the adequacy and certainty of the means of collection,—in our own domestic securities, upon the courts and the sheriff.

I might begin by saying that up to this time there is no adequate and certain international court, and certainly no international sheriff to collect international loans.

So our loans must be made with that in view.

Will to Pay

Remember always, as I have already said, the most important element in the repayment of foreign loans is the debtor's will to pay. It is, I believe, demonstrable that during the war period many debtor governments, perhaps most of them in number, have had sufficient dollar exchange to pay the service—interest and sinking fund—on their obligations, but they have stubbornly refused to do so, preferring—inspired by our peace-time deficit spending policy—to use their funds in their own country, not infrequently for grandiose schemes and plans that will be social luxuries in their countries for a long time to come. This lack of the will to pay was, for most of them, the real reason for the non-service of their bonds for years before the war. I repeat again, this attitude, practically universal in the governmental borrowing field, constitutes a real hazard to international lending that is of particular importance when the lender is putting out other peoples' money—the taxpayers' money whenever the government loans—instead of his own.

Purpose of Making Foreign Loans

The purposes for which a loan is made is another matter to be carefully considered. With all due respect to our governmental departments and those who man them, one can be reasonably certain that the dominating element in making the loans by government will, in many cases, be the political element, and political loans are always a highly hazardous venture. No loan is likely to be made to the fellow we do not like, no matter how sound he may be financially, and loans will be made to the fellow we do like, without too much scrutiny about his financial responsibility, providing he promises to play our game. Making such loans would mean our control of the domestic policies of every country willing to sell out to us. Thus we would become not only the monitor, but the dictator of every little country in the world, we would be trying to control their national, economic, even cultural life, to meet the ideas of the official staffs and their civilian cronies of our own departments. To do this we shall have to dictate who shall govern the borrowing countries. Now we have had our foreign favorite individuals even in the very recent past, and we did what we could to further their interests. Along with that we had, of course, our personal enemies that we wished to punish, and we have done the best we could at that. Sometimes we have been gloriously disappointed; in the vernacular "we bet on the wrong horse," so suffering a serious, humiliating rebuff. We shall frequently bet on the wrong horse if we finance by public lendings, because our very backing of a favorite will normally create such a reaction as to defeat our scheming. Thus government lending will involve us in a career of imposition and interference that will bring upon us the deserved hatred and fear of the world, to the destruction of the good will that should obtain among nations and that must obtain if we are to have peace.

This government lending plan, and certainly any collection plan of the monies lent, will in addition, because of the dislike we shall breed, tend to destroy much, perhaps a good part of our trade and commerce with the nations affected, for nations do not buy, any more than individuals buy, from those they do not like, if there be any other place where they can get what they want, and we shall have plenty of trade and financial competition in the years to come.

Ours Not the Only Way

There is a good deal of talk about remaking the world to conform to our standards of life and living, as to food, clothing, education, economics, culture, government, and what not.

We must give up this idea too many of us have, that our way of life and living is not only the best, but often the only true way of life and living in the world, that we know what everybody else in the world should do and how they should do it. We must come to realize that every race and every people have their own way of doing things, their own standards of life, their own ideals, their own kinds of food and clothing and drink, their own concepts of civil obligation and honor, and their own views as to the kind of government they should have. It is simply ludicrous for us to try to recast all of these into our mold.

Furthermore, we must come to acknowledge and accord to every people, the divinely given right to live their own lives as they wish to live them. We claim this for ourselves; we must yield it to others.

Sovereignty

This may be a good place to say a word or two about sovereignty, which I shall not define, but which, for our purpose, can be said to be full, complete national independence, with no overlordship by any other power. The effect of full sovereignty was stated by Chief Justice Marshall, 120 years ago. He said:

> No principle of general law is more universally acknowledged than the perfect equality of nations. Russia and Geneva have equal rights. It results from this equality that no one can rightfully impose a rule on another. Each legislates for itself, but its legislation can operate on itself alone. A right, then, which is vested in all by the consent of all, can be divested only by consent. . . . As no nation can prescribe a rule for others, none can make a law of nations. (Henry Wheaton, *Reports of Cases . . . in the Supreme Court . . . ,* 11 vols. [New York, 1816–26], 10:22)

All states, all nations, belonging to the family of nations—an association that has existed in the world for hundreds of years—are sovereign states.

The Atlantic Charter—which it now appears was never a formal document and never signed, though we were once told it was a solemn international undertaking—affirmed:

> Third, they respect the right of all peoples to choose the form of government under which they will live; and they wish to see sovereign rights and self government restored to those who have been forcibly deprived of them.

In his Central Park speech, the President declared, in dilute paraphrase of the Atlantic Charter: "We believe in the eventual return of sovereign rights and self-government to all peoples who have been deprived of them by force."

Both the Charter and the President's dictum leave us in doubt about Puerto Rico, Egypt, and the Boer South Africa, the Dutch East Indies, India, the Philippines, and other countries.

But all I want out of these statements now is to show we admit the principle of sovereignty, and in principle the non-infringement thereof by others.

Our Excuse for Government

Now when the proposals are made to make these government loans to foreign countries, we shall be told they are for this, that, or the other humanitarian purpose, or for bringing the blessings of needed transportation, or for indispensable port facilities, or to increase production so that the standard of living shall be raised, and so on through a long list of similar *prima facie* beneficial enterprises.

How shall we be sure that the moneys lent will be spent for the purposes specified? Someone will remember that in the past, moneys lent to certain countries for prescribed purposes have been frittered away or completely subverted stolen when they reached the confines of the borrowing nation.

Supervising Expenditure of Loan Funds

This problem will be answered by the affirmation that we will supervise the expenditure, we will see the money is honestly spent for the right purpose. Of course, we have not been too proficient ourselves along this line in spending our own moneys in our own country. But we can do it somewhere else, we say. Of course, we shall not be able efficiently to supervise loan expenditures, and if we undertake it, we shall sooner or later be faced with a scandal that will make us blush with shame, and discredit us before the whole world. Already we are being twitted about the wasteful expenditure, some call it by a worse name, of U.N.R.R.A. funds.

But this is where sovereignty comes in: No sovereign state permits another sovereign state to come into its jurisdiction and exercise sovereign functions, and there is no higher sovereign function than the direction of the expenditure of sovereign funds, as these loan funds would be when they gave us their I.O.U.'s, and we turned the money over to them. The public treasury is the life blood of every state. But some again will say, we will not turn over the money to them, we will retain it and spend it. That is, we would think we could go into another country, with our supervision, perhaps equipment, and construct something they might or might not want, and then send them the bill to pay. Such an arrangement would almost surely precipitate a revolution in the borrowing country that would overturn the borrowing administration and install another that would repudiate the whole transaction as an infringement upon their sovereignty. So we would be back to the place of beginning,—unless we used force, and that would obviously be a violation of sovereignty, such a violation as would set-by-the-ears against us every little nation in the world—for we would not treat the big nations thusly. This would mean the complete destruction of international good will towards us, and also our power and prestige among the nations; and we have none to spare now.

Collection of Loans

But suppose the loans are made, and the money expended properly. What about collecting the loans, for we must assume we are not intending to give the money away—we are hardly in a position to do that.

As I have already indicated to you, on December 31, 1944, there were in default on one or another bond issue six out of every seven of all debtor countries owing us money. With that record and with the "gimme" complex thoroughly imbedded in the international mind, we must expect some defaults. Then, what are we going to do about it?

Well, the custom of nations is pretty well crystallized on this.

In the first place, in theory, you might be able to bring suit in the debtor's courts for the default. But for one sovereign to sue another sovereign in the latter's own courts is such an unconventional, not to say, discourteous proceeding, that merely the bringing of the suit would arouse more resentment than the default might be worth, so this would hardly be a practicable measure.

Furthermore, if suit were brought and successfully prosecuted and judgment obtained, how could recovery be had? The enforcement officer could hardly break into the public treasury to fetch us the gold, and there would probably be no gold there to fetch. You might say: levy on the national palace or the capitol building. But how would you realize? In the United States a judgment against the government must normally be satisfied by a Congressional appropriation, and experience shows this may take two generations or more to secure. So the court route seems out.

In theory, our government might exercise some diplomatic pressure to get payment. But here you run into a deeply imbedded international rule that distinguishes between tort claims, for example claims for personal injury or destruction of property, and contract claims, including bond claims. Governments do exercise diplomatic pressure in behalf of tort claims, but not usually for contract claims, because the latter are supposed to have a remedy in the courts. But we have just seen how illusory this remedy might be. It might be here said that of all contract claims, bond claims are at the bottom of the list as to diplomatic intervention. So diplomatic pressure is out. We call this initial pressure unofficial good offices.

If nothing happened from this pressure, the next remedy in order would be formal representation. But since sovereigns would be involved on both sides, it is hardly likely formal representation would accomplish anything where the informal had not.

Your next step would be breaking off diplomatic relations, but as again as sovereigns were directly involved, the respective positions would have been discounted long before this, and each would probably stand pat.

The foregoing having failed we could ask for arbitration; this could have been done earlier if it had been considered by either party desirable, that is, if the party proposing it felt it could certainly win.

All of these having failed, we could next proceed to what are called measures of force short of war.

You could first parade the fleet outside one of their ports, if they had one, to show how big and powerful we were. They would probably have discounted that long before this stage was reached.

If the fleet did not scare them, we might put reprisals into effect. This could be worked out, if the debtor were an importer to us of his goods, by sequestering his dollar credits here and applying them to repayment of his loan. But that would seriously interfere with trade relations and all our importers and exporters would make so much fuss, we would not likely try that. Great Britain tried that against Frederick of Prussia way back in those days, in connection with the Silesian loan, but gave it up.

Then reprisal failing, you might institute a so-called pacific blockade (as did certain European powers against Venezuela at the beginning of this century). That enterprise caused the framing of the Drago doctrine (Dr. Drago was an Argentinean), which lays it down that force shall not be used for the collection of bond debts,— a doctrine which Latin America particularly has ever since insisted upon.

I ought to mention here that in order to forestall a legal excuse for the interposition of a sovereign in behalf of his subject or citizen whom another sovereign was injuring by violating contract rights, another Argentinean, Dr. Calvo, formulated a clause, since bearing his name, by which the alien concessionaire covenants as a condition to the granting of his contract, that he relinquishes all right to the protection of his government in connection with the contract or any violation thereof.

But all the foregoing remedies failing, the final remedy is war. In the last analysis, that seems the only real sanction which can be effectively used against a recalcitrant debtor. But is 10 millions or 100 millions or 100 billions of debt worth a war? That question answers itself.

So, in fact, there is no procedure known in international relations by which the collection of a bond obligation can be certainly made.

The attitude and conduct of the run of existing debtor governments are not such and have not been such over the years as to warrant an assumption that they will pay their debts except as their convenience may suggest. The bulk of the debtors in numbers are now, and many have been for years, in default. They show no inclination to pay. They seek, not facilities to pay, but devices to avoid payment.

Governments now debtor to us are not now safe risks for further Treasury loans from us.

If you add to this fact the further ones that we are in no position nationally to make Treasury loans unless we either substantially raise, not lower our taxes, or resume our peace-time deficit spending—that is, float more government bonds—neither of which alternatives is desirable, and each may be ruinous, I say, unless we go forward on either or both of these bases, we are in no position to make loans to foreign governments from our national funds.

Whatever further financing of foreign governments is to be done by dollar lendings should be done only by lendings made in the conventional way of privately purchased foreign bonds by persons willing to take the hazard. It should not be done by Treasury lendings with taxpayers' money whether that money be obtained by further taxation or by the sale of our own government obligations, or by some scheme which may be proposed of our own government guaranteeing bonds issued directly by foreign governments.

Cuba and Khrushchev

19 September 1960

JRC drafted this brief memorandum "apropos [the] visit of Khrushchev and his communist fellow leaders in New York at the General Assembly of the United Nations." Box 263, Folder 9, JRCP.

Their attendance shows they have neither the instincts of gentlemen nor the wisdom and astuteness of statesmen. We have not been too prolific in wisdom ourselves. Our leaders, seeking to follow the popular trend as they saw it, have been easy victims to the blandishments and duplicity of foreign nations and their skillful representatives. When they have cooed with the sweetness of the mourning dove, we have been wooed by the sweetness of the song and have failed to note the tanglewood of trouble we would have entered if we followed their beautiful, mournful bidding to come.

For example, when we gave Cuba her independence, Cubans, exultant with the cry of victory and flushed with high hopes of independence, yet knowing their own weakness, besought, and we gave it to them, a solemn international agreement which they incorporated in their Constitution, a covenant to which we became a part, that we might intervene in their domestic affairs whenever such intervention was necessary to preserve in Cuba a government adequate for the protection of life, liberty, and property, in order to establish and maintain such a government.

This was the status of our relations for upwards of half a century. Cuba grew, prospered, and was independent to all intents and purposes in all her governmental activities. There was great progress and development in Cuba. Then came a time in our domestic affairs when our National Executive seemingly for reasons primarily his own, which fed his vanity and his reputation for international broadmindedness, decided, upon the plausible but specious representations of the then Cuban authorities, to relinquish this right of ours which was really one of the bases of the Cuban state and we lost any right of control. This right of control was to our far-seeing statesmen, an indispensable element in the relationship between ourselves and an alien government almost within cannon-shot of our shores. While the situation stood thus we had no trouble. Then the Cuban blandishments persuaded our Executive that this control was unnecessary in this day, and we relinquished it. Now we have the sad situation existing at the present moment, when Cuba has become the ally of a foreign government (we forgot the Monroe Doctrine) and we have the malignant disease which now threatens us.

Index